Magical Interpretations, M: Realities

Witchcraft is alive and well in Africa today both among the disenchanted and downtrodden as well as the educated elite. This volume sets out recent thinking on witchcraft in Africa, paying particular attention to variations in meanings and practices. It examines the way different people in different contexts are making sense of what witchcraft is and what it might mean.

Clearly, the promises of countless western social theorists – that such 'enchant-ments' would die a sudden death with 'modernity' – have not come to pass. In fact, despite growing democracy and development throughout the region, the general sentiment on the continent is that witchcraft is increasing. Indeed, witchcraft is routinely implicated in modern state politics, free markets and legal systems. But why, and why now?

Using recent ethnographic materials from across the continent, the volume explores how witchcraft articulates with particular modern settings, for example: the State in Cameroon; Pentecostalism in Malawi; the university system in Nigeria and the International Monetary Fund (IMF) in Ghana, Sierra Leone and Tanzania. The editors provide a timely overview and reconsideration of long-standing anthropological debates about 'African witchcraft', while simultaneously raising broader concerns about the theories of the western social sciences. This book will be widely read and used by anthropologists, social scientists, development theorists and policy makers.

Henrietta L. Moore is Professor of Anthropology and **Todd Sanders** is a Research Fellow, both in the Department of Anthropology at the London School of Economics.

Magical Interpretations, Material Realities

Modernity, witchcraft and the occult in postcolonial Africa

Edited by Henrietta L. Moore
and Todd Sanders

London and New York

First published 2001
by Routledge
11 New Fetter Lane, London EC4P 4EE

Simultaneously published in the USA and Canada
by Routledge
29 West 35th Street, New York, NY 10001

Routledge is an imprint of the Taylor & Francis Group

Typeset in Goudy by Exe Valley Dataset Ltd, Exeter
Printed and bound in Great Britain by The University Press, Cambridge

British Library Cataloguing in Publication Data
A catalogue record for this book is available from the British Library

Library of Congress Cataloging in Publication Data
Magical interpretations, material realities: modernity, witchcraft,
and the occult in postcolonial Africa / edited by Henrietta L. Moore
and Todd Sanders.
    p. cm.
  Includes bibliographical references and index.
  1. Witchcraft – Africa, Sub-Saharan. I. Moore, Henrietta L.
  II. Sanders, Todd, 1965–

BF1584.A357 M34 2001
133.4′3′096 – dc21   2001048185

ISBN 0–415–25866–9 (hbk)
ISBN 0–415–25867–7 (pbk)

In Memory of Bwire T.M. Kaare
1954–2000

Contents

Figures

Contributors

Adam Ashforth is Visiting Associate Professor of Social Science at the Institute for Advanced Study, Princeton. He is the author of *The Politics of Official Discourse in Twentieth Century South Africa* (Clarendon Press 1990) and *Madumo, A Man Bewitched* (Chicago University Press and David Philip 2000) as well as articles exploring the dynamics of witchcraft in post-apartheid Soweto.

Misty L. Bastian is an Associate Professor of Anthropology at Franklin and Marshall College in Lancaster, Pennsylvania. She has published widely on gender, popular culture, media, religious practice and political economy in southeastern Nigeria. Her most recent publications include articles in *Anthropological Quarterly*, *Ethnology* and the volume *Great Ideas for Teaching about Africa* (Lynne Rienner 1999), edited with Jane L. Parpart.

Cyprian F. Fisiy is the Social Development Sector Manager for the East Asia and Pacific Region of the World Bank. Fisiy joined the Bank in 1994. He has undertaken several social impact assessments and mitigation planning for Bank-funded projects. Before joining the Bank, Fisiy obtained his Ph.D. in Legal Anthropology at the University of Leiden, and was also a post-doctoral fellow at the Agricultural University in Wageningen, the Netherlands. He has published extensively on witchcraft and sorcery, and continues to publish and lecture on development issues in Sub-Saharan Africa.

Peter Geschiere is Professor of African Anthropology at Leiden University and the University of Amsterdam. Recent publications include *The Modernity of Witchcraft: Politics and the Occult in Postcolonial Africa* (University of Virginia Press 1997); *Containing Witchcraft*, special issue (co-edited with Diane Ciekawy) of *African Studies Review* 41, 3 (1998); and, with Francis Nyamnjoh, 'Capitalism and autochthony: the seesaw of mobility and belonging', in Public Culture 12, 3: 423–453 (2000).

Henrietta L. Moore is Professor of Social Anthropology at the London School of Economics and was Director of the Gender Institute at the LSE from 1994 to 1999. Her recent books include *Anthropological Theory Today* (Polity 1999) and *Those Who Play with Fire: Gender, Fertility and Transformation in East and Southern Africa* (with Todd Sanders and Bwire Kaare; Athlone 1999). Her interests include social and feminist theory, the anthropology of east and central Africa and psychoanalysis and anthropology.

Isak Niehaus is a Senior Lecturer in Anthropology at the University of Pretoria, South Africa. He is the author of *Witchcraft, Power and Politics: Exploring the Occult in the South African Lowveld* (Pluto 2001). He has published widely on witchcraft in South Africa, and is currently writing a book on the intersections of masculinity, sexuality and power.

Francis B. Nyamnjoh is Associate Professor in the Department of Sociology at the University of Botswana. He has researched and written extensively on Cameroon, where he was Head of Department of Sociology and Anthropology at the University of Buea. He has published widely on media and communication issues in Cameroon and Africa; his most recent book is *Media and Democratisation in Africa* (forthcoming). Nyamnjoh also writes fiction, and his novels include: *Mind Searching* (1991), *The Disillusioned African* (1995) and *A Nose for Money* (forthcoming). He is member of council for the International African Institute in London, and also an editorial board member of *Critical Arts, Ecquid Novi, Pula* and *International Journal of Comic Art*. His current research interests include globalization and identity politics in Africa.

Jane Parish is Lecturer in Anthropology at Keele University. Her research looks at the relationship between witchcraft and misfortune. Her most recent publications include 'The dynamics of witchcraft and indigenous shrines among the Akan,' *Africa* 69: 426–448 (1999); and 'From the body to the wallet: conceptualising Akan witchcraft at home and abroad', *Journal of the Royal Anthropological Institute* 6: 487–500 (2000). She has also co-edited with Martin Parker the collection, *Age of Anxiety: Conspiracy and Social Science Theorising* (Blackwell 2001).

Susan Rasmussen is Professor of Anthropology at the University of Houston. She has researched and authored a number of articles and two books on topics in anthropology of religion, gender, symbolism, ritual, and the life cycle, based on nearly twenty-five years of fieldwork among the Tuareg of Niger, West Africa, and more briefly, in France. She currently has a third book in press, *Healing in Community: Medicine, Contested Terrains, and Cultural Encounters among the Tuareg* (Greenwood 2001).

Todd Sanders is a Research Fellow at the London School of Economics and Political Science in the Department of Anthropology and the Gender Institute. He has published (with Henrietta Moore and Bwire Kaare) *Those Who Play with Fire: Gender, Fertility and Transformation in East and Southern Africa* (Athlone 1999) as well as a number of articles on gender symbolism, ritual, witchcraft, modernity and colonialism in Tanzania and Kenya. He is currently writing a book on gender in Africa.

Rosalind Shaw is Associate Professor of Sociocultural Anthropology and Director of the Africa and the New World Interdisciplinary Minor Program at Tufts University. She has conducted research in Sierra Leone since 1977 on memory, ritual, religion, dreaming, and gender, and is co-editor of *Syncretism/Anti-Syncretism: The Politics of Religious Synthesis* (Routledge 1994) and *Dreaming, Religion and Society in Africa* (E.J. Brill 1992). Her latest book is *Memories of the Slave Trade: Ritual and the Historical Imagination in Sierra Leone* (University of Chicago Press 2002). She is currently conducting research on religion and grassroots processes of reconciliation in Sierra Leone.

Rijk van Dijk is an anthropologist and researcher at the African Studies Centre, Leiden University, the Netherlands. He has done extensive research and published several articles on Pentecostalism in Malawi and Ghana. He is the author of *Young Malawian Puritans* (Utrecht , ISOR Press 1993), and has co-edited with Richard Fardon and Wim van Binsbergen *Modernity on a Shoestring* (London, SOAS/Leiden, ASC 1999) and with Ria Reis and Marja Spierenburg, *The Quest for Fruition* (James Currey 2000). His interests include the relationship between politics and Pentecostalism in Malawi, the topic of his latest article: 'Secret worlds, democratization and election observation in Malawi', in J. Abbink and G. Hesseling (eds) *Election Observation and Democratization in Africa* (Macmillan 2000). His current research focuses on the relationship between Ghanaian Pentecostals in Accra and those in the diaspora.

Chapter 1

Magical interpretations and material realities

An introduction[1]

Henrietta L. Moore and Todd Sanders

In April 1944, a middle-aged Scotswoman called Helen Duncan was convicted under the 1735 Witchcraft Act and sentenced to ten months in Holloway Prison, London (Gaskill 2001). Winston Churchill was reported as indignant that so much time and money had been spent on 'all this obsolete tomfoolery'. Helen Duncan was a well-known psychic and such conjurers of ectoplasm and conversers with the dead were more normally prosecuted under the 1824 Vagrancy Act, providing a concrete link between the practices of spiritualism and the poverty and distress that provided its fertile ground. Spiritualism flourished in the context of other occult beliefs. The First World War of 1914–1918 had dealt death arbitrarily and on a massive scale. It had disrupted the flow of generations and the form of family life, and was speedily followed by further economic disaster. The popular followers of Helen Duncan were facing hardship and social transformation in equal and large measure, and somehow the limits of this world were all too apparent. Yet perhaps surprisingly, spiritualism was not a manifestation of 'tradition' or a hangover from the past, but a new quest for meaning in the context of rapid industrialization, large-scale war and the major advances of Victorian and early twentieth-century science. The Society for Psychical Research was founded in 1882 by a group of eminent Victorians. Seances, then popular, were occasions when sleights of hands, trickery and fraud were all in play, but the audience, for all their credulity, were always asked to see and hear for themselves; not only to experience strange events, but to witness their proof. Ghost hunters and other sceptics set about proving the opposite, but science and spiritualism – far from being simple opposites – were conjoined investigators.

Spiritualism in its Victorian and early twentieth-century form died out as something of mass popular interest from the 1950s onwards: a period of notable economic growth and social confidence in the United Kingdom. Today, however, at the dawn of a new millennium, newspapers advertise weekend 'Psychic Fayres' where gullible audiences listen to tarot card readings and the voices of the dead. In the intervening years, popular belief in flying saucers, New Age Spiritualism, millennial cults, Gaia, crop circles and aliens has waxed and waned, but never died out. Nor have compulsory education and an increase in the popular understanding of science done much to dent the popularity of science fiction or indeed to prevent perfectly sane individuals from claiming that we are all descended from lizards. Science and the occult have never been entirely separate. Not then. Not now. It is enough to recall – evolutionary theory is one such case – that serious sciences have often started off as forms of imaginative 'metaphysics'.

Around the turn of the nineteenth century, anthropologists and other westerners frequently (mis)took 'witchcraft' in Africa and elsewhere for evidence of 'primitive' or 'pre-logical' thinking (Lévy-Bruhl 1926); for something Europeans themselves had, in times past, endured, but had now outgrown. African witchcraft thus served as an unmistakable marker of 'the primitive other'. This idea, popular in its day, meshed neatly with European social evolutionary thinking – underpinned as it was by those grand, Enlightenment-inspired notions of progress, development and modernization (Frazer 1959 [1890]; Tylor 1913 [1871]). Social evolutionary theory, like all theories, made a number of assumptions. Principle among them was that all societies have an in-built telos, allowing or even causing them to 'evolve' along a linear path from 'primitive' to 'modern'. This movement logically implied an eventual convergence of societies everywhere, and that this was a 'natural' process.

As societies 'evolved', a number of things allegedly happened: scientific understandings grew; instrumental rationality increased; a secular world view triumphed; 'superstitions' like witchcraft vanished; and people made an ever-clearer distinction between facts and fictions, objective Truth and subjective falsehoods. Social evolutionary theory suggested that Europeans had somehow 'evolved' quite a bit further than had Africans or other 'primitives'.

Such evolutionary notions of course sprang directly from eighteenth-century European Enlightenment thinking, and also underpin the works of later, foundational social theorists: Marx's inevitable move from precapitalist social formations through to communism; Durkeim's transition from mechanical to differentiated, organic forms of social cohesion; Weber's modern capitalism in which 'religious and ethical reflections upon the world were increasingly rationalized . . . [and] primitive and magical notions were eliminated' (Gerth and Mills 1958: 275).

Yet it should not surprise us that education and science, the two most potent symbols and purveyors of progress and modernity, should not eradicate belief in the unseen, in the magical, in powers that transcend ordinary human control and comprehension. Since the 1980s, there has been an upsurge of popular and academic interest in 'witchcraft' in Africa – as it has been generally termed – in occult powers, ritual murders, the commoditization of body parts, and the role of God and the Devil as opposing forces in the world. This volume sets out recent work on such phenomena, and pays particular attention to variations in meanings and practices, and to the way different people in different contexts are making sense of what 'witchcraft' is and what it might mean. Key questions include whether 'witchcraft' is appropriate as a catch-all, general term, why incidences of witchcraft accusation, witch-finding, and occult practices might be on the increase, and how these discourses and experiences can be explained in relation to socio-economic transformation, growing inequalities and the perception of modernity and globalization by local actors.

One thing that is very clear is that the African experience may have caught the imagination of anthropologists, politicians and journalists, as well as local administrators, business people, civil servants and ordinary citizens in Africa and elsewhere, but it is not unique. Africans have no monopoly on witchcraft, occult forces and discourses (cf. Brown 1997; Comaroff 1994; Greenwood 2000; Melley 2000; Morris 2000; Stewart and Harding 1999; Scheper-Hughes 2000). Moreover, contemporary witchcraft, occult practices, magics and enchantments are neither a return to 'traditional' practices nor a sign of backwardness or lack of progress; they are instead thoroughly modern manifestations of uncertainties, moral disquiet and unequal rewards and aspirations in the contemporary moment (Comaroff and Comaroff 1999). The very familiarity of such practices begs questions that are difficult to answer, principle among them: 'What do we mean by the terms we use'?

What is witchcraft?

What is clear from contemporary work on Africa is that the term 'witchcraft' has been generally used to cover a variety of activities, often of the nefarious sort, and that in much of the literature it is used almost interchangeably with terms like the occult, magic and enchantment. Anthropologists have justified this more capacious and shapeless use of the term with reference to the widespread local use of the term in Africa and, in particular, in print and electronic media on the continent and elsewhere. Geschiere (1997: 13–15) makes this very valid point, and argues that as social scientists we cannot afford to distance ourselves from complex, on-the-ground realities. While this is undoubtedly true, difficulties remain.

For one thing, there is the question of what exactly witchcraft is. Earlier anthropological work dedicated a certain amount of ink to trying to distinguish between witchcraft and sorcery: where the former was a mystical and innate power, and the latter was an evil magic consciously practised against others, sometimes deploying objects, 'medicines' or 'tools' (Middleton and Winter 1963; Harwood 1970). Problems of translation immediately raise questions, since the usual French translation of the English term 'witchcraft' in anthropological texts is *sorcellerie*. Such distinctions have on the whole in anthropology been disregarded in favour of a more contextualized approach. In many earlier texts, then, witchcraft refers to local beliefs about good, evil, causation, divination and healing that provided 'a coherent ideology for daily living' (Fortes 1953: 18; Evans-Pritchard 1937; Gluckman 1944). This is in itself a very broad definition, and clearly accounts for the easy extension of the term 'witchcraft' to cover such things as zombies, ritual murder, sale and manipulation of body parts, general occult powers and magic. It also draws attention to Crick's point that the term 'witchcraft' is an historical one: its meanings, deriving from a particular period and culture, cannot be meaningfully transferred to another (Crick 1970: 343). Crick's view is that witchcraft beliefs are inextricably tied up with moral systems, 'evaluatory ideas' and 'systems of belief' and have to be understood in context (ibid.: 347).

While all the authors in this volume contextualize 'witchcraft' in this way, situating it soundly within particular ethnographic and historical settings, several also make the point that witchcraft is perhaps best understood as a matter of social diagnostics rather than belief. This is because, for many people in Africa, witchcraft is not so much a 'belief' about the world as it is a patent feature of it, a force that is both self-evident and solemnly real – a point Francis Nyamnjoh (Chapter 2) makes clear in his discussion of the popular epistemological order of Cameroon and beyond: 'an order that marries the so-called natural and supernatural, rational and irrational, objective and subjective, scientific and superstitious, visible and invisible, real and unreal' (see p. 29). In the contexts of Nigeria, Malawi and South Africa, the respective chapters of Misty Bastian, Rijk van Dijk and Adam Ashforth (Chapters 4, 5 and 10) all make a similar point by showing how witchcraft pervades and saturates a number of separate yet interrelated social and cultural domains. Across the continent, people see witchcraft less as extraordinary than as everyday and ordinary (Ashforth 1996), forming as it does an integral part of their daily lives.

Recent commentators have observed that local terms associated with witchcraft, magic and power have very specific meanings, not all of them associated with harmful activities. Thus, rather than translating local terms as 'witchcraft' or 'sorcery', which often conjure only negative images and associations in the western mind, it may be sensible to use 'a more neutral term like "occult forces"; this leaves open the question of whether the force is used for evil or for good' (Geschiere 1997: 14). Bongmba (1998: 168), for instance, discusses how the Wimbum people of Northwest Cameroon employ three different terms for the phenomenon glossed as witchcraft to refer to 'an overarching conception of local knowledge, power and interpretation of misfortune', and there are both positive and negative uses of such knowledge and power. Particularly attuned to the problem of translation, Susan Rasmussen (Chapter 7) similarly shows that the Tuareg of Niger have four distinct notions of occult forces – both negative and positive – which defy simple English glosses and understandings (also Rasmussen 1998). One of the points being made here is that seeing contemporary witchcraft and occult practices in Africa through the prism of a particular European historical experience runs the risk of serious misapprehension (Crick 1979), and overemphasizes negative power and malevolent forces at the expense of local understandings based on ambiguity, where understandings change contextually: 'the same techniques may be moral and approved in one context but immoral and outlawed in another' (Krige 1947: 12; see also Nyamnjoh, Chapter 2; Sanders, Chapter 8; Ashforth, Chapter 10; Fisiy and Geschiere,

Chapter 11).[2] Indeed, many scholars have noted that local African terms are not direct translations of the English term 'witchcraft'; and that local terms frequently run the gamut from 'good' to 'bad' mystical forces. Godfrey Wilson noted in 1936 for the Nyakyusa that they had one word, *ovolosi*, meaning aggressive witchcraft that was bad, and another, *amanga*, meaning defensive witchcraft that was good, as well as a phrase 'the breath of men' which meant the power of witchcraft used in accordance with general public opinion (Wilson 1936: 85). Oyler noted for the Shilluk that they believed in the management of occult powers by both good and evil medicine men (Oyler 1920). The major argument here is that power and its operation in and across everyday and occult realms is ambivalent, and people's views of its workings and consequences are ambiguous (Arens and Karp 1989; Geschiere 1997; Rowlands and Warnier 1988: 121; Sanders 1999; West 1997; 2001).

As Africanist anthropologists have increasingly problematized the relationship between 'mystical' and 'mundane' forms of powers, exposing in particular ethnographic settings the subtle and ambivalent operation of occult forces and discourses (Ellis 1993; Ellis and ter Haar 1998; Feierman 1990; Murphy 1998; Packard 1981; Sanders 1998; Strandsbjerg 2000), they have simultaneously drawn attention to how witchcraft is sometimes seen as something more than just good or bad forces. For example, Rijk van Dijk (Chapter 5) shows how Pentacostalists in Malawi often understand witchcraft as being about humour or irony, which thus carries connotations of scepticism. Such views offer a compelling critique of Horton's (1970) notion that witchcraft is a 'closed' system, incapable of engaging meaningfully with people's social worlds. Above all else, the point of interest is that speaking of 'witchcraft' in general terms, and conflating it with European historical experience, reconfigures it as something 'backward', anti-scientific and/or 'traditional', and imposes a specific view of the relationship between modernity and witchcraft that obscures the nature of such practices and beliefs in the contemporary moment (Pels 1998; Olivier de Sardan 1992).

The question of translation is however much more complex. Since Africans themselves use both the English and French terms for 'witchcraft', 'sorcery' and *sorcellerie* and have done since colonial times – that is, for the last one hundred years or more – the meanings of these terms have evolved; they have not stayed static. In addition, processes of urbanization and migration have meant that local people have adopted indigenous terms from neighbouring groups or from those whose languages have become the lingua franca or national language of different countries. There is therefore no easy discussion about the simple translation of indigenous terms into English or French. A further and important point has been the influence of Christianity on witchcraft belief, and the deployment of dualistic thinking surrounding the powers of God and the Devil (e.g. Niehaus *et al.* 2001: ch. 2). This has proved particularly relevant for an understanding of the rise of Pentecostal and other charismatic churches in Africa (van Dijk, Chapter 5; Meyer 1999; MacGaffey 1983). Witchcraft in Africa is a complex historical phenomenon that is specific to local contexts, has evolved and changed markedly over time and is specifically tied to African forms of modernity.

A brief history of witchcraft: anthropology's ghosts

Though early anthropologists, administrators and others had written a good deal about African witchcraft from the turn of the nineteenth century, none of these writings matched in clarity of exposition or eloquence Evans-Pritchard's *Witchcraft, Oracles and Magic among the Azande*, first published in 1937. Built on a solid foundation of earlier explorations (Evans-Pritchard 1928, 1929, 1931, 1932a, 1932b, 1933, 1934, 1935), this tome was the first major treatise on African witchcraft which would fire the anthropological imagination on a number of issues, and which has served as an anthropological benchmark to this day.

In an implicit argument with Lévy-Bruhl (1926), who adamantly argued that Africans were mired in a mystical, 'prelogical' mentality, Evans-Pritchard claimed that Azande thinking was no less rational than European thinking. Azande witchcraft, rather, was a highly coherent and engaged system of meanings – an African epistemology – that made logical sense once one understood the basic premises upon which it was based. Evans-Pritchard thus took a 'cultural' or 'symbolic' approach to witchcraft, in that his principal concern was with the sociology of knowledge and systems of thought.

So why did the Azande believe in witchcraft? His answer: because it explained the inexplicable. Witchcraft offered explanations for misfortunes, explanations that addressed the 'why' more than the 'how' questions. Thus, to recall one particularly well-known example, when free-standing granaries occasionally collapsed and killed those sitting under them, the Azande knew as well as Europeans that termites had eaten and thus weakened the legs, thus occasioning the unfortunate event. This answered the *how* question. But Azande witchcraft probed somewhat deeper, asking questions like: *why* had that particular person been sitting under the granary when it collapsed, and *why* had it collapsed at that particular moment? In some ways, then, Azande witchcraft dealt with the Big Questions in life – which were, at once, ontological and cosmological in nature – questions that called for answers of quite a different order to the narrow answers 'science' could provide.

In making this argument, Evans-Pritchard did at least two things. First, he demonstrated the rationality of witchcraft, suggesting it could not be taken as a marker of muddled, mystical thinking. The Azande were every bit as rational as their European counterparts; their respective mental make-ups and reasoning abilities were no different. This had the effect, second, of calling into question grand evolutionary teleologies which suggested that Africans were somehow inferior, mentally or otherwise, to Europeans. If the purportedly prelogical was perfectly logical after all, then any supposed evolutionary move from the former to the latter was utter nonsense. Following Evans-Pritchard, an entire generation of anthropologists aimed to demonstrate, in varied ethnographic locales, that 'witchcraft is something more than meaningless superstition' (Krige 1947: 8).

Later generations of anthropologists would similarly seek to 'make sense' of African witchcraft. And their answers, though frequently different to Evans-Pritchard's answer, would similarly subvert – sometimes implicitly, sometimes explicitly – European notions of unilinear progress.

Witchcraft, Oracles and Magic was published in the late 1930s, but it was not until the after the Second World War, in the 1950s and 1960s, that the topic of African witchcraft once again received sustained analytic attention. One of the most concerted efforts came from the Manchester School – Max Gluckman (1956: ch. 4), Victor Turner (1957), Clyde Mitchell (1956), Max Marwick (1965) and the like – who had their own ways of 'making sense' of African witchcraft. Unlike the general thrust of Evans-Pritchard's writings, the Manchester approach highlighted the social rather than the metaphysical sense in witchcraft.

By using the extended case study approach and by focusing on patterns of witchcraft accusations, Manchester anthropologists sought to demonstrate how witchcraft led to fissions and, less often, fusions in a range of 'traditional' African societies. Here, 'witchcraft accusations were an idiom in which the painful process of fission could be set going' (Douglas 1970: xviii). Witchcraft accusations were analysed as a 'social strain-gauge' (Marwick 1964), linked to social control and change. The general view was that witchcraft accusations tended to occur in situations where social relations were ill-defined or abrasive. The initial impetus for such work had come from Evans-Pritchard's work on the Azande where he had suggested that witchcraft accusations appeared where other mechanisms for resolving tensions between neighbours failed. The Manchester School's concern was thus less with why Africans believed in witchcraft than with the effects that such beliefs had on local social structures. Witchcraft may have been philosophically meaningful, but it was also meaningful because it *did* things: it led to the formation of new villages and lineages, and to the ruin of old ones. Witchcraft made sense because it 'functioned' (Middleton 1960, 1963; Mitchell 1956; Turner 1957).

Underpinning this view was the idea that witchcraft accusations were generally made against specific individuals and by those who were involved in specific networks of social relationships with them. Hence witchcraft and kinship became indissolubly linked in the anthropological imagination: among the Azande (Evans-Pritchard 1937); Pondo (Hunter 1936); Lovedu (Krige and Krige 1943); Amba (Winter 1965 [1959]); Cewa (Marwick 1952a, 1952b, 1965); Gusii (Mayer 1954); Ndembu (Turner 1957); Lugbara (Middleton 1960, 1963); Kaguru (Beidelman 1963); Suku (Kopytoff 1964); Yao (Mitchell 1956), Tonga (van Velson 1964). This despite the occasional report that witchcraft accusations were never made between kinsfolk or only between certain categories of kinsfolk under certain conditions (Wilson 1936; Lienhardt 1951: 312). A related argument was made with regard to gender relations, and patterns of witchcraft accusation were traced to forms of descent reckoning, the position of wives, and the practice of uxorilocal marriage in matrilineal societies (Turner 1957; Colson 1958; Nadel 1952; Mitchell 1956; Gluckman 1956; Mayer 1954; Middleton 1960). These views have retained their hold on anthropologists to a significant extent, even though the structural-functional framework within which they were first expressed is no longer popular: 'As long as the family remains the main basis of social security, the enigmatic discourse on witches and their secret forces will continue to mark people's reactions to modern changes in Africa' (Geschiere 1997: 214).

While in some respects structural-functionalist approaches failed to do justice to the complexity and subtleties of Evans-Pritchard's work, and Evans-Pritchard himself deplored the crude functionalism of many interpretations of witchcraft (Douglas 1970), they did make useful advances in certain areas. Arguably the most important was the sustained focus on social change – a topic that, somewhat ironically, recent scholars have vehemently charged structural-functionalism with ignoring. Witchcraft accusations and the social tensions and fissions they generated, quite literally, made history. However, the emphasis on the normative and moral aspects in the context of mechanisms to maintain the stability of society resulted in an emphasis on homeostasis: witchcraft was a pressure value, a means for relieving tensions so that change would not occur. The result was a strangely ambivalent relation to the general question of social change.

In such a system, witchcraft was itself controlled. However, this led structural-functionalist accounts to explain situations in which witchcraft accusation or witch-finding appeared to be increasing as ones in which social stability was itself breaking down. Hence, structural functionalist authors routinely linked apparent increases in witchcraft to the negative effects of colonialism, wage labour, migration, Christianity and urbanization. Audrey Richards was often explicit on this point: 'native belief in witchcraft, and the widespread use of protective magic and counter-charms of all kinds . . . I believe to have been actually increased by contact with white civilization, and the resultant economic and social changes in Northern Rhodesia' (Richards 1935: 460).

Witch-cleansing or finding movements were a notable feature of colonial Africa, and were generally interpreted as being the result of new institutions and modern forms of socio-economic breakdown: 'Missionaries all over Africa are teaching a religion which casts out fear, but economic and social changes have so shattered tribal institutions and moral codes that the result of white contact is in many cases an actual increase in the dread of witchcraft, and therefore in the whole incidence of magic throughout the group' (Richards 1935: 458). The idea that 'the west' or 'modernity' has occasioned outbreaks of witch-cleansing cults and occult beliefs has remained popular (e.g. Auslander 1993), and throughout the decades, such outbreaks have often been billed as 'modern', since they often incorporate new styles and symbols of state institutions and translocal economic processes into older rituals and regimes of value (Richards 1935; Marwick 1958; Auslander 1993; but see Green 1997). Evans-Pritchard recorded the witchfinding and witchcraft-related movements that were sweeping the Belgian Congo and the Sudan in the 1930s, and that were both invoking the symbols and values of the colonial state and simultaneously subverting state authority (Evans-Pritchard 1937: 511ff.; cf. Fields 1985; van Binsbergen 1981).

The rise of sorcery, witchcraft and the occult was frequently linked to: colonial meddling in traditional authority structures; increased travel and commerce (Wilson 1936: 94); the prevalence of venereal disease, especially in certain mining districts; the jealousies surrounding new forms of production (Field 1940: 141); the increased social insecurity and social differentiation evident in African townships (Aquina 1968); and social change in general:

> Thus it appears that in Ashanti ten years ago increased European contact, an extension of social scale, rapid economic advance, political change, and the spread of Christianity and school education had been accompanied not simply by the persistence of witchcraft beliefs but by their very considerable increase, and by the emergence of new cults designed to deal with them.
>
> (Ward 1956: 47)

In short, witches in Africa and their possibly increasing influence/incidence have long been associated with new forms of consumption, production and political control: 'Wherever modern changes have brought about situations for which there are no indigenous precedents, and problems of tribal rules of thumb can offer no solution, these tensions arise and are often expressed in terms of witchcraft' (Marwick 1958: 112).

The structural-functionalist writers of the 1950s and 1960s, as well as their predecessors, have thus turned out to have much in common with contemporary writers on witchcraft who also explain both the nature and the prevalence of witchcraft on changed relations of power, production and consumption. Yet the evidence from the period 1930–1970 was by no means clear cut, and as Douglas pointed out: 'The general proposition that an increase of witchcraft accusations occurs as a symptom of disorder and moral collapse was superbly untestable' (Douglas 1970: xx). There was no baseline data that would allow scholars to decide whether witchcraft was really on the rise, and the very fact of accusation and cleansing movements could be taken as an indication of moral resistance to socio-economic change rather than as a symptom of breakdown and disruption in traditional society. Many contemporary accounts of witchcraft suffer from these problems also, but what is noticeable is that although the way anthropologists have supported their claims about rising occult practices and beliefs has varied considerably, the reasons given for those increases have been remarkably uniform. 'Research from every part of Africa reports that there is a feeling that bad magic – i.e. sorcery rather than witchcraft – is on the increase. We can relate this feeling directly to the increase in opportunities for advancement and promotion' (Brain 1982: 382). The impact of increasing social differentiation brought on by modernity (Rowlands and Warnier 1988; Drucker-

Brown 1993) and 'the troublesome articulation of local means of production with more distant (often international) sources of power and value' (Comaroff 1997: 10) have provided the background for interpretation.

The view that witchcraft is on the increase has been with us since at least the 1940s: 'The present state of things is that, as far as we can assess the matter ourselves, *boloki* is not decreasing its hold on the people's minds, rather the reverse' (Viccars 1949: 228). It is, of course, demonstrably easier to document the fluctuations of certain occult-related activities than others. Witch-cleansing and witch-finding movements, for instance, are highly public spectacles that have come and gone at particular historical moments (cf. Auslander 1993; Douglas 1999; Green 1997; Richards 1935; Ward 1956; Willis 1968). Another way anthropologists have attempted to establish that witchcraft is rising is by noting its increased prevalence in public rumours and gossip, or in the popular media (Bastian 1993: 155–156; Geschiere 1997). The question of whether witchcraft and resort to occult forces is on the increase in contemporary Africa is difficult to answer definitively. Yet what *is* clear is that many people across Africa – indeed across the globe – are experiencing what they believe to be an upsurge in witchcraft and occult activity. Occult beliefs and practices, in the Comaroffs' words, 'are widely *experienced* throughout the world as intensifying at a frightening rate at present' (Comaroff and Comaroff 2000: 316, emphasis in original; forthcoming).

Witchcraft and modernity

More recently, beginning in the late 1980s (Geschiere 1988; Rowlands and Warnier 1988; Warnier 1988; Fisiy and Rowlands 1989), and given further impetus in the early 1990s (Comaroff and Comaroff 1993b), the study of 'African witchcraft' has experienced a decisive revival. And it has come with some new theoretical, methodological and topical twists. As ever, these innovations have come side-by-side with anthropology's ongoing concern to 'make sense' of witchcraft. In the process anthropologists have also sought – more vocally than ever before – to unsettle the western teleologies of social change.

One of the main contentions of recent work is that because the powers of witchcraft are ambivalent, they can easily reinvent themselves in novel situations: 'It is precisely through this ambivalence that discourses on the occult incorporate modern changes so easily' (Geschiere 1997: 13). Consequently, witchcraft is dynamic and engaged with the world and is, for this reason, eminently modern (Auslander 1993; Comaroff and Comaroff 1993a; Bastian 1993; Geschiere 1988; Shaw 1997b). 'The modernity of witchcraft' (Geschiere 1997) is often presented as a critique of earlier theorists who, like Lévy-Bruhl, saw witchcraft as primitive and prelogical or, as earlier anthropologists so often seemed to imply, as a static and tightly-bounded tradition. Related to this is the claim that previous scholars misunderstood witchcraft by failing to look beyond small-scale, village-level communities (Geschiere 1997: 12). Finally, given witchcraft's inherent dynamism, and its everlasting engagement with the modern moment, recent scholarship has highlighted the historicity of witchcraft discourses and practices – suggesting that they are forever changing, alive to the basic rhythms of our world over the *longue durée* (Shaw 1997b; Green 1997; Colson 2000; cf. Ardener 1970). In this volume, this latter point is argued forcefully by Rosalind Shaw (Chapter 3), and by Cyprian Fisiy and Peter Geschiere (Chapter 11). Shaw shows how local images of cannibalism and occult forces in Sierra Leone are both historically-informed and modern, and how these images have continually (re)produced themselves through ongoing, translocal transactions over many centuries. Similarly concerned with historical process, Fisiy and Geschiere problematize the relationship between witchcraft and development in Cameroon from the 1960s to the present, showing how local understandings of witchcraft have shifted historically from 'levelling' to 'accumulation'. At different times, in different places, and in different ways, the occult and modernity have gone hand-in-hand.

The claims recent scholars have been making about witchcraft – that it is 'modern' not 'traditional'; wide-ranging not 'local'; historical not static – are all very important. But it is also worth noting that these claims are not altogether novel, even if they are sometimes presented as though they were. As we saw in the previous section, earlier anthropologists were concerned with witchcraft as a response to social change, and writings on witch-cleansing movements in many ways anticipated recent developments by focusing on the region-wide spread and movement of witchcraft. Moreover, while it may be true that many earlier works were village-focused, others also focused on occult beliefs and practices in urban settings, or at rural–urban interstices (Hellman 1935: 59–60; Mayer and Mayer 1961: ch. 9; Mitchell 1965; Hammond-Tooke 1970; Swartz 1970; Gamble 1973/74). In fact, some recent studies have themselves been criticized for taking as their starting and ending points 'the village and its limited microcosmos' (van Dijk 1995: 172).

Overall, then, it appears that witchcraft, for many anthropologists, has long been part engaged with modernity, if not exactly a part of it (Richards 1935). Anthropologists have long known that witchcraft does not whither under 'modernity': in fact, as they have frequently noted, witchcraft and other occult beliefs and practices are often mustered to 'resist' changes and are creatively refashioned to suit new situations. For this reason it would be wrong to suggest, as plenty of social theorists have, that '[m]odernity destroys tradition' (Giddens 1994: 91); or that modernity leads to secularization (Voyé 1999).

Even so, recent works on witchcraft are *not* simply repeating what has already been said. For today's problematique differs markedly in some respects, and has provided additional theoretical purchase over our previous understandings of witchcraft. Where recent scholars of witchcraft part company from their predecessors is not in their insistence on social change, or even on the notion that witchcraft is a response to social change, but in their insistence that witchcraft operates as part and parcel of modernity itself. In other words, contemporary scholars of witchcraft cast occult beliefs and practices as not only contiguous with, but constitutive of modernity.

One recent development that signals a definitive shift in contemporary approaches to witchcraft is the notion of modernity that is deployed. In stressing that witchcraft is modern, it has also been common to note that modernities are multiple (Comaroff and Comaroff 1993a), and that witchcraft and occult beliefs and practices articulate differently with different trajectories of modernity. As Bastian (Chapter 4) asks in her discussion of the cosmological contours of Nigerian modernity, 'Can people's experiences of being modern ever be homogenous, when their histories, societies and basic cosmological under-standings are not the same?' This question has been raised increasingly – and not just by anthropologists studying witchcraft – with the explicit aim of undermining teleologies.[3] This it does in several ways. For one, it makes plain the lack of convergence across the globe: modernity does not conform to a single plan or follow a single trajectory. For while it is undoubtedly true that '[m]odernity is everywhere' (Gaonkar 1999: 1) and is 'at large' (Appadurai 1996), our world has not become one, and it seems unlikely that it ever will. This is one reason why, following recent poststructuralist concerns with pluralities, fragmentation and anti-telos, a number of scholars have suggested the notion of 'multiple modernities' (Comaroff and Comaroff 1993a; Fischer 1999: 459; Taylor 1999: 162–165).

Modernity comes with no single built-in telos, no single rationalizing *raison d'être*: modernity, if it ever was a single entity, has gone in innumerable and often unanticipated directions. To assume multiple modernities is to assume the world is best seen 'as a story of continual constitution and reconstitution of a multiplicity of cultural programs' (Eisenstadt 2000: 2). As such, the notion of multiple modernities is a firm refutation of 1950s and 1960s modernization theories as well as dependency theories, all of which assume societal and eventually global convergence. It explodes the mythology about globalization which wrongly suggests the world, with modernity, will become one. More helpful still, the notion of multiple modernities refocuses social theory on questions of heterogeneities, differences, structural and other inequalities and competing discourses about power (Escobar 1995; Ferguson 1994, 1999). This has usefully allowed for the continued study of 'globalization', and the very real structural inequalities generated therein, without the presupposition that the world is becoming one.

Since modernity has not led to the wholesale convergence of societies and cultures, it is plain that there is nothing particularly 'natural' or inevitable about it. Modernity is not simply the logical outcome of an inevitable unfolding of structures and ideas. Rather, modernity turns out to have been cultural all along. The notion of multiple modernities, then, is useful 'to remind ourselves that our pretended rationalist discourse is pronounced in a particular cultural dialect – that "we are one of the others"' (Sahlins 1993: 12). It allows us to problematize modernity: to see it as a deeply cultural project, to treat its claims to rationality not as natural, universal truths but as particular discourses about truth that require explanation.[4]

Seeing modernity(ies) as a cultural project has allowed anthropologists concerned with witchcraft to refocus our discipline's analytic gaze back on ourselves, and draw parallels between the operation of 'occult economies' (Comaroff and Comaroff 1999) the world over. In the process, it has also freed up a valuable conceptual space for self-critique. The focus has shifted to certain dynamics of power, to how hidden forces shape everyday worlds in specific cultural forms. Juxtaposing the west and the rest – considering witchcraft and conspiracy theories (West and Sanders n.d.), child abuse and satanic rites (La Fontaine 1992, 1998; Comaroff 1997), spirit possession in Asia (Geschiere 1998a), and American spin-doctors (Geschiere 1998b) as kindred beliefs about the world's workings – is important because it shows that 'witchcraft', and the particular dynamic of power it presupposes, are not just African phenomena. They operate in similar fashion the world over, albeit in different modernities and different culturally-inflected guises. Also, by rendering such beliefs and processes parallel, many recent scholars have suggested that 'occult economies' critique the varied modernities of which they form a part. The crucial point is that this particular project has allowed anthropologists to do what we have long excelled at: to render familiar the unfamiliar 'other', while standing our ordinary western world on its head.

Important though this agenda undoubtedly is, the notion of 'occult econo-mies' is not without its difficulties. For one thing, as Sally Falk Moore (1999) has suggested, the comparative notion of 'the occult' is very broad. This raises the questions, On what basis can we compare and analyse such disparate events and phenomena under a single heading? The second difficulty is whether such approaches are prone to overstate the relationship between the occult and modernity. After all, being within modernity and being about modernity are not logically the same (Englund 1996: 259; Sanders n.d.). Is witchcraft, or the occult more generally, offering a critique of globalization and modernity? Must it do so (van Dijk, Chapter 5)? Is witchcraft really about symbolic politics (cf. Auslander 1993; Green 1997; Englund 1996)? Could it be that anthropologists are telling a popular liberal tale through 'others' and, in the process, inadvertently reinscribing the very 'us'–'them' dichotomies we seek to dismantle? It seems most unlikely that, in all cases and places, people are resisting or critiquing the technologies and conveniences of modernization, and they are certainly not shy of the capitalist relations needed to acquire them. Instead, what many are after 'is the indigenization of modernity, their own cultural space in the global scheme of things' (Sahlins 1999: 410). In the end, we need to pay close attention to witchcraft in specific social and historical settings rather than assume monolithic meanings. In rightly dis-missing one of modernity's central master narratives – that of unilinear progress – we should not be duped into uncritically accepting another (Englund and Leach 2000).

Witchcraft and globalization

In recent studies of witchcraft, the broadening of scope in historic terms has been matched by a broadening of scope in geographical terms, a decisive shifting in the scale of study. As already noted, recent studies criticize structural-functionalists for restricting their analyses to village-level events, and for implying that witchcraft is the sole product of specific, bounded cultures like 'the Azande' (Geschiere 1988: 39–40, 1997: 12). This is an attack, above all, on the level of analysis, suggesting that previous generations either did not look far enough to answer the questions they raised, or that their questions were too narrowly framed from the start. It seriously calls into question earlier claims that 'witchcraft beliefs are likely to flourish in small enclosed groups, where movement in and out is restricted, when interaction is unavoidably close, and where roles are undefined or so defined that they are impossible to perform' (Douglas 1982 [1970]: 108). From the contemporary perspective, witchcraft forms part of a much broader ethnographic context; it is shaped, or even produced by, translocal 'others' and images, connected as it is to a vastly-expanded universe of values and meanings. Practically, this idea has led analysts to do 'ethnography on an awkward scale' (Comaroff and Comaroff 1999: 282), to range freely from one level of analysis to another, from local-level politics to rural-urban linkages to the nation-state and the global system (Geschiere and Meyer 1998; Geschiere and Nyamnjoh 1998; Parish 2000). These expanded analytic horizons have led, in turn, to an increased concern to problematize local–global interstices (Shaw, Chapter 3; Weiss 1998).

In this expanded universe of value, some have argued, witchcraft can be seen as indigenously-inflected critiques of modernity(ies), capitalism and globalization, and the inherently problematic relations of production that accompany them (Comaroff 1997: 10, 1994: 11; Parish 2000: 488; Auslander 1993: 189; Meyer 1992: 118, also 1995). Thus, witchcraft is not only implicated in and moulded by the global system; it goes further, according to some analysts, and provides a metacommentary on the ill-doings of capitalism and globalization.

But is today's world really so different from previous times? Has there been an identifiable rupture, a definitive sociohistorical break with the past? On the one hand, there *does* seem to be something categorically different about today's world – with its rapid flows of people, goods and ideas around the globe (Appadurai 1996; Hannerz 1996: 19; Tambiah 2000: 164). On the other, at the same time, there are undeniable historical continuities in our world (Mintz 1998), and we should be extremely careful not to overplay the contrasts between past and present, then and now, static and active, bounded and unbounded, since to do so threatens to reassert the very dichotomies anthropologists have worked so hard to call into question (Piot 1999: 22). One of the central preoccupations of social theorists has been how to make sense of today's world of pluralities – multiple modernities, ever-expanding cultural flows and the ever-present tensions between forces of homogeneity and heterogeneity. Witchcraft is related here, argue recent theorists, since it is often the product of such translocal flows of information, people and goods (Comaroff and Comaroff 1999, 2000; Masquelier 1999, 2000; Shaw 1997b; Scheper-Hughes 2000).

Illicit accumulation

A large body of evidence from Africa suggests that witchcraft and other occult practices are intimately bound up with people's ideas about production, exchange and consumption. The flows of information, goods and people characteristic of globalization are seen as incorporating some and excluding others: the processes of differentiation and privation that result are viewed as predatory and illicit forms of exchange. The terms of exchange equate people and their body parts with commodities, their life-force with ill-gotten wealth and their fertility with immoral consumption (Nyamnjoh, Chapter 2; Bastian, Chapter 4; Sanders, Chapter 8; Comaroff and Comaroff 1999; Scheper-Hughes 1996, 2000).[5] Stories of zombies, cannibalism and headhunting are imaginative, moral frameworks for making sense of wage labour, consumption, migration, productive regimes, structural adjustment programmes, development policies and the functioning of markets (Shaw, Chapter 3; Shaw 1997b; Comaroff and Comaroff forthcoming; Masquelier 2000; Niehaus 1995: 537). Such frameworks do not exist in isolation. There are other forms of discourses and types of explanation that provide understandings of how these processes work, where they are going, their value structures and their impact on people. These include, of course, the discourses on economic growth, development, globalization, the knowledge society, civil society and democratic participation (many of which are informed by teleological notions of 'natural' progress). Such discourses are themselves part of the globalized world they seek to describe, and whilst they may have originated in particular academic, institutional and entrepreneurial settings, they are also to a greater or lesser extent part of local discourses available on the radio (*Radio Trottoir*, for example), in newspapers, in rumours and through participation in development projects, structural adjustment initiatives, credit schemes, schools and hospitals (Sanders, Chapter 8; Fisiy and Geschiere, Chapter 11).

For instance, Adeline Masquelier (2000) shows how stories of cannibalism and headhunting are part of Nigerien peasants' experience of migrancy, smuggling and marketing, and are connected to their understandings of how capitalism, globalization and international relations (with Nigeria) work. Masquelier argues that these economies of terror and violence, where kinsfolk trade their relatives to Nigerian cannibals who consume their life-force in order to get rich, are linked to people's ideas about improper accumulation and illicit wealth: to the production of wealth through mysterious means and apparently without normal forms of labour (Masquelier 2000: 91). The Nigerien economy is subordinate to that of the wealthy Nigeria, but Nigerien peasants are under no illusion that theirs is a world of tradition and morality, while that of Nigeria is a land of modern and despicable ogres. The rural communities of Niger recognize that there are Nigeriens who are just as involved in the production of illicit wealth, who suffer from a hunger, an insatiable desire to consume. The threat to personal and social integrity is that people may turn into uncontrolled consumers, or worse still, consumable commodities. The rumours of cannibalism are thus a moral mediation on the effects of global markets on local economies: 'For the victims as well as the beneficiaries of the large abstraction we choose to call capitalism . . . the experience itself arrives in quite personal, concrete localized, mediated forms' (Scott 1985: 125).

In such stories of cannibalism, capture, headhunting and trading in humans, links are made between occult forces and production and consumption. The stories and accounts themselves are forms of historical consciousness or social memory (Shaw, Chapter 3 and 1997a, 1997b), ways of making sense of experiences and ideas that are current in specific places at specific times. A key feature here is the idea that people often experience modernity as a lack, as something from which they are 'abjected' (Ferguson 1999), or that others have access to via nefarious means. Thus, for instance, Sanders (Chapter 8) shows that many Tanzanians have experienced their recent involvement in 'the free market' with great ambivalence since some have greatly enriched themselves, while the vast majority have instead been excluded from novel forms of wealth. This has led to increased speculation – in idioms of occult-related trafficking in human skins – about new relations of production, accumulation and consumption, and people's differential access to these processes through occult means.

Such views are not simply a misrecognition of capitalism or the workings of the economy, but metaphysical speculations about the origins of value. Consider Birgit Meyer's (Meyer 1998a) work on Pentecostalism in Ghana. She relates the amazing spread of Pentecostal Churches in Africa to, among other things, their ability to provide people with the solution to their ambivalence about new consumer goods. Pentecostalism takes people's fears seriously and links particular global commodities to the work of the Devil. It also provides a ritual to purify them, so that such commodities may be consumed without danger (Meyer 1998a). Indeed, Meyer claims that one of the reasons for the extraordinary popularity of the Pentecostal Church is its claim to be able to reveal the occult forces behind money, power and goods. Pentecostalism became popular in Ghana just after the Rawlings 'revolution' when the state completely failed to deliver services and goods to people. The Pentecostal emphasis on success and wealth, but through Godly means, later helped to make sense of the fact that even with structural adjustment and the availability of western goods, life for ordinary Ghanaians remained one of hardship (Meyer 1998b). The dualistic theology of Pentecostalism emphasizes the struggle between God and the Devil, and witchcraft and other occult practices are explicitly recognized as the Devil's work. In this context, modern Christianity has not displaced ideas about witchcraft and the occult, but provided a new context in which they make perfect sense (see van Dijk, Chapter 5).

Jane Parish's chapter (Chapter 6) raises yet another set of concerns about the linkages between occult and globalizing forces, and draws our attention, once again, to the above-mentioned issues of translation/meaning and the ambivalence of occult powers. In the context of Ghana, Parish shows how, on the one hand, 'young marketeers' see anti-witchcraft shrines as legitimate forms of occult powers and use them to gain access to new forms of wealth, while on the other, 'young aristocrats' see (some of) these shrines as models of 'a true African past' that should not be exploited for personal gain in the present. Furthermore, the young aristocrats denounce many of these shrines as fulfilling 'the white man's worst prejudices about witchcraft'. Thus, while all concerned actively engage with local understandings of 'tradition', 'modernity', 'power' and 'witchcraft', they simultaneously draw global, master narratives on unilinear progress into their discussions and debates.

Adam Ashforth (Chapter 10) raises similar issues in his discussion of 'spiritual insecurity' in Soweto, South Africa. There, people experience a multifaceted sense of danger, doubt and fear about witchcraft, and are faced with an overabundance of local and global interpretive authorities, few of whom agree on the nature of occult forces, and how best to manage them (see also Ashforth 1998a). Understanding such conditions of chronic uncertainty – by no means unique to South Africa – further elucidates, for instance, why HIV/AIDS in Africa is often interpreted across multiple registers and from competing epistemological perspectives, witchcraft being one of them (Yamba 1997; Ashforth 2001).

Illicit power

Witchcraft and related occult activities have often been thought of as outside the law, both in Europe and in Africa. However, contemporary witchcraft and anti-witchcraft practices in Africa need to be understood in terms of state power, actual political processes, and local political institutions (see Nyamnjoh, Chapter 2; Bastian, Chapter 4; Niehaus, Chapter 9; Fisiy and Geschiere, Chapter 11; Green 1997). Anti-witchcraft practitioners, as noted above, often claim to be working with God and/or Christian Saints. They may also claim to be working for development and for the state by combating the reactionary and backward, not to say baleful, nature of witchcraft and its work against modernity (Green 1994: 32, 1997). Such claims depend not just on local understandings of modernity and development, but also on local perceptions and knowledge of political processes, and the relationship between local-level politics and the state. It is no surprise to find witchcraft and anti-witchcraft practices bound up with ideas about power since witchcraft and other occult practices are themselves about hidden forces in the world, as well as part of a more general discourse on morality, sociality and humanity. Geschiere (1988: 37) has argued that in many African contexts sorcery and witchcraft play a central role in the tensions between state and society, and that this is particularly relevant as forms of the modern state are themselves bound up with new forms of power and wealth. In many contexts, the oppressive nature of the state, combined with corruption and the continuing impoverishment of local populations raises questions about how wealth is produced through the exercise of illegitimate or illicit power. The effects of structural adjustment and development projects are seen in many cases as further examples of the relationship between wealth and illicit power under the patronage of the state and/or local political appointees. Rowlands and Warnier (1988) demonstrated how crucial sorcery is to modern politics in Cameroon and that the link between forms of power and forms of domination – a link that earlier anthropologists were able to demonstrate as working through witchcraft – is at the heart of both local political processes and state building in the contemporary period (also Ellis 1993; Ellis and ter Haar 1998; West 1997, 2001).

Writers on the relationship between witchcraft and occult activities and the state tend to take one of two positions. Popular beliefs about witchcraft are seen as a form of political action from below, where witchcraft accusations are used as levelling mechanisms preventing social inequalities from developing beyond the point of community control. However, because witchcraft and the occult are ambiguous and ambivalent forms of power, they can also be deployed to protect the accumulation of power (Geschiere 1997) – hence the mass of contemporary evidence from Africa that local populations, in both rural and urban contexts, see political leaders and elites as involved in the nefarious deployment of occult powers to gain and maintain political power (see Nyamnjoh, Chapter 2; Bastian, Chapter 4; Fisiy and Geschiere, Chapter 11). State power is itself associated with witchcraft and occult power, and the evident desire of many African states to link economic and political control to cultural domination is clear from, amongst other things, the involvement of the media in the political manage- ment of popular sentiment and comprehension (see Nyamnjoh, Chapter 2).

However, the link between state power and occult forces has been reinforced in the popular imagination – starting in colonial times and continuing to the present day (Orde Browne 1935: 485; Bukurura 1994: 65; Ciekawy 1998; Gray 2000; Melland 1935: 496; Roberts 1935: 488–489) – by the state's attempt to outlaw witchcraft, often resulting in the law taking action against those who accused and perhaps punished or killed witches, rather than against the witches themselves: 'Many Africans view these measures [outlawing the killing of witches] as indications that modern state apparatuses have aligned themselves on the side of evil because from their standpoint these measures have obviously been designed to protect witches and sorcerers against retaliation by their innocent victims' (Middleton and Winter 1963: 21; also Winter 1963: 286; cf. Abrahams 1994: 18–19). The perception that the state is in league with witches and the occult is today reinforced not just by rumour and reporting in the media, but by the ambivalent relation of the modern state to 'culture', 'belief' and 'tradition'. As Isak Niehaus compellingly argues (Chapter 9), the South African state reinforced this ambivalence first through the Ralushai Commission inquiry into witchcraft and second through an evident desire to take witchcraft beliefs seriously, whilst punishing attacks on apparently innocent individuals (cf. Fisiy and Geschiere, Chapter 11; Ashforth 1998b: 531). Thus while some postcolonial states have revamped or removed colonial witchcraft legislation, this has often reinscribed rather than eroded conceptual linkages people make between the occult and the state. Fisiy and Geschiere (1990) note that although state courts in the Cameroon have regularly convicted witches since the end of the 1970s, the courts work with local 'witchdoctors', and it is through their collaboration that witches are brought to court and convicted (also Fisiy and Rowlands 1989; Geschiere and Fisiy 1994; Fisiy 1998). Witchcraft and the occult are thus not just about popular ways to resist the state. They are constitutive of state power and legal process.

Conclusion

Why have beliefs in the occult and occult-related practices not died out? How can such things remain in our modern and modernizing world? The authors in this volume demonstrate that these questions, though frequently asked, are fundamentally misframed. For we can only think such 'enchantments' should whither and die if we think in narrow teleological terms of progress, development and modernization. However, once we admit to 'multiple modernities', to the idea that 'progress', 'development' and 'modernity' are multiplex, undecidable and contextually specific, there is no reason to suppose that the occult *should* vanish. Such a question would seem no more or less pressing than one that asks why any other feature of our contemporary global landscape might wax or wane.

We might equally pose the question: when will western faith in grand teleologies of progress vanish, given there is a world – quite literally – of evidence that they lack explanatory value? Should it not concern us that western teleological models bare no obvious resemblance to our multiply-modern empirical world? And are western teleological beliefs about progress, development, rationality and modernity – those ready-made explanations for social change that provide answers to the Big Questions in life – really so different from the idea that occult forces move the world? What, after all, is the driving force behind 'progress' or 'development'? Could it be 'the market' and Adam Smith's invisible hand, or some other similarly enigmatic notion? When, in short, will our own occult beliefs about the motor of our contemporary world be given up?

As anthropologists have long known, there is nothing particularly natural or objective or amoral about social change – or, for that matter, about markets, currencies, commodities and their workings. Rather, all are deeply embedded in social, cultural and political processes and institutions (Appadurai 1986; Comaroff and Comaroff 1993a; Parry and Bloch 1989; Ferguson 1995; Geschiere 1992). Indeed, as often as not, claims to 'naturalness' serve more to justify than to explain (Butler 1990; Ferguson 1994; Sanders 1998; Williams 1999; Yanagisako and Delaney 1995).

Witchcraft and the occult in Africa are a set of discourses on morality, sociality and humanity: on human frailty. Far from being a set of irrational beliefs, they are a form of historical consciousness, a sort of social diagnostics. In this sense, they strongly resemble other forms of social, economic and political diagnostics, originating in the academy and without, that try to explain why the world is the way it is, why it is changing and moving in a particular manner at the moment. These theories, most of them originating in the social sciences, are equally concerned with value and growth, with consumption and power, and with the impact of the world on the lives of individuals and communities: in short, with the major concerns of witchcraft.

Notes

1 We would like to thank the ESRC for funding which has made this volume possible.
2 See Keesing 1985 for a general discussion of problems of translation in anthropology.
3 On varied notions of 'African modernity' see Moore 1996 and Piot 1999. More generally, see the special issues of Dædalus (2000, vol. 129, no. 1) and Public Culture (1999, vol. 11, no. 1) on 'multiple modernities' and 'alter/native modernities' respectively. See also the interesting work by Mayfair Yang (2000) that deals with the question of 'multiple capitalisms'.
4 A number of scholars have viewed capitalism in this way: 'Western capitalism in its totality is a truly exotic cultural scheme, as bizarre as any other, marked by the subsumption of material rationality in a vast order of symbolic relationships' (Sahlins 1993: 12; also Sahlins 1976; Mintz 1985; Comaroff and Comaroff 2000).
5 See Sharp 2000 for an excellent overview of the commodification of the body and its parts.

Bibliography

Abrahams, R.G. (1994) 'Introduction', in R.G. Abrahams (ed.) *Witchcraft in Contemporary Tanzania*, Cambridge: African Studies Centre.

Appadurai, A. (ed.) (1986) *The Social Life of Things: Commodities in Cultural Perspective*, Cambridge: University Press.

—— (1996) *Modernity at Large: Cultural Dimensions of Globalization*, Minneapolis: University of Minnesota Press.

Aquina, M. (1968) 'A sociological interpretation of sorcery and witchcraft beliefs among the Karanga', *NADA* ix, 5.

Ardener, E. (1970) 'Witchcraft, economics and the continuity of belief', in M. Douglas (ed.) *Witchcraft Confessions and Accusations*, London: Tavistock.

Arens, W. and Karp, I. (1989) 'Introduction', in W. Arens and I. Karp (eds) *Creativity of Power: Cosmology and Action in African Societies*, Washington DC: Smithsonian Institution Press.

Ashforth, A. (1996) 'Of secrecy and the commonplace: witchcraft and power in Soweto', *Social Research* 63, 4: 1183–1234.

—— (1998a) 'Reflections on spiritual insecurity in a modern African city (Soweto)', *African Studies Review* 41, 3: 39–67.

—— (1998b) 'Witchcraft, violence, and democracy in the New South Africa', *Cahiers d'Études africaines* 150–152 xxviii, 2–4: 505–532.

—— (2001) 'AIDS, witchcraft, and the problem of public power in post-apartheid South Africa', School of Social Science Occasional Paper, Princeton, Institute for Advanced Study.

Auslander, M. (1993) '"Open the wombs!": the symbolic politics of modern Ngoni witchfinding', in J. Comaroff and J. L. Comaroff (eds) *Modernity and its Malcontents: Ritual and Power in Postcolonial Africa*, Chicago: University of Chicago Press.

Bastian, M.L. (1993) '"Bloodhounds who have no friends": witchcraft and locality in the Nigerian popular press', in J. Comaroff and J.L. Comaroff (eds) *Modernity and its Malcontents: Ritual and Power in Postcolonial Africa*, Chicago: University of Chicago Press.

Beidelman, T.O. (1963) 'Witchcraft in Ukaguru', in J. Middleton and E. Winter (eds) *Witchcraft and Sorcery in East Africa*, London: Routledge and Kegan Paul.

Bongmba, E.K. (1998) 'Toward a hermeneutic of Wimbum *Tfu*', *African Studies Review* 41, 3: 165–191.

Brain, J.L. (1982) 'Witchcraft and development', *African Affairs* 81, 324: 371–384.

Brown, M.F. (1997) *The Channeling Zone: American Spirituality in an Anxious Age*, Cambridge, MA: Harvard University Press.

Bukurura, S. (1994) 'Sungusungu and the banishment of suspected witches in Kahama', in R. Abrahams (ed.) *Witchcraft in Contemporary Tanzania*, Cambridge: African Studies Centre.

Butler, J. (1990) *Gender Trouble: Feminism and the Subversion of Identity*, London: Routledge.

Ciekawy, D. (1998) 'Witchcraft in statecraft: five technologies of power in colonial and postcolonial coastal Kenya', *African Studies Review* 41, 3: 119–141.

Colson, E. (1958) *Marriage and the Family among the Plateau Tonga of Northern Rhodesia*, Manchester: University Press.

—— (2000) 'The father as witch', *Africa* 70, 3: 333–358.

Comaroff, J. (1994) 'Contentious subjects: moral being in the modern world', *Suomen Antropologi* 19, 2: 2–17.

—— (1997) 'Consuming passions: child abuse, fetishism, and "The New World Order"', *Culture* 17, 1–2: 7–19.

Comaroff, J. and Comaroff, J.L. (1993a) 'Introduction', in J. Comaroff and J.L. Comaroff (eds) *Modernity and its Malcontents: Ritual and Power in Postcolonial Africa*, Chicago: University of Chicago Press.

—— (eds) (1993b) *Modernity and its Malcontents: Ritual and Power in Postcolonial Africa*, Chicago: University of Chicago Press.

—— (1999) 'Occult economies and the violence of abstraction: notes from the South African postcolony', *American Ethnologist* 26, 2: 279–303.

—— (2000) 'Millennial capitalism: first thoughts on a second coming', *Public Culture (special issue: Millennial capitalism and the culture of neoliberalism)* 12, 2: 291–343.

—— (forthcoming) 'Alien-nation: zombies, immigrants, and millennial capitalism', in G. Schwab (ed.) *Forces of Globalization*, New York: Columbia University Press.

Crick, M. (1970) 'Recasting witchcraft', in M. Marwick (ed.) *Witchcraft and Sorcery: Selected Readings*, London: Penguin Books.

—— (1979) 'Anthropologists' witchcraft: symbolically defined or analytically undone?', *Journal of the Anthropological Society of Oxford* 10: 139–146.

Douglas, M. (1970) 'Thirty years after *Witchcraft, Oracles and Magic*', in M. Douglas (ed.) *Witchcraft Confessions and Accusations*, London: Tavistock.

—— (1982 [1970]) *Natural Symbols: Explorations in Cosmology*, New York: Pantheon Books.

—— (1999) 'Sorcery accusations unleashed: the Lele revisited, 1987', *Africa* 69, 2: 177–193.

Drucker-Brown, S. (1993) 'Mamprusi witchcraft, subversion and changing gender relations', *Africa* 63, 4: 531–549.

Eisenstadt, S.N. (2000) 'Multiple modernities', *Dædalus* (special issue: *Multiple Modernities*) 129, 1: 1–29.

Ellis, S. (1993) 'Rumour and power in Togo', *Africa* 63, 4: 462–476.

Ellis, S. and ter Haar, G. (1998) 'Religion and politics in sub-Saharan Africa', *The Journal of Modern African Studies* 36, 2: 175–201.

Englund, H. (1996) 'Witchcraft, modernity and the person: the morality of accumulation in Central Malawi', *Critique of Anthropology* 16, 3: 257–279.

Englund, H. and Leach, J. (2000) 'Ethnography and the meta-narratives of modernity', *Current Anthropology* 41, 2: 225–239.

Escobar, A. (1995) *Encountering Development: the Making and Unmaking of the Third World*, Princeton: University Press.

Evans-Pritchard, E.E. (1928) 'Oracle-magic of the Azande', *Sudan Notes and Records* xi: 1–53.

—— (1929) 'Witchcraft (*mangu*) amongst the A-Zande', *Sudan Notes and Records* xi: 163–249.

—— (1931) 'Sorcery and native opinion', *Africa* iv, 1: 22–55.

—— (1932a) 'The Zande corporation of witchdoctors, part I', *Journal of the Royal Anthropological Institute* lxii: 291–336.

—— (1932b) 'The Zande corporation of witchdoctors, part II', *Journal of the Royal Anthropological Institute* lxiii, 1: 63–100.

—— (1933) 'The intellectualist (English) interpretation of magic', *Bulletin of the Faculty of Arts (Egyptian University, Cairo)* 1, pt. 2: 1–21.

—— (1934) 'Lévy-Bruhl's theory of primitive mentality', *Bulletin of the Faculty of Arts (Egyptian University, Cairo)* 2, pt. 2: 1–26.

—— (1935) 'Witchcraft', *Africa* viii, 4: 417–422.

—— (1937) *Witchcraft, Oracles and Magic among the Azande*, Oxford: Clarendon Press.

Feierman, S. (1990) *Peasant Intellectuals: Anthropology and History in Tanzania*, Madison: University of Wisconsin Press.

Ferguson, J. (1994) *The Anti-Politics Machine: 'Development', Depoliticization, and Bureaucratic Power in Lesotho*, Minneapolis: University of Minnesota Press.

—— (1995) 'From African socialism to scientific capitalism: reflections on the legitimation crisis in IMF-ruled Africa', in D.B. Moore and G.J. Schmitz (eds) *Debating Development Discourse: Institutional and Popular Perspectives*, New York: St Martin's Press.

—— (1999) *Expectations of Modernity: Myths and Meanings of Urban Life on the Zambian Copperbelt*, Berkeley: University of California Press.

Field, M.J. (1940) 'Some new shrines of the Gold Coast and their significance', *Africa* xiii, 1: 138–149.

Fields, K. (1985) *Revival and Rebellion in Colonial Central Africa*, Princeton: University Press.

Fischer, M.M.J. (1999) 'Emergent forms of life: anthropologies of late or postmodernities', *Annual Review of Anthropology* 28: 455–478.

Fisiy, C.F. (1998) 'Containing occult practices: witchcraft trials in Cameroon', *African Studies Review* 41, 3: 143–163.

Fisiy, C.F. and Geschiere, P. (1990) 'Judges and witches, or How is the state to deal with witchcraft? Examples from Southeast Cameroon', *Cahiers d'Études africaines 118* xxx, 2: 135–156.

Fisiy, C.F. and Rowlands, M. (1989) 'Sorcery and the law in modern Cameroon', *Culture and History* 6: 63–84.

Fortes, M. (1953) 'The structure of unilineal descent groups', *American Anthropologist* 55, 1: 17–41.

Frazer, J. (1959 [1890]) *The Golden Bough*, Garden City: Anchor Books.

Gamble, D.P. (1973/74) 'Temne witchcraft beliefs in rural and urban settings in Sierra Leone', *Africana Research Bulletin* 4, 4: 3–13.

Gaonkar, D.P. (1999) 'On alternative modernities', *Public Culture* 11, 1: 1–18.

Gaskill, M. (2001) *Hellish Nell: Last of Britain's Witches*, London: Fourth Estate.

Gerth, H.H. and Mills, C.W. (eds) (1958) *From Max Weber: Essays in Sociology*, New York: Oxford University Press.

Geschiere, P. (1988) 'Sorcery and the state: popular modes of action among the Maka of Southeast Cameroon', *Critique of Anthropology* 8, 1: 35–63.

—— (1992) 'Kinship, witchcraft and "the market": hybrid patterns in Cameroonian societies', in R. Dilley (ed.) *Contesting Markets: Analyses of Ideology, Discourse and Practice*, Edinburgh: University Press.

—— (1997) *The Modernity of Witchcraft: Politics and the Occult in Postcolonial Africa*, Charlottesville: University Press of Virginia.

—— (1998a) 'Globalization and the power of indeterminate meaning: witchcraft and spirit cults in Africa and East Asia', *Development and Change* 29, 4: 811–838.

—— (1998b) 'On witch-doctors and spin-doctors: the role of "experts" in African and American politics', Working Paper, University of Leiden.

Geschiere, P. and Fisiy, C. (1994) 'Domesticating personal violence: witchcraft, courts and confessions in Cameroon', *Africa* 64, 3: 323–341.

Geschiere, P. and Meyer, B. (1998) 'Globalization and identity: dialectics of flow and closure', *Development and Change* 29: 601–615.

Geschiere, P. and Nyamnjoh, F. (1998) 'Witchcraft as an issue in the "politics of belonging": democratization and urban migrants' involvement with the home village', *African Studies Review* 41, 3: 69–91.

Giddens, A. (1994) 'Living in a post-traditional society', in U. Beck, A. Giddens and S. Lash (eds) *Reflexive Modernization: Politics, Tradition and Aesthetics in the Modern Social Order*, Cambridge: Polity Press.

Gluckman, M. (1944) 'The logic of African science and witchcraft', *Human Problems in Central Africa* 1: 61–71.

—— (1956) *Custom and Conflict in Africa*, Oxford: Basil Blackwell.

Gray, N.A. (2000) 'The legal history of witchcraft in colonial Ghana: Akyem Abuakwa, 1913–1943', PhD dissertation submitted to Columbia University.

Green, M. (1994) 'Shaving witchcraft in Ulanga', in R. Abrahams (ed.) *Witchcraft in Contemporary Tanzania*, Cambridge: African Studies Centre.

—— (1997) 'Witchcraft suppression practices and movements: public politics and the logic of purification', *Comparative Studies in Society and History* 39, 2: 319–345.

Greenwood, S. (2000) *Magic, Witchcraft and the Otherworld: An Anthropology*, Oxford: Berg.

Hammond-Tooke, W.D. (1970) 'Urbanization and the interpretation of misfortune: a quantitative analysis', *Africa* 40: 25–39.

Hannerz, U. (1996) *Transnational Connections: Culture, People, Places*, London: Routledge.

Harwood, A. (1970) *Witchcraft, Sorcery and Social Categories among the Safwa*, London: Oxford University Press.

Hellman, E. (1935) 'Native life in a Johannesburg slum yard', *Africa* viii: 34–62.

Horton, R. (1970) 'African traditional thought and western science', in B. Wilson (ed.) *Rationality*, Oxford: Blackwell.

Hunter, M. (1936) *Reaction to Conquest*, Cape Town: David Philip.

Keesing, R. (1985) 'Conventional metaphor and anthropological metaphysics: the problematic of cultural translation', *Journal of Anthropological Research* 41: 201–217.

Kopytoff, I. (1964) 'Family and lineage among the Suku of the Congo', in R.F. Gray and P.H. Gulliver (eds) *The Family Estate in Africa*, London: Routledge and Kegan Paul.

Krige, E.J. and Krige, J.D. (1943) *The Realm of a Rain-Queen: A Study of the Pattern of Lovedu Society*, London: Oxford University Press.

Krige, J.D. (1947) 'The social function of witchcraft', *Theoria* 1: 8–21.

La Fontaine, J.S. (1992) 'Concepts of evil, witchcraft and the sexual abuse of children in modern England', *Ethnofoor* 5, 1–2: 6–20.

—— (1998) *Speak of the Devil: Tales of Satanic Abuse in Contemporary England*, Cambridge: University Press.

Lévy-Bruhl, L. (1926) *How Natives Think*, London: Allen and Unwin.

Lienhardt, G. (1951) 'Some notions of witchcraft among the Dinka', *Africa* xxi, 4: 303–318.

MacGaffey, M. (1983) *Modern Kongo Prophets: Religion in a Plural Society*, Bloomington: Indiana University Press.

Marwick, M.G. (1952a) 'The social context of Cewa witch beliefs', *Africa* xxii, 2: 120–135.

—— (1952b) 'The social context of Cewa witch beliefs', *Africa* xxii, 3: 215–233.

—— (1958) 'Another modern anti-witchcraft movement in East Central Africa', *Africa* xx, 2: 100–112.

—— (1964) 'Witchcraft as social strain-gauge', *Australian Journal of Science* 26: 263–268.

—— (1965) *Sorcery in its Social Setting: a Study of the Northern Rhodesian Cewa*, Manchester: University Press.

Masquelier, A. (1999) '"Money and serpents, their remedy is killing": the pathology of consumption in southern Niger', *Research in Economic Anthropology* 20: 97–115.

—— (2000) 'Of headhunters and cannibals: migrancy, labor, and consumption in the Mawri imagination', *Cultural Anthropology* 15, 1: 84–126.

Mayer, P. (1954) *Witchcraft*, Grahamstown: Rhodes University.

Mayer, P. and Mayer, I. (1961) *Townsmen or Tribesmen: Conservatism and the Process of Urbanization in a South African City*, Cape Town: Oxford University Press.

Melland, F. (1935) 'Ethical and political aspects of African witchcraft', *Africa* viii, 4: 495–503.

Melley, T. (2000) *Empire of Conspiracy: The Culture of Paranoia in Postwar America*, Ithaca: Cornell University Press.

Meyer, B. (1992) ' "If you are a devil, you are a witch and, if you are a witch, you are a devil": the integration of "pagan" ideas into the conceptual universe of the Ewe Christians in Southeastern Ghana', *Journal of Religion in Africa* xxii, 2: 98–132.

—— (1995) ' "Delivered from the power of darkness": confessions of satanic riches in Christian Ghana', *Africa* 65, 2: 236–255.

—— (1998a) 'Commodities and the power of prayer: Pentecostalist attitudes towards consumption in contemporary Ghana', *Development and Change* 29, 4: 751–776.

—— (1998b) 'The power of money: politics, occult forces, and Pentecostalism in Ghana', *African Studies Review* 41, 3: 15–37.

—— (1999) *Translating the Devil: Religion and Modernity among the Ewe in Ghana*, London: Edinburgh University Press.

Middleton, J. (1960) *Lugbara Religion: Ritual and Authority among an East African People*, London: Oxford University Press.

—— (1963) 'Witchcraft and sorcery in Lugbara', in J. Middleton and E.H. Winter (eds) *Witchcraft and Sorcery in East Africa*, London: Routledge and Kegan Paul.

Middleton, J. and Winter, E.H. (1963) 'Introduction', in J. Middleton and E.H. Winter (eds) *Witchcraft and Sorcery in East Africa*, London: Routledge and Kegan Paul.

Mintz, S. (1985) *Sweetness and Power: the Place of Sugar in Modern History*, London: Penguin Books.

—— (1998) 'The localization of anthropological practice: from Area Studies to Transnationalism', *Critique of Anthropology* 18, 2: 117–133.

Mitchell, J.C. (1956) *The Yao Village: A Study in the Social Structure of a Malawian People*, Manchester: University Press.

—— (1965) 'The meaning of misfortune in urban Africa', in M. Fortes and G. Dieterlen (eds) *African Systems of Thought*, London: Oxford University Press.

Moore, S.F. (1996) 'Post-socialist micro-politics: Kilimanjaro, 1993', *Africa* 66, 4: 587–606.

—— (1999) 'Reflections on the Comaroff lecture', *American Ethnologist* 26, 2: 304–306.

Morris, R.C. (2000) *In the Place of Origins: Modernity and its Mediums in Northern Thailand*, Durham: Duke University Press.

Murphy, W.P. (1998) 'The sublime dance of Mende politics: an African aesthetic of charismatic power', *American Ethnologist* 25, 4: 563–582.

Nadel, S.F. (1952) 'Witchcraft in four African societies: an essay in comparison', *American Anthropologist* 54, 1: 18–29.

Niehaus, I.A. (1995) 'Witches of the Transvaal Lowveld and their familiars: conceptions of duality, power and desire', *Cahiers d'Études africaines 138–139* xxxv, 2–3: 513–540.

Niehaus, I.A., with Mohlala, E. and Shokane, K. (2001) *Witchcraft, Power and Politics: Exploring the Occult in the South African Lowveld*, London: Pluto Press.

Olivier de Sardan, J.-P. (1992) 'Occultism and the ethnographic "I": the exoticising of magic from Durkhiem to postmodernism', *Critique of Anthropology* 12, 1: 5–25.

Orde Browne, G.S.J. (1935) 'Witchcraft and British colonial rule', *Africa* viii, 4: 481–487.

Oyler, D.S. (1920) 'The Shilluk's belief in the good medicine men', *Sudan Notes and Records* iii: 110–116.

Packard, R.M. (1981) *Chiefship and Cosmology: An Historical Study of Political Competition*, Bloomington: Indiana University Press.

Parish, J. (2000) 'From the body to the wallet: conceptualizing Akan witchcraft at home and abroad', *Journal of the Royal Anthropological Institute* 6, 3: 487–500.

Parry, J. and Bloch, M. (eds) (1989) *Money and the Morality of Exchange*, Cambridge: University Press.

Pels, P. (1998) 'The magic of Africa: reflections on a Western commonplace', *African Studies Review* 41, 3: 193–209.

Piot, C. (1999) *Remotely Global: Village Modernity in West Africa*, Chicago: University of Chicago Press.

Rasmussen, S. (1998) 'Ritual powers and social tensions as moral discourse among the Taureg', *American Anthropologist* 100, 2: 458–468.

Richards, A.I. (1935) 'A modern movement of witch-finders', *Africa* viii, 4: 448–461.

Roberts, C.C. (1935) 'Witchcraft and colonial legislation', *Africa* viii, 4: 488–503.

Rowlands, M. and Warnier, J.-P. (1988) 'Sorcery, power and the modern state in Cameroon', *Man* 23: 118–132.

Sahlins, M. (1976) *Culture and Practical Reason*, Chicago: University of Chicago Press.

—— (1993) 'Goodbye to *Tristes Tropes*: ethnography in the context of modern world history', *Journal of Modern History* 65: 1–25.

—— (1999) 'Two or three things that I know about culture', *Journal of the Royal Anthropological Institute* 5: 399–421.

Sanders, T. (1998) 'Making children, making chiefs: gender, power and ritual legitimacy', *Africa* 68, 2: 238–262.

—— (1999) 'Modernity, wealth and witchcraft in Tanzania', *Research in Economic Anthropology* 20: 117–131.

—— (n.d.) 'Disregarding modernity, reaffirming tradition: bewitching the rain in postcolonial Tanzania', unpublished manuscript.

Scheper-Hughes, N. (1996) 'Theft of life: organ stealing rumours', *Anthropology Today* 12, 3: 3–10.

—— (2000) 'The global traffic in human organs', *Current Anthropology* 41, 2: 191–224.

Scott, J.C. (1985) *Weapons of the Weak: Everyday Forms of Peasant Resistance*, New Haven: Yale University Press.

Sharp, L.A. (2000) 'The commodification of the body and its parts', *Annual Review of Anthropology* 29: 287–328.

Shaw, R. (1997a) 'Cosmologers and capitalism: knowing history and practising sorcery in Mayotte', *Cultural Dynamics* 9, 2: 183–194.

—— (1997b) 'The production of witchcraft/witchcraft as production: memory, modernity, and the slave trade in Sierra Leone', *American Ethnologist* 24, 4: 856–876.

Stewart, K. and Harding, S. (1999) 'Bad endings: American apocalypsis', *Annual Review of Anthropology* 28: 285–310.

Strandsbjerg, C. (2000) 'Kérékou, god and the ancestors: religion and the conceptions of political power in Benin', *African Affairs* 99: 395–414.

Swartz, M.J. (1970) 'Modern conditions and witchcraft/sorcery accusations', in M. Marwick (ed.) *Witchcraft and Sorcery*, London: Penguin.

Tambiah, S.J. (2000) 'Transnational movements, diaspora, and multiple modernities', *Dædalus* (special issue: *Multiple Modernities*) 129, 1: 163–194.

Taylor, C. (1999) 'Two theories of modernity', *Public Culture* (special issue: *Alter/native modernities*) 11, 1: 153–174.

Turner, V. (1957) *Schism and Continuity in an African Society: A Study of Ndembu Village Life*, Manchester: University Press.

Tylor, E.B. (1913 [1871]) *Primitive Culture*, London: Murray.

van Binsbergen, W. (1981) *Religious Change in Zambia: Exploratory Studies*, London: Kegan Paul.

van Dijk, R.A. (1995) 'Fundamentalism and its moral geography in Malawi: the representation of the diasporic and the diabolical', *Critique of Anthropology* 15, 2: 171–191.

van Velsen, J. (1964) *The Politics of Kinship: A Study in Social Manipulation among the Lakeside Tonga*, Manchester: University Press.

Viccars, J.D. (1949) 'Witchcraft in Bolobo, Belgian Congo', *Africa* xix, 2: 220–229.

Voyé, L. (1999) 'Secularization in a context of advanced modernity', *Sociology of Religion* 60, 3: 275–288.

Ward, B.E. (1956) 'Some observations on religious cults in Ashanti', *Africa* xxvi: 47–61.

Warnier, J.P. (1988) 'L'Economie politique de la sorcellerie en Afrique Centrale', *Revue de l'Institut de Sociologie* 3–4: 259–271.

Weiss, B. (1998) 'Electric vampires: Haya rumors of the commodified body', in M. Lambek and A. Strathern (eds) *Bodies and Persons: Comparative Perspectives from Africa and Melanesia*, Cambridge: University Press.

West, H.G. (1997) 'Creative destruction and sorcery of construction: power, hope and suspicion in post-war Mozambique', *Cahiers d'Études africaines* 147 xxxvii, 3: 675–698.

—— (2001) 'Sorcery of construction and socialist modernization: ways of understanding power in postcolonial Mozambique', *American Ethnologist* 28, 1: 119–150.

West, H.G. and Sanders, T. (eds) (n.d.) *Conspiracy and Transparency*, unpublished manuscript.

Williams, D. (1999) 'Constructing the economic space: the World Bank and the making of *Homo Oeconomicus*', *Millennium* 28, 1: 79–99.

Willis, R.G. (1968) 'Kamcape: an anti-sorcery movement in south-west Tanzania', *Africa* 38: 1–15.

Wilson, G. (1936) 'An African morality', *Africa* ix, 1: 75–99.

Winter, E.H. (1963) 'The enemy within: Amba witchcraft and sociological theory', in J. Middleton and E.H. Winter (eds) *Witchcraft and Sorcery in East Africa*, London: Routledge and Kegan Paul.

—— (1965 [1959]) *Beyond the Mountains of the Moon: The Lives of Four Africans*, Urbana: University of Illinois Press.

Yamba, C.B. (1997) 'Cosmologies in turmoil: witchfinding and AIDS in Chiawa, Zambia', *Africa* 67, 2: 200–223.

Yanagisako, S. and Delaney, C. (eds) (1995) *Naturalizing Power: Essays in Feminist Cultural Analysis*, New York: Routledge.

Yang, M.M.-H. (2000) 'Putting global capitalism in its place: economic hybridity, Bataille, and ritual expenditure', *Current Anthropology* 41, 4: 477–509.

Chapter 2

Delusions of development and the enrichment of witchcraft discourses in Cameroon

Francis B. Nyamnjoh

Development: of dominant and dormant systems of knowledge

A western epistemological export that marries science and ideology in subtle ways for hegemonic purposes has dominated social science in and on Africa, and coloured perceptions of Africa even by Africans. This dominant epistemological export has not always been sensitive to new perspectives that question conventional wisdom and myopic assumptions. It has largely remained faithful to a type of social science induced and informed more by fantasies, prejudices, stereotypes, ideologies and biases about Africa and Africans. Given its remarkable ability to reproduce and market itself globally, this epistemological export has emptied academia of the power and impact of competing systems of knowledge by Africans (Mudimbe 1988: x–xi). Yet, only by re-integrating sidelined epistemologies can African studies graduate from scholarship by analogy to scholarship informed by African worldviews and historical processes (Mamdani 1996: 12–13).

Under the dominant epistemological import from the west, most accounts of African cultures and experiences have been generated from the insensitive position of power and quest for convergence and homogeneity. Explicit or implicit in these accounts is the assumption that African societies should reproduce western ideals and institutions regardless of the feasibility or contextual differences. Few researchers of Africa have seriously questioned the theories, concepts and basic assumptions that inform the dominant epistemological import. The tendency has been to conform to a world conceived in the image of the west without the rest (cf. Abdel-Malek 1967: 250–264; Chinweizu 1987). The looks they have generally brought to bear on the continent and its realities have been mainly condescending, and have tended to devalue or reject many social experiences Africans value. Mudimbe notes that 'Even in the most explicitly "Afrocentric" descriptions, models of analysis explicitly or implicitly, knowingly or unknowingly, refer' to 'categories and conceptual systems which depend on a western epistemological order' as if 'African *Weltanschauungen* and African traditional systems of thought are unthinkable and cannot be made explicit within the framework of their own rationality' or 'epistemological locus' (Mudimbe 1988: x). Often missing are perspectives of the silent majorities deprived of the opportunity to tell their own story their own way or even to enrich others' defective accounts with their own life experiences. Correcting this entails paying more attention to the popular epistemology on which ordinary people draw daily, and the ways they situate themselves in relationship to others within that epistemology.

To understand the importance of witchcraft and its relationship to development or the lack thereof in Cameroon, we must understand the popular epistemological order to which Cameroonians subscribe. Under the dominant western export, reality is presented as anything whose existence has, or can be, established in a rational, objective manner. According to this export, the world is dichotomous: there is the real and the unreal. The real is the rational, the natural, and the scientific; the unreal is the irrational, the supernatural and the subjective. Such a dichotomy has also been used to categorize whole societies, countries and regions, depending on how these 'others' were perceived in relation to western Cartesian rationalism and empiricism.

The popular epistemological order in Cameroon and most of Africa does not subscribe to the same dichotomies. On the contrary, it builds bridges between or marries the so-called natural and supernatural, rational and irrational, objective and subjective, scientific and superstitious, visible and invisible, real and unreal; making it impossible for anything to be one without also being the other. It is an epistemological order where the sense of *sight* and *physical evidence* have not assumed the same centrality, dominance or dictatorship evident in the western export's 'hierarchies of perceptual faculties' (van Dijk and Pels 1996: 248–251). It has equal space for all the senses, just as it does for the visible and the invisible. The real is not only what is observable or what makes cognitive sense; it is also the invisible, the emotional, the sentimental (Redfield 1997). In this epistemology emphasis is on the whole, and truth is something consensual, not the result of artificial disqualification, dismemberment or atomization.

In this popular system of knowledge, the opposite or complement of presence is not necessarily absence, but invisibility. Thus, as Mbembe (1997) argues, understanding the visible is hardly complete without investigating the invisible. We misunderstand the world if we 'consider the obverse and the reverse of the world as two opposite sides, with the former partaking of a "being there" (*real presence*) and the latter as "being elsewhere" or a "non-being" (*irremediable absence*) or, worse, of the order of unreality'. The obverse and its reverse are also linked by similarities which do not make them mere copies of each other, but which unite and at the same time distinguish themselves according to the Cameroonian or African 'principle of *simultaneous multiplicities*' (Mbembe 1997: 152). In other words, far from merely being the other side, the mask or substitute of the visible, the invisible is in the visible, and vice versa, 'not as a matter of artifice, but as *one and the same* and as external reality simultaneously – or as the image of the thing and the imagined thing at the same time' (Mbembe 1997: 152).

Following this 'principle of simultaneous multiplicities', we can understand why, for example, few conflicts make sense without understanding the role of supernatural powers and those witches, diviners and (oc)cult members who wield them. A person who wishes to harm or influence another through witchcraft or other occult means need not bother with the victim's physical absence when something of his or hers (hair, cloth or whatever) can serve as a substitute. One may be visible and physically present, at the same time that one's spirit has temporarily left the body to hunt for game in the likeness of a predator, to commit mischief, or to wreak havoc on others and their property. This speaks not only of the multi-dimensionality of life, but also of the fact that all of life's dimensions can be articulated simultaneously at various levels, visible and invisible.

Writing about Togo and Liberia, Ellis (1993, 1999: 220–280) argues that a powerful person is one who can convince others he or she controls a complex array of visible and invisible forces. For 'just as a person known to have political power is presumed also to have power over the spirit world, so a person who successfully manipulates the symbols of spiritual control is assumed also to be in possession of political power' (Ellis 1993: 471). In a context where wealth, prestige and power are in limited supply and intensely sought after, one must be ingenious in one's quest for these things. And 'acquiring the strength of others through eating their vital organs or drinking their blood' after ritual killings, could be a sure technique for acquiring or maintaining all three (Ellis 1999: 265). Appearances can indeed be deceptive.

This popular epistemological order is also at variance with the tendency in the western export to minimize the power of society, social structures, communal and cultural solidarities by 'trumpeting instead the uncompromising autonomy of the individual, rights-bearing, physically discrete, monied, market-driven, materially inviolate human subject' (Comaroff and Comaroff 1999a: 3). It refuses to see individuals and social structures as passive and easily detachable from one another, to be manipulated into compliance with the expectations of those who know best. It stresses instead a mix between individual rights and interests on the one hand, and the rights and interests of groups and collectivities, on the other.

In discussions of development in Africa, the narrow insistence on individual rights, freedoms and aspirations even among academics has impaired understanding of the interconnectedness of peoples, cultures and societies refusing to see individuals as products, melting-pots and creative manipulators or jugglers of 'multiple identities' (Werbner 1996). Imported western discourses on development and democracy tend to recognize individuals and nation-states as *real*, but either ignore the existence of intermediate communities, or treat these as backsliding on the long march towards modernity. Discussing agency and development in Africa demands careful scrutiny of individual and collective cultural identities. Indigenous African ideas of freedom need to feed into the current sterility of the dominant western epistemological export on the continent. It is traditionally African to see and treat the individual as a child of the community, as someone allowed to pursue his or her needs, but not greed. The individual's creativity, abilities and powers must be harnessed, in order to be acknowledged and provided for. Agency has meaning only as domesticated agency, by which is meant agency that stresses negotiation, interconnectedness and harmony between individual interests and group expectations. In other words, with domesticated agency, the freedom to pursue individual or group goals exists within a socially predetermined framework that emphasizes conviviality with collective interests while simultaneously allowing for individual creativity and self-fulfilment. Social visibility or notability derives from being interconnected with others in a communion of interests. Given life's vicissitudes, it pays to be modest about personal success, and measured in one's ambitions.

Through domesticated agency, the collectivity shares the responsibility of success and the consequences of failure with the active and creative individual, thereby easing the pressure on individuals to prove themselves in a world of ever-diminishing opportunities. Domesticated agency does not deny individuals the freedom to associate or to be self-reliant or independent, but rather puts a premium on interdependence as insurance against the risk of dependence, where people face the impermanence of independent success. Achievement is devoid of meaning if not pursued within, as part of, and on behalf of a group of people who recognize that achievement. For only by making their successes collective can individuals make their failures a collective concern as well. Such domestication emphasizes negotiation, concession and conviviality over maximization of pursuits by individuals or by particular groups in contexts of plurality and diversity. Appreciation should be reserved and room created for excellence, especially for individuals who demonstrate how well they are ready to engage with collective interests. Individuals who refuse to work towards enhancing their community are those most likely to be denied the public space to articulate their personal desires.

And faced with the vicissitudes, temporality or transience of personal success in the context of African modernity, even the most achieving and cosmopolitan or diasporic of individuals hesitates to sever links with kin entirely. They strive instead to make their village community part of their successes and good fortunes in the world beyond, so that, in return, the community will help them in times of individual failure and misfortune. The city and the 'world out there' are perceived as hunting grounds; the home village the place to return to at the end of the day. Investing in one's home village is generally seen as the best insurance policy, and a sign of ultimate success, for it guarantees survival even when one has lost everything in the city, and secures and manifests success in satisfying obligations (Nyamnjoh 2000). Thus, although successful urbanites may not permanently return to or retire in their home villages, most remain in constant contact with them, and some wish to be buried or re-buried there (Geschiere and Nyamnjoh 2000). Even those who have no ties with village kin and are permanently trapped in urban spaces often reproduce the village and localist styles in subtle and imaginative ways. No one, it seems, is too cosmo-politan to be local as well.

Witchcraft and the occult in Cameroon

African epistemology has important implications for the study of witchcraft and how it relates to development. Scholars inspired by the dominant western epistemological import have tended to be dichotomous in their approaches to witchcraft. When not simply dismissed as superstitious beliefs and practices by primitives, witchcraft has tended to be confined to rural or village communities where individuals are still supposedly trapped by custom and tradition. The expectation has been that once de-contaminated, disinfected, exorcized or enlightened by science through education and urbanization, the village African should abandon, as a matter of course, his or her penchant for witchcraft beliefs and practices, accusations or counter-accusations, just as Europeans are *presumed* to have done. The city or town has tended to be excluded, *a priori*, from studies of witchcraft; city dwellers have either been assumed to be rational, civilized and scientific in their outlook and behaviour, or the victims of witches and wizards from their backward-looking home villages. Often tantalized by such assumptions, cosmopolitan Africans have found themselves pretending to be Cartesian rationalists in public or declaration, and epistemologically autochthonous and/or indigenous in private or practice (Nyamnjoh 1991).

However, witchcraft and the occult have no sacred spaces. They are as practised in urban spaces as in rural ones, as much by the most cosmopolitan as by the most localist. They may assume new forms and new uses (Geschiere 1997), but witchcraft and occult practices form part of everyday life in urban Africa (e.g. Ashforth 1996, Chapter 10; Bastian, Chapter 4; van Dijk, Chapter 5). Even a casual perusal of newspapers makes plain that the urban elite, those who publish and read these papers, are obsessed with witchcraft and the occult, especially in the context of globalized consumerism (cf. Comaroff and Comaroff 1999b, 1999c).

In contemporary Africa, development is presented as the way to salvation, promising concrete and visible results; but the more it is pursued, the greater an illusion it becomes. High expectations are not matched by positive results, and disappointment grows by leaps and bounds. Development or modernity seems to excel in churning out 'malcontents' (Comaroff and Comaroff 1993) through unilinearity and zombification. A world where development is promised to many, but where only a few reap the rewards, is bound to baffle and disappoint. It is also bound to intensify questioning of Cartesian rationalism as a solution. And even if the elite leadership cannot afford to pursue this questioning openly and aggressively for fear of turning off the tap of development assistance, then their private lives continue to bridge the artificial chasms between science and witchcraft, and between the individual and community. Faced with repeated detours and derailments on the way to the Calvary of Development or

Modernity, the African elite have opted for the more realistic and reassuring alternative of straddling the visible and invisible worlds which the popular epistemology has always treated as complementary parts of reality, the pursuit of which any inclusive science ought to make its mission.

In this light, we can understand the widespread belief in and resilience of sorcery or occult forces in Cameroon not so much in terms of the inability of Cameroonians to modernize their beliefs and rituals, but as reflecting collective preoccupations with the conflictual relationships between competing agentive forces in societies where promises of development are fast becoming broken dreams for all but an elite few (cf. Ferguson 1999). Sorcery can be as much a source and resource of personal and collective power or powerlessness as it is a call for domesticated agency against various forms of exploitation, marginalization, inequality and individualism (Ardener 1996: 243–260; Rowlands and Warnier 1988: 121–125; Warnier 1993a: 139–162; Geschiere 1997; Fisiy and Geschiere 1996: 193–197; Geschiere and Nyamnjoh 1998). Indeed, the fact that sorcery accusations usually occur between family members or kin is indicative of how much ordinary Cameroonians cherish the solidarity of domesticated agency and how ready they are to protect it from aggression and the harmful pursuit of personal success (see Geschiere 1995: 7–35; Fisiy and Geschiere 1996: 197; Geschiere and Nyamnjoh 1998). For what use is a social system that glorifies personal success but in reality has little space for all who seek it? Success attainable only at the expense of others' humanity is not considered worth pursuing.

Witchcraft and politics in urban Cameroon: animality and power

Let us look at some allegations of mystical connections in urban Cameroon, the veracity of which has generally been accepted. In 1994, following a double slash in civil servants' salaries and a 50 per cent devaluation of the Franc CFA, rumours of mystical occurrences connected with sex and sexuality were common-place – quite understandable in a country where *phallocracy* has become a dominant mode of power, and where men use wealth and office to debase and extract maximal libidinal pleasure from women (cf. Mbembe 1992, 1997). In Limbe, rumours suggested that Igbo businessmen from Nigeria were making local men's sexual organs shrink or disappear, simply by shaking hands with them. Limbe women were rumoured food for Nigerian business tycoons' penises. These stories were, and are, widely reported and widely believed. Around the same time, it was rumoured that two girls from the University of Yaounde fell victim to a foreign tycoon. Stories claimed the girls dated the man, and later returned to his posh residence in the Bastos area. Rather than sleeping with the girls, the foreigner chose one, and allegedly transformed himself into a boa constrictor and began to swallow her. When the other girl realized what was happening, she hastily departed and alerted the police. The police investigation supposedly revealed that this was common practice for this man. This story circulated widely in the press, on *Radio Trottoir* and by word of mouth, and was generally believed. Today, thousands of such stories about mystical boa constrictors circulate around the country.

Professor Gervais Mendo Ze, General Manager of Cameroon Radio Television (CRTV) since the early 1990s, has masterminded most of the manipulation that has kept President Biya recycling and perfecting the insensitivities of illegitimate power. He has also been at the centre of numerous rumours connecting him with straddling religions – being both a committed Catholic who propounds the virtues of the Virgin Mary (*mariologie*) on the one hand, and a Rosicrucian whose mystical totem is a boa constrictor that sucks the blood of young virgins whom he entices with money and expensive gifts of necklaces (*serpentologie*) on the other. Rumour has it he drinks his victims' menstrual blood. On 15 February 1999, a girl known simply as 'cousine Elise' phoned the Yaounde FM94 *A Coeur Ouvert* presenter Joly Nnib Ngom, to accuse 'a well placed personality of the Republic' whom she had dated for six to seven months of having given her a boa constrictor in the form of an expensive gold necklace.[1] Rumour immediately associated Mendo Ze with the girl, and matters worsened when Mendo Ze suspended the programme's presenter. The rumour was given extensive coverage in the private press and was widely disseminated in public places. Although the presenter was eventually reinstated, the rumour remained, and Mendo Ze has since been given the nickname of *serpentologue*, to go with *mariologue*. The reputation he had gained as Deacon and expert on the Virgin Mary was subsequently dented when Christians protested against his alleged occult practices with mysterious snakes, and the Catholic authorities banned him from giving communion.

In Yaounde on Christmas day 1999, four children went missing. Three days later, they were found dead in an abandoned car with their genitals cut off.[2] Rumours started that Professor Mendo Ze had hired someone to carry out the ritual killing, since he allegedly trafficked in human body parts (Sanders, Chapter 8). A few months later, Magistrate Louis Ndzie was savagely murdered in Yaounde. Purportedly he was the one handling the murdered children's file, and he had vowed to catch Mendo Ze for his diabolical acts. Having failed to influence the magistrate through his wife (with whom Mendo Ze was said to have had an affair) and with a bribe of several million Francs CFA, Mendo Ze reportedly asked the wife to hire thugs to eliminate her magistrate husband. Shocked, Yaounde magistrates threatened a strike action, which was only averted by a hurried countrywide reshuffle of magistrates, ordered by President Biya. The late magistrate's wife was reportedly detained at the Kondengui Central Prison in Yaounde.

Why is there the tendency to believe these stories without *proof*? To those who subscribe to the popular epistemology where reality consists of the visible and the invisible, these stories make perfect sense. Since the early 1990s, President Biya, with the assistance of Mendo Ze and others, has thwarted popular aspirations for democracy. The elite have stood their ground against the Cameroonian majority, remaining insensitive to calls for change. Even when beaten in the polls they have remained obstinate. This is not natural, and cannot be explained simply in terms of Cartesian rationalism. How can a handful of people defy the will of the majority of Cameroonians? There must be some unseen forces, a face behind the mask, that imbues them with power and confidence beyond the ordinary; power and confidence that have succeeded, quite strangely, in hypnotizing masses of angry, hungry and disaffected Cameroonians during a more than ten-year clamour for democracy.

As recently as July 2000, Professor Gervais Mendo Ze boasted that *his* CRTV journalists were *Les Lions Indomptables de l'audio-visuel*. At the 1992 presidential elections, Paul Biya presented himself as *l'homme Lion*, imbued with the power, courage and intentions of protecting Cameroon from *les marchands d'illusions*; the main opposition leader John Fru Ndi and his Social Democratic Front (SDF) were presented as champions by CRTV. In taxis, market places, bars, chicken-parlours and elsewhere, ordinary people saw Biya's message as a corruption of reality. He was a lion, no doubt. But his mission was not to save but to devastate, for five more years, Cameroon and her people. This alternative interpretation never made its way to national radio and television, not even through the other presidential candidates, whose campaign broadcasts were heavily monitored and censored. Jean-Jacque Ekindi, for example, a 1992 presidential candidate, who had baptized himself the foremost *chasseur du Lion* (lion hunter), had his trenchant campaign counter-offensives banned by CRTV. Crowning CRTV the 'Indomitable Lion' of the broadcast media while the government was pretending to be liberalizing broadcasting, was a timely reminder to the information-hungry public not to take the government's rhetoric on liberalization too seriously. Cameroon, in short, had space for only three Indomitable Lions: President Biya, the CRTV, and the national football team, whose victories and fame the President and CRTV were simulating through manipulation and corruption.[3]

The tendency to believe in a hidden hand is akin to an indictment of liberal democracy and its illusions of empowerment and development. Liberal democracy and the version of development it inspires promise political, economic and cultural enrichment for all. But in reality a hidden hand (of capital, the west, etc.) determines who among the many shall be provided for. Its rhetoric of opening up, and of abundance, is sharply contradicted by the reality of closures and of want for most of its disciples. The hidden hand of global capital and its concerns, for example, through the IMF, World Bank and national interests of Western partners, make it possible for autocracy to pay lip-service to democracy and development in exchange for guaranteeing the political stability needed by investors to venture into the periphery. In exchange for having weak foreign relations, autocratic regimes like Cameroon's are afforded the ability and protection to flex their muscles within their own countries, in a perplexing and mystical manner. Hence, instead of democracy and development for ordinary people who want such things, one finds myriad ways people's rights and dignities are bargaining away. Cameroonians and Africans, who are well aware of this contradiction, realize that pursuing undomesticated agency is a very risky business. There is an ever-looming possibility, even for the most successful and cosmopolitan, of the sudden unexplained failure, and of having to cope alone; hence, nearly everyone's eagerness to maintain kin networks they can turn to in times of need. Even those who have severed kin links entirely seek such solidarity in kin of another type: for some ruling elite, these alternative networks are provided by membership in mystical cults such as Rosicrucianism and Freemasonry. These alternative networks purport to offer them double protection: against the harmful expectations of village kin; and against the vicissitudes or impermanence of success in the modern world. Hence whether one is entirely localist or cosmopolitan, or both, witchcraft and the occult seem always to provide solutions to otherwise insurmountable problems, both for those modernity has by-passed and for those on whom it has smiled. The sort of uncertainties and anxieties people feel in modern life simply cannot be attended to by the imported pseudo-scientific doctrine of Cartesian rationalism and empiricism alone. This is obvious even to the most learned (in Cartesian rationalist and empiricist terms) and cosmopolitan.

Examples of mystical happenings associated with the powerful are countless. One could easily write volumes just on allegations and rumour about the invisible and political power in Cameroon. In February 1997 an oil-filled train derailed in Yaounde. It was rumoured that the indigenes, the Ewondo (of the same ethnic origin as President Biya and his closest collaborators), barred all non-indigenes from recovering for themselves any spilt oil. They reputedly claimed the oil belonged to the autochthons alone. A disaster occurred when someone inadvertently struck a match, and hundreds of people died. This, like other accidents and deaths, was also linked to the ruling Cameroon People's Democratic Movement (CPDM) party and the President, whom it was alleged usually made mystical sacrifices of ordinary militants and supporters before a major political event, which in this case was the imminent parliamentary elections scheduled for May 1997. On previous occasions, the deaths of family members (e.g. Jeanne-Irene Biya) and close collaborators of President Biya (e.g. Motaze Roger, a presidential cook, Jean Assoumou and Jean Fochive), have been connected with rumour that they had been sacrificed to occult forces so that the President could survive difficult political spells. Political survival, according to such rumours, is predicated upon human sacrifices to occult forces. In a context where the vote has been rendered impotent by greed and ulterior motives, legitimacy has to be conferred by less visible mechanisms than formal elections.

Cabinet reshuffles are always preceded by rumours of occult sacrifices, visits to fortune-tellers and witchcraft practices. Incumbents and aspirants are said to scheme for cabinet positions, and to employ natural and occult forces to this end. Various lodges and fraternities allegedly play a major part in determining who stays and who becomes what. Among the key players are Rosicrucianism and Freemasonry, both of which are influenced and implanted from France, a major and not-so-hidden hand in Cameroonian politics. It was even rumoured that President Biya financed the construction of a Rosicrucian lodge in France, and that he moved his membership between lodges depending on his political fortunes.[4] He might be a Catholic and even an ex-seminarian whose family has been personally blessed by Pope John Paul II on two consecutive visits to Yaounde, but this does not stop him, nor apparently contradict his allegedly cultivating mystical identities to buttress his political power base.[5]

If the reality of politics were limited to the apparent and the transparent as prescribed by liberal democracy, there would hardly be reason to explain success or failure otherwise. In general, if people had what they merited, and merited what they had in liberal democratic terms, there would be little need for a hidden hand of any kind, real or imagined. But because nothing is what it seems, the invisible must be considered to paint a full picture of reality.

Kinship, development and witchcraft in the Bamenda Grassfields

The following two cases offer insights into understandings of success and development in the Bamenda Grassfields of north-west Cameroon (cf. Rowlands 1994, 1995). Again, this is an understanding informed by the popular episte- mology as discussed above and revisited below.

Case one

Mr X came from Guzang in the Northwest Province and lived in Mutengene, Southwest Province. He had close relatives (his brother's children) in Ekona, a few miles from Mutengene. Until his brutal murder in July 1999, he was the local headman or chief of the Metah community in Mutengene, a position he had earned for his long residence there, his good character and his reputation for friendliness and charity. He was also considered rich, owning a large compound, several houses and an off-licence bar. Mr X was a Presbyterian, and an active member in the Christian Men's Fellowship (CMF); he reportedly loaned them nine million Francs CFA for their uniforms.

Though some thought Mr X became rich from his prolonged service as a driver with the now-defunct Marketing Board, his kin in Ekona claimed it was because he had joined an occult group. This suspicion was strengthened by an account of a fellow Metah man who had paid a casual visit to his residence and found a glittering cross on the door. This man was so terrified that he had fortified himself by ingesting some earth (a practice thought to prevent bewitchment) before drinking what his host had served.

The following concerns the savage killing of Mr X by his relatives following accusations of witchcraft. The accusations attest not so much to the inexplic- ability of death, as to the sense that a person's life is inextricably intertwined with kin. For it is in this context that a person achieves successes and failures, and where these 'achievements' are visible and invisibly noted.

Several of Mr X's kin in Ekona had died mysteriously, all allegedly from his witchcraft. The latest was a young man. Mr X was away in his native village, Guzang, at the time. This time, the kin in Ekona vowed not to bury the corpse, but to leave it for Mr X to deal with on his return. Unfortunately for the kin in Ekona, Mr X was delayed so they were forced to bury the corpse themselves. When Mr X eventually returned, he decided, as is customary, to visit his kin to mourn the loss. When he and his two wives arrived at Ekona, their greetings were answered with an unwelcome silence. Shunned by his kin, Mr X decided he and his wives should leave. But before they did, the 'silent kin' confronted him and told him he must visit the deceased's grave. Mr X said that if he did, he would do so of his own volition, not under obligation. This infuriated the relatives, who insisted more adamantly that he visit the grave. When he made it clear that he would not go, however, his relatives beat him and accused him of being responsible for the young man's death. The beating, they argued, was punishment for being vicious (selling his kin to *Nyongo*) to his relatives. They stabbed him with knives and other weapons; one female relative even stabbed him in the eyes. His first wife was also allegedly assaulted, since she was an accomplice to her husband's occult practices. She was only rescued by the intervention of another relative who claimed that Mr X, not she, was the real perpetrator. She then quickly fled and alerted the police, but only too late. By the time they arrived, Mr X was dead.

Sometime prior to all this, Mr X had a serious accident on the Limbe – Mutengene road, damaging his pickup irreparably. He survived unscratched, which again people saw as mysterious. He had been taken to hospital where he spent some time but eventually left without any problems. Rumour had it that the accident was caused by his fellow occult members who had demanded that he sacrifice a victim, which he was reluctant to do. The young boy's death in Ekona was therefore seen as providing this sacrifice, to forestall the threat to his own life by his occult associates.

Case two

The following is the story of Mrs BX, wife of Dr MX, professor in a Cameroonian state university. As in the preceding story, we see the tensions between various communities in which people vest their successes and failures, and the importance of negotiation of individual agency through conviviality. We see, too, the complex epistemological framework of cause and of power within which these tensions take form and negotiations take place.

Mrs BX comes from a strongly Catholic Grassfields family and is well-educated. Both her parents are highly-qualified, long-time primary and secondary school teachers. She was one among five brothers and two sisters; though in 1980 her eldest brother died, and in 1998 she lost her immediate junior brother. All her siblings have either studied or worked in Europe. Her immediate older brother, ZP, went to study in Britain in 1982 and returns home only for brief visits. He has a doctorate, a well-paying job, a British passport, owns a house in London, and recently married a woman from his native Grassfields. Through him, three brothers and two sisters have reached Europe as well, including the one who died in 1998. All are reasonably comfortable, and keep in regular phone and e-mail contact with their parents and sister in Cameroon. They routinely send home modern consumer goods, and sometimes money, for village projects. Mrs BX would have joined them in Europe, were she not happily married and the mother of six children. Like her parents, she is a secondary school teacher, but with a higher qualification from the University of Yaounde.

The following is what Mrs BX, a family friend, kindly shared with me after the loss of her brother in June 1998. Her story not only highlights the point made throughout this chapter about the visible and invisible as complementary in the popular epistemology, but also a common understanding of what it means to succeed. Personal success or achievement counts for very little unless it also includes one's extended family. Focusing merely on the immediate family (parents and siblings) is insufficient.

> When YY, my maternal uncle died, I was a high school student in Kumba. He came and stood by my bed in my sleep. His lips firm, he looked at me for a long time. One week later my eldest brother, QN, died. Just before BV, my junior sibling died in June this year, I had the same dream. My brother QN came and stood by my bed in my sleep, tears in his eyes, but they did not roll down his cheeks. He came with a car, a pickup. There was something in it, which I couldn't quite figure. I called him and asked: 'QN, what's the problem, why have you come to me with such a sad face?' He didn't talk. Then I called him by his nickname, and he looked at me and drove off. The following day my maternal cousin in Douala, LA, came with news that BV's dead. My siblings in Europe called her and told her this. BV died in a car accident, the only one of five passengers to lose his life in the mysterious accident.
>
> When ZP came with the corpse from Europe to the village, papa CC, my father's paternal first cousin, was so happy that he even distributed free drinks to people in an off-licence bar. He went to the stream to fetch water and met some women there and was also happily telling them about BV's death. He swore that my father hadn't seen anything yet – that is how the children will be coming back home one after the other, in coffins. Just as he was about to return home with his water, he fell and seriously fractured his leg. The women present said: 'You see how God is punishing him? How can you rejoice over the death of your brother's child?' They called some nearby men who rushed him to the hospital where he stayed for a month. One of his sisters also said my father wanted to show off his riches, the fact that he has children abroad. 'These are they coming back in coffins,' she rejoiced. [. . .]
>
> After the death ceremony my cousin, LA, in Douala, went and met a female diviner from Bafang based in Douala. This diviner revealed to her

the cause of BV's death and what was to come in the future. She asked for my mother to come to Douala immediately. Cousin LA sent word to my mother and she came and met the diviner. The diviner told her about my youngest brother, UT, how my father's cousins were planning to send an old woman to Italy by witchcraft. This old woman would be walking on the road and someone driving, in an attempt to dodge her, would hit UT and kill him. The diviner asked that my mother should go to the village and bring certain things for her to use to stop the accident from happening. My mother was to bring UT's clothes, gather stones and 5 Francs CFA and throw them into the sea in Douala. The diviner would use the clothes to invoke UT's double to appear. While my mother was still at the motor park [waiting] for a lift to Bamenda, the diviner sent LA to call for her. She said the old woman had already been sent to Italy and within that week the accident was to occur, that she was going to use another method to stop it. She said she couldn't do it alone, since the treatment was to take a week and within that time she was to have her period [menstruation]. So she had to go to the north of the country to meet her fellow diviner to continue the work, because she is not supposed to do any work when she is having her period.

Before she went to the north, the diviner asked my mother to go and bring soil from our compound in Bamenda, from the front and back of the house, and also from papa CC's compound. But when my mother got up by five o'clock, papa CC was already in front of his house. This confirmed what the diviner said that whatever my mother was doing, papa CC was aware of it. However, she managed to get the soil. While in the north, the diviner and her partner also discovered other revelations about us. She said that they wanted to distract my husband from me and to make me and the children suffer, and [that] eventually I will go mad.

Just before ZP returned for his wedding in October this year, the diviner warned that ZP should be very careful because they would be out to get him this time. So my mother asked that my cousin, LA, come with the diviner to the village to explain to my father her findings, and also to work on ZP [fortify him against evil forces]. The diviner also did something in the compound, to protect it from mysterious happenings. Because of her presence in the compound, my father's female cousins did not come for the wedding. As for papa CC, he had not visited the compound for five years.

A few weeks ago, I had a dream that papa CC gave ZP some T-shirts and asked him to distribute them, and whoever got these T-shirts would automatically be taken to Nyongo [sacrificed to the occult]. So when I saw ZP with the T-shirts I shouted at him: 'Why did you accept these T-shirts? Don't you know the implications of these shirts?' So ZP held the shirts and didn't know what to do with them. This same dream recurred two or three nights later. In the third dream, ZP's hands were tied behind him and to a chair; his mouth was tied as well. And they asked him to call his mother to come and help him. I was so frightened in the dream that I awoke abruptly. All of these dreams happened before the death of papa CC last week.

In my thinking, I thought that papa CC wanted to do something but was pre-empted. There is also a male diviner in Bamenda whom my mother met. My mother and father and this diviner went to the outskirts of the village, killed and buried a dog and performed certain rites. In the course of burying this dog, the diviner said that anybody who tried anything against us would die like that dog. Even the Bafang diviner from Douala buried something – a lock – in the compound, and said that anybody who tried to unlock it would fail and then die.

In a telephone conversation the other day, I told ZP in London about the dreams and he told me that he also had a similar dream in which he was given a cap, not T-shirts. And he recalled having been given caps when he came home with BV's corpse. So immediately he went and looked for the caps and said he was going to burn them. He advised me that whenever I have a dream in which I am fighting with a snake or a dog or anybody, I should make sure I kill them or I overcome the person. If it is water or a canoe I shouldn't enter any of them. There is always the belief that when you have a dream and you are fighting and you don't overcome a person and the person overcomes you, it is a bad sign.

These two accounts both concern people from the Bamenda Grassfields of Cameroon, whose ideas of personhood, agency and success are illustrative of the popular epistemology. Both cases present development or modernity as a bazaar to which many are drawn but few rewarded. In the first case, Mr X educates his brother's children under the delusion that education would bring them salvation and success. They migrate to urban areas with certain 'expectations of modernity' (Ferguson 1999). But this has led to unemployment, disillusionment and anxieties. Paradoxically, Mr X, a man of little education himself, continues to accumulate riches to the point that he can loan the Christian Men's Fellowship nine million Francs CFA for luxuries like uniforms. The education he gave his brother's children has proved of little value, and the children are bound to wonder if his apparent generosity was not a con after all – a suspicion only compounded by the fact that the very nephews and nieces he supposedly cares for are dying mysterious deaths while his own children remain untouched. At the end of the day, far from being the source of salvation as he had hoped, he is treated instead as the family's curse, someone who has chosen personal success to the detriment of collective welfare. He has failed to domesticate his agency as an individual, and proceeds to consume his kin instead. For his greed, he must pay the ultimate price: a brutal death, the fate he supposedly reserved for his kin, those for whom he pretended to care.

In the second case, it is obvious that Grassfielders are intolerant of narrow definitions of success or of family. Although Mrs BX's parents have achieved a lot in educating their children who, in turn, have shown gratitude by maintaining family solidarity and redistributing the fruits of their success, it is evident that the wider family is critical of their narrow definition of family and success. As long as the larger family is not integrated clearly and unambiguously, as long as they are not made to feel part of that success, there is a problem. Again we see development or modernity in the Grassfields as an essentially inegalitarian process wherein few rejoice, even when there is limited success. Mysterious deaths and death threats are supposed to instil reason in all that capricious modernity must be encountered jointly to ensure that individuals and their kin triumph together, or comfort one another if they fail.

Domesticated agency and the management of success

In the Grassfields, people's meticulous distinction between good and bad persons of all types speaks eloquently of a conviction that no agency is rewarding for the collectivity, or even, ultimately, for the individual if undomesticated. Undomesticated agency is greed, and success that comes from greed can only be achieved by sacrificing others or their interests, as my study of the notions of *Awung* (an ambivalent type of clairvoyance and clairvoyant) and *Msa* (a dangerous, mysterious and attractive world of infinite possibilities and abundance) in Bum show (Nyamnjoh 1985). Apart from variations in appellation, the notions of *Awung* and *Msa* are common throughout the Bamenda Grassfields. Understanding them is key to understanding ideas of success in the area. In general, Grassfielders tend to believe that 'personal success is essentially destructive unless seen to be acting for the good of all and this ensures that such achievements should be accompanied by egalitarian redistributory mechanisms' (Rowlands 1994: 17).

In his study of personal success in the Bamenda Grassfields, Michael Rowlands points out that, in this region, people believe that personal success always comes at the expense of others. 'Someone who suddenly acquires wealth or good fortune has done so at the expense of close relatives or friends', who are usually thought to have been 'made into zombies' and 'given to societies of sorcerers to work for them and produce wealth in return for the good fortune given to one of their members' (Rowlands 1994: 15). It is believed, he observes, that 'if someone has success in business or politics, has many wives, many goats, or a bountiful harvest of yams or groundnuts, . . . that success must necessarily have been at the expense of someone else's career or that he/she will have sucked the fertility out of the families, livestock or fields of someone else' (Rowlands 1994: 15–16). Thus his conclusion that the Bamenda area

> shares a mercantilist philosophy according to which resources are in a fixed and limited supply and what someone has 'eaten' is appropriated at the expense of the whole society. Life in itself is part of the bargain, and if someone is sick or dies, it must be that someone has sucked away his/her life to feed on it. The wealthy will have to take this into consideration and

should people experience misfortune or die among his kin and neighbours, accusations may arise.

(Rowlands 1994: 17)

Agency as the ability to manipulate oneself into a position of abundance while others struggle to get by, is perceived as destructive to others and, ultimately, to the accumulating individual too, as discussions below of the ambivalence of Msa and *awung* further demonstrate. It is not enough to belong to a group or community; such belonging must impact positively on one's kin to be recognized. So while it could be argued that even the villains and sorcerers described below identify with communities at Msa or form communities of *awung* respectively, the fact that they are considered destructive to their own kin and communities, means they are neither recognized nor legitimated.

This ethos is well-articulated in ideas of personhood and agency in the Grassfields. The beliefs and categories explored below are of course neither static nor uncontested. Nonetheless, they are widely shared and invoked, particularly in times of stress, misfortune and uncertainties (Geschiere and Nyamnjoh 1998). In what follows, it is evident that Msa and *awung* are central to common understandings of, and beliefs about, how the world should be organized to maximize everyone's interests. Since people are born with different abilities, and because shortage is a fact of life, it is important for the extra-gifted to harness their *awung* and knowledge of Msa so the less well-endowed can benefit too. Using one's talents for personal gratification alone is likely to occasion more conflict and pain than satisfaction and pleasure for all, talented or not.

Most people in the Bamenda Grassfields believe in a supreme God (*Fyen*) who is responsible for creation. He endows some individuals with clairvoyance (*seba* = two eyes), others with innocence (*seimok* = one eye). The 'clairvoyant' are said to be endowed with an ability (sing. *fintini*; plur. *fintitu*) to see and do certain things that their 'innocent' counterparts cannot. Clairvoyants are commonly called clever people (sing. *wutatoffana* = person of sense; plur. *ghetatoffana*), meaning manipulative and slippery. The innocent is associated with short-sightedness, incapability and, at times, foolishness. The verb 'to see' (*yen*) is sometimes used to distinguish between the clairvoyant and the innocent, and means the ability to perceive, even the invisible. The former sees (*yenalo*), and the latter sees not (*yenawi*).

To those who share this belief, 'clairvoyant' and 'innocent' are the only two categories of person: everyone is born one or the other. However, each category has two subcategories. A clairvoyant might be associated either with Awung or Msa. Awung (pl. *uwung*) are further subdivided into two: Wise person (sing. *awungadzunga* = good *awung*; pl. *uwungudzungu*); and Sorcerer (sing. *awungabe* = bad *awung*; pl: *uwungube*). Msa or Cunning (sing. *wutamsa* = person of Msa; pl. *ghetamsala*) is the appellation of the second subcategory of clairvoyant, which is also subdivided into two: Sly (sing. *wutamsamdzung* = good person of Msa; pl. *ghetamsamdzunga*); and Villain (sing. *wutamsamba* = bad person of Msa; pl.

ghetamsambe). The innocent fall into either of two subtypes: Medium (sing. *wut-ni-toffotu* = person with intelligence; pl. *gheta-ni-toffotu*); or Inept (sing. *ayung, ngwo, mumu* = person capable of nothing great; pl: *wuyung, wungwo, wumumu*).

People believe that *awung* is practised the world over. Sorcerers are generally associated with lies, gossip, treachery, jealousy, egoism and wickedness. According to some of my informants, a person who publicly disagrees with the majority must be a sorcerer, for no one else would dare. *Awung* is identified through a person's actions and words most of the time, since no one has ever ordinarily seen another actually eating human flesh. Sorcerers eat or deplete their victims mysteriously at night, because, an individual may be said to have been eaten, when in reality he/she is still alive and going about his daily activities. However, it is said that even then, the victims are just like shadows of themselves, their hearts having been taken out and eaten, their life-essence gone. They may be visible but they have been killed in the world of the invisible.

Sorcerers are seen as destructive, jealous people, opposed to progress. They tend to hunt in the house rather than in the bush. Sorcerers, like villains, must choose their victims among their kin, and are expected to prove intimacy by removing their victims' amulets; it is very dangerous for a sorcerer to remove someone's amulet with whom he or she has no kinship ties. Sorcerers can enhance their clairvoyance with medicine or magic. This further empowers them and makes them less vulnerable to other sorcerers, or to diviners, of whom they are very suspicious. Sorcerers' relationships with diviners are marked by mutual fear and distrust, and people say that sorcerers would not hesitate to poison diviners they see as traitors. If sorcerers are those who have severed links with the community of kin entirely, diviners are those with a foot in both worlds, straddling the realities of the kin and the undomesticated agency of the sorcerers.

From the foregoing discussion of personhood, it is evident that *Msa* represents an important dimension in certain mainstream understandings of agency in the Grassfields. Most people believe *Msa* to be a mysterious world of abundance and infinite possibilities. It is present everywhere – at home, in a river, and the bush – and can be made visible by 'Cunning' individuals. It is sometimes called *Kunta, Nyongo, Famla*, or *Kupeh*, following exposure to new forms of witchcraft by those who have migrated to the cities and plantations in search of a better life (cf. Ardener 1996). Only 'Cunning' individuals can visit *Msa* anytime, anywhere. *Msa* is a world of beauty, abundance and marvels, where everything can be found. It is inhabited by its own people who look no different from ordinary people. The people of *Msa* live in even better houses, but speak local languages; just as the people of *Msa* of other communities speak the respective languages of these areas. *Msa* can be found everywhere in the world. But its inhabitants are very wicked, hostile and vicious; they are what people call devils (*deblisu*).

Villains, when they want something valuable, take their victims to *Msa* to be tethered like goats. *Msa* is like a market, complete with traders and buyers, a bazaar where many come but where few are rewarded. To get what one wants, one must bargain and pay for it. But the only currency in *Msa* is human beings, variously referred to as 'goat' or 'fowl'. At *Msa*, villains can only get what they want after complete payment. Villains who fail to honour their debts must pay with their own lives. The number of 'fowls' or 'goats' to be paid, once agreed upon, cannot be revoked. This is why, while at *Msa*, the more sensible 'Sly' individuals are hesitant to promise payments or to enter into debt.

People also believe that anything that comes from *Msa* multiplies or proliferates. *Msa* is, above all, an ambivalent place – full of good and bad, pleasure and pain. As *Beben* Ktteh of Fonfuka put it:

> At *Msa*, you are first shown only the good, the fantastic, the marvellous. This normally attracts you. Then you are trapped and caught. And you die. It is after death that you are shown the other phase of it – the bad and distasteful aspect of it. At *Msa*, after your death, you are enslaved completely: You are ill-treated, overworked, discriminated against and so on. Sometimes its inhabitants use you as a pillow on their beds, ask you to work on their farms, to carry water for them, wash their dishes and so on. And you do all this work when their own children and themselves do just nothing.

Msa is a world of extremes. In it, there is more good than one can imagine, and more evil than the imagination can grasp. *Msa* is both good and evil, and no one can have one without the other. Yet *Msa*'s most problematic aspect is that evil is seemingly enveloped in goodness; one often gets more than one sees. The personal success *Msa* appears to offer is ultimately an illusion; so, also, is the semblance of a new solidarity and a counter-community it creates in individuals by encouraging them to sacrifice their own kin and traditional alliances. When life becomes hard, *Msa*'s true ethos – greed and callous indifference – come to the fore, and individuals must make the ultimate sacrifice: giving their own lives. In other words, there is no group spirit, solidarity or collective consciousness at *Msa*; only individuals seeking to maximize their greed, and sometimes paying the ultimate price. Interdependence, interconnectedness and intersubjectivity seem to threaten the very existence of *Msa*; hence its violent opposition to all attempts at conviviality between the individual and his or her community of origin. The surest and safest way to benefit from *Msa* without becoming trapped by its evils is to be a 'Wise person'; that is, choosing not to belong fully to *Msa* but to act as a bridge between the two worlds. In other words, domesticating one's connections with *Msa* is the surest way of survival for *Msa*, the individual and his or her kin.

From the foregoing, it is hard to resist seeing *Msa* as analogous to modern capitalism, especially as experienced on the periphery (cf. Warnier 1993a: 159–162; Ardener 1996: 243–260): its rhetoric of emancipation and empowerment for the individual who sacrifices family and custom to embrace modernity, on the one hand, and the harsh reality of exploitation, zombification, debasement, depletion and disenchantment it occasions, on the other. Many scholars have explored the relationship between persistent beliefs in Msa and other forms of witchcraft and the changing nature of capitalism and its effects on the periphery. While local beliefs in Msa predate the transatlantic slave trade, and communication between the Grassfields and the coastal regions predates colonialism and plantation agriculture, current discourses or narratives on witchcraft in the Grassfields are heavily coloured by the symbols and associations of capitalism. Most recent analyses have explained the resurgence of witchcraft beliefs in mysterious centres of accumulation in Cameroon and elsewhere in Africa, with the globalization of poverty, uncertainty, and anxiety generated by consumer capitalism. While witchcraft cannot be explained by the impact of capitalism alone, neither can we ignore it, since the tremendous expansion of the market economy in recent years 'has given a new impetus to the idioms of accumulation and dis-accumulation through various kinds of leakages' (Warnier 1993b: 310).

The ideas of Msa and awung can be seen as statements both against undomesticated agency, as well as against capitalism's illusion of the permanence of personal success. Like capitalism, Msa and awung, when unharnessed, bring power and opportunities to only a few – those with the clairvoyance and greed to indulge in them. Like global capitalism which caters to the needs of investors, advertisers and affluent global consumers, the undomesticated pursuit of Msa and awung enhances the self-seeking individuals at the expense of family and the wider community. It is only by marginalizing family and collective interests – by manipulating, exploiting or taking advantage of others – that the selfish pursuit of clairvoyance can afford for its disciples personal success (Rowlands 1994, 1995; Warnier 1993a: 163–196). But such success is merely an illusion because, like consumer capitalism, Msa and awung are seemingly eternal cycles of indebtedness, manipulation, zombification and the never-ending search for fulfilment. The appetites Msa and awung bring only grow stronger, and those who yield to their allure are instantly trapped and ultimately consumed, but not before consuming their own and others' sociality. This impermanence of success even at the personal level is indicative of how agency as independence only creates dependence, and provides further evidence for interdependence or domesticated agency as the only way of curbing the 'radically widening chasm between rich and poor', and the 'uneasy fusion of enfranchizement and exclusion, hope and hopelessness' (Comaroff and Comaroff 1999a: 19), that Msa, global capitalism or modernity seems to bring about in marginal communities.

Conclusion

This chapter has argued that there is much to be gained by going beyond the dominant western epistemological export for understanding witchcraft and occult practices in Africa. It points to the popular epistemology among ordinary Africans as the way towards a more comprehensive understanding of these phenomena and how they have informed alternative appreciations of development or modernity on the continent. Far from contradicting the western epistemological import, the popular epistemology actually complements or completes it. The chapter argues for a more rounded picture of reality, one that provides for both the visible and invisible dimensions of our world. Not doing this means subscribing to the dichotomies or dualisms that limited and limiting social science as ideology has imposed on Africa in terms of theory and methodology. How we understand witchcraft and its relationship to development depends critically on one's theoretical and methodological perspective. In other words, it depends on one's epistemological assumptions about reality.

Notes

1 See *La Nouvelle Expression*, No. 494, 24 March 1999, p. 5; *Le Messager*, No. 899, 7 April 1999, p. 6; *L'Anecdote*, No. 084, 6 April 1999, pp. 5–9; *Mutations*, No. 207, 1 April 1999, p. 10; *Dikalo*, No. 424, 30 March 1999, p. 3; *Perspectives Hebdo*, No. 185, 26 March 1999, pp. 2–9.

2 See *The Herald*, No. 854, 29 December 1999, pp. 1 and 3.

3 This guarantees that the Indomitable Lion of politics shall appropriate the victories and fame of the Indomitable Lions of football, thanks to facilitation and manipulation by the Indomitable Lion of broadcasting. It makes it possible for government to feed the people not with facts but with opinions only, so that they remain incapable of thinking for themselves. Truth, the Indomitable Lion of politics [Biya] has never tired of affirming, comes from above and rumour from below (*la vérité vient d'en haut, la rumeur vient d'en bas*). Hence the constant exhortation for Cameroonians to take for truth everything communicated to them by CRTV and *Cameroon Tribune* or by writings published in honour of the system by pro-establishment academics. They are in turn to shun 'untruths disseminated by certain media, with scant regard for the most elementary of journalistic ethics and at variance with the rules and means of seeking the truth'. Information from any source other than these official media, 'the most trustworthy and credible sources', could only be, as Paul Biya himself termed it, by 'insensitive and ill-intentioned people . . . who want to claim an importance that they haven't got' (*Cameroon Tribune*, No. 3080, 21 September 1984).

   To mark his importance as premiere vehicle of 'truth from above', Mendo Ze as director of CRTV has physically located his office on the 11th floor of the CRTV production centre at Mballa II in Yaounde, and has also reserved a lift for himself. In this way, his authority is practically reinforced by the feeling of physically sitting on everyone of his journalists, producers and support staff. Supplemented by mystical or occult powers, he and President Biya could see themselves as metaphorically sitting on all Cameroonians, big and small, willing and reluctant. Under Biya, CRTV assumed the same dictatorial and insensitive stature that Radio Cameroon had assumed under Ahidjo. And with this has come an arrogance unmitigated by ignorance on the part of politicians in high office and journalists in their service. From the public's perspective, only someone super endowed with more than meets the eye could display with impunity the arrogance and insensitivity of President Biya and such acolytes as Mendo Ze. One requires more than ordinary political or bureaucratic power to do what they do, and get away with it. Such power is invisible and is provided by witchcraft and occult practices in which they indulge with the assistance of the stifling misery of their victims.

4 *Nouvelle Expression*, 15 January 1999 and 24 March 1999.
5 Nor are such rumours just a 1990s phenomenon. See Rowlands and Warnier 1988: 128.

Bibliography

Abdel-Malek, A. (1967) 'Sociologie du développement national: problèmes de conceptualisation', *Revue de l'Institut de Sociologie* 2, 3: 249–264.

Ardener, E. (1996) 'Witchcraft, economics and the continuity of belief', in S. Ardener (ed.) *Kingdom on Mount Cameroon: Studies in the History of the Cameroon Coast, 1500–1970*, Oxford: Berghahn Books.

Ashforth, A. (1996) 'Of secrecy and the commonplace: witchcraft and power in Soweto', *Social Research* 63, 4: 1183–1234.

Chinweizu (1987) *The West and the Rest of Us: White Predators, Black Slavers and the African Elite*, Lagos: Pero Press.

Comaroff, J. and Comaroff, J.L. (eds) (1993) *Modernity and its Malcontents: Ritual and Power in Postcolonial Africa*, Chicago: University of Chicago Press.

—— (1999a) 'Introduction', in J. and J.L. Comaroff (eds) *Civil Society and the Political Imagination in Africa*, Chicago: University of Chicago Press.

—— (1999b) 'Alien-nation: zombies, immigrants, and millennial capitalism', *Codesria Bulletin* 3/4: 17–28.

—— (1999c) 'Occult economies and the violence of abstraction: notes from the South African postcolony', *American Ethnologist* 26, 2: 279–303.

Ellis, S. (1993) 'Rumour and power in Togo', *Africa* 63, 4: 462–475.

—— (1999) *The Mask of Anarchy: The Destruction of Liberia and the Religious Dimensions of an African Civil War*, London: Hurst and Company.

Ferguson, J. (1999) *Expectations of Modernity: Myths and Meanings of Urban Life on the Zambian Copperbelt*, Berkeley: University of California Press.

Fisiy, C. and Geschiere, P. (1996) 'Witchcraft, violence and identity: different trajectories in postcolonial Cameroon', in R. Werbner and T. Ranger (eds) *Postcolonial Identities in Africa*, London: Zed Books.

Geschiere, P. (1995) *Sorcellerie et Politique en Afrique*, Karthala: Paris.

—— (1997) *The Modernity of Witchcraft: Politics and the Occult in Postcolonial Africa*, Charlottesville: University Press of Virginia.

Geschiere, P. and Nyamnjoh, F. (1998) 'Witchcraft as an issue in the "politics of belonging": democratization and urban migrants' involvement with the home village', *African Studies Review* 41, 3: 69–92.

—— (2000) 'Capitalism and autochthony: the seesaw of mobility and belonging', *Public Culture* 12, 2: 423–452.

Mamdani, M. (1996) *Citizen and Subject: Contemporary Africa and the Legacy of Late Colonialism*, London: James Currey.

Mbembe, A. (1992) 'Provisional notes on the postcolony', *Africa* 62, 1: 3–37.

—— (1997) 'The "thing" and its double in Cameroonian cartoons', in K. Barber (ed.) *Readings in African Popular Culture*, Oxford: James Currey.

Mudimbe, V.Y. (1988) *The Invention of Africa: Gnosis, Philosophy, and the Order of Knowledge*, London: James Currey.

Nyamnjoh, F.B. (1985) 'Change in the concept of power amongst the Bum', unpublished Maîtrise dissertation, FHSS, University of Yaounde.

—— (1991) *Mind Searching*, Awka: Kucena Publishers.

—— (2000) '"A child is one person's only in the womb": domestication and agency in the Cameroonian Grassfields', paper presented at PhD and Post-doctoral seminar on Personhood and Agency in African Studies, Leiden, 27–29 September 2000.

Redfield, J. (1997) *The Celestine Prophecy*, New York: Warner Books.

Rowlands, M. (1994) 'Predicting personal success in Bamenda', unpublished manuscript.

—— (1995) 'The material culture of success: ideals and life cycles in Cameroon', in J. Friedman (ed.) *Consumption and Identity*, London: Harwood Press.

Rowlands, M. and Warnier, J.-P. (1988) 'Sorcery, power and the modern state in Cameroon', *Man* 23, 1: 118–132.

van Dijk, R. and Pels, P. (1996) 'Contested authorities and the politics of perception: deconstructing the study of religion in Africa', in R. Werbner and T. Ranger (eds) *Postcolonial Identities in Africa*, London: Zed Books.

Warnier, J.-P. (1993a) *L'Esprit d'Entreprise au Cameroun*, Paris: Karthala.

—— (1993b) 'The king as a container in the Cameroon Grassfields', *Paideuma* 39, 303–319.

Werbner, R. (1996) 'Introduction: multiple identities, plural arenas', in R. Werbner and T. Ranger (eds) *Postcolonial Identities in Africa*, London: Zed Books.

Chapter 3

Cannibal transformations
Colonialism and commodification in the Sierra Leone hinterland

Rosalind Shaw

> Last month I went as usual to trade in Freetown. Ere I return Chief Bey Simerah and people concocted together and arrange to put an end to my life by charging your poor servant with Cannibalism, they have got as much ill disposed persons to prove me, and bring me under the crime of being an Alligator. A Charge that your petitioner is quite innocent of.
>
> (Testimony of Kiyelleh, 1892, in Milan Kalous 1974: 217)

Historicizing cannibalism stories

In the literature on modernity and the occult imaginary, such creatures as Human Alligators, zombies, witches, and cannibals are usually located in an age of postcolonial states and structurally adjusted economies.[1] These images speak eloquently of the ruptures of postcoloniality, the contradictions of modernity, the 'eating of the state' (Geschiere 1997), and the 'violence of abstraction' (Comaroff and Comaroff 1999). At the same time, in a different strand of scholarship on postcoloniality, others have commented on the ways in which various kinds of postcolonial experiences reinscribe colonial ones.[2] In this chapter, I wish both to tie these strands together and to push the implications of the second strand further, arguing not only that many of today's images of occult extraction are mediated by colonial memory, but also that in some parts of Africa, experiences of colonialism were themselves configured by memories of earlier transregional processes, such as the Atlantic slave trade. Postcoloniality may be simply the most recent historical predicament in which commodification and rupture are experienced in images of cannibalistic or vampiric occult beings – images that have been continually refashioned, creating accounts that are both 'new' and 'old' (Shaw 2002).

At a particularly turbulent point in Sierra Leone's colonial past, during the late nineteenth and early twentieth centuries, accounts of ritual murder multiplied in the Sierra Leone hinterland. The epigraph above comes from a series of accusations and confessions concerning the 'cannibalism' of deadly were-animals – 'Human Crocodiles', 'Human Leopards', and (later) 'Human Chimpanzees' – that were described as capturing and ritually slaughtering people in order to make wealth-producing medicines from their victims' vital organs. Accounts such as these, as White (2000) demonstrates in her remarkable analysis of vampire stories in East and Central Africa, mark a way in which relationships entailed by colonial rule could be debated, evaluated, and commented upon. But in addition, as I hope to trace in this chapter, these colonial Human Crocodile and Leopard accounts in the Sierra Leone hinterland reworked memories of still earlier rumours of 'Atlantic' cannibals – rumours that spoke to morally deleterious forms of power and commerce in Sierra Leone's slave-trading past.

Tracing stories of cannibalism historically and exploring them as forms of social memory, however, grates against a longstanding axiom in both anthropology and history that we cannot 'explain' a cultural idea or practice in terms of its origins (White 2000: 15–21). This is a critique of nineteenth-century arguments that reduce cultural phenomena to generic, unchanging forms disconnected from specific sociohistorical concerns as they persist through time. But it is time to reexamine this oft-reiterated axiom about 'explanation' and 'origins' in the light of social memory, given that the work of memory is hardly that attributed to the 'origin' of a phenomenon in such arguments – that of determining its own static passage down the years through passive human vectors. Moreover, an overwhelming focus on the mutability of the past ('the politics of the past in the present') in both anthropology and history has tended to obscure the mutability of the present – the ways in which memories form a prism for the configuring of present experience. Instead of a process of reduction, the work of memory entails a process of historical sedimentation in which inherited cultural ideas and practices mediate the ways in which relationships, actions, and events are envisioned – and these ideas and practices are themselves reconfigured in turn.

Thus in Sierra Leone, stories and accusations of cannibalism have long been (and still are) a dynamic part of inherited cultural images that configure visions of extractive relationships. These are, of course, different stories, told in different ways, at different times, and in different sociohistorical contexts. Yet I suggest that successive stories about human consumption in a particular place do not simply arise *sui generis*, born again and again in different circumstances, disconnected from memories of earlier stories. Viewing a history of Sierra Leone through the lens of cannibalism stories may, I suggest, enable us to see how people tie experiences of commodification and extraction to memories of earlier experiences even as they rework those memories today.

Cannibalism and conquest

'And even when they kill their enemies in battle they cut pieces of them and dry and smoke them and cook them with rice and eat it', wrote Valentim Fernandes of the inhabitants of Sierra Leone at the turn of the sixteenth century

(1951 [1506–1510]: 94–95; English translation by Alice Clemente). Fernandes obtained his information from an informant called Alvaro Velho, who had lived in Sierra Leone for eight years. We do not know if Velho had witnessed the cannibalism he outlined (unlikely, in view of the sparse details he gave of a practice that would presumably have been startling to him), or reporting a rumour, or giving a literal interpretation to the image of 'eating' as a metaphor for defeat. All we can be sure of in this reference from five centuries ago is that there existed local ideas of cannibalism that were linked in some way with defeat and capture in war.

Earlier in Fernandes' account, we find another reference to cannibalistic consumption – and this time, man-eating is attributed to European slave traders. Fernandes tells of a group of Portuguese further north, on the Gambia River, who were met by a fleet of canoes whose occupants shot arrows at them. When the Portuguese managed to find a group of their assailants who would speak to them through an interpreter, the Portuguese explained that they had come not to make war but to trade, as they did already with the people of the *Canaga*, and had brought a gift for their king on behalf of the king of Portugal. Their adversaries were not impressed:

> They replied that they knew well how we had dealt with people in the *Canaga*, and that the Christians ate human meat and that all the slaves that they bought were carried away to be eaten. And because of that they did not want our friendship but they wanted to kill us all and to make a gift of them to their king who lived three days' from there. And they shot them with arrows.
>
> (Fernandes 1951 [1506–1510]: 34–35; English
> translation by Alice Clemente)

In this story of the cannibalism of European traders we can, I suggest, catch a glimpse of the early incorporation of the Atlantic trade into local meanings of 'eating'. Although we know next to nothing of these meanings in this time and place, it is clear that for this belligerent group on the Gambia at the turn of the sixteenth century, rumours of the European consumption of slaves identified trade with 'Christians' as a form of predation. In an area that had been incorporated into long-distance trade flows well before the coming of Europeans (Brooks 1993; Rodney 1970), this was hardly a reaction of 'isolated' Africans to sudden commercial contact with the outside world. Rather, it was specifically the *kind* of trade – a trade that fed the 'Christian' appetite for the consumption of humans – that was viewed as problematic.

We have a slightly better idea of the sociohistorical context of a later set of cannibalism stories in Sierra Leone: those told about the conquest and rule of this area by a group called the Mane in the sixteenth and early seventeenth centuries. When Mane raiders arrived on the coast of Sierra Leone in the second half of the sixteenth century and subsequently imposed their form of kingship upon peoples of the area, Portuguese and other foreign contemporaries reported recurring stories that the Mane practised cannibalism (Brooks 1993: 305). In Manuel Alvares' account, for instance, captive concubines are slaughtered and cooked; captives are made to eat each other; a baby is seized from its mother, stuffed with rice, and roasted on the fire; a father-in-law is fed (unbeknown) to his own daughter at a banquet in his honour; a child is fed the meat of his slaughtered compatriots; and a local, non-Mane governor who criticizes the king is invited by the latter to a banquet in which he is to be the intended meal (Alvares 1990 [c.1615], II, ch.11: 1–4). Some of these stories recapitulate the association between reports of cannibalism and defeat and capture in warfare that were present in Fernandes' account a century earlier. Others concern violations that erase and invert bonds of concubinage, companionship, affinity, kinship, and political office. If we note that Alvares wrote when local peoples were subsumed within Mane political structures and were assimilating Mane military and cultural practices, while at the same time they were also incorporating their Mane conquerors through marriage (Brooks 1993: 303–305), these stories would seem to highlight contradictions in these processes of mutual absorption across marked disparities of power. The descriptions of meals and cooking depict acts of commensality that (we can probably assume) ordinarily created and maintained relationships, but are here turned around to attack the very basis of moral connection among people: 'Not only do we consume you', the Mane are made to say in these stories, 'but we also make you consume each other.'

There was a further context for these stories: a symbiotic relationship had developed between Mane warfare and the Atlantic slave trade (Brooks 1993: 293–294; Rodney 1970: 102). The warfare that was frequently associated with stories of Mane cannibalism – stories that may, moreover, have played off earlier stories of the 'eating' of war captives – was itself the means by which local African bodies were captured and 'consumed' by the slave trade. If the stories about cannibalistic cooking and meals and gruesomely inverted commensality expressed concerns about incorporating the Mane conquerors into local communities through affinal ties, these concerns would seem an appropriate response to the dangerous paradox of forging moral relationships with foreign overlords who have sold large numbers of people from your locality. Whether or not Mane cannibalism stories also drew upon earlier stories of the cannibalism of the Atlantic trade, the 'eating' of humans is a powerful image for the articulation of Mane warfare and state-building with a form of commerce in which 'consumable' bodies were captured and sold before disappearing forever.

Atlantic cannibals

Other stories, circulating not just in Sierra Leone but along the length of Africa's Atlantic coast, were focused not on African intermediaries such as the Mane, but on the Europeans who carried people away in the Atlantic trade. In contrast to the gruesome particulars in reports of Mane cannibalism, nameless and faceless Europeans are simply described as eating African slaves, either on the slave ships themselves or at their distant destinations: there are no specifics of food preparation, cooking, banquets, or captives forced to eat their own kin and companions. If accounts of Mane cannibalism convey the difficulties of building affinal and other relationships with people who have conquered you and made your relatives and neighbours disappear into slave ships, the spare depictions of European cannibalism on those ships or across the ocean convey the idea of predatory foreigners with whom there is little or no direct relationship.

These stories of white cannibalism were focused not on the European traders who had settled on the coast, but on unsettled Europeans who carried captives away in ships, and those who received them at distant destinations. It was thus Europeans in conjunction with the forms of transatlantic mobility and transport they controlled who were important in these stories.[3] Here were foreigners and vessels whose transatlantic passage reconfigured the boundary of the ocean as a space of deadly transformation, materializing the chilling convertibility of human bodies, money, and foreign commodities as they moved back and forth across the water (cf. Auslander 1993; Bastian 1992: 148–208; Masquelier 2000; Weiss 1996: 179–219; White 2000: 122–147). Although these vessels wove connections between particular African places and the country of Europeans through the foreign goods they brought, these connections did not reduce the experiential separation between 'there' and 'here' because the people carried away did not come back. The opaqueness of the exchanges that these ships mediated across the ocean, moreover, was objectified in the opaqueness of their own hulls, inside which the experience of the Middle Passage was hardly less nightmarish than the imagined scenario of African bodies being broken down into food (Curtin 1967: 313).

Most of these stories about European cannibalism seem to have been unelaborated but persistent and transregional, circulating in the west African interior, on the coast, on slave ships, and even in the New World on the other side of the ocean (Palmie 1995): these were Atlantic stories. Within their usually sparse details, however, we can sometimes discern particular local meanings (e.g. Ceyssens 1975: 528–529). Thus in John Matthews' late eighteenth-century account of Sierra Leone, we are told that understandings of Atlantic cannibalism in the Sierra Leone hinterland extended beyond those of simple eating. An African captive sold to a European, Matthews claims, 'imagines the white man buys him either to offer him as a sacrifice to his God, or to devour him as food; and I have seen some of these poor wretched beings so terrified with apprehensions of their expected fate, as to remain in a state of torpid insensibility for some time' (1966 [1788]: 152). If these rumours of European cannibalism in the region of Sierra Leone entailed ideas of sacrifice – the *ritual* consumption of a victim – that would distinguish them from more generic stories of Atlantic consumption. Let us explore this further.

Ideas of Europeans who kill and consume captives as part of a sacrifice carry a different – although no less grotesque – set of meanings from those of Europeans devouring people for food alone. While I do not know the specific meanings of sacrifices in the Sierra Leone hinterland two hundred years ago, animal sacrifices (both in contemporary Sierra Leone and elsewhere) commonly engender beneficial and enabling transformations through the exchange of the victim's life for blessings and benefits (or, in the case of apotropaic sacrifice, for freedom from harm) from an extra-human force to whom this life is offered. The rumours that Matthews reports depict a reversal of the position of Africans within that exchange, turning them from ritual participants into offerings. Instead of being those who benefit from a sacrifice's generative circulations, African captives become the victims whose ritual slaughter benefits European others – a prospect so appalling as to throw many captives into 'a state of torpid insensibility', Matthews (1966 [1788]) tells us. What sort of boon the white man was viewed as receiving from 'his God' for such a sacrifice remains undisclosed. But whatever it was, these stories made it part of a European ritual process that integrated the transport of African bodies across the Atlantic into a further set of transactions with the Europeans' God – a process that ultimately channelled a return flow of foreign commodities and money back to the rulers and big traders on the coast and rivers of Sierra Leone.

The conviction that slaves carried away in the Atlantic trade were eaten by Europeans persists in Sierra Leone to this day, although it is not linked to the idea of sacrifice. That linkage between cannibalism, sacrifice, and predatory trade does, however, resonate in intriguing ways with ideas of the ritual cannibalism of Human Leopards and Crocodiles that circulated in the Sierra Leone hinterland a century after Matthews' account.

Colonial power and 'cannibal crimes'

These cannibalism stories of the late nineteenth century erupted nearly seventy years after British authorities in the Crown Colony of Sierra Leone, based in Freetown, had replaced the Atlantic slave trade with a 'legitimate trade' in products such as palm oil, palm kernels, camwood, and timber. The stories entered the colonial record as rumours and reports of suspicious killings, as part of the correspondence between hinterland chiefs and colonial authorities, and as accusations and confessions in colonial court cases. The accounts were not specific to any particular linguistic group. Instead, reports of these killings were common 'in those parts of the forest zone most thoroughly transformed by commercial contacts' (Richards 2000: 89), especially in communities along the coastal Sherbro area in the southwest and the major trade routes inland. In most of these accounts, the human victims' blood and organs were used either to create or to 'enliven' powerful medicines, while the killings themselves often simulated attack by leopards, crocodiles ('alligators'), and chimpanzees ('baboons'). Human Leopards, for example, were accused of ritually slaughtering their victims with a five-pronged 'leopard knife' in order to imitate the signs of a leopard attack. Human Crocodiles were described as using a medicine containing a tiny model canoe (Kalous 1974: 83) that empowers humans to enter and animate either a crocodile skin (Kalous 1974: 76) or a 'submarine canoe' that resembles a crocodile in the water.

Murder by shape-shifting into leopards and crocodiles, termed 'the witchcraft of the leopard' (ra-ser ra an-sip) and of the crocodile (an-kuy) in Temne, was a well-known form of witchcraft long before the late 1800s (Matthews 1966 [1788]: 130–132).[4] Such understandings were not merely abstract ideas; they formed part of a divinatory process in which people accused and convicted as witches were sold into the slave trade by chiefs and other leaders (Shaw 1997). But during the nineteenth century, after the Atlantic slave trade was abolished, the colonial government made treaties with hinterland chiefs (Wylie 1977: 73–74) in which the internal sale of slaves was prohibited. Thus severed from the process of the commodification of persons, witchfinding divinations that had for several centuries turned people into slaves by convicting them as witches eventually tapered off.[5] But in the Human Leopard scare in the last quarter of that century, a different form of accusation developed in which established ideas of the shape-shifter's witchcraft were synthesized with ideas of harmful ritual action by malefactors in the more concrete form of Human Leopards. And this time, as we shall see, these stories were levelled *against* chiefs more often than by them.

For the colonial authorities who recorded and acted upon these accounts, the stories seemed readily appropriable into European conceptions of 'cannibalism' and 'Fetish Custom' (Kalous 1974: 269), confirmations of '[t]he extraordinary ignorance and superstition of the Aborigenes' (Kalous 1974: 32). As Abraham (1976) points out, such conceptions were used as justifications for colonial rule (Kalous 1974: 9, 279, 291, 304, 306). But ironically, these accounts of cannibalism that were used to authorize the imposition of colonial force were stories that spoke directly to the consequences of the colonial political economy (Abraham 1976; Jackson 1989). Let me begin, then, to outline these consequences.

Cannibalism and colonial commerce

Throughout the nineteenth century (especially toward its end), the Colony authorities advanced their penetration of the hinterland, signing treaties, inserting themselves (where possible) into processes of chiefly succession, intervening in 'trade wars', sending punitive military expeditions, and forcibly annexing territory (Ijagbemi 1968; Jones 1983: 131–161; Wylie 1977: 91–189). Many of the struggles between the chiefs and the colonial government were over control of the legitimate trade: chiefs considered it their right to regulate commerce, levy tribute on trade goods, and assert their authority over traders by blocking the roads, much to the disapproval of the Colony (Wylie 1977: 74–75, 91–128). Chiefs at that time had had a long history of collaboration with (and control of) foreign traders, successively drawing in such strangers as sixteenth- and seventeenth-century Portuguese private traders and eighteenth-century

Muslim merchants through intermarriage. While such collaboration between chiefs and traders remained strong during the legitimate trade (Richards 2000), chiefs were also aware that the wealth derived from this commerce gave traders the opportunity to become 'big men', to pay their own professional warriors, and thereby to challenge the chiefs (Ijagbemi 1968; Wylie 1977: 178; Jones 1983: 128–130). When chiefs tried to assert their authority over both trade and traders, however, the colonial government often stepped in to restrain them (Wylie 1977: 178).

These struggles among chiefs, wealthy traders, and Colony were intensified in the 1870s, when the demand for palm kernels increased rapidly (Mitchell 1962: 205), and the rivers that were essential for the transport of palm products became the foci of violent commercial rivalries. At that time domestic slavery, slave-raiding, and warfare formed the nuclei of massive contradictions in the workings of the legitimate trade. Domestic slaves, obtained by raiding weaker neighbours, were critical both for the production and porterage of cash crops for the trade, and for the cultivation of food crops to provision the chief's body of warriors (Ijagbemi 1968; Lenga-Kroma 1978; Wylie 1977). Chiefs and big men established small hamlets, called *fakay*, away from the town, and settled them with slaves (Abraham 1975: 135; Wylie 1977: 77), concealing them from raiders from other chiefdoms who sought to seize both people and crops (Dorjahn 1960: 115 and 121, n. 3). Chiefs then sold the cash crops and forest products produced by the slaves in these *fakay* in the legitimate trade, thereby enabling them to keep their warriors armed with the weapons that would maintain the flow of captured slaves (Wylie 1977: 85). At the same time, chiefs' capacities to defend their chiefdoms from the raids of others depended on their warriors' capacities for warfare and raiding, and therefore on the chiefs' capacities to arm their warriors through the legitimate trade and to feed them by acquiring and controlling domestic slaves (Ijagbemi 1968: 181–213; Lenga-Kroma 1978, I: 76–78, 153ff.; Wylie 1977: 85). The British, for their part, sought to eliminate all of these interconnected processes – warfare, raiding, and internal slavery – that the legitimate trade had helped engender, and on which it depended. Thus ironically, as Wylie notes, '[t]he very wars and raids which [the British] wanted to end provided . . . the only capital which many of the smaller societies . . . could generate in order to make the system of exchange function; that capital was slaves' (1977: 86).

If these conditions meant a crisis of power and authority for the chiefs, they meant terror for the chiefs' subjects. It was at this time of intensifying contradictions and accelerating violence in the last two decades of the nineteenth century that accounts of Human Leopard and Crocodile killings multiplied. The globalizing connections forged in pursuit of the legitimate commerce – linking together chiefs and Colony, warfare and enslavement, rural production and river transport, slave settlements and the global market – were experienced in terms of the violent disconnection of vital parts of the human body (Sanders, Chapter 8).

In 1896, the British imposed a Protectorate on the Sierra Leone hinterland in order to control the trade more directly and to suppress the warfare disrupting it (which, ironically, the trade had itself engendered). After this, the contradictions of the legitimate trade took a different form: the Colony continued to promote the trade, but forbade chiefs and big men from engaging in warfare, raiding, and the internal trade in slaves. Although trade in slaves was prohibited, however, slavery itself was allowed to continue until 1929. Pragmatism forced the Colony to compromise with the chiefs and big men over internal slavery, given that the Colony still needed the trade with the Protectorate for its own economic survival (see Rashid 1999: 215). The chiefs' access to labour was nevertheless considerably eroded by the prohibition on raiding and internal slave-trading, prompting them to seek alternative sources of labour and wealth.

Many Protectorate chiefs found these sources in their capacity, through their new position as agents of Government, to 'eat their chiefdom' (Dorjahn 1960: 111). While in relation to the Government itself their powers had been curtailed, the checks and balances that had formerly curbed abuses of chiefly power over their subjects were gone. For southern Temne chiefs – sacred figures who should not be allowed to die a natural death – the most important constraint had lain in the powers of their counsellors and subchiefs (e-kaper), who were empowered to kill the chief when he fell ill. In practice this had meant, as Dorjahn points out, that minor illnesses were overlooked in a popular chief, while 'a wicked man was dispatched after the slightest decline in health or well-being' (1960: 114). This important sanction against a despotic chief was eliminated by the establishment of the Protectorate, while other powers of the kaper subchiefs were eroded, thereby removing the major checks on the chief's ability to 'eat his chiefdom'.

For many Temne chiefs in the Protectorate era, the 'eating' of their own chiefdoms effectively replaced their warriors' slave raids on other chiefdoms in the previous century. This 'eating' now took the form of monetized levies on their subjects that supplanted the tribute in food normally given (for example) after the harvest, of extortionate court fees and fines, extra-judicial fining, and the attachment of their own additions to the colonial tax (Dorjahn 1960: 130–135). It also took the form of labour levies for the cultivation of cash crops on the chief's farm – a farm that tended to grow larger and larger through land obtained in pledge, or through seizure following dubious rulings in the chief's own court (Dorjahn 1960: 134; Kalous 1974: 81). Additional labour could likewise be obtained through the court, as the chief would lend people money for the court's exorbitant fees if the plaintiffs were willing to pawn a son as security for the debt – an arrangement that became permanent when the court case was lost (Dorjahn 1960: 135).

In the Protectorate era, then, trade with the Colony no longer entailed a system of exchange that functioned through war, raiding, capture, and enslavement. Instead it now entailed chiefs' 'eating' the land, pawned youths, and forced labour of their own subjects – subjects whose experiences of their powerful patrons, I suggest, found expression in the continued salience of Human Leopard, Crocodile, and Chimpanzee scares in the Protectorate era.[6]

The Leopards of the legitimate trade

Instead of the anonymous and generalized European cannibals of the Atlantic trade, accounts of Leopard, Crocodile, and Chimpanzee killings identified *known* individuals: substantial numbers of chiefs and headmen were accused of being alien were-animals outside the bounds of moral human existence.[7] Certain of their accusers claimed that the killings had been committed to 'make [the chief] powerful to govern the whole country' (Kalous 1974: 107, also 94, 166). Chiefs, in turn, claimed that such accusations against them were the fabrications of discontented subjects ('My countrymen do not like me as a Chief' [Kalous 1974: 277, also 132–133]). Some chiefs (and, more rarely, subchiefs) levelled accusations against their rivals – other chiefs, contenders for chiefly office, and wealthy subjects (Kalous 1974: 137, 195, 217, 225, 236).

Several traders in the legitimate commerce were also accused, either as collaborators with (see Richards 2000) or rivals of the chief, including 'a trader in palm kernels' (Kalous 1974: 98), 'a trader in a fairly large way at Bonthe' (Kalous 1974: 303), 'a Merchant and paramount chief of Poro' (Kalous 1974: 85), and the trader Kiyelleh with whose testimony this chapter began, and who was 'blessed in cattle and many things sufficient to be regarded as a rich man' (Kalous 1974: 217). Like Kiyelleh, and in important contrast to those accused of witchcraft during the Atlantic trade, those identified as Human Leopards or Alligators were often wealthy: 'Poor people are not accused of being human leopards', stated a witness, '[i]t is only rich people with property' (Kalous 1974: 196, also 194, 204, 219).

Often, chiefs' and big men's ritual advisors were included in this indictment. These were usually Muslim specialists, known in Sierra Leone Krio as 'mori men' (Temne *an-more*) who divined, healed, and made amulets for rulers and other leaders. In Leopard accusations, the potency of 'mori-men's' ritual knowledge was perceived as having been turned to their patrons' sinister purposes; their divination techniques ('Bundu proposed that Abdulai should be employed to look country fashion to find the woman' [Kalous 1974: 137]), their sacrificial skills ('The prisoner was a "medicine man", and murdered the child' [Kalous 1974: 111]), their written amulets ('The man who has [this writing] must get money, and it will make him a Chief' [Kalous 1974: 107]), and their liquid Qur'anic medicine ('Nessi is a medicine made by the Murri men and is used by the human leopard society' [Kalous 1974: 161]) were all viewed as carrying the potential for extractive, 'cannibalistic' rituals of individual empowerment and enrichment.[8]

Significantly, those who accused chiefs, traders, and diviners of Leopard, Crocodile, and Chimpanzee killings often located those they denounced within the problematic transactions of trade with the Colony. Witnesses made repeated connections between cannibalism, human sacrifices, and the production of wealth, often invoking the white man and trade with the Colony as the source of that wealth (Kalous 1974: 91, 93–94, 104, 116, 125, 170–172). A few also claimed that the ritual substances and practices in question deflected colonial surveillance (see Abraham 1976; Jackson 1989; Kalous 1974: 112).

Human Leopards, Crocodiles, and Chimpanzees, moreover, were accused of catching and ritually consuming their prey in sites of rural production and along routes of transport for the legitimate trade. Instead of the European cannibals of the Atlantic trade, who sacrificed and devoured their human victims in an alien place – the enclosed interiors of slave ships, or the cannibal country of Europeans – the local cannibals of the legitimate trade operated in the bush near isolated farms and hamlets (*fakay*). Farms, Richards (2000) observes, are always somewhat hazardous places for children during busy times of year, when chimpanzees may snatch unsupervised babies left at the edge of the bush, and 'mug' children running an errand between farm and village; but during the Atlantic trade and the legitimate trade, he suggests, these hazards of agrarian life took on a far more sinister significance (Richards 2000: 85). Indeed, the accounts gathered by Kalous confirm that it was the remote *fakay* in which slaves and other dependants cultivated cash crops for their patrons that became particular sites of disappearance from which women and children – especially slaves' children – would vanish under suspicious circumstances ('I came to the town and you made me go back to the farm: look how people have now caught my son' [Kalous 1974: 127, also 43, 97, 121, 141, 224, 271]). Collecting palm kernels – the principal crop of the legitimate trade at that time – became a task of particular dread ('No one can be enter into the bush or field under the palm trees for the purpose of getting the Kernels' [Kalous 1974: 34, also 40]). Likewise, the routes of transport along which these and other products were carried to the Colony became conduits for stalking Leopards and deadly 'Alligator canoes' ('the brooks and high ways are inaccessible unless under guard with guns and cutlasses' [Kalous 1974: 218, also 69, 70, 189–190]).

The bush, the roads, and the navigable rivers had long been part of a landscape of death and disappearance during the Atlantic slave trade. But now this threat was transformed as the spatial separation between disappearance 'here' and acts of cannibalism in a European 'there' had collapsed; now, in addition to catching their prey, the 'cannibals' carried out their wealth-producing disassemblage of the human body 'here'. Instead of Atlantic conversions of human bodies into foreign wealth across the ocean, the legitimate trade's transactions between Colony and hinterland entailed comparable conversions 'at home', turning familiar places into sites of visceral extraction. Cannibals no longer abducted their prey to another world; now they walked among ordinary humans, transforming the known world – just as they themselves had become transformed – through processes of grotesque production and consumption.

The animal predators that the cannibals became – leopards, crocodiles, and chimpanzees – are, Richards (1996a, 2000) points out, the only animals in the upper Guinea forests that will stalk and eat or mutilate humans. Richards also suggests that peoples' experiences of these predators were changed by the legitimate commerce, given that the expansion in trade in forest products and the swelling river traffic led to increased human encroachment upon these animals' respective habitats (1996a, 2000). There are further reasons why these animals were prominent in the occult imaginary during the political-economic transformations of the legitimate trade. In Temne chiefdoms, for instance, leopards are 'royal' animals to whom the chief is sometimes compared (in coronations, for example), and hunters are obliged to give the skin, teeth, and claws of a leopard they kill to the chief of the chiefdom in which it is caught. In a sense, then, the chief is already a 'human leopard' – but one whose power and stealth is supposed to protect and benefit his subjects. The transformative leopardskin clothing described for Human Leopards ('the leopard skin . . . covered his whole face and was tied down at the back' [Kalous 1974: 55, also 58 and 62]) would thus seem to suggest the presence of chiefly power turned rogue.

As for crocodiles, Richards (2000) presents the intriguing argument that they may index the relationship between traders and chiefs. He was told (in a Mende-speaking locality) that the smaller broad-nosed crocodile in upland forest streams is 'mother's brother' to the more dangerous Nile crocodile of the larger rivers toward the coast – a kinship terminology that, he argues, suggests the historical relationship established through marriage between the chief and 'Mandingo' merchants involved in the slave trade (2000: 94). I would add that this image of a kinship connection between coastal and upriver predators may also recall intermarriages throughout the Atlantic trade era between chiefs' families and European slave traders – with the latter typically settled by the rivers and plying the waterways upstream for slaves to deliver to the coast. While these kin ties might have 'domesticated' the strangers, they also integrated the chiefs into predatory commercial flows down the waterways.

Chimpanzees, for their part, are known both by rural Sierra Leoneans and by primatologists, according to Richards (2000), for their occasional but serious attacks on young, vulnerable humans – 'mugging' children, snatching babies, and sometimes biting victims on or near the genitals. Such behaviour, Richards suggests, is disturbingly reminiscent of that of the raiders who, for several centuries, kidnapped young people in the Sierra Leone hinterland and sold them into slavery (2000: 85).[9] This association between raiders and chimpanzees was echoed in a striking narrative I collected from the former ritual subchief of Bombali Seborah Chiefdom, the late Pa Kaper Bana. Pa Kaper told me of a 'First World' (an-daru ra-totoko) that existed before this present one, whose angry, warlike inhabitants had habitually seized children and sold them; these people, he said, 'were people who had hair on their skin, like the chimpanzee. They were not of the same height as us. The first people were short, short, short, short'.[10] Thus not only do chimpanzee attacks trigger incidental memories of fighters who emerge from the bush to carry off children, but in Pa Kaper Bana's narrative the memory of those fighters has also been reworked in the image of the chimpanzee.

Divining Leopards

In several cases, Leopard, Crocodile, and (later) Chimpanzee accusations were made in the context of rivalries between chiefs and wealthy traders: the trader Kiyelle, for instance, claimed that Bay Simera had had him accused of being an Alligator because this chief envied Kiyelle's wealth (Kalous 1974: 217). To control the process of conviction, certain chiefs now called divinations to find Leopards and Crocodiles among their subjects (e.g. Kalous 1974: 77, 194, 196–197, 204, 218–219, 221). Given that the export slave trade was no longer viable, these chiefs did not enslave and sell those identified by the diviners, but instead seized the accused's property and slaves, fined their kin 'according to [the accused's] rank and fortune' (Kalous 1974: 214), and in some cases had those convicted burned to death (the latter finally causing the colonial authorities to intervene [Kalous 1974: 217–219; Wylie 1977: 184]). These chiefs thereby not only increased their wealth, but also eliminated their rivals.

Yet as we have seen, chiefs were themselves accused at least as much as they accused others – and their accusers were not only their wealthy rivals. Many dependants became witnesses against their powerful patrons in the colonial courts, thereby using the colonial government for their own purposes – turning it, perhaps, into a kind of colonial diviner they could use to make visible the predatory acts of chiefs and big men. 'People are ready to come forward with these charges on the slightest provocation', wrote a District Commissioner in 1931 (Kalous 1974: 66). While the colonial authorities placed emphasis on their own benign intervention in Leopard cases, we also need to recognize the agency of those who enabled (and often initiated) this intervention by recounting to colonial agents their narratives of Leopards and Crocodiles, cannibalism and wealth, human sacrifice and bad medicines. Many slaves denounced their owners (Kalous 1974: 225): an Assistant District Commissioner in Moyamba complained that 'the only people who were prepared to come forward and give evidence were Mendi slaves' (Kalous 1974: 16).[11] In some cases slaves accused their masters of having compelled them to give up their children to pay a 'debt' ('If we have any child, it belongs to you and I cannot refuse you' [Kalous 1974: 139, also 120]). In coming forward, slaves and other dependants risked being arrested themselves, but even then they were able to make graphic confessions that subsumed their own actions within the malevolent agency of their patrons ('Pa Neng . . . came back to own . . . that it was Bai Sherbro who had always sent him to practice the catching of people in the shape of an alligator' [Kalous 1974: 80]).

The localizing of cannibals

In these accusations and confessions, wealthy patrons (or their lackeys) are situated within a moral discourse of witchcraft. Some of these accounts –

especially in Temne-speaking areas – are explicit depictions of acts of witchcraft that take place beyond ordinary human embodiment ('it [the victim] was there in the form of a spirit' [Kalous 1974: 89, also 231]), and by implication in dreams (see Shaw 1992).[12] More usually, however, these accounts suggest concrete translations of these ideas of witchcraft: acts ordinarily understood as taking place in dreams and 'in spirit' are fully materialized in the waking actions of malefactors in the visible human world. Thus instead of (or as well as) shape-shifting into a leopard, Human Leopards don leopard skins and wield 'leopard knives'. Instead of invisibly consuming their victims' blood and internal organs in dreams, these 'cannibals' take blood and internal organs in fully enfleshed form to create or 'feed' wealth-producing medicines. And instead of belonging to a witches' association in which each member incurs an obligation (a 'debt') to provide a victim in turn for a nocturnal feast in the other world (failing which the member will be killed and consumed instead), the malefic ritual actions of Human Leopards are located within a secret 'Leopard Society' with an identical 'debt' arrangement, and whose nocturnal feasts are held in this world.

Accounts of 'materialized' witchcraft, of apparently visible, tangible, and this-worldly acts of cannibalism, effectively translate witchcraft into a 'language of the concrete' that was more closely commensurable with the language of 'physical evidence' in the colonial courts. Yet this language of the concrete in Human Leopard accounts seems never to have been fully substantiated in concrete objects and events in the material world, much to the puzzlement of colonial officials who were confronted with corpses but were never able to find the paraphernalia of Leopard, Crocodile, and Chimpanzee disguises. These objects had been described again and again in accusations and confessions, and were sometimes even constructed as models: 'No District Commissioner has ever been able to get hold of the Leopard dress, or knives', wrote the Acting Attorney General, 'altho' models have been made from descriptions given by the accomplices' (Kalous 1974: 289 and see 58). The material reality of the submarine 'Alligator canoe' was equally mysterious. Accounts of this vessel in the 1950s depict a fabulous but deadly vehicle with mysterious powers of mobility and a simultaneously animal and machine-like appearance. Covered with animal skins (Kalous 1974: 85) and fitted with a hinged glass front 'like the glass windows of a car' (Kalous 1974: 82, 72–73), it moved without paddles, and its occupants inside were able to 'travel all night' under the water (Kalous 1974: 84). 'How air is supplied, or how the hinged door can be open or closed when the canoe is under water, I cannot attempt to explain', mused one official (Kalous 1974: 73).

But one important aspect of Human Leopard accounts does not fit this picture of cannibalism as concretely realized witchcraft. The killings that activate 'bad' medicines are often identified as sacrifices, a ritual form that does not, to my knowledge, ordinarily figure in understandings of witches' invisible activities. Ordinarily, animal sacrifices (Temne *as-athka*) such as those I attended in Temne-speaking communities from the late 1970s to the early 1990s are open, transparent, daytime events that – ideally, if not always in practice – connect kin and affines together when participants eat the cooked meat of the sacrificed chicken or sheep. The life (*an-nesem*) of the victim, embodied in the blood, heart, and liver, is released and consumed by the appropriate spirits and ancestors, as well as by God (*K-uru*), engendering the beneficial flow of (for example) abundant rice and healthy children to promote the continuity and collective prosperity of the lineage or town.

In contrast, the accounts of sacrifice that form part of Human Leopard accusations entail the ritual offering of humans by those who are, in a sense, 'animals'. In hidden and nocturnal cabals in the bush, these ritual participants rob households, lineages, and settlements (sometimes their own) of their younger members – a theft that has especially serious consequences for upland rice-farming communities whose subsistence depends upon the coordination of labour (Richards 2000: 84). Thus instead of promoting the growth of healthy rice and children in the community, sacrifice by Human Leopards robs the victim's family and community of their capacity to feed, perpetuate, and renew themselves. Severed from the living body, the life concentrated in the sacrificial victim's blood, heart, and liver – life that would have sustained the growth of the child into a productive (and reproductive) adult – now produces a flow of power and money for chiefs and big men. Meanwhile, severed from its young member, the victim's family is left with a diminished capacity to produce and reproduce its future.

If this aspect of Human Leopards' noxious ritual actions represents a departure from ideas of 'ordinary' witchcraft, however, it also represents a convergence with earlier stories of the Atlantic trade in which 'the white man' buys a captive 'either to offer him as a sacrifice to his God, or to devour him as food' (Matthews 1966 [1788]: 152). Thus while accounts of Human Leopards play off understandings of witchcraft, they also, I suggest, entail the work of memory, drawing upon ideas of wealth-producing but perverted forms of sacrifice from a prior 'cannibalistic' trade. But in contrast to the indeterminate, almost abstracted Atlantic sacrifices by generic white men, the sacrificial transactions of the legitimate trade are given detailed depiction. Specific offerings are enumerated ('the Murri men had told them to pull some "salaka". . . [of] a black cow, a black fowl and a crazy person' [Kalous 1974: 163]); particular body parts ('the genitals' [Kalous 1974: 66]) are used to prepare specific medicines ('they had a fetish. . .the Bofima' [Kalous 1974: 112]); and named ritual specialists prescribe the sacrifice and prepare the medicines ('Abdulai said to him: ". . .the only way to get it is to kill your daughter or your sister"' [Kalous 1974: 137]).

Thus just as the invisible cannibalism of witches was made tangible in accounts of the fully embodied cannibalism of Leopards, Crocodiles, and Chimpanzees, the remote human sacrifices enacted by Europeans left their Atlantic locations and were incorporated, in Leopard accusations, into accounts of a local corpus of clandestine ritual practice controlled by chiefs, big men, and their ritual specialists. The Atlantic trade's replacement by the legitimate trade did not, then, result in the disappearance of 'cannibals', but in their becoming more *locally* embedded.

These accounts and images of colonial-era cannibalism, shaped through the prism of Atlantic memory, contributed just as surely to the making of a transformed colonial world as did the new imperatives for the production and transport of 'legitimate' goods, and the world markets in which these goods circulated. Leopards, Crocodiles, and Chimpanzees did not merely clothe colonial transformations in figurative cultural images; these images of entrepreneurial were-animals helped form the colonial world itself.

Postcolonial power and occult consumption

If rumours of Atlantic cannibals were reconfigured during the colonial era in more localized images of Human Leopards, this was not the end of their metamorphosis: accounts of Leopard, Crocodile, and Chimpanzee murders are now colonial memories that have been reworked in postcolonial Sierra Leone, both before and during the current rebel war. And this time, their latest incarnations are rumours about political elites and combatant leaders.

Seven years after Independence, in 1968, the long rule of the All People's Congress (APC) began: this political party went on to preside over twenty-five years of economic decline and escalating political corruption (see Reno 1995; Zack-Williams 1989). By the time I arrived in Sierra Leone for my first period of fieldwork in 1977 and 1978, many ordinary Sierra Leoneans were describing the rapacity of APC politicians and other 'big persons' in similar terms to those in which subjects in the colonial era had spoken of Protectorate chiefs who 'ate their chiefdoms'. Politicians and their covert foreign business partners, I was often told, consumed both Sierra Leone's diamond wealth and the foreign aid intended for the poorest people of Sierra Leone, diverting it for the exclusive use of their own families. A Freetown diviner I knew, Pa Yamba, complained, for instance, that 'when they send money to this country from outside for the poor people, it goes to the big people. They sit on it, and their families eat it.' Thus instead of channelling the flow of benefits to their communities, big people arrest it by 'sitting on it', and thereby turning proper circulation into improper accumulation. As Bayart (1993) and Geschiere (1997) have documented for ideas about (respectively) 'the politics of the belly' and 'the eating of the state' in contemporary Cameroon, this pattern of insatiable accumulation and consumption by politicians was (and is) for many Sierra Leoneans I knew a sign of sinister occult predation (see Nyamnjoh, Chapter 2).

Specifically, those politicians, top civil servants, and other big people who are viewed as especially rapacious are – like colonial-era chiefs – often the subjects of rumours about ritual murder. These rumours have been recast since colonial times: with rural production for export shifted from forest crops to diamond digging, with foot and canoe traffic replaced by motorized transport, and with the near-disappearance of both leopards and crocodiles, only rarely are postcolonial predators associated with forest animals (see Richards 2000). But the imagery of human commodification through sacrifice has been readily appropriable as a commentary on the new forms of power wielded by those who (both officially and unofficially) control the state, its institutions, and its 'shadow' economies. Thus rumours highlight covert connections between postcolonial leaders and sinister diviners who are suspected of performing human sacrifices in order to obtain medicines of power and enrichment for their patrons (Shaw 1996, 2002). In these stories, medicines derived from vital organs are described as making political leaders 'shine' (Richards 1996a: 143–145; Ferme 1999: 170). Like the Human Leopard accusations of the legitimate trade, such rumours concerning the use of human body parts (especially reproductive organs, and especially those of children and young women) make powerful statements about the appropriation of others' productive and reproductive capacities. Those few who, by enriching themselves through dubious means, have greatest access to the products and privileges of globalized modernity in the form of western consumer goods and high-tech international mobility, are thereby associated with images that have come to carry both meanings of 'backwardness' and memories of the malignant spiritual powers behind rapacious leaders.

Even diviners themselves participate in this discourse. Some of the diviners I knew – specialists who not only practised divination but also healed and prepared medicines – affirmed that they had prepared medicines to create or sustain the power of big persons, the ingredients for which were revealed by the tutelary spirit behind their powers. Once prepared, such medicines could be applied by eating or drinking them, washing with them, boiling them and inhaling the steam, rubbing them into incisions in the skin, dropping them in the eyes, wearing an undershirt soaked in them, sewing them inside a belt tied around the waist, or enclosing them in an amulet (Temne *an-sebe*) hung around the neck.

Those diviners who claim to have been 'behind' the success of a big person have to tread a fine line between affirming their occult powers and yet disclaiming the malefic use of such powers. One way of making such a disclaimer is to make use of stereotyped images of 'bad' ritual specialists in order to underscore the differences between the latter and themselves. Pa Yamba, the diviner I quote above, put it this way during my 1992 visit:

> PY: What I do is the work of God (*K-uru*). I have seen them [the politicians and other leaders] call big Muslim diviners (Temne *an-lefa*) to come to this country. He says he wants power; he tells the diviner. Ah, Satan (*Sethani*)! The diviner says 'I want blood'. Well, I who have power, now, I call the members who are behind me, if I'm a minister. Any power I get, they will get it too. They will go and find a person to kill.
>
> RS: Where do the diviners come from?
>
> PY: Some come from Guinea, some from other countries. This work, I don't want it. It's the money of Hell (*an-kala na ro-yanama*).

Pa Yamba thus appropriated the discourse that demonizes diviners for the purpose of his own castigation of other specialists, using it to condemn powerful foreign diviners outside Sierra Leone's borders. The latter, he suggested, are an external evil drawn in from beyond the nation's boundaries by an internal corruption within the government. These foreign diviners from the Republic of Guinea to the north (especially, he added, from the Futa Jallon area) are the modern counterparts of Muslim strangers who came and settled in the eighteenth and nineteenth centuries as ritual advisors to chiefs in the Sierra Leone hinterland. The 'wonderful' literate Islamic knowledge for which these specialists are renowned is still recognized as superior, but is now indelibly associated with the excesses of the most corrupt and nefarious political leaders. A strong moral dualism distinguished Pa Yamba's own divinely-derived work ('the work of God') from their 'Satanic' activity and its diabolic reward ('the money of Hell'). But even these 'Satanic' strangers, he pointed out, were driven by the (literally) consuming ambitions of local politicians and their followers.

Through the transgressive forms of sacrifice and medicine that Pa Yamba and others described, the ritual consumption of a human being's life and potential is viewed as giving the politician – and through him, the diviner 'behind' his power – access to the consumption of the wealth of the state. Thus 'eating' people ritually, through the mediation of a diviner, confers the capacity to 'eat' people politically, through the apparatus of the state (Shaw 1996, 2002). Non-discursive memories of human commodification during the Atlantic and colonial eras, I suggest, have structured the agency of postcolonial subjects as they experience the opacity and dangers of national politics, and reflect upon the opportunities the modern state provides for its own forms of extraction.

These forms of memory have, tragically, been rendered especially relevant during Sierra Leone's current rebel war, in which rumours circulate of the cannibalism of the rebels (see, e.g., Richards 1996b: 92) and of human sacrifices made by combatant leaders.[13] Once again, such rumours are fitting expressions of the human costs of a war financed by diamonds and fought with the extracted labour of young people who are treated – by all sides – as commodified resources (Richards 1996b, 2000). Richards suggests, in fact, that the moral critique developed in cannibalism stories might provide a useful basis for local debates about how to limit abuses of patronage and rethink patrimonial political culture in Sierra Leone (1996b: 160–161). Whether or not such debates take place, we would do well to listen to what the discourse of cannibalism tells us about the memory of Atlantic commodities and the modernity of a twenty-first century war.

Notes

1 See, e.g., Auslander 1993; Bastian 1993; Ciekawy and Geschiere 1998; Comaroff and Comaroff 1999; Fisiy and Geschiere 1996; Geschiere 1997; Masquelier 2000; Meyer 1998; Weiss 1996.

2 E.g. Dirks 1992: 7; Cole 1998; De Boeck 1998; Ranger 1996; Stoller 1995; Werbner 1998.
3 In various parts of the Atlantic coast and its hinterland, images of cannibalism were triggered by travel towards the coast, or by the presence of the sea, of a ship, and of Europeans (see, e.g., Park 1817, I: 484; Curtin 1967: 331).
4 We should not assume, however, that the capacity to metamorphose into a wild animal is (or was) always viewed as an unambiguously negative quality (see Jackson 1989: 102–118).
5 Although the external trade in slaves was greatly reduced, however, it did not disappear (see Jones 1983: 83–85; Kalous 1974: 185–186; Wylie 1977: 83–84).
6 In 1954, the chiefs' persistent 'eating' of their chiefdoms gave rise to 'Disturbances' in the form of an uprising of youth in the Northern Province (Dorjahn 1960: 111, 139).
7 See, e.g., Kalous 1974: 13, 32, 55–56, 78, 82, 85, 88, 89, 102, 107, 118, 121, 133, 139, 161, and 277.
8 See also Kalous 1974: 60, 67, 83, 129, 130, 133–137, 141–142, 148, 161–172.
9 Raiders did not, of course, bite captives on their genitals. They did, however, 'mutilate' the reproductive capacity of the families whose young people they stole by severing them from their next generation.
10 October 1989, Petbana Masimbo.
11 Some accusations were, in fact, made by chiefs and big men against domestic slaves (Kalous 1974: 63, 89). Yet such accusations tended to rebound upon the accusers (Kalous 1974: 91).
12 This raises the question of how many of the accusations and confessions in the colonial records are dream narratives (cf. Baum 1983).
13 One such rumour that circulated in 1999 (the year of the Lome Peace Accord) described Foday Sankoh, the leader of the RUF rebels, as having presided over the sacrifice and consumption of several albinos, together with several black cows, in order to ensure that the rebels would remain rebels forever. See Ellis (1999) on cannibalism stories in the Liberian civil war.

Bibliography

Abraham, A. (1975) 'The pattern of warfare and settlement among the Mende of Sierra Leone in the second half of the nineteenth century', *Kroniek van Africa* 2: 130–140; reprinted as Occasional Paper No.1, Institute of African Studies, Fourah Bay College.
—— (1976) 'Cannibalism and African historiography', in *Topics in Sierra Leone History: A Counter-Colonial Interpretation*, Freetown: Leone Publishers.
Alvares, M. (1990 [c.1615]) *Ethiopia Minor and a Geographical Account of the Province of Sierra Leone*, P.E.H. Hair (trans. and ed.), Department of History, University of Liverpool, mimeograph.
Auslander, M. (1993) '"Open the wombs!": the symbolic politics of modern Ngoni witch-finding', in J. Comaroff and J. Comaroff (eds) *Modernity and its Malcontents: Ritual and Power in Postcolonial Africa*, Chicago: University of Chicago Press.
Bastian, M. (1992) 'The world as marketplace: cosmological, historical and popular constructions of the Onitsha market', unpublished PhD dissertation, University of Chicago.
—— (1993) '"Bloodhounds who have no friends": witchcraft and locality in the Nigerian popular press', in J. Comaroff and J. Comaroff (eds) *Modernity and its Malcontents: Ritual and Power in Postcolonial Africa*, Chicago: University of Chicago Press.
Baum, R.M. (1983) 'Crimes of the dream world: French trials of Diola witches', paper presented at the University of Warwick, conference on the History of Law, Labour, and Crime.

Bayart, J.-F. (1993) *The State in Africa: The Politics of the Belly*, London: Verso.

Brooks, G.E. (1993) *Landlords and Strangers: Ecology, Society and Trade in Western Africa, 1000–1630*, Boulder: Westview Press.

Ceyssens, R. (1975) 'Mutumbula. Mythe de l'opprimé', *Cultures et Développement* 7: 483–550.

Ciekawy, D. and Geschiere, P. (1998) 'Containing witchcraft: conflicting scenarios in postcolonial Africa', *African Studies Review* 41: 1–14.

Cole, J. (1998) 'The uses of defeat: memory and political morality in east Madagascar', in R. Werbner (ed.) *Memory and the Postcolony: African Anthropology and the Critique of Power*, London: Zed Books.

Comaroff, J. and J.L. Comaroff (1999) 'Occult economies and the violence of abstraction: notes from the South African postcolony', *American Ethnologist* 26: 279–303.

Curtin, P. (ed.) (1967) *Africa Remembered: Narratives by West Africans from the Era of the Slave Trade*, Prospect Heights, IL: Waveland Press.

De Boeck, F. (1998) 'Beyond the grave: history, memory and death in postcolonial Congo/Zaire', in R. Werbner (ed.) *Memory and the Postcolony: African Anthropology and the Critique of Power*, London: Zed Books.

Dirks, N.B. (1992) 'Introduction', in N.B. Dirks (ed.) *Colonialism and Culture*, Ann Arbor: University of Michigan Press.

Dorjahn, V.R. (1960) 'The changing political system of the Temne', *Africa* xxx: 110–140.

Ellis, S. (1999) *The Mask of Anarchy: The Destruction of Liberia and the Religious Dimension of African Civil War*, New York: University Press.

Ferme, M.C. (1999) 'Staging *politisi*: The dialogics of publicity and secrecy in Sierra Leone', in J.L. Comaroff and J. Comaroff (eds) *Civil Society and the Political Imagination in Africa*, Chicago: University of Chicago Press.

Fernandes, V. (1951 [1506–1510]) *Description de la Côte Occidentale d'Afrique (Sénégal au Cap de Monte. Archipels*, trans. and notes by Th. Monod, A. Teixera da Mota and R. Mauny, Bissau, Portugal: Centro de Estudios da Guine Portuguesa (No. 11).

Fisiy, C. and Geschiere, P. (1996) 'Witchcraft, violence and identity: different trajectories in postcolonial Cameroon', in R. Werbner and T. Ranger (eds) *Postcolonial Identities in Africa*, London: Zed Books.

Geschiere, P. (1997) *The Modernity of Witchcraft: Politics and the Occult in Postcolonial Africa*, Charlotteville: University Press of Virginia.

Ijagbemi, E.A. (1968) 'A history of the Temne in the nineteenth century', unpublished PhD thesis, University of Edinburgh.

Jackson, M. (1989) *Paths Toward a Clearing: Radical Empiricism and Ethnographic Inquiry*, Bloomington: Indiana University Press.

Jones, A. (1983) *From Slaves to Palm Kernels: A History of the Galinhas Country (West Africa) 1730–1890*, Wiesbaden: Franz Steiner Verlag.

Kalous, M. (1974) *Cannibals and Tongo Players of Sierra Leone*, Aukland, NZ: Wright and Carman.

Lenga-Kroma, J.S. (1978) 'A history of the southern Temne in the late nineteenth and early twentieth centuries', unpublished PhD thesis, University of Edinburgh.

Masquelier, A. (2000) 'Of headhunters and cannibals: migrancy, labor, and consumption in the Mawri imagination', *Cultural Anthropology* 15: 84–126.

Matthews, J. (1966 [1788]) *A Voyage to the River Sierra Leone, on the Coast of Africa*, London: B. White and Son.

Meyer, B. (1998) 'The power of money: politics, occult forces, and Pentecostalism in Ghana', *African Studies Review* 41: 15–37.

Mitchell, P.K. (1962) 'Trade routes of the early Sierra Leone protectorate', *Sierra Leone Studies* (new series) 16: 204–217.

Palmie, S. (1995) 'The taste of human commodities: experiencing the Atlantic system', in S. Palmie (ed.) *Slave Cultures and the Cultures of Slavery*, Knoxville: University of Tennessee Press.

Park, M. (1817) *Travels in the Interior Districts of Africa*, vol. I. London: J. Murray.

Ranger, T. (1996) 'Postscript: colonial and postcolonial identities', in R. Werbner and T. Ranger (eds) *Postcolonial Identities in Africa*, London: Zed Books.

Rashid, I. (1999) '"Do dady nor lef me make dem carry me": slave resistance and emancipation in Sierra Leone, 1894–1928', in S. Miers and M. Klein (eds), *Slavery and Colonial Rule in Africa*, London: Frank Cass.

Reno, W. (1995) *Corruption and State Politics in Sierra Leone*, Cambridge: University Press.

Richards, P. (1996a) 'Chimpanzees, diamonds and war: the discourses of global environmental change and local violence on the Liberia-Sierra Leone border', in H.L. Moore (ed.) *The Changing Nature of Anthropological Knowledge*, London: Routledge.

—— (1996b) *Fighting for the Rain Forest: War, Youth and Resources in Sierra Leone*, Oxford: James Currey.

—— (2000) 'Chimpanzees as political animals in Sierra Leone', in J. Knight (ed.) *Natural Enemies: People-Wildlife Conflicts in Anthropological Perspective*, London: Routledge.

Rodney, W. (1970) *A History of the Upper Guinea Coast 1545 to 1800*, London: Oxford University Press.

Shaw, R. (1992) 'Dreaming as accomplishment: power, the individual and Temne divination', in M.C. Jedrej and R. Shaw (eds) *Dreaming, Religion and Society in Africa*, Leiden: E.J. Brill.

—— (1996) 'The politician and the diviner: divination and the consumption of power in Sierra Leone', *Journal of Religion in Africa* xxvi: 30–55.

—— (1997) 'The production of witchcraft/witchcraft as production: memory, modernity, and the slave trade in Sierra Leone', *American Ethnologist* 24: 856–876.

—— (2002) *Memories of the Slave Trade: Ritual and the Historical Imagination in Sierra Leone*, Chicago: University of Chicago Press.

Stoller, P. (1995) *Embodying Colonial Memories: Spirit Possession, Power and the Hauka in West Africa*, New York: Routledge.

Weiss, B. (1996) *The Making and Unmaking of the Haya Lived World*, Durham, NC: Duke University Press.

Werbner, R.P. (1998) 'Beyond oblivion: confronting memory crisis', in R. Werbner (ed.) *Memory and the Postcolony: African Anthropology and the Critique of Power*, London: Zed Books.

White, L. (2000) *Speaking with Vampires: Rumor and History in Colonial Africa*, Berkeley: University of California Press.

Wylie, K.C. (1977) *The Political Kingdoms of the Temne: Temne Government in Sierra Leone, 1825–1910*, London: Africana Publishing Company.

Zack-Williams, A.B. (1989) 'Sierra Leone 1968–85: the decline of politics and the politics of decline', *International Journal of Sierra Leone Studies* 1: 122–130.

Chapter 4

Vulture men, campus cultists and teenaged witches

Modern magics in Nigerian popular media

Misty L. Bastian

'At Okokomaiko-Lagos, I was a witness to the story of a cat that transformed into a human being (an aged woman)', avers Nigerian editorialist Amaechi Ukor (1997), writing in a piece meant not only to be placed in a local newspaper but to be posted on the World Wide Web for a global audience. What is more, Ukor and his colleagues at the *Post Express Wired* want this global audience to know that such transformations are not 'traditional' in a simple sense but are as much a part of their fractured experience of modernity as is their ability to reach both national and transnational readers. Indeed, the general theme of Ukor's editorial is that modern Nigeria has become a place of 'horrifying realities', where people are daily outraged by events and practices unheard of in the precolonial period. The unsettling quality of Nigerian life at the beginning of the twenty-first century is marked by a different attachment to material reality – whether through virtual relationships, mediated by the electronic press, or through signs of another virtuality on Nigerians' home ground: the seeming ubiquity of what evangelical Christians see as satanic witchcraft and magic in the country's teeming cityscapes. In this chapter, I will therefore consider three different subgenres of Nigerian popular press narratives about magical modernity, seeking to understand why Nigerians mark their experiences of modernity differently from most westerners – if, indeed, they do.

The first of these popular subgenres has to do with witchcraft and bodily transformation within Nigerian cities. Narratives of bodily transformation, I will argue, speak to the sense of many urban Nigerians that the anonymity of city life and the rapid change inherent to city relationships have destabilized people's understandings of space, place and even of personhood (cf. Watts 1996; Ashforth 1998, Chapter 10). This discussion of anonymity and social transformation is meant to be rather different from Benjamin's (1969: 172) classic characterization of the *flâneur* – the man of leisure who masters and patrols the crowded urban streets in search of sensations, but who transcends his surroundings and is never transformed by them. Comparing Nigerian narratives of bodily transformation with Benjamin's ideas about metropolitan flâneurship therefore may tell us something significantly different in the experiences of modernity at different times and in different locations.

In the second set of narratives, I will examine the pervasive fear of 'cultism' in Nigeria's university system. Although Nigeria's universities were once the pride of sub-Saharan Africa, they have – during an extended period of military rule – undergone a process of degeneration in terms of infrastructure, the quality of teaching and the attitudes of young people who attend them. Stories about university cults speak to a growing disenchantment with the empty promises of late capitalism for Nigeria's youth – as well as to the anxieties that adults feel about the activities of educated but jobless, often prospectless, young men. These stories of violence within an academic setting demonstrate the liminal circumstances not only of young men but of one of the supposed motors of modernity and 'development' within Nigeria, the educational system itself.

Finally, I will discuss a subgenre of narratives about an *arriviste* category of Nigeria's magical population: the teenaged (usually female) witch. In this section, media stories of young women who embrace witchcraft will be considered, demonstrating how witchcraft can be glamorized as a 'profession' for urban girls, who are represented as having an inordinate amount of leisure as well as an insatiable desire for the trappings of material success. This part of the chapter will highlight the gendered nature of Nigerian modern magics, discussing the way young women are subjected – at least in the Nigerian imaginary – to control and bodily discipline when they demonstrate a propensity to move beyond normalized gender boundaries. It will also suggest that the claim of witchly powers may be one method for urban women to counter the control of their elders and the misogynist attitudes of their male peers.

Important themes to be addressed throughout the chapter include urban African life at the beginning of the twenty-first century; expressions of alienation, desire and fragmented social relations in contemporary Nigeria; representations of masculinity under conditions of late capitalism; the militarization of Nigerian society; and the continued development of Nigerian versions of modern western social categories. By addressing these themes, the chapter will demonstrate how Nigerian representations of witchcraft, modernity and development necessarily speak to the recent history of the Nigerian state and to the separate cultures that inhabit it.

Vulture men: human to animal transformations in Nigeria's cities

During my first field experience during the late 1980s, I often heard urban legends about mysterious transformations in places like Lagos and Onitsha, the southeastern Nigerian city where I was working. Such stories began with a normal animal witnessed performing abnormal feats, whether walking on two legs, speaking or appearing suddenly in an unusual location. When people who saw this phenomenon were moved to act, they invariably tried to attack the uncanny beast. If the animal was wounded or killed, there were two possible consequences. The first was that the uncanny being managed to escape or disappeared in magical fashion. The second was that the beast was immobilized, suddenly turning into a person known to onlookers. The denouement of the first version is that the same wounds were invariably found on some suspected person the next morning – or that person was found dead in her (or, more rarely, his) bed, with wounds that corresponded exactly to those inflicted on the werebeast.

In such narratives, city streets, or other public spaces, were peculiarly prone to infestation with uncanny fauna, and urban spaces at night were most often the sites for hybrid, human-bestial behaviour. People reported such sightings to me both as first-hand observations (much like that of Mr Ukor above) and as choice market gossip. A few urban sceptics considered these only to be tales from the more credulous or 'illiterate' of their countrymen. However, most people who related such narratives were sure of the stories' veracity, pointing to specificities in the tales in order to legitimate their truth-quality. Such specificities, however, are the hallmarks of the urban legend, combined as it often is in Nigeria (or throughout the west) with a more vague sense of when this event took place and who, exactly, was present to corroborate it.

Stories about animals with human characteristics have long had their place in southern Nigerian folklore (cf. Amadi 1982: 22). Wily snake-men who seduce beautiful but arrogant maidens, as well as witches who fly about as nocturnal birds, looking to cause harm to ordinary people, are staples of both Igbo and Yoruba folktales.[1] However, in most of the standard folkloric narratives about trickster animals or creatures out of category, the uncanny beasts work their magical transformations in the forest. This is a place where human beings are at a distinct disadvantage, but where animals and other wild spirits are at home.

In contemporary Nigeria, as in other parts of the world, urban dwellers have a more fraught relationship, not only with animals in the forest, but with the countryside more generally (cf. Bastian 1993). Nonetheless, this estrangement between country and city would seem to have produced, within the stories circulating throughout Nigeria's cityscapes about human-animal transformations, a displacement of forest magic into the very centres of town. But is this really as ironic as it might appear, or could there be an internal logic to forest-based tricksters taking on urban dress and performing their magics in spaces that would seem antithetical to them? To answer this question, we will examine one, more recent story from the Nigerian electronic media, that of the 'vulture man' of Port Harcourt (Brown 1999).

During late August 1999, rumours circulated in the southeastern coastal city that a child had knocked down a flying vulture that subsequently transformed into a man. Adebayo Brown, a reporter for the *Post Express Wired*, tells us that police were called in when a group of people encircled the 'vulture man', intending to kill him. The man was hospitalized because of the beating he sustained before the police could break up the 'angry mob action', remaining in protective custody a week after the event. The man's transformation into a vulture was taken seriously not only by those passers-by who claimed to be its witness but by the local media. Some reporters went so far as to question the

Rivers State Commissioner of Police, A. J. Peters, if the prisoner had attempted any further animal transformations while in custody (Brown 1999). Peters then scolded journalists at a press conference for seeking out sensational stories 'for sale of newspapers, and entertainment on television', and averred that the supposed vulture man was actually of 'unsound mind'.

Whatever the official position of the Port Harcourt police's Swift Operations Squad, however, people in town were less sure about the vulture man – and remained interested in him and his fate. It was not that vulture men, or other human-animal hybrids, were perceived as so rare in Nigerian cities, but that the capture of a living specimen and its preservation by the police offered much food for thought. Madness is understood both as a medical and a spiritual condition in contemporary Nigeria. Psychiatric hospitals and 'herbal homes', as the shrines of healer-diviners are often known, have long histories and not always separate adherents among Nigeria's urban populations. While southern Nigerians have their own symptomologies of madness, including seeing animals that no one else can see (Sadowsky 1999: 14, 88), southerners do not consider people caught performing an animal–human transformation to be mad. There are other categories for those capable of such a feat: witches, members of secret societies and elders with special powers, gained from connections to powerful medicines.

It would be difficult to say which of these categories of person causes the most anxiety among urban dwellers. Witches, as noted above, become animals when on their nightly errands – carrying out their murderous plans disguised as predators. Members of contemporary secret societies are thought to take on the animal forms of the societies' forest patrons, including vultures, civet cats and leopards. In the Port Harcourt area, for instance, leopards are historically associated with the *Ekpe/Ekpo* secret societies that once punished Igbo and Ibibio people who transgressed local prohibitions (Offiong 1991: 2, 62–63). Early twentieth-century colonial reports are also rife with popular rumours having to do with 'leopard men' who terrorized both 'natives' and colonial officials alike.[2] Elders, whose persons have been medicated by magical practitioners, are often viewed in the modern urban context as regressive agents of rural power, and their appearance in towns is a cause for unease among West African city dwellers (cf. Bastian 1993; Geschiere and Nyamnjoh 1998).

Vultures, however, have been positively valued in Ibibio religious practice, as they were once considered to be representatives and sometimes even incarnations of ancestral forces (Talbot 1967 [1923]: 173–174). Their appearance at rituals of sacrifice was absolutely required; any sacrifice that did not draw the carrion birds was considered unsuccessful. Among southern Igbo-speakers (another significant part of the Port Harcourt population), vultures have both positive and negative symbolic associations. As scavengers of the marketplace, they are considered 'useful' animals – beings who help to keep the market clean and beautiful (Bastian forthcoming a). Conversely, the birds are perceived to be polluted and polluting because they eat the kills of other animals. This view is conducive to the worst Igbo 'reading' of vultures as cannibal beings who live off the bodies of the more productive or less fortunate. Such readings can help to explain why the notion of a 'vulture man' flying over the skies of Port Harcourt would be both so fascinating and repellent to urbanites. The idea of ancestors manifesting themselves as vultures might also take on a more problematic status if we consider how ill-prepared to face ancestral forces, or any other powers connected with older modes of rural life, most urban dwellers feel themselves to be.[3]

In southern Nigerian discourse the spiritual forces of the forest have never confined themselves strictly to the wild, but always seek to infiltrate civilized human spaces. At the beginning of the twenty-first century, Nigeria's urban areas are not so privileged by global modernity that they can claim immunity from this infiltration. If anything, the modern cityscape offers new avenues for the creativity of the forest and its denizens. Where people living in even a relatively populous village-group can be familiar, at least by sight, to most of their neighbours, the Nigerian urbanite is mobile, less rooted and finds it more difficult to know those who live and work in close proximity. Other city dwellers' personal histories are a mystery, only to be learned by dint of great effort, and intimate connections have to be *made*. They cannot be taken for granted. The sheer numbers of people around the urbanite makes it impossible for him or her to feel secure about the motivations and interests of others. Strangers do not, as in the rural areas, come from outside. They live next door or even in the next room.

Vulture men therefore need not find an excuse for their presence; the buildings and complex, badly marked streets are as good a cover as the trees of the subtropical forest once were. The cities and their suburban satellites indeed have replaced many of the old, forested areas of southern Nigeria, opening up space only in one sense. The loss of the trees and underbrush did not, in the imaginary of southeasterners, necessarily mean the loss of spiritual entities that once made these areas their home.[4] Instead of becoming disenchanted, Nigeria's cities have taken on a modern magic: with forest creatures reinventing themselves as entrepreneurs and fashion victims, the better to snare their old prey, human beings.

What is more disturbing to southern Nigerians than the notion that their cities are homes to such creatures is that the state is implicated in the animal-human hybrids' plots and machinations. In 1980s urban legends about human animals, after all, the best solution offered to the paradox of hybridity was xenocide, but in Brown's report the 'vulture man' was not destroyed by mob action because the police protected him. This is probably one reason why the story received such extensive coverage in the local and electronic press. Many Nigerians distrust the officials who supposedly protect them, but who require expensive bribes to do the minimum for ordinary citizens – and, indeed, might be seen as bureaucratic vultures, picking over the barely-breathing body of Nigerian civil society.

If magic is valuable to the modern West African state – and we have many reasons to believe it is (Shaw 1996; Geschiere 1997; Meyer 1998) – then it is understandable why Port Harcourt inhabitants and members of the Nigerian press might find it suspicious that state functionaries were so eager to characterize the 'vulture man' as mad.[5] The mixture of magic and the state makes regular Nigerians anxious, because they know that there is political currency in the occult – whether that currency is imaginary or not (Comaroff and Comaroff 1999). As we will see in the next section on 'campus cultists', even the most fantastic of conspiratorial ideas can become too painfully real in a society where modernity's most basic promises are subverted. Vulture men may be good to think with – a part of the nation's consideration of what modern cities mean – but cults and secret societies on the nation's campuses speak to the unthinkable: the potential breakdown of all modern civility, at the very moment of its gestation.

'Spilling blood all in the name of brotherhood': campus cultists, or gangsters in the ivory tower?

We have always wanted to be tough, to be feared and obeyed. Rough life is welcome, it is considered manly. In our dictionary, that is. Which is why we got together and formed the Great Fraternity . . . There would always be cults after us because there were cults before us. Consider how we came into existence. Each of us used to belong to some fraternity until it became clear that independence was inevitable. We were not at home with some of their *modus operandi*. For instance, the conservative members of the parent organisation believed in using machets for *hits*. We subscribe to guns. We love guns. There's a finality to that word, and dirty jobs get done in a clean way – no mess ups. We could not understand why the other members were reluctant to move with the times.

Of course there would always be cults. They used to belong to youths from poor backgrounds – as a way to combat the oppressions by the rich. Not anymore. Some of us are from very wealthy homes. Interestingly, our fathers used to be cult members and some still are – although we place 'oc' before the 'cult' for you to understand the dimension of their clandestine preoccupation.

The occultic is like the doctorate programme for young frat boys like us. While we learn the ropes within the school environment through regular fraternities, our fathers are consolidating our position in the big-time league pending our graduation. And it's rather ridiculous to hear people suggest that our mothers do not know of our fathers' involvement in secret societies. How the heck did they meet?...Why is society forever persecuting us? Why does it continually delude itself with half-hearted attempts at cleansing the campuses? Policemen and soldiers and government agents parading the school like there's a state of emergency. Tut tut. Is it possible to prosecute the IG's [Inspector General's] son or an Army General's son?

(Anonymous 2000)

During the 1960s, the first full generation of educated Nigerian youth were able to attend university in their own country (Crowder 1973: 305–388; Zachernuk 2000: 128–129). The immediate post-independence period was a heady time for the universities, and there was great optimism about Nigeria's future as a 'developed' country, one of the 'giants' of contemporary Africa and a leader in the non-aligned movement of so-called Third World states.[6] Universities – first in the southwestern region of Nigeria, then in both the north and the southeast – were thought to be the motors for the new nation's inevitable prosperity. Education more generally was celebrated as the sovereign means for social transformation and the spread of development and modernization ideologies – what Ferguson (1999: 13–14) calls the 'modernization myth' – throughout the population (cf. Escobar 1995: 45). The last thing that was expected by those who contemplated the burgeoning Nigerian university system at its inception was that universities would become notorious hotbeds for what partisans of modernization would stigmatize as 'superstition'.[7] Certainly no one imagined the resurgence of violent, masculinist rituals within the universities, syncretic of local and foreign men's associations.

What Nigerians now refer to as 'campus cultism' began during the 1950s, when nationalist fervour was at its height. Some even point to Nobel Laureate Wole Soyinka as the founder of the early fraternity movement (Nzediegwu 1999).[8] Soyinka's Pyrate Confraternity at the University College of Ibadan was one of the first such associations, and its membership constituted a late colonial, intellectual elite who would go on to work in international scholarly circles as well as in Nigerian journalism and politics (cf. Zachernuk 2000: 135–138). The point of the Pyrate fraternity was conviviality and, quoting editorialist Emmanuel Nzediegwu (1999), 'to put pressure on the colonialists, shake off colonial mentality, assert the identity of true independence and to instil university culture into members'. Although Soyinka and his colleagues took as their mascot the bloodthirsty pirate, the playful spelling of their organization's name gives a good sense of the style of the fraternity. Sophisticated English verbal games were of far greater interest than mayhem, although serious topics were discussed by the fraternity members who understood themselves to be in preparation for political and social independence from the British.

The best-educated sons of Nigeria's (mostly southern) indigenous professionals, the Pyrates wished to be part of Nigeria's future and did not model themselves directly on institutions from what they considered very much the country's past. There is no space in the present chapter to go into the contentious history of Nigerian intellectuals on the cusp of independence (see Zachernuk 2000), so all that I will say here is that the Pyrates soon split apart under the pressure of competition within the fraternity. Other groups formed as offshoots of the original Pyrates, and yet more fraternities developed along with the expansion of the university system throughout the tumultuous civil war period of the 1960s and Nigeria's Oil Boom in the 1970s. These fraternities seem to have remained relatively benign and true to the intent of Soyinka and his peers, although their names emphasized the more sensationalistic and violent aspects of transatlantic popular culture: Buccaneers, Blood Suckers, Black Cat, Vikings Confraternity, Mafia, Red Devils, Black Berets, Green Berets, the Black Axes and the Neo Black Movement among others (Nzediegwu 1999).

Young Nigerian men who were the products of the university system during its heyday maintained contact with each other after graduation and professional training, much in keeping with the ties created by contemporary North American fraternities (Nuwer 1999). These now senior men also developed ties with younger men who were involved in fraternity life on campus. They acted as mentors to their juniors and encouraged their male relations to take part in masculine secret associations as an initiation into the modernizing rubrics of 'university culture'. However, college confraternities were no more immune to the growing difficulties faced by Nigeria's population in the era of extended military rule and Oil Bust (1980s–1990s) than were other Nigerian institutions. If anything, we might suggest that they were actually more sensitive than some organizations of Nigeria's increasingly 'uncivil' society, because their member-ship was particularly at risk in the climate of kleptocracy, brain drain and systemic unemployment. Unlike the members of fraternities from the 1940s onwards, the 'brothers' of the 1980s and 1990s did not find their university coursework and degrees an automatic passport to well-paid positions in the government bureaucracy or the 'Nigerianized' petrochemical industry. Indeed, young men during the latter two decades of the twentieth century were educated by a university system under severe strain.

During the Oil Boom, as an attempt to appease any ethnic discontent remaining from the Biafran civil war, alternating Nigerian civilian and military regimes pursued a policy of establishing new, often underfunded universities throughout the country. In the 1980s I heard these new universities referred to as 'mushroom campuses', because they had sprung up – in quite unlikely locations – overnight. Unlike the older, established universities at Ibadan or Ile-Ife (now known as Obafemi Awolowo University), the mushroom campuses suffered from shoddy and sometimes inadequate construction, strained relations between local faculties and outsider administrations, as well as ongoing financial crises. Students attended overcrowded lectures, taught by postgraduate students and faculty members who no longer looked forward to regular paycheques, much less to the subsidized housing and transport of Nigeria's Oil Boom academe. University libraries contained mainly out-of-date publications, when books or journals were to be had at all, and students could neither afford nor obtain textbooks for their courses. During the late 1980s, student dormitories in the new universities were regularly without electrical power and running water, while the student cuisine of necessity was dry *gari* (cassava) mixed with heated water and sugar – if the last two commodities were available.

It was into this climate of scholarly and national deprivation that campus fraternities were reborn as campus cults. Whereas the original confraternities were elite organizations, the college male organizations of the 1970s onwards took on a different character. In the aftermath of universal primary education programmes and expanded access to secondary schools (Falola 1996: 85–87, 150), young men *and* women from less lofty social backgrounds were able to take advantage of the Oil Boom expansion of the university system, entering tertiary education in ever-increasing numbers.[9]

Male youth coming to the universities directly from rural areas and less privileged households may have seen the fraternity system as close kin to the age grades, men's masquerade and other secret societies with which they were familiar. According to the anonymous (2000) features writer for *Sunday Vanguard* quoted at the beginning of this section, these young men, anxious about their future prospects and present, liminal class positions, banded together in collegiate 'cults' in order 'to combat the oppressions by the rich'. While class-based resistance may have motivated the formation of certain counter-fraternities, by the late 1980s rumours abounded among educated young people that elite undergraduates were taking over the leadership and developing 'gangs' from among the disaffected male majority in the universities (cf. Bastian 1999).

Whether gangs, cults or counter-fraternities, such groups were associated in the minds of my youthful informants in the 1980s with the burgeoning drug and weapons trade in the southeast. This trade in illegal but highly lucrative commodities was, among other things, considered by many to be a direct consequence of IMF structural adjustment requirements and the lengthening shadow of military rule throughout Nigeria (Apter 1999). Nigerian media has been sensitive to the possible connection between young university men's increasing violence in the past two decades and what one *Post Express Wired* editorialist (Onunaiju 1999) calls 'the militarisation of the country's political process and the consequent de-intellectualisation of [its] university life'.

Certainly it became clear to Nigeria's intelligent male youth during the 'permanent transition' from General Babangida's military tricksterism (Apter 1999) to General Abacha's state of terror that weapons, brutal intimidation and illicit trade were the means to political and social power in the country. Civilian elections could be set aside, civilian candidates and their kin could be jailed or permanently silenced by mysterious bombs or highway ambushes, and men claiming to live on the salaries of the military command ranks could amass foreign bank accounts with balances numbering in the billions of US dollars. The lesson was sufficiently pointed, even for students whose classes were constantly cancelled because of faculty strikes or government shutdowns of the universities for 'subversion' and 'indiscipline'.

While the military regimes of the 1980s and 1990s suppressed university activism alongside the trade union and other socially conscious movements, all in the *name* of national discipline, campus cults became more entrenched in university life. Many civic-minded Nigerians began to join editorialist Charles Onunaiju (1999) in his question: 'Did [the military rulers] not prefer the production of thugs, to patriots who will raise questions about their rascality with power?' However, such questions could only be spoken in the most subdued tones under General Abacha, a military dictator who showed a propensity for the parapolitical tactics of disappearance, torture and extra-judicial execution – all, not coincidentally, also the modus operandi of campus cultists. Campus thugs, some argued, were in training for their future roles in the military take-over of the Nigerian polity, and the most intimate familial connections between the military and campus cult leaders were sometimes postulated, as in the anonymous quote (2000) above.

An important part of media and ordinary Nigerian discourse about campus cults during the last decades of the twentieth century was an understanding that university violence was carried out on several levels, including that of the occult. Discussions of the fraternities invariably lead Nigerians to rumour about fraternity/cult initiations, which are thought to require physical violence and terror, often against women on campus,[10] as well as 'medicines', other power objects, and even the standard ritual accoutrements of European Masonry or Satanism. Once initiated, university cult members were (and are) believed to have a supernatural immunity to gunshot wounds, to possess a superhuman sexual potency and appetite and to have a magical ability to influence the minds of others (Iloduba 1999). In the latter case, members are supposedly able to use what appear to be ordinary, everyday objects like handkerchiefs or cigarettes to bewitch people and force them to do the cults' bidding (cf. Bastian 1992, 1998).

Rumours about campus occultism are directly tied to ideas about the magical activities of Nigerian politicians, military and businessmen. Cult violence at the universities does not occur only in the Nigerian imaginary, but has exploded into an all too real epidemic of rape, physical (as well as psychological) wounds and death on campus during the past decade. Such violence is perceived by many Nigerians to be determined by the more generally violent environment of the country.[11] Cultism therefore reflects forms of violence already present in society, but it also perpetuates and even creates an escalating environment of immorality, carrying that immorality and its material consequences into the next generations.

When cult members leave the campus, they are rumoured to have two trajectories. If of an upper-class background, young cultists go into elite secret societies like the Reformed Ogboni Fraternity. This is a Yoruba-based group that now boasts a membership crossing all ethnic boundaries and is said to be behind the ascent of many Nigerians into the higher echelons of government administration, the judiciary and multinational corporations (cf. Agbroko 1996). Although once an elders' society, limited to the Yoruba-speaking areas of the country and meant to act in the capacity of moral guardianship for the community, including the *oba* or king (Amadi 1982: 9–10; Apter 1992: 83, 90; Matory 1994: 265, n. 16), the Reformed Ogboni Fraternity is now considered – at least by those who do not belong to the organization – to be at the bottom of Nigeria's most entangled conspiracies.

Ogboni members I knew in the late 1980s, however, denied involvement in national conspiracy and told me that their group was really meant for elite networking and socializing. They were uniformly proud of their membership, but would only hint at the rigours of their initiation and investiture into Ogboni, mainly suggesting it was, in the English words of one member, 'costly, very costly'. The continuing costs of Ogboni membership are an issue of great interest and anxiety among ordinary Nigerians today, particularly evangelical Christians. Stigmatized by Christian leaders as 'public sinners . . . who cannot be [members] of the body of Christ' (Esele 1996), there has been a growing sense that Ogboni, Freemasons and other secret societies mean ill for their fellow human beings. Just as campus cultists are sometimes rumoured to sacrifice human beings (or parts of their own bodies; cf. Anonymous 1999), there is a conflation in Nigerian conspiratorial imaginaries between groups like the Reformed Ogboni Fraternity and the supposedly wealthy practitioners of 'satanic acts' or *juju* (Iloduba 1999).

Graduates of lower social background have little hope of immediate entrance into Nigerian secret societies like the Ogboni. Unlike the children of Ogboni members, lower class ex-cultists without connections may seek patronage from 'big men' in their home areas or may trade upon associations begun with elite graduates from their universities. Some consider the recent explosion of armed robbery within the southern half of Nigeria to be directly connected to the numbers of ex-cultists who have weapons, ruthless patrons as well as the experience of university brutality behind them (Emeh 1997). Unemployed after graduation and with few prospects, since their university degrees (if granted) now offer little in the way of social mobility, lower class ex-cultists have very few other options. They may enlist in the military and expect to serve as 'peacekeepers' in African locations of civil strife like Sierra Leone, where the temptation to take part in the violent corruption associated with the illicit diamond and weapons trade is great.[12] They may try to return to their impoverished hometowns, where there will be an equally great temptation to use campus cultist skills – including mystical skills – to become more important personages among their peers. The result of this latter prospect may be seen in the spate of kidnappings for money and disappearances of children, possibly for use in 'ritual murder', in the city of Owerri during the mid-1990s (Bastian 1999; Smith forthcoming).

Equipped by their college cult education, not for continued modernization or the development of civil society in Nigeria, but to shore up the nation's kleptocratic elite, some young men are moving into what we might call postgraduate violence. What they have learned is pertinent to the Nigerian version of modernity that stresses the importance of (para)militarized power and terror and contributes to the material *and* spiritual insecurity (Ashforth 1998, Chapter 10) of everyday life in contemporary Nigeria. In a haze of hyper-masculinity and without much sense of any future worth considering, ex-cultists leave the campus but not the cult behind, and it is not only the universities but Nigerian society as a whole that suffers for it.

(Teen) witches invade Nigeria: young women in magical modernity

> My name is Augustina Uzora from Imo State. I am an Ogbanje, agent of satan. I am from River Niger. I have five powers. One of this is in my private part and I use it to destroy. Each man who makes love with me would have his family wrecked because my spiritual husband gave me power to destroy men. My private part usually disturbs me whenever I see a man because of the power I have there. I use my heart to think evil about people and it happens like that[.] I also use my mouth to curse many people including my brother, who is here. I used my mouth to curse them because they used to beat me because of my stubbornness. I am stubborn because of the powers I have. My nose and my eyes also have powers of destruction. Please, I have killed a lot of people.
>
> (from a transcript of 'ogbanje' confessions at the Synagogue Church in Ikotun, Lagos, published in *Conscience International*, June 1998, p. 6)

In 1998 a Nigerian weekly newsmagazine, *Conscience International*, published an article on the plague of young women 'ogbanje' (*ogbaanje*; cf. Bastian 1997, forthcoming c) infesting Lagos, the country's former capital. Complete with photographs of the confessing ogbaanje speaking into microphones and holding up evangelical literature, it is apparent that these are youthful, well-dressed and lovely women, hardly the stereotype of aged, powerless women often seen as the victims *par excellence* of African mystical accusations (see Figures 4.1 and 4.2).[13] These young women *are* confessing – under the pressure of a new fashion, 'born again' Christianity – to the interference with physical and social reproduction often associated with witchcraft and other mystical acts on the continent (Austen 1993). However, as in the example above, they are confessing to a peculiarly modern conflation of overwhelming sexuality and reproductive blockage rather than to the antisexual powers and supposed jealousies of age.

Augustina Uzora, self-confessed ogbaanje and 'agent of satan' as quoted above, claims five 'powers', all lodged at various sites in her body.[14] These powers have been given to Uzora by her 'spiritual husband' – which in the present case probably means the ambigendered spiritual force known as Mami Wata (Bastian 1997) – and they are used to ensnare, then destroy, men. The mode of this destruction is made clearer by Uzora's sister ogbaanje, Georgina Nwokwa (Figure 4.3): 'I don't go for poor guys. I go for rich men. Anytime I have fun with them, their business will start collapsing. Even if he is very wealthy, the man will start having problems'. Uzora claims that the power resident in her vagina 'disturbs' her when she sees such a successful man. It is as though her dangerous sexuality calls out, not for satisfaction, but for revenge. Once she and Nwokwa 'have fun' with their male victims, the men are no longer rich and their families are 'wrecked'. In the more explicit words of another confessing ogbaanje, Ngozi Nwosu (Figure 4.4), who proclaims herself 'the queen of the coast, a Cobra':

Figure 4.1 Iyabo Akindele, who claims to have seven ogbaanje powers in her body. She supposedly uses her powers to entrap wealthy businessmen.

Figure 4.2 Ifeoma Ejiogu of Festac Town, Lagos 'with Ogbanje power all over her body'.

'The power in my vagina is the one I use to destroy men[.] I destroy their sperm so that they will become impotent and their business will not prosper. I'll just make them useless'.

Although Uzora seems to wish to lose her powers, and to have come to the Synagogue Church for just this purpose, she also appears to be proud of those powers. There is a sense in her brief confession that she has taken charge of a life that otherwise was intolerable, a life where, among other things, she was beaten by male relatives because of her 'stubbornness'. As is common with the confessions of other ogbaanje in the *Conscience International* article, Uzora first boasts about what she can do with her powerful body, then submits it to the ministrations of Pastor T.B. Joshua for exorcism. To understand better the confessions (and Christian submission) of these youthful Nigerian women, we need to discuss the more general situation of young women in the country – particularly their gendered experiences of modern social life.

As I have argued elsewhere (Bastian 2000; forthcoming b), not only gender but youth is a constructed category in contemporary Nigeria, with a history directly connected to European colonial and mission incursions. Missions were especially implicated in the development of separate 'spheres' for gendered

Figure 4.3 Georgina Nwokwa, who coun-
sels young men that 'girls with
demonic powers . . . will surely
destroy their lives'.

Figure 4.4 Ngozi Nwosu, self-described
'queen of the coast, a Cobra'.
She tried to seduce Pastor T.B.
Joshua but failed when he
sprinkled holy water on her.

youth during the colonial period. Mission education played a key part in the
construction of a protracted 'girlhood' or female adolescence during which
young, colonial women could be kept from marriage and (their own) house-
keeping in order to become modern, Christian and female subjects. An unin-
tended consequence of these educational activities, however, was that – as
young Nigerian women developed these looked-for, modern Christian sub-
jectivities – they also developed an interest in personal, individuated advancement. Young women necessarily imbibed some of the rubrics of secularism along
with their modern studies, especially once some of them could read in English
and discovered genres of literature that were not first approved by the missionaries. Formal literacy was hardly the only means for young women to learn
modernity, however.

New, embodied disciplines of dress and hygiene were forced upon missionized
women in the colonial period; once tested, these same disciplines were actively
embraced by Nigerian women everywhere. Young women in particular were
encouraged by missionaries to adopt what the Europeans thought of as modest
dress, 'frocks' constructed on sewing machines. In adopting European-style
fashion, youthful Nigerian women also learned the new fashion technology as a

means for cash employment and were drawn further into modern practices of consumption. Colonial notions of hygiene were frequently directed towards African women's sexuality and its social consequences (cf. Schmidt 1992; Shaw 1995; Hunt 1999; Bastian 2001). Women in the mission schools of southern Nigeria were taught not only to cover their bodies but to wash, groom and otherwise maintain their body boundaries to minimal European standards. Again Nigerian women were required to engage in wider patterns of consumption, including the purchase of imported soaps, pomades, lotions, combs and other products meant to 'civilize' their African, unruly and sexual bodies, bringing them more in line with the European feminine norm (cf. Burke 1996 for a similar process in Northern Rhodesia).

Not all southern Nigerian women, of course, wholeheartedly embraced colonial and mission projects during the twentieth century. Some women – notably those based in rural communities – actively resisted colonial incursion (Bastian forthcoming a, 2001), including western commodities and practices of consumption. Women living in the colony's urban areas were more implicated in the first wave of missionization, and it was urban life in Nigeria, as in Europe or North America, that gave greater scope for women's attachment to modern products and the ideas embedded in them. Young women began to live outside lineage compounds and control, acting as an important part of the money economy within southern Nigerian towns as early as the 1920s. They also developed relatively independent social lives through contacts made among neighbours and co-workers in the urban areas, social lives that included sexuality not always tied to marriage. When marriage did concern this emerging class of young, female, colonized moderns, it was often couched in Christian, mono-gamous terms – at exactly the same time that mission-educated, male nationalists were beginning to question monogamy as anti-African.[15]

By the independence period, young southern Nigerian women were flocking to the cities. Along with this more educated, although less affluent (in relation to their male counterparts) population came an increased commodification of urban women's sexuality, not only through prostitution but through less profes-sional interactions. Women were said to trade sexual favours for kind as well as cash. Urban men, also living away from their lineage bases in the rural areas, were both without their accustomed modes of domesticity and suddenly aware of the sheer numbers of sexual partners possible.[16] Men had greater access to employment and commodities, particularly as they were offered opportunities in the new, state-run industries, military or government bureaucracy. There-fore they found that women were sexually available in the city without the commitment of (or public scrutiny associated with) marriage.

Women in the cities of independent Nigeria suffered from less consistent employment and education, although they continued to make significant gains in both. Indeed, contemporary Nigeria can boast of prominent women in all sectors of government, education and business. Nonetheless, these elite women constitute only a small minority of the overall Nigerian female, urban population – and their achievements are not always seen positively. In southern societies, powerful, important women have long been stigmatized as witches, whose nightly, covert meetings take place at the tops of trees (Henderson 1969: 301; Apter 1992: 113).[17] Such witches, like the vulture man (pp. 73–76), are said to transform themselves into nocturnal birds, and they are associated with psychic cannibalism and blocked lineage reproduction. However, night birds may also promote the general wealth of a town, and the witches' society – sometimes amusingly and tellingly called 'the Air Force' in present-day Nigeria – may offer a protective power against outsiders.

The sexuality of elder witches is suspect, mainly in that it is exercised to the detriment of patrilineage fertility. Contemporary urban 'sugar mummies' are considered probable candidates for membership in the occult Air Force. They keep youthful, virile men from mates of their own age and class and are rumoured to generate their continuing beauty and seemingly bottomless bank accounts from sexual rituals performed with these youths. While such women are chastised in popular discourse (including the print media; e.g. Kebby 1988), their behaviour is often represented in indulgent, even patronizing tones. The manners and mores of older women, especially those beyond the years of child-bearing, do not seem to threaten patriarchal social structures deeply. Indeed, menopausal women in Nigerian cities who accumulate money, lovers and power may even shore up patriarchal relations in that they emulate the career trajectory of elite men, but are not in serious competition with male elders for resources or status.[18]

The rise of youthful women with rumoured sexual and mystical sway over older, successful men, however, is perceived to be more of a problem for masculinist urban Nigeria. These young women are portrayed in media and rumour as nubile, bored and rapacious – but also as canny and not only willing, but able, to trick men into doing their bidding. Self-absorbed and secure in their sexual potency, able to support themselves through the commodification of their bodies or alliances with the wild spiritual forces that, as we have seen, are believed to roam city streets, youthful witches (or ogbaanje) offer a new threat to the status quo. An urban legend recently collected in Nigeria speaks interestingly to men's concerns about mobile, modern and beauty-obsessed female youth:

> There is a story going around Lagos that illustrates the lethal cocktail produced when ignorance and superstition are combined with poverty. It begins with the driver of a motorcycle taxi, called an Okada, who picked up a female passenger one day and handed her a helmet. The helmet is the first clue that this is not your usual Okada story. No one in Lagos, Nigeria's largest city, wears a helmet while riding a motorcycle.
>
> The passenger didn't put on the helmet; she wanted to protect her hairstyle. She placed the helmet on the head of the driver instead. No sooner had she done this than he vanished and the motorcycle crashed.
>
> Drivers swarmed around. Someone recognised the driver's bike, but his

body was nowhere to be found. A group went to his house to break the news to his family.

There, they found the driver, stretched out on his bed, in a zombie-like state. And from the mouth of this zombie came money, more money than any of them had ever seen before.

(Drohan 2000)

The bald, western newspaper account only hints at the richness of the original story, told to me by Canadian journalist Madelaine Drohan, recently returned from a month's visit to Nigeria.[19] In the oral version of the narrative, I had a sense of the beautiful, richly dressed young passenger, her hair just relaxed and swept up in the latest fashion; of her indecision about what to do with the unaccustomed helmet, and the speed with which she and the mysterious Okada driver darted in and out of Lagos's notorious 'go-slows' (traffic jams). There was also the denouement of the young woman's decision to jam the helmet down on her driver's head, told as if in slow-motion: the motorcycle going out of control, and the passenger thrown onto the street, rising to look for the missing driver, unable to believe the evidence of her eyes. Finally the tale was replete with vignettes of other Okada taximen, looking for their colleague along the street, recognizing his bike and demanding that the young woman accompany them to the driver's home as surety that she had not stolen the valuable vehicle and come to grief on it. There, after forcing their way into the driver's house, all eyes were met with the final horror: the dead but animate body stretched out on the bed, money pouring out of its mouth in streams. All realized immediately that this was to be the fate of the young woman herself – and understood that this was probably not the first body to lie helpless on the bed, vomiting out its life's productivity (or, as local people say, 'making money the easy way' for its mystical owner; cf. Bastian 1992; Masquelier 2000).

Besides being one of a vast array of West African urban legends about *juju*, this tale clearly represents the futility some men feel about gaining access to and controlling the sexuality of young women in the cities. The Okada taxidriver is a stock villain of modern Nigerian magic: he is a money magician, preying on the unwary and their need for cheap, rapid transport through Lagos streets, disguised as an honest, even humble entrepreneur. The promise of speed and efficiency, elusive commodities in the land of the 'go-slows', is a ruse to lure young women under the medicated helmet. With their powerful heads imprisoned and vision obscured, the women disappear off the liminal space of the road and reappear suggestively, without consciousness or volition, on the magician's bed – where their valuable (and already commodified?) bodies produce the cash that a motorcycle taxidriver would otherwise never earn.

What is new about this story is that the young woman inadvertently foils her mystical assailant through her vanity. She appears the perfect victim; she is young, beautiful and alone on the Lagos streets. She is more aware of her costume and personal grooming than of the potential danger of her surroundings.

But it is this self-absorption that saves her: rather than give herself 'hat hair' after all the time and money that has gone into her coiffeur, the young woman impatiently puts the helmet on the driver's head, sending him to the fate he had reserved for her. The money magician does not control her body; she controls his. The passenger renders her driver (a businessman of sorts) as 'useless' as Ngozi Nwosu, above, makes her unwary sexual partners.

To some extent outside of patriarchal boundaries, refusing or unwilling to submit to masculine authority, able to use the power of their abundant sexuality for their own purposes, 'stubborn' or simply clueless, the young women who take on occult powers in early twenty-first century Nigerian social imaginaries challenge male verities. This does not mean that these young witches and ogbaanje are conscious, resisting agents of Nigerian feminism. The ogbaanje who have reportedly 'destroyed' 4,000 Nigerian men have come to the male-dominated church of Pastor T.B. Joshua to try his prophetic powers (and, in the case of the queen of the coast, to try his chastity) and have been defeated through prayer, Christian faith and holy water. Their sexual potency and magical alliances end at the door of the Synagogue Church, where they are forced to submit to an unabashedly masculinist interrogation and to part with the forces that once animated their powerful, young bodies. The young woman who thwarts the money magician can never feel as safe on the streets of her city, nor as ready to ignore the world's dangers in favour of her own beauty. That mirror is smashed forever by her new-found knowledge of the extent to which some men will go to dominate and commodify her very existence.

Women's modern magics, while feared, are thus ultimately tamed in the Nigerian imaginary and brought under the surveillance and control of senior, masculine forces. Overwhelming sexuality and satanic avarice in these narratives invariably are drawn and yield to the power of evangelical Christianity. Young women with too much leisure, interest in consumption and mobility become the prey of money magicians. In both cases, women's embodied pleasures must be yielded up or there is a threat that their lives (mortal or immortal) will be taken from them by the very powers they embrace. Whether renouncing Satan or learning to be afraid of public transportation, the teenaged witch is put solidly back into her place in these narratives: that of the properly fertile, properly submissive, no longer magical girl. Buffy the Vampire Slayer has not yet come to Nigeria, although her hereditary enemies are well entrenched.

Conclusions

Nigeria's populous cityscapes resonate with many forces, for good or ill. Some of those forces westerners would immediately recognize as indicative of urban modernity (cf. Williams 1973; Giddens 1990; Miller 1994; Felski 1995; Appadurai 1996; Hall et al. 1996). Nigerians are quite familiar with free-wheeling, globalized capitalist commerce and consumption, social, individual and physical mobility, agencies of state-level surveillance and control, belief in and reliance on abstract systems, the proliferation of technologies, the sometimes pleasurable, sometimes terrifying anonymity of city life, criminals, deviants, madmen and proponents of radical dissent, and an avant-garde of artists and other culture brokers who propel socially creative innovations. But is the modernity of Lagos exactly the same as that of New York or London? Can people's experience of being modern ever be homogeneous, when their histories, societies and basic cosmological understandings are not the same? Indeed, should we call the experiences of those outside the western world 'modern' at all?

Naturally I pose these questions in full awareness of an emerging critique of the ethnography of modernity (Englund 1996; Appadurai 1996; Hannerz 1996; Englund and Leach 2000; Ferguson 1999) and agree with some of its premises – notably the necessary centrality of the ethnographic method, even when one works from textual materials as I do here. I also see a good deal of sense in Hannerz's (1996: 51) representation of the 'metaculture' of similarity: in which western theorists constantly seek to homogenize the world in order better to categorize and understand it. However, I take issue with critics Englund and Leach when they suggest that all ethnographic work on modernity, or multiple modernities, 'represent[s] variation against something that is *invariable*' (2000: 228, their italics). The laundry list of urban modernity above is just that: a partial accounting of the social garments available. Western (and westernized) societies may well experience all of the rubrics above and understand them, in part, to constitute 'modernity', but it is their particular, historically specific combinations with other, equally valid and important social experiences that give a group its own, modern identity. Such lists are necessarily incomplete, situational and contextual, just as I would posit southern Nigerian understandings of what it means to be modern to be. Variation is thus at the heart of modernity, even if obscured by what philosopher of technology Andrew Feenberg (1995: 221) calls the 'necessary illusion' of reason's autonomy in modern systems.[20]

As we have seen in this chapter, Nigerian urban experiences of modernity may include a sense that rural-based elders have access to transformative abilities that can threaten the well-being of their city kin and even strangers, or that cities themselves maintain a cosmographic continuity with the forested areas they have displaced physically but not conceptually. Supposed 'motors' of modernization and development, like the university system, may harbour organizations that are both 'modern' in their use of the technologies of destruction and 'retrograde' in their insistence on the extremes of male solidarity and dominance. Secret societies may flourish at the same time a nation-state embraces the rhetoric of civil society and official transparency. Young women – whose social status has, perhaps, been the most changed over the course of Nigeria's tumultuous twentieth century – are expected to be gendered consumers *par excellence* but also to rein in their problematic sexuality and desire for personal agency, both of which can be connected to the history of colonial commodities and ideas. Hovering over all of this is a *Nigerian* metanarrative of forces that are both inside and outside of nature and persons, that break down carefully constructed, external rubrics of modernity and make them recognisable and palatable to local people. Even more than that, what is variably Igbo, Yoruba, Ibibio or simply urban in Nigeria encompasses global modernity in their own metacultures of similarity – taming, categorizing and making modernity local people's own.

Acknowledgements

The author would like to thank all those who gave their comments and support for this chapter, especially Brad Weiss, Michael Lambek, Adeline Masquelier, Rosalind Shaw and the editors of this volume, Todd Sanders and Henrietta Moore. The illustrations in this chapter were reproduced by kind permission of *Conscience International* magazine.

Notes

1   Such stories have a wider currency in West Africa more generally. See, for instance, Gottlieb 1992: 98–115 for Beng folklore relating to clairvoyant dogs and the highly ambiguous hyena. The Mande epic corpus also includes a number of tales having to do with transforming animals or human-animal hybrids. See Niane 1965, Bird 1972, Austen 1999, Conrad 1999 and Johnson 1999. Willis (1975) gives a number of stories about the supposed spirit connection to various beasts in Eastern Africa and discusses the important problem of human-animal classificatory systems in anthropological thought more generally.

2   Cf. Talbot 1967 [1923]: 88 for Ibibio notions of 'were-beasts,' Hives 1940 [1930]: 69–70 on the transformative abilities of Aro Igbo, as well as Butt-Thompson 1970 [1929] for a similar set of stories in colonial Sierra Leone. More recently, historian Nancy Rose Hunt (1999: 30) notes that the nearby Congo was considered – at least by colonialists – to be 'a . . . world of leopard-men and crocodile-men' during the 1930s.

3   Smith (forthcoming) also provides a story of evil vulture transformations in the Owerri Igbo area, just to the north of Port Harcourt. His understanding of the symbolic nature of vultures is clearly coloured by the negative 'reading' of vulture behaviour.

4   In neighbouring Niger, spirits from the bush are said not only to follow the unwary into the town (Masquelier 1999: 37) but to transform themselves into automobiles or other vehicles and attempt to murder people who stray onto rural roads at night (Masquelier 1992: 57).

5   Nigerian media writers are well aware of the importance of the occult for West African and, indeed, for international political economy. As Mma Agbagha (1997) noted in his *Post Express Wired* editorial on the subject: 'Today in several embattled African countries [Agbagha is being circumspect in the face of the Nigerian military regime], it is the soothsayer that has the last word in the formulation and implementation of policy, both personal and national, as far as the leader is concerned. And like the case of Macbeth, these fortune-tellers worm their way into the heart of the leader through initial self-fulfilling prophesies. Thereafter, the leader of a whole nation is at their mercy.'

6   A textual sample of this early, educated enthusiasm for Nigeria and its potential can be found in Sam Epelle's (1960) *The Promise of Nigeria*, published in the United Kingdom as informative propaganda for the new state. Zachernuk (2000: 125–174)

discusses the intellectual climate of the immediate pre-colonial and colonial period at some length. However, see Ihonvbere and Shaw (1998: 144–147) for a critique of Nigerian intellectual conservatism and retreat to the 'ivory tower,' even in the period of the 1960s.

7 A moving testimonial to the optimism, nationalist fervour and modernization orientation of students during this period can be found in Amuta (1999): 'Now at mid-life, I can look back at those years [in college at the University of Ile-Ife, now Obafemi Awolowo] with a certain degree of nostalgia as, perhaps, the years of greatest hope and optimism for my generation. It was an optimism in the power of knowledge to transform reality. We literally charged at knowledge as the only tool for changing our society and transforming our individual lives.' Amuta's sense of outrage at a spate of campus cult-related executions at Obafemi Awolowo University during 1999, he tells us, is all the sharper because of the expectations he took away from his sojourn there.

8 Professor Ogbu Kalu (personal communication 1999) has also suggested to me that Soyinka's early fraternity at what became the University of Ibadan was the first and most influential of the academic men's associations. Professor Kalu has written an unpublished report on campus violence and cultism for the Nigerian Social Science Research Council.

9 See Ogundipe-Leslie (1994), Okeke (2001) and Bastian (forthcoming b) for more on women's problems in Nigerian education.

10 See, for instance, the *Better Lover* magazine story (Anonymous 1998a). In this narrative, a young woman of a lower class background is seduced by a prominent and elite member of a campus cult. Although she believes that she has found romance and upward mobility, she is actually being targeted for a gang rape during the cult's upcoming initiation. Her return to a 'proper' class orientation after the brutal assault is signalled in the subtitle of the piece: 'I'm through with UNILAG [University of Lagos] students and their cults Wahala, Oshodi traders here I come.' While we have no means for evaluating the truthfulness of sensationalistic periodical stories like this one (which is couched as a 'problem page' story, asking for reader advice, I am convinced that the topics of such narratives are important for gauging indigenous popular consciousness. Certainly such topics sell newspapers and magazines, and they find their way into the Nigerian electronic media with great frequency. I make no claim for the veracity of this particular story, but am interested here more generally in the pervasiveness of campus cultism and gang rape within current Nigerian popular discourse. See Gumpert 1987, Bird 1992, Turner 1993, Dégh 1994, and Bordo 1997 for more on folkloric and popular narratives in the Euro-American sensationalist press. I consider such stories to have a similar hold over western popular consciousness.

11 In one of the worst incidents documented of cult violence in recent years, six students at Obafemi Awolowo University were murdered, a number of others injured and the wife of the Vice Chancellor was kidnapped in early July, 1999. See Ndiribe 1999 and Nwandu 1999 for more on the OAU killings.

12 For a more positive perspective on Nigerian peacekeeping in Sierra Leone, see Richards 1996: 20–21.

13 For several examples of this Africanist stereotypy, see Marwick 1970 (particularly the chapters by Schapera, Krige and Wilson). In a more contemporary Africa, see Comaroff and Comaroff 1993 (especially Apter, Auslander and Austen).

14 All ogbaanje confessions quoted in this section are from Anonymous 1998b.

15 This dichotomous marital discourse continues to the present day in Nigeria; see Bastian forthcoming b and Okeke 2001.

16 'Walk-about' women or the *femmes libres* of the African cities of the 1950s onwards

are well-known figures in anthropological literature. See, for example, Little 1973, La Fontaine 1974, Schuster 1979, Obbo 1980, Dinan 1983 and Gondola 1997. White (1990) has also written a telling history of sex traders' contribution to urban male domestic comfort in Nairobi during the colonial period.

17 Yoruba-speaking people refer to these important witches respectfully as *awon iya wa* ('our mothers'; Drewal 1992: 178). See Barber 1991: 233–236 for short biographies of a couple of Yoruba women who were both admired and considered possible witches.

18 Senior women who might compete with men for socially approved goods/wealth are often coopted directly into the male system of title-taking and secret societies. Several older women I knew in Onitsha during 1987–88 were 'titular males' (women for whom bridewealth would no longer be received) and were encouraged to take part as patrons of masquerade societies and to attend certain masculine functions. They were not, however, allowed to be official advisors of the *Obi* (king) of Onitsha or to take the most prestigious of male titles.

19 Personal communication, 23 September 2000. Drohan, a columnist for the Toronto *Globe and Mail*, contacted me to ask for my perspective on the urban legends she heard while in Nigeria. This story, told to her by a Nigerian journalist, took her fancy, but she was not sure what might be behind it. A somewhat truncated version of our conversation ended up in the article she eventually wrote for the paper.

20 I most heartily do *not* agree with Feenberg on some of his other conclusions about technology and modernity, but the notion of necessary fictions in modern life has always been attractive to me (cf. Bastian 1992).

Bibliography

Agbagha, M. (1997) 'Soothsayers and the way forward', *Post Express Wired* (editorial, 17 July) <http://www.postexpresswired.com> (accessed 23 March 2001).

Agbroko, G. (1996) 'Ogboni vs. Methodist Church: trouble in God's house', *Theweek* 5, 6: 10–15.

Amadi, E. (1982) *Ethics in Nigerian Culture*, Ibadan: Heinemann.

Amuta, C. (1999) 'Campus mobsters and the endangered university', *Post Express Wired* (editorial, 15 August 1999) <http://www.postexpresswired.com> (accessed 23 March 2001).

Anonymous (1998a) 'Grammar no be money: I'm through with UNILAG students and their cults "wahala", Oshodi traders here I come', *Better Lover* 12: 34–38.

Anonymous (1998b) 'Witches invade Nigeria – over 4,000 men allegedly destroyed', *Conscience International* 2, 1: 5–7, 10.

Anonymous (1999) 'The power behind the cultists', *Post Express Wired* (editorial, 27 July) <http://www.postexpresswired.com> (accessed 23 March 2001).

Anonymous (2000) 'Getting cult', *Vanguard* (Penchant column, 17 August) <http://www.vanguardngr.com> (accessed 3 September 2000).

Appadurai, A. (1996) *Modernity at Large: Cultural Dimensions of Globalization*, Minneapolis: University of Minnesota Press.

Apter, A. (1992) *Black Critics and Kings: The Hermeneutics of Power in Yoruba Society*, Chicago: University of Chicago Press.

—— (1999) 'IBB=419: Nigerian democracy and the politics of illusion', in J.L. Comaroff and J. Comaroff (eds) *Civil Society and the Political Imagination in Africa*, Chicago: University of Chicago Press.

Ashforth, A. (1998) 'Reflections on spiritual insecurity in a modern African city (Soweto)', *African Studies Review* 41, 3: 39–67.

Austen, R.A. (1993) 'The moral economy of witchcraft: an essay in comparative history', in J. Comaroff and J.L. Comaroff (eds) *Modernity and its Malcontents: Ritual and Power in Postcolonial Africa*, Chicago: University of Chicago Press.

—— (1999) 'The historical transformation of genres: Sunjata as panegyric, folktale, epic and novel', in R.A. Austen (ed.) *In Search of Sunjata: the Mande Oral Epic as History, Literature, and Performance*, Bloomington: Indiana University Press.

Barber, K. (1991) *I Could Speak Until Tomorrow: Oriki, Women and the Past in a Yoruba Town*, Washington DC: Smithsonian Institution Press.

Bastian, M.L. (1992) 'The world as marketplace: historical, cosmological, and popular constructions of the Onitsha market system', unpublished PhD dissertation, University of Chicago.

—— (1993) '"Bloodhounds who have no friends": witchcraft and locality in the Nigerian popular press', in J. Comaroff and J.L. Comaroff (eds.) *Modernity and its Malcontents: Ritual and Power in Postcolonial Africa*, Chicago: University of Chicago Press.

—— (1997) 'Married in the water: spirit kin and other afflictions of modernity in southeastern Nigeria', *The Journal of Religion in Africa* xxvii, 2: 116–134.

—— (1998) 'Fires, tricksters and poisoned medicines: popular cultures of rumour in Onitsha, Nigeria and its markets', *Etnofoor* xi, 2: 111–132.

—— (1999) '"Diabolic realities": narratives of conspiracy, transparency and "ritual murder" in the Nigerian popular print and electronic media', paper presented at the workshop Transparency and Conspiracy: Power Revealed and Concealed in (the) Global Village(s)', London School of Economics and Political Science, 28–29 May.

—— (2000) 'Young converts: Christian missions, gender and youth in Onitsha, Nigeria 1880–1929', *Anthropological Quarterly* 73, 3: 145–158.

—— (2001) 'Dancing women and colonial men: the *Nwaobiala* of 1925', in D.L. Hodgson and S. McCurdy (eds) *'Wicked' Women and the Reconfiguration of Gender in Africa*, Portsmouth, NH: Heinemann.

—— (forthcoming a) '"Vultures of the marketplace": southeastern Nigerian women's discourse about the *Ogu Umunwaanyi* (Women's War) of 1929', in J. Allman, S. Geiger and N. Musisi (eds) *Women and African Colonial History*, Bloomington: Indiana University Press.

—— (forthcoming b) 'Acadas and fertilizer girls: young Nigerian women and the romance of middle class modernity', in D.L. Hodgson (ed.) *Gendered Modernities: Ethnographic Perspectives*, New York: St Martin's Press.

—— (forthcoming c) 'Irregular visitors: narratives about *ogbaanje* (spirit children) in Nigerian popular writing', in S. Newell (ed.) *Readings in African Popular Fiction*, Bloomington: Indiana University Press.

Benjamin, W. (1969) *Illuminations*, New York: Schocken Books.

Bird, C. (1972) 'Heroic songs of the Mande hunters', in R.M. Dorson (ed.) *African Folklore*, Bloomington: Indiana University Press.

Bird, S.E. (1992) *For Enquiring Minds: A Cultural Study of Supermarket Tabloids*, Knoxville: University of Tennessee Press.

Bordo, S. (1997) *Twilight Zones: The Hidden Life of Cultural Images from Plato to O. J.*, Berkeley: University of California Press.

Brown, A. (1999) 'Police dispel rumors of man's transformation', *Post Express Wired* (news article, 28 August) <http://www.postexpresswired.com> (accessed 23 March 2001).

Burke, T. (1996) *Lifebuoy Men, Lux Women: Commodification, Consumption, and Cleanliness in Modern Zimbabwe*, Durham: Duke University Press.

Butt-Thompson, F.W. (1970 [1929]) *West African Secret Societies: Their Organisations, Officials and Teaching*, Westport, CT: Negro Universities Press.

Comaroff, J. and Comaroff, J.L. (eds) (1993) *Modernity and its Malcontents: Ritual and Power in Postcolonial Africa*, Chicago: University of Chicago Press.

—— (1999) 'Occult economies and the violence of abstraction: notes from the South African postcolony', *American Ethnologist* 26, 2: 279–303.

Conrad, D.C. (1999) 'Mooning armies and mothering heroes: female power in the Mande epic tradition', in R.A. Austen (ed.) *In Search of Sunjata: the Mande Oral Epic as History, Literature, and Performance*, Bloomington: Indiana University Press.

Crowder, M. (1973) *The Story of Nigeria*, London: Faber and Faber.

Dégh, L. (1994) *American Folklore and the Mass Media*, Bloomington: Indiana University Press.

Dinan, C. (1983) 'Sugar daddies and gold-diggers: the white-collar single women in Accra', in Christine Oppong (ed.) *Female and Male in West Africa*, London: George Allen and Unwin.

Drewal, M.T. (1992) *Yoruba Ritual: Performers, Pay, Agency*, Bloomington: Indiana University Press.

Drohan, M. (2000) 'Gruesome tales show Nigeria's desperate state', *Globe and Mail* (Toronto, Canada; 25 September).

Emeh, O. (1997) 'The cult problem', *Post Express Wired* (editorial, 15 November) <http://www.postexpresswired.com> (accessed 23 March 2001).

Englund, H. (1996) 'Witchcraft, modernity and the person: the morality of accumulation in central Malawi', *Critique of Anthropology* 16, 3: 257–279.

Englund, H. and Leach, J. (2000) 'Ethnography and the meta-narratives of modernity', *Current Anthropology* 4, 2: 225–248.

Epelle, S. (1960) *The Promise of Nigeria*, London: Pan Books.

Escobar, A. (1995) *Encountering Development: the Making and Unmaking of the Third World*, Princeton: University Press.

Esele, A. (1996) 'Public sinners in the church', *Theweek* 5, 6: 13.

Falola, T. (1996) *Development Planning and Decolonization in Nigeria*, Gainesville: University Press of Florida.

Feenberg, A. (1995) *Alternative Modernity: The Technical Turn in Philosophy and Social Theory*, Berkeley: University of California Press.

Felski, R. (1995) *The Gender of Modernity*, Cambridge, MA: Harvard University Press.

Ferguson, J. (1999) *Expectations of Modernity: Myths and Meanings of Urban Life on the Zambian Copperbelt*, Berkeley: University of California Press.

Geschiere, P. (1997) *The Modernity of Witchcraft: Politics and the Occult in Postcolonial Africa*, Charlottesville: University Press of Virginia.

Geschiere, P. and Nyamnjoh, F. (1998) 'Witchcraft as an issue in the "politics of belonging": democratization and urban migrants' involvement with the home village', *African Studies Review* 41, 2: 69–92.

Giddens, A. (1990) *The Consequences of Modernity*, Stanford: University Press.

Gondola, C.D. (1997) 'Popular music, urban society, and changing gender relations in Kinshasa, Zaire (1950–1990)', in M. Grosz-Ngate and O.H. Kokole (eds) *Gendered Encounters: Challenging Cultural Boundaries and Social Hierarchies in Africa*, New York: Routledge.

Gottlieb, A. (1992) *Under the Kapok Tree: Identity and Difference in Beng Thought*, Bloomington: Indiana University Press.

Gumpert, G. (1987) *Talking Tombstones and Other Tales of the Media Age*, New York: Oxford University Press.

Hall, S., Held, D., Hubert, D. and Thompson, K. (eds) (1996) *Modernity: An Introduction to Modern Societies*, Oxford: Blackwell Publishers.

Hannerz, U. (1996) *Transnational Connections: Culture, People, Places*, London: Routledge.

Henderson, H.K. (1969) 'Ritual roles of Onitsha Ibo women', unpublished PhD dissertation, University of California, Berkeley.

Hives, F. (1940 [1930]) *Juju and Justice in Nigeria*, Harmondsworth: Penguin.

Hunt, N.R. (1999) *A Colonial Lexicon of Birth Ritual, Medicalization, and Mobility in the Congo*, Durham: Duke University Press.

Ihonvbere, J.O. and Shaw, T. (1998) *Illusions of Power: Nigeria in Transition*, Trenton: Africa World Press.

Iloduba, K. K. (1999) 'Cult membership: all the details', *Post Express Wired* (feature, 12 November). <http://www.postexpresswired.com> (accessed 23 March 2001).

Johnson, J.W. (1999) 'The dichotomy of power and authority in Mande society and in the epic of Sunjata', in R.A. Austen (ed.) *In Search of Sunjata: the Mande Oral Epic as History, Literature, and Performance*, Bloomington: Indiana University Press.

Kebby, M. (1988) 'Seduction: most unfair', *Lagos Weekend* (*Weekend Magazine* feature, 22 January), p. 7.

La Fontaine, J. (1974) 'The free women of Kinshasa: prostitution in a city in Zaire', in J. Davis (ed.) *Choice and Chance: Essays in Honour of Lucy Mair*, London: Athlone.

Little, K. (1973) *African Women in Towns: an Aspect of Africa's Social Revolution*, Cambridge: University Press.

Marwick, M. (ed.) (1970) *Witchcraft and Sorcery*, Harmondsworth: Penguin.

Masquelier, A. (1992) 'Encounter with a road siren: machines, bodies and commodities in the imagination of a Mawri healer', *Visual Anthropology Review* 8, 1: 56–69.

—— (1999) 'The invention of anti-tradition: Dodo spirits in southern Niger', in H. Behrend and U. Luig (eds) *Spirit Possession: Modernity and Power in Africa*, Oxford: James Currey.

—— (2000) 'Of headhunters and cannibals: migrancy, labor, and consumption in the Mawri imagination', *Cultural Anthropology* 15, 1: 84–126.

Matory, J.L. (1994) *Sex and the Empire That Is No More: Gender and the Politics of Metaphor in Oyo Yoruba Religion*, Minneapolis: University of Minnesota Press.

Meyer, B. (1998) 'The power of money: politics, occult forces, and Pentecostalism in Ghana', *African Studies Review* 41, 3: 15–37.

Miller, D. (1994) *Modernity: An Ethnographic Approach*, Oxford: Berg.

Ndiribe, O. (1999) 'OAU's black Saturday . . . a grisly tale of cold-blooded murder', *Post Express Wired* (feature, 17 July) <http://www.postexpresswired.com> (accessed 23 March 2001).

Niane, D.T. (1965) *Sundiata: An Epic of Old Mali*, London: Longman.

Nuwer, H. (1999) *Wrongs of Passage: Fraternities, Sororities, Hazing, and Binge Drinking*, Bloomington: Indiana University Press.

Nwandu, T. (1999) 'Taking cultism to a dangerous height', *Post Express Wired* (feature, 22 July) <http://www.postexpresswired.com> (accessed 23 March 2001).

Nzediegwu, E. B. (1999) 'Secret cults in our schools', *Post Express Wired* (editorial, 18 June) <http://www.postexpresswired.com> (accessed 23 March 2001).

Obbo, C. (1980) *African Women: their Struggle for Economic Independence*, London: Zed Books.

Offiong, D.A. (1991) *Witchcraft, Sorcery, Magic and Social Order among the Ibibio of Nigeria*, Enugu: Fourth Dimension Publishers.

Ogundipe-Leslie, M. (1994) *Re-Creating Ourselves: African Women and Critical Transformations*, Trenton: Africa World Press.

Okeke, P.E. (2001) 'Negotiating social independence: the challenges of career pursuits for Igbo Women in post-colonial Nigeria', in D. Hodgson and S. McCurdy (eds) *'Wicked' Women and the Reconfiguration of Gender in Africa*, Portsmouth, NH: Heinemann.

Onunaiju, C. (1999) 'The military and cultism', *Post Express Wired* (editorial, 4 September) <http://www.postexpresswired.com> (accessed 23 March 2001).

Richards, P. (1996) *Fighting for the Rain Forest: War, Youth and Resources in Sierra Leone*, Portsmouth, NH: Heinemann.

Sadowsky, J. (1999) *Imperial Bedlam: Institutions of Madness in Colonial Southwest Nigeria*, Berkeley: University of California Press.

Schmidt, E. (1992) *Peasants, Traders, and Wives: Shona Women in the History of Zimbabwe, 1870–1939*, Portsmouth, NH: Heinemann.

Schuster, I.M.G. (1979) *New Women of Lusaka*, Palo Alto: Mayfield Publishing Company.

Shaw, C.M. (1995) *Colonial Inscriptions: Race, Sex and Class in Kenya*, Minneapolis: University of Minnesota Press.

Shaw, R. (1996) 'The politician and the diviner: divination and the consumption of power in Sierra Leone', *Journal of Religion in Africa* xxvi: 30–55.

Smith, D.J. (forthcoming) 'Ritual killing, "419" and fast wealth: inequality and the popular imagination in southeastern Nigeria', *American Ethnologist*.

Talbot, P.A. (1967 [1923]) *Life in Southern Nigeria: The Magic, Beliefs and Customs of the Ibibio Tribe*, New York: Barnes and Noble.

Turner, P. A. (1993) *I Heard it through the Grapevine: Rumor in African-American Culture*, Berkeley: University of California Press.

Ukor, A. (1997) 'Our time's horrifying realities', *Post Express Wired* (editorial, 30 December) <http://www.postexpressedwired.com> (accessed 23 March 2001).

Watts, M. (1996) 'Islamic modernities? Citizenship, civil society and Islamism in a Nigerian city', *Public Culture* 8, 2: 251–290.

White, L. (1990) *The Comforts of Home: Prostitution in Colonial Nairobi*, Chicago: University of Chicago Press.

Williams, R. (1973) *The Country and the City*, London: Oxford University Press.

Willis, R. (1975) *Man and Beast*, St Albans, UK: Paladin.

Zachernuk, P.S. (2000) *Colonial Subjects: An African Intelligensia and Atlantic Ideas*, Charlottesville: University Press of Virginia.

Chapter 5

Witchcraft and scepticism by proxy

Pentecostalism and laughter in urban Malawi

Rijk van Dijk

With hindsight, urban Malawi of the late 1980s and early 1990s was a veritable spectacle of power. These were the last years of the dictatorial regime of president Kamuzu Banda and in the various townships of a city like Blantyre, the country's largest commercial centre, the political machinery was intensifying its coercive presence in a variety of ways. There were the *Ayufi* (youth-league of the ruling party) who by positioning themselves overtly near such places as markets, bus stations and hospitals embodied the presence of the state. People were flogged if they did not obey orders. Township residents were coerced into attending compulsory party meetings where the display of political power by party-bosses was required to be observed with awe and respect. People disappeared as a result of the many eyes and ears which those in power sent out secretly through the townships to control dissent or open criticism. Perhaps even more intimidating than the *Ayufi* were the Malawi Young Pioneers (MYP), Banda's elite troops – well trained, well armed and parading in their splendid uniforms. It was as if no one could control the display of violence they would unleash on township residents if disobedience had been noted by those in power. Even the chiefs (*mfumu*) in the local residential areas shivered and shook when MYPs or the *Ayufi* entered their areas in search of dissention, as cries of agony came closer and closer. The noise of deliberately broken cooking pots as well as the sound of the destruction of small gardens were, on such occasions, heard through a township, provoking much anxiety. And in the Blantyre Kamuzu Stadium, President Banda would occasionally dance with the *Zinyau*, the masked representatives of the *Nyau* secret society. The young dancers of this society, to which only initiated men of the Chewa- and Mang'anja-speaking groups of Central and Southern Malawi belong, are commonly referred to as *zilombo*, that is, wild animals from the bush. They were notorious for spreading a reign of violent terror in the villages (see also Kaspin 1993; Englund 1996b). Their occasional appearance on the city's outskirts invariably caused great alarm and distress.

While the eyes and ears of Banda were perceived as omnipresent and the visual presence of the various features of the political machinery loomed large, there was another spectacle of power becoming increasingly evident. Banners and flyers called for redemption and obedience to the word of God; they spoke of the need to banish sin and, even more, all Satanic influence. Amidst the turmoil in townships, markets and bus stations, street-preachers stepped forward, many of them teenagers, calling on people to repent before it was too late, before the wrath of God was unleashed on all unbelievers (van Dijk 1992a, 1992b, 1993, 1998). Large revival meetings were held where fire and brimstone preachers would mollify all who stopped to listen. Many would publicly kneel in front of these preachers and repent their sins. This might have been interpreted as a youthful parody of well-respected (religious) authority if their public performance had been less convincing or less effective. However, the shouts and cries of those caught up in the atmosphere of excitement these religious meetings produced were clear signs of the power that these youths commanded. Their Christian fundamentalist message always touched on the issue of witchcraft as the centre of innate evil. It fostered the imagery of a satanic power that their preaching could work against, in particular, to cleanse urban society. Their highly emotional displays of 'fighting' and of 'casting out' evil spirits created much awe and respect. Indeed, they touched a central nerve. Witchcraft made people disappear, it made people suffer, it made ordinary township residents fall victim to the evil powers of a nocturnal world, producing in the process one haunting question: are politics and witchcraft one of a kind?[2] Although these young preachers were unrelated to the political power of the party youth organizations, and often had a different background than these age-mates, they effectively placed themselves in the domain of these powers and the imagery they produced (van Dijk 1999b).

Under such tense circumstances, in this situation fraught with fear, it might appear odd to discuss scepticism and ridicule. This general social anxiety, produced by the frantic search for dissidents by militant youth as well as by the ecstatic search for sinners of witchcraft by preaching youth, may seem to leave little space for such demotive discourses. However, Mbembe has argued incisively for the banality of power in the postcolony, the playfulness, conviviality and laughter by which 'ordinary people bridle, trick and actually toy with power instead of confronting it directly' (Mbembe 1992: 22). Whereas examples abound of such forms of scepticism in the field of political power, very little has surfaced in a similar vein in the study of witchcraft in the Southern African region. In most accounts of witchcraft, horror reigns over humour, scare over scepticism. Recent studies emphasize the modernity of witchcraft in Africa and are inclined to demonstrate how discourses on occult forces, in fact, address Africa's modern predicament. Many scholars emphasize the ambiguities, anxieties and aspirations many people face in postcolonial societies (Comaroff and Comaroff 1993, 1999; Geschiere and Fisiy 1994; Geschiere 1997; Shaw 1997). These studies, ranging from Sierra Leone to Cameroon and to South Africa, explore how witchcraft beliefs are not an archaic residue likely to disappear from African societies as modernity progresses, but must be seen as a domain where simultaneously the magical lure as well as the anxiety about the modern world with its capitalist relations and unimaginable wealth are addressed. In zombie-scares, panics about the occult trade in body parts and new witchcraft eradication movements these studies read deep-seated anxieties about the exposure to a wider world engulfed in a capitalist and therefore dehumanizing system (see, for instance, Fisiy and Geschiere 1991; Auslander 1993; Englund 1996a; Meyer 1999; Comaroff and Comaroff 1999).[3] In this context, witchcraft is solidly and exclusively represented as a domain of the fantastic and horrific.[4]

This chapter, however, draws attention to experiences of witchcraft which allow for laughter and local scepticisms whilst acknowledging the advancement that has been made by post-modern studies. In investigating the above-mentioned street-preachers in one of the townships in Blantyre, it became clear that witchcraft appeared as a salient domain of conviviality and playfulness. It spoke much less to the kind of imagery that reveals modernity's malcontents or a mystique of the world market *per se*. Rather, the Pentecostal ideology presented by these preachers and their charismatic fellowships created the space to experience witchcraft in terms of mockery, laughter and amusement.

Over the last two decades, Pentecostalism has become a very popular form of Christianity in Malawi's major cities (see van Dijk 1992b, 1995, 1998; Von Doepp 1998). Reviewing earlier fieldwork material of a Pentecostal fellowship reveals the sense of amusement that became part of many instances of witchcraft self-confession that took place. In some cases this humour became more meaningful than 'just' entertainment. Pentecostalism appeared to foster a kind of scepticism towards the domain of power that the discourse on witchcraft referred to. In the suburb I studied, known as Chilomoni, both the representatives of the nation-state as well as the 'traditional' authorities of the chief and of the historical Christian churches had great difficulties coming to terms with the capricious nature of the self-confessional style of witchcraft affairs in the Pentecostal fellowship. Whereas over the past decade or so, many studies have explored the rise of this new brand of Pentecostalism across Sub-Saharan Africa,[5] attention to this aspect of its ideology has been minimal. This chapter calls for a more nuanced investigation of the scepticism that sometimes surrounds witchcraft in the context of emerging Pentecostalism as a dominant context of identity formation as was the case in the Malawian situation. The chapter concludes by underscoring the need for a socioculturally-inspired analysis of the sceptical style that emerges as the distinguishing mark of such modern religious formations.

Pentecostal street-preachers in Malawi

In Malawi, the younger generation has largely supported the spread of a new kind of charismatic Pentecostalism (van Dijk 1992a, 1993, 1995, 1998). From the mid-1970s it became increasingly popular among university and college students. Small groups of itinerant preachers began moving around in Malawi's largest cities. In townships they organized revival meetings, usually attended by large numbers of local residents, where they propounded an ideology in which a new but very rigid moral code would play a crucial role. It stressed the need not only for every individual to cleanse him or herself of sin, but also for the nation as a whole to purge itself of its vices: heavy drinking, smoking, violence, promiscuous sexual conduct and so on. This moral code also implied clear-cut notions of which forces should be held responsible for all these seemingly rampant evils. All kinds of spirits, ranging from ancestral spirits to the 'spirit of witchcraft', as they called it, were rigidly classified as representations of Satan. The young preachers held these demonic forces responsible for the lack of progress and prosperity individuals and Malawi as a whole were experiencing. The large revival meetings they conducted concentrated on deliverance of demons and the protection against witchcraft. Their calls for purification seemed to resonate with a collective memory of earlier *mchape* witchcraft-cleansing movements as well, to which I return below.

Before turning to this issue, however, some remarks are in order about the history of this form of Pentecostalism in colonial and postcolonial Malawi in relation to the advent of young revival preachers. To a large extent this movement of preachers can be interpreted as the most recent stage in the development of independent Christianity and Pentecostalism in this society. This has been underway since the first decade of the twentieth century (see also Schoffeleers 1985). The first Pentecostal churches established in the country were of the so-called 'full gospel' type, including such denominations as the Assemblies of God and Full Gospel Church of Christ. Usually led by white missionaries from the UK, the US and South Africa and occasionally by missionaries from black pentecostal communities in the US, these churches made their way to the then protectorate of Nyasaland from South African cities. In a way they were 'latecomers', as missionization in various parts of this region by Presbyterian and Roman Catholic churches had been well underway since the 1870s. These evangelistic and pentecostal churches, however, developed specific and counter-acting forms of Christianization. They preferred to approach young converts to act as itinerant preachers (*alaliki*, literally 'sayers') who would be employed to organize massive revival meetings in what was then Nyasaland (now Malawi) as early as 1920. They acted zealously against what they perceived as heathenism, greatly alarming chiefs and colonial authorities alike (Fields 1985: 43). Many such churches, including early Watchtower movements, regarded these young converts as an excellent class of daring preachers. They were prepared to penetrate remote areas, usually under the most difficult circumstances. From 1910 to 1930 waves of mass revivalism occurred in areas belonging to both present-day Zambia and Malawi which particularly alarmed many white missionaries of the established Christian churches (who regarded this development as running against their own expansion and conversion efforts [Ncozana 1985: 199–202]).

Many of the preachers' activities went hand-in-hand with witchcraft-cleansing. Their work had been so effective, in fact, that when in the late 1920s and early 1930s the young *mchape* witch-finders began their eradication practices in southern Malawi, they regularly skipped those villages that had been 'Christianized' through these revivals.[6]

During the same period myriad African Independent Christian churches also appeared. Many scholars would interpret the proliferation of Pentecostal churches as belonging to the overall development of these forms of syncretic Christianity – of which many so-called prophetic-healing churches are part – that took place in the early decades of the twentieth century. In Malawi this led to the establishment of large numbers of Zion and Apostolic churches, but also those of the Providence Industrial Mission which played a crucial part in the first uprising against the colonial regime in 1905.

However, there are a number of crucial differences which are important to make sense of the rise of the movement of Pentecostal street-preachers in the 1970s and 1980s. As many scholars have shown, the rise of 'independent Christianity', particularly in the form of the prophetic-healing churches, implied a syncretization of religious discourse and practice. Many of these churches incorporated important elements of local cosmologies, healing practices and styles of leadership. They often merged elements of missionary Christianity (the Bible, hymns, styles of dress and uniforms) with a range of healing and cleansing practices that related directly to 'traditional' forms. Their healing prophets catered for a wide array of problems perceived to be caused by occult powers, evil spirits and the like which the established white missionary churches were prone to dismiss as unreal, heathen, superstitious and the product of ignorance. Hence, these churches offered many people what missionary churches could not, or would not.

However, the Pentecostal churches, from which the street-preachers have arisen, have always maintained a critical distance from both the healing churches and the established missionary churches. Effectively, they took a third way from which much of their present-day popularity may be explained. They critiqued the missionary churches for denying what was so obviously a part of everyday African life: occult forces. These were and still are in Pentecostal ideology understood as manifestations of satanic power. It was also on this account that these Pentecostal churches have remained dismissive of the healing churches' syncretic practices. As the 'traditional' practices for healing, protection or exorcism may in themselves be contaminated by demonic influences, it followed that these churches could not be trusted either. Instead, the Pentecostal churches began stressing ecstatic deliverance sessions in which prayer healing and possession by the Holy Spirit is sought. Herbs, candles, water, fire or other substances that are commonly used in both traditional healing practices and in healing churches tend not to be found among these Pentecostal churches, nor in the practices of the street-preachers.

The variety of Full Gospel churches and the Assemblies of God in Malawi, all belonging to this brand of charismatic Christianity, began to Africanize their leadership and essential elements of ideology and ritual practice in the 1950s, without resorting to the form of syncretism that healing churches did. It is from these Africanized 'full gospel' type of churches that the first 'pioneers' of the movement of born-again Pentecostal preachers have sprung, starting something new and much more 'charismatic' in outlook.[7]

By the late 1970s the preachers had established small organizations, usually called 'fellowships' or 'ministries'. Numerous prayer meetings were organized at many places in town, at different hours of the day throughout the week. This 'grid' of meetings enabled confirmed Pentecostal born-again believers to maintain a kind of constant spiritual guidance. It gave them the opportunity for regular communication with the benevolent heavenly powers they needed to tap into and sustain a sufficient level of 'sealing off' (*kutsirika*) against evil, outside forces. Some of the fellowships gradually turned into churches, with formal membership and an established leadership.[8] As has been reported across Africa, this form of Pentecostalism usually leads to a wide proliferation of hundreds of churches.[9] The personal acumen of the Pentecostal leaders amounts to much and the church, the ministry or the affiliated business ventures are, in a real sense, his property (it is noticeable that women do not often hold similar positions).

Within only a few years, these Pentecostal groups managed to attract a large following in Malawi's urban areas. Initially they appealed to the young and emergent urban middle classes, but gradually they expanded to include groups of the less educated and less fortunate. Following in the steps of these successful preachers, in the expanding urban townships, other young people, often without higher education and without the prospects of a secure position in life, began forming similar fellowships for their activities as inspired preachers. All of a sudden, in a city like Blantyre in the 1980s, dozens of these preachers could be found. The youngest I met was only 9 years old.

The first group of preachers has 'produced' over time well-known names and national figures such as Madalitso Mbewe. In the month leading up to the general and presidential elections of 15 June 1999, he organized the first ever 'presidential prayer breakfast' which was attended by the state president, Bakili Muluzi. The second cohort of preachers was far less prolific in the national public realm. The exception here is a young woman by the name of Linley Mbeta who, aged 19, created the Redemption Voice Ministries in 1989 and became president Banda's personal spirit-healer in the final years of his regime (see van Dijk 1994b). Her preaching sessions often took the form of a witchcraft-eradication event where people were searched for their witchcraft-related amulets (*zitumwa*). There was massive, popular interest in these sessions, which very much recalled a kind of collective memory of the *mchape* witchcraft-cleansing ceremonies organized by young men in the 1930s.[10]

Although young preachers of this second cohort remained confined to the poorer urban areas, this did not mean that they had less access to the Pentecostal rhetoric that had become so essential in the overall success of this 'Pentecostal wave' in the first instance. This will be demonstrated in the next section by discussing the Miracle Power of God-Fellowship that operated in Blantyre's Chilomoni township. Noteworthy is how well-versed these leaders were and still are in the current Pentecostal discourse which their highly educated 'predecessors' produced, which often contains transnational features like addressing their followers in English, and referring to international literature like Emmanuel Eni's *Delivered from the Power of Darkness* which was produced in Nigerian Pentecostal circles.[11]

To date, this Pentecostal ideology has stressed a religiously-inspired dichotomy between 'tradition' and the 'past' versus the 'modern' and the present-day world, the inferior against the superior (Meyer 1998). The exorcist and spirit-healing sessions organized by the preachers include an inspection of a person's life, his or her place within the family and the family's spiritual background. By stressing the 'born-again' experience the preachers aimed to sever a person from his or her past life and therefore from a history of involvement in, for example, ancestral veneration, spirit possession or spirit-healing rituals. Preachers urged their audiences to seek what they call the 'infilling' of the Holy Spirit (*Mzimu Woyera*, lit. the White Spirit). This protects people from the powers of their past that may continue to haunt them in the present. As a result, for the true born-again believer (*abadwo mwatsopano*), taking part in rituals where ancestral deities are venerated, such as in funeral ceremonies, has become problematic.

Witchcraft and evil spirits are frequently seen to originate from either the immediate family and/or from some of the rituals in which the person had participated in the past. These include, for example, initiation rituals or healing through 'traditional' forms. *Asing'anga*, the healers and herbalists, are invariably classified by these preachers as 'witchdoctors'. They emphasize the ambiguous nature of their healing powers by claiming that demons are always involved in what is administered to the person. 'Traditional' healing was declared an inferior mode of solving problems which are perceived as being caused by real and powerful demonic and occult forces. Witchcraft is therefore not considered mere superstition, a position long held by the established churches. Neither is it a problem for which the *asing'anga*, the local healers and witchdoctors, would need to be consulted. Much of the power to fight witchcraft afflictions is put in the hands of the confirmed believer him/herself. Through prayer sessions, deliverance hours and fasting it is believed that the identity of the afflicting witch will be revealed, as well as what can be done about it.

Public testimonies of witchcraft afflictions are common practice during Pentecostal prayer meetings. Often people confess to having been involved in witchcraft; Satan is held ultimately responsible for such behaviour. In Pentecostalism both the accused and the afflicted find a relatively safe haven for counteracting in the spiritual realm the forces that haunt them. As discussed earlier, prayer-sessions are perceived as a method of putting in place spiritually protective walls against witchcraft (again indicated by the term *kutsirika*). To this end the street-preachers, after the initial stages of their movement, established 'intercession groups' and 'prayer towers' where people devoted much of their time to ecstatic prayer (this is also the background of the fellowship, as discussed in the following section).

The mission churches have always remained critical of the success of the many Pentecostal churches that emerged in the 1950s and 1960s. They became even more alarmed by the youthful appeal of the street-preachers in the 1980s. The charismatic preachers began to gain a massive following, particularly among the young membership of churches such as the Church of Central African Presbyterian (CCAP). It is beyond the scope of this chapter to detail how and why conflicts developed and what it meant for the established churches to lose their far-reaching spiritual control over the younger generation when many turned to the Pentecostal, charismatic groups. However, it is important to note that, for many, the advantage was and is that the fellowships did not require them to resign their membership of the established churches and thereby run the risk of losing the potential benefits of membership. The street-preachers made their fellowships 'interdenominational' and made clear that their only goal was the elimination of satanic forces from society.[12]

The Pentecostal street-preachers' movement was and still is fundamentally a movement from within. It is an attempt to rejuvenate Christianity, public morale and to campaign effectively against witchcraft. It became accepted in a Malawian society which, at that time, was already deeply aware, both historically and politically, of the power youths can muster. Both the power of the militant youth bodies as well as the spiritual power of the street preachers were deeply 'modern', and even though each ventured to make its presence felt in the same urban space, they never collided directly. Any direct criticism of how the regime used young people as instruments of political coercion was too dangerous. Rather, in the way the Pentecostal preachers treated witchcraft – humorously and playfully ridiculing how youths were often enlisted in the service of witches – they affected political power in a less confrontational way. As the following case will show, in Pentecostal groups scepticism of certain witchcraft cases became an important element in their exercise of spiritual power.

The Miracle Power of God-Fellowship

At the age of 16 Peter Mbepula decided to move from his small home village near the city of Zomba (approximately a one hour drive from Blantyre) to Chilomoni-township in Blantyre. His maternal uncle (*malume*) had offered to pay his secondary school fees, which his parents could no longer afford. He demanded that Peter come and live near him in the township's remote Mulunguzi area. Although Peter and his uncle were Yao-speakers by birth (the Yao ethnic group is the largest Islamized unit in Malawi, Islam comprising about 18 per cent of the total population), their family had not converted to Islam. Soon after arriving in Mulunguzi, Peter came into contact with Pentecostal Christianity, through meetings organized by a nearby branch of the United Apostolic Faith church, and particularly by a number of Pentecostal ministries in the city centre. Soon he experienced a mystical 'rebirth' and became an enthusiastic participant in many such meetings.

His schooling was not a success, as Peter started to experience visions and revelations. He predicted misfortune ('hindsight', as he called it) for some Mulunguzi residents. Further, as he started laying on of hands, people reported that they had been miraculously healed of certain ailments. Within two years of his arrival, it was clear to many people that Peter had developed special charismatic gifts, and that Mulunguzi was becoming a special place because of his presence. He proclaimed that he had received from God a 'discerning spirit'. This enabled him to see, via the spiritual realm, those residents who practised witchcraft and those who had been affected and afflicted by it. A small group of Mulunguzi residents formed to support him in his preaching and cleansing 'ministry'. Outside the Mulunguzi area of Chilomoni, Peter began preaching in various parts of Blantyre (the Central Market in particular). In addition he went with his support group and organized 'crusades' in and around Zomba (van Dijk 1995).[13]

The activities outside Mulunguzi can be interpreted as a kind of 'outreach' for his moral message. However, inside Mulunguzi, his activities were of a different nature. Here they took the form of a witchcraft-cleansing project. To avoid making open witchcraft accusations he developed a practice of visiting neighbourhood houses which he searched for witchcraft-related objects, in particular, the so-called *zitumwa* (sing. *chitumwa*). These are the kind of amulets believed to contain a *chizimba*, considered the active ingredient in the *chitumwa*. An amulet containing the *chizimba* may give its owner unimaginable power or wealth, but there is a dark side. This is the sort of esoteric material that can only be obtained by partaking in the nocturnal witches' activities where human 'meat' is harvested and body parts are taken from the corpses of those killed through witchcraft. The person will be commanded to kill a close relative to obtain the right kind of body parts and must consume human corpses at nocturnal orgies (i.e. become a witch).

Peter's discerning spirit, he claimed, allowed him to see 'hyenas (*afisi*) standing on their hind feet at night', a sign that witchcraft was present. It also led him into the houses of possible culprits in search of *zitumwa*.

With this activity some people began moving from Mulunguzi by the end of the 1980s. Although the local ruling party chairman (the most powerful political authority in the area) received some complaints by members of other churches, particularly the Seventh Day Adventists, overall a relaxed and even cheerful atmosphere predominated. People joked about what Peter saw in his visions of certain people's nocturnal activities and these stories were at times a source of hilarity and laughter. The group, which named itself the 'Miracle Power of God-Fellowship', built a wattle and daub meeting place in the centre of Mulunguzi where its 'prayer-tower' was held. Around it the same atmosphere of 'relaxation' was evident as I experienced at the public meetings of the above-mentioned Linley Mbeta. Although she pointed openly at people during her meetings as possible candidates of witchcraft-involvement, this was at the same time discussed in an ambivalent mixture of hilarity and fear, mockery and anxiety, jokes and images of the frightening. In her and Peter's case laughter accompanied the discussions and gossip of how a certain individual was involved in *kutamba*, that is, the naked dancing at night while devouring human flesh as witches reputedly do during their orgies. Or how another person would moan like a zombie, magically enslaved by witches for their feasts. Both Linley Mbeta (on a wider level) and Peter Mbepula (on a smaller scale in Mulunguzi) appeared to be experts at conjuring up the image in their speeches of laughing at fear, of playing with chilling images, of turning witchcraft into an element of entertainment. Linley Mbeta took great pride in pointing at 'sinners' during her preaching sessions and of bringing these people forward so that everybody could 'take a good look at them'. Roaring laughter usually accompanied such instances when people were brought up and requested to kneel before Linley Mbeta. While most of these 'sinners' laughed too, the audience's or Peter's laughter following at Mulunguzi was more than just enjoyment at somebody else's expense. There was something genuinely relaxing about it, something equally recognizable in many other Pentecostal groups of young street-preachers in Blantyre. Witchcraft, *kutamba* and similarly ambiguous images could be turned into a source of parody by the superior spiritual powers that the Pentecostal faith could muster. Some of these groups even performed drama plays on stage and acted out, with a great sense of humour, the fears and anxieties involved.

However, another event at Peter's Fellowship made me aware of a further dimension in this play of ambiguity in the construction of the 'witch' (*mfiti*). Gradually it appeared that, without necessarily being the same, laughter and amusement turned into scepticism. A sceptical attitude towards some manifestations of the occult (i.e. the force itself and not just its bearer) became apparent with regard to the boys' behaviour.

One day I was informed that the Fellowship had received two boys, around 12 years old, who had been sent to Mulunguzi from relatives of Peter in his home village. The two boys soon turned out to be great sources of amusement for the few hundred inhabitants of Mulunguzi. The local traditional authority (*mfumu*), the party chairman and other dignitaries were all greatly interested in meeting these boys. They initially enjoyed listening to their otherwise gruesome stories (albeit with a touch of mockery too) and many came to see the two boys to be amazed by their experiences of witchcraft. The boys related to anybody who would listen their stories that, at night, they played football with their relatives' heads. These relatives suffered from bruises, swellings and terrible headaches when, at dawn, their heads were magically re-attached to their bodies after a 'good' night's football match. Roars of laughter could be heard when the two boys described what the rumpled faces looked like after a number of kicks during the witches' match.

However, dead silence invariably fell once the boys began giving further details of other witchcraft activities. They told of how they tore out their victims' hearts, kidneys or uteruses. Or how they constructed aeroplanes from human bones and blood – the planes' skeleton and fuel – and put a stolen silver coin in the middle of the plane to make it fly to South Africa. And even how they would open graves and feast on the corpses, or eat close relatives 'from the inside' to gain control over their life-power. A wide range of witchcraft themes appeared to belong to their repertoire.

For several weeks people flocked to Mulunguzi to hear with their own ears the boys' stories, clearly demonstrating their fascination with this mixture of horror and humour. But there was suddenly a turning point in the boys' success. This can be understood by the following. The boys were clearly placed into the hands of Peter Mbepula and under the care of the Miracle Power of God-Fellowship. In Peter's home village their stories had caused some turmoil; too much talk of witchcraft, villagers felt, might provoke worse happenings in the community. Peter's and the Fellowship's reputation for sealing off (*kutsirika*) the area against outside evil had spread to this village. Pentecostal fellowships, their prayer towers and intercession groups served to contain evil, to cast it out and thus to operate as purgatory devices. Evil cannot easily return to those places from which it has been eradicated.

But these are also places of 'truth', of transparency, where ultimately nothing remains hidden. Even innate evil through the born-again experience of 'infilling' by the *Mzimu Woyera* (lit. the White Spirit) will always transpire (in stressing that transparency, both Linley Mbeta and Peter Mbepula for instance tended to dress in white). From the perspective of the relatives in the village, the Mulunguzi Fellowship in its urban location was a 'white' place; a place where the truth behind the boys' witchcraft experiences would eventually come out. The haunting question was obviously who was to be held responsible for these young children's involvement in such horrific and heinous behaviour. However, where there was fear in the village there was laughter in the urban location.

Initially, neither Peter nor the Fellowship was very interested in discovering who was behind their proclaimed evil. This changed abruptly when after some weeks the boys began naming names. Laughter quickly turned into disbelief and the one was in no way synonymous with the other. One of those they named, a man the boys claimed had appeared in their visions and nocturnal 'adventures', was Peter Mbepula's father, who still lived in his home village. Here, the boys had apparently overstepped the boundary and now found people sneered at them. Sceptical views of their activities and stories now dominated. Previously such views were one among many 'voices' present during the discussions and, above all, during moments of laughter about the boys. But now people openly wondered: 'How could this be true?' For weeks the Fellowship was in turmoil as the scepticism produced by the young boys' conduct raised questions of how truth can be ascertained. No one doubted the reality of witchcraft. Rather, they were concerned with its manifestations and how God's 'wonder-working power' could be enlisted to provide the kind of transparency required. Members of the Fellowship now met at the small prayer hut more than three times a day – some even decided to stay away from work to participate – and held extended prayer sessions throughout the night. After all, if the boys were not telling the whole truth, the Devil must be in their midst. To laugh about the truth is one thing, but to joke with deception is quite another!

Consequently, Peter organized a 'crusade' to his home village. A crusade is the common organizational form by which born-again groups 'reach out' from their urban locales to remote rural places (van Dijk 1995). It is an attempt to stamp out occult forces in what may almost look like a military campaign.[14] Before leaving with a number of members of the Fellowship, Peter publicly distanced himself from his father. He claimed that he 'hated him' and stated that it was time that all the witchcraft in which these elders were involved in Chindenga village was eradicated once and for all. Although he encountered difficulties with this crusade with the local chief and particularly with the local Presbyterian minister (from the nearby Songani parish) he returned after a few weeks very much satisfied with what he had accomplished. The boys were sent back to the village, thoroughly cleansed, and Peter's reputation was even stronger.

Interpretation: scepticism by proxy

Gable (1995) has argued incisively that local manifestations of scepticism are often interpreted by anthropology as a (by-)product of modernity. Scepticism reflects the operation in society of destabilizing notions, ideas and perceptions that often find inspiration in non-local, extraneous cultural resources and which often have the sublevel effect of undermining dominant discourses and practices. Gable notes that it is commonly argued that local scepticisms of authority, of spiritual manifestations and other beliefs – as he found among the Manjaco in Guinea Bissau – are part of the cultural orientation of those members of society who have been exposed to a modern, urban and western form of life. Modern social formations, which have their roots in the colonial experience of western power and knowledge systems, missionization, media and the like create a kind of distanced viewpoint. Pentecostalism, I argue, is very much part of how the experience of modernity produces local convictions and traditions as outmoded, superstitious or backward. In common anthropological interpretations, such modern ruptures allow for the emergence of sceptical views of the local and the traditional.

This view, however, fosters a denial on two accounts. First, it excludes the possibility of 'indigenous' sceptical discourses about 'traditions' such as the kind of debates Gable drew anthropology's attention to in his study of the Manjaco chieftaincy. Second, it tends to exclude the possibility of the increase of local scepticism *vis-à-vis* the modern. In this section I argue that the stories the two boys told and the boys' involvement with nocturnal witch orgies can be interpreted in this light. The growing scepticism towards the boys, the laughter that became less friendly and more biting, also contained a message for the modern postcolonial Malawian state and the way in which it instrumentalized youth for its power politics. This perspective allows us to see the modernity of witchcraft not only for how it negotiates the 'doom' that the encroachment of modern life brings to local communities, but also for how witchcraft makes modernity itself the object of scepticism. We need not take witchcraft as 'dead serious', as many studies lead us to believe the 'natives' do.

So there are two issues at hand: one concerns the possibility of laughter in witchcraft cases, the other is the possibility of that laughter being turned into something more meaningful than mere entertainment when an element of scepticism enters. Many studies emphasize that modern manifestations of witchcraft express and give meaning to people's anxieties surrounding their incorporation into a wider world of capitalist markets, exploitative labour relations and western consumption and production patterns (see Geschiere 1997). In this view, witchcraft does not joke with modernity.

Although many critical remarks can be made about the postmodern study of witchcraft, the point I wish to emphasize is that it does not allow for scepticism, humour and conviviality alongside the horrific.[15] In such approaches the materialist condition of encroaching capitalism, modern power and similar issues appear to exclude parody and mockery. Still, this is exactly what Pentecostal ideology and praxis in the case of the boys brought to the fore. It produced not only a context for laughter, but also provided the grounds for a sceptical attitude. How did it do this?

To begin with, Pentecostalism was and is widely experienced as presenting the believer with clear-cut dichotomies: between the good and the bad, the benevolent and the malevolent, the Christian and the non-Christian and, above all, between an inferior past against a superior future. A person's and a society's past life is the domain of vices, whereas the present and the future have the prospect of (civic and moral) virtue. By becoming a born-again the individual is believed to be liberated from the ties that bind him or her to the past and tradition. Severing those ties and becoming 'born-again' offers the promise of progress and prosperity. In Malawi (van Dijk 1998) and elsewhere (Meyer 1998) Pentecostal practice subjects a person's past and the social and ritual representation of cultural traditions to close moral scrutiny. Pentecostal leaders frown upon participation in all types of cultural traditions, for instance, relating to funerals, as these are regarded as sanctified by the ancestors and other spirits, and are thus unequivocally condemned as 'demonic'. On this basis Pentecostalism creates a critical view of cultural heritage.

In the Malawi of that period, however, the Banda postcolonial state made itself the custodian of a selective range of traditions and called for the preservation of Malawi's pre-colonial cultural heritage (Vail and White 1989; Kaspin 1993; Forster 1994). President Banda's *Nyau* dances at the Kamuzu Stadium in Blantyre were in fact a celebration of that attempt to retrieve a cultural past in the service of a state's project of creating a distinctive Malawian nationhood (Vail and White 1989; Kaspin 1993). This nationhood, furthermore, was based on a kind of (re-)interpretation of Chewa culture, the dominant ethnic group to which Banda belonged. It also entailed, as Banda was proclaimed the *Nkhoswe* Number One,[16] a specific circumscribed position of the younger generation (van Dijk 1999b; Tengatenga 1996). Briefly, the form of Chewa nationhood Banda envisioned was inspired by the notion of making the younger generation subservient to the matriclan, to their custodians and elders.[17] Both the *Ayufi* and the Malawi Young Pioneers were manifest forms of a kind of national gerontocratic rule in which they, as youths, would serve their elders and thus preserve Malawian cultural heritage. It meant that on an everyday level much of the coercive political and social power was in the hands of party chairmen and loyal chiefs who had at their disposal these very effective youth organizations (see also Englund 1996b).

In addition to holding these everyday political powers, elders were and still are generally perceived as being *kukwhima*, 'ripened' in the affairs of the nocturnal world. Their powers usually provoke awe and respect, and are always assumed to be present when they successfully exercise their authority and impose their will on others. Some Pentecostal preachers, such as Peter Mbepula or Linley Mbeta, talk about the older generation in general terms like *ntakhati*, that is, experts in the things from below the earth, i.e. the realm of the dead (*zinthu za kunthaka*, lit. the 'things of the earth'). Their fears of the elders' nocturnal powers bespoke a more general anxiety of being turned overnight into will-less creatures, known as *ndondocha*. In the service of the elderly's occult powers youths felt they could be turned into such zombies, whose feet and tongues are magically chopped off to prevent them from running away or wanting their friends (cf. Comaroff and Comaroff 1999). It is in this sense that youth found in Pentecostalism a modus to negotiate the overall gerontocratic mode of social and political authority. Within such Pentecostal fellowships as those of Peter Mbepula, scepticism called into question on moral grounds the legitimate basis of the elders' authority without confronting it head-on. While Pentecostalism in its deliverance ideology and praxis has never been sceptical about the powers that lie behind manifestations of social, political or even religious authority, the bearers of those powers tend to meet in Pentecostal praxis a lot of parody and ridicule: a form of indirect contestation.

Pentecostal preachers needed to operate with the utmost caution, since it is risky in such instances of parody and ridicule to name, as Linley Mbeta did, specific persons or to single them out from an audience. In general terms, most of the Pentecostal preachers I met did not feel the political regime was restricting them in their preaching activities in the cities, provided their messages did not confront political power and authorities directly. Their calls for moral virtues did not directly incite political authorities, nor in particular the militant youth organizations to take action against them as a kind of general public policy. To the contrary, the Pentecostal ideology in its public manifestations appeared to produce the kind of acquiescent, a-critical rhetoric which superficial studies of 'right wing' religious movements tend to perceive as a kind of common denominator (Gifford 1991).

On a local level, as illustrated by Peter Mbepula's Miracle Power of God-Fellowship, a different picture emerges. Here the relationship with the political authority of the party representatives became increasingly tense. Some Mulunguzi inhabitants filed complaints against Peter's witchcraft-findings activities; those in power and in influential positions grew increasingly uneasy with these activities. In addition, the township of Chilomoni was targeted for a number of compulsory party rallies in the late 1980s and early 1990s. Mulunguzi, as part of Chilomoni, was confronted numerous times in that period by local authorities, frequently elderly men from the party and the 'traditional' chiefs, who flexed their political muscle by sending in *Ayufi* to enforce local participation. They also sent the message to Mulunguzi that 'Pentecostals hold too many meetings', hence disapproving of unauthorized absence from these public party meetings. Although direct confrontation with these people of authority was not an option for Peter Mbepula and his supporters, he nevertheless deliberately 'disappeared' by holding 'crusades' elsewhere. This risky behaviour demonstrated his independence from the overall social authority structure in which youths were supposed to be subservient. Mulunguzi people generally saw this flouting of authority as a sign of his very special spiritual powers; an area in which not even the party chairman, the local *mfumu* or any other religious leaders could directly interfere.

It was in this context that the two boys arrived to Mulunguzi. After a while their witchcraft stories clearly indicated that elderly relatives had involved them in occult practices in the village and at that point the laughter within Peter Mbepula's Fellowship changed to something much more sceptical. The boys' stories about being used as mindless creatures in the witchcraft affairs of their village elders opened up what I would interpret as a manipulative space for scepticism by proxy. For everyone it was clear that the boys' witchcraft was manipulated by their elders (including Peter's own father) and that laughing at them implied ridiculing the implicated village elders as well. This laughter did not deny the seriousness of the occult powers lurking behind these boys' behaviour. Nor did it dismiss the frightening occult grip the elders may have had over the younger generation. However, it sent a message that counteracting power both in the daily and the nocturnal realm was possible. In particular, it disqualified the way elders are perceived to use the younger generation as an instrument for their own interests. By laughing at the two boys, the gerontocratic structure of authority was mocked without denying the seriousness of the forces these elders presumably commanded. While this laughter eventually implicated the gerontocratic authority structure, through its conviviality the local party chairman and other authority holders initially participated in the general atmosphere of hilarity. At that stage laughing with and laughing about authority were both ambiguously present. The boys, after all, were demonstrating how foolish it is of elders to think that they can enlist the services of youth for their nocturnal escapades. 'You see, this is what the elders try to do to us', a younger helper of Peter Mbepula explained to me.[18] The fact that these boys managed to come to Mulunguzi to reveal these hideous things, fed the Pentecostal-inspired sceptical attitudes within the Fellowship concerning the effectiveness and moral legitimacy of gerontocratic authority. Peter Mbepula's neglect of the orders and obligations set out by local party authorities and the chieftaincy was already a clear sign that within the Pentecostal domain the powers of the elderly had lost much of their sway.

However, when the boys – probably encouraged by their apparent success – began naming names, this mode of scepticism by proxy changed. Their proclamations became unambiguously confrontational and might have jeopardized the entire Fellowship to which these boys were entrusted. Public witchcraft accusations were and still are a serious legal offence.[19] Furthermore, they are a source of turmoil which would have likely provoked the party chairman to take vicious action. The change from laughter to utter disbelief the boys experienced from the side of the Fellowship, should therefore be interpreted primarily as a form of self-protection. It was a way to create a distance from this particular witchcraft case. The fact that Peter Mbepula set out on a 'crusade' to the boys' village shows again that there were no doubts about the true source of this evil. Satan lurks particularly in the villages. Those who fall victim to satanic powers, such as his own father, are to be both ridiculed and pitied.

Conclusion

The question remains as to whether dominant discourses, such as those on witchcraft in Malawian society, contain the seeds of their own negation. Two studies published in the early 1970s were crucial in critically engaging the then dominant functionalist perspectives of witchcraft (Sansom 1972; Wyllie 1973). It was particularly Wyllie's study that drew attention to the increasing popularity of self-confession among new religious groups in Africa. Although drawing heavily on kinship systems and ideologies to explain why particular women among the Fante of Ghana were involved in self-confessions of witchcraft, it bore witness to the notions of identity and personhood that come into play. From a structural-functionalist perspective, Wyllie followed closely on from Lewis' (1975) interpretation of peripheral possession cults. Women's self-confession, he argued, could be explained as a forceful call for attention from their husbands and other kin. It provides the structurally suppressed with a method of asserting their position in social structures. This allowed the women some leverage for material gains and to improve their status.

This is an instrumentalist interpretation, and it played a role in critiquing much of the research that had been done on witchcraft which emphasized accusations and the accused. It had other advantages as well. Although little elaborated in these terms, these studies were some of the first to hint at the relationship between witchcraft and identity. Self-confession produces witchcraft as a creative space where, in the Pentecostal case, identities of being 'born-again', of being 'delivered' from the bonds with a past, are produced. These studies were thus able to show that witchcraft discourses also contain the ground for a reflexive distance in which witchcraft is not only seen as destroying identities but also of fostering new ones with which confirmed Pentecostal believers can demonstrate their spiritual superiority over the occult.

Although Wyllie emphasized the instrumentality of self-confessive witch-craft, he did not elaborate on how in Pentecostalism born-again believers' identities are rhetorically produced through negotiations over meanings and intentions of the witchcraft to which a person has confessed. Witchcraft confessions go further than issues of status and reward alone. They actually create the ideological space where the modern born-again believer is pitted against an inferior past: a past in which a person's life was engulfed by occult and harmful practices. Pentecostalism's fascination with horrific witchcraft stories plays a role in the construction of a critical politics of identity. It destabilizes other frameworks of identity production, such as the modern Malawian postcolonial state, seeking to enhance its dominion over its citizens through a specific project of nationhood.

On the other hand confessions of witchcraft are also 'enlisted' by Pentecostal groups, such as the Miracle Power of God-Fellowship, to create a favourable distance with domains of life that are perceived to be 'traditional', particularly those referring to gerontocratic forms of authority. It is this distancing from both the 'modern' and 'traditional' that allows the modes of scepticism discussed concerning the two boys in Mulunguzi to emerge. Scepticism is not only produced by the modern (cf. Gable 1995). It may also critically engage with it, as in this case, where Pentecostalism clearly engages with the modern Malawi nation. This is not to deny that there is a relationship between witchcraft and modernity, as a massive recent literature underscores. This relationship, however, may entail not only witchcraft as the domain where modernity is negotiated in terms of enticement or anxiety, but where the modern is placed under sceptical revision as well.

Notes

1 Fieldwork in Blantyre, on which this chapter is based, took place from 1989 to 1992 and was financed by the Dutch Organisation for Social Science Research in the Tropics (WOTRO), to which I am greatly indebted. I would like to acknowledge Wim van Binsbergen, Nina Tellegen and Todd Sanders for their valuable comments and suggestions on earlier drafts of this chapter.
2 See also Geschiere 1997, Ciekawy 1998, and Geschiere and Nyamnjoh 1998 for further elaboration on the links between politics and witchcraft elsewhere in Africa.
3 Outside Africa important insights can be gained in this respect from Taussig 1980, 1987.
4 An exception is Bastian (1993), who stresses the element of satire in Nigerian tabloid's commentary of witchcraft cases that frequently affect the status of local politicians.
5 Examples can be found on Ghana (Meyer 1998, 1999; van Dijk 1997, 1999a), Nigeria (Marshall 1993), Zimbabwe (Maxwell 1998), Zambia (Gifford 1998), Kenya (Gifford 1993) and Malawi (van Dijk 1992a, 1998).

6   During the first years of Malawi's independence this also applied to the witchcraft eradication activities that emerged in the Southern districts of the country (see Ross 1969).

7   A well-known case of a 'pioneer' of the first years of the movement is Madalitso Mbewe of the then-called Pentecostal Revival Crusade Ministry (PRC) whose father was a renowned Assemblies of God pastor in southern Malawi.

8   For instance, a fellowship led by the famous preacher Stanley Ndovi turned into the Living Waters Church during the mid-1980s and the Pentecostal Revival Crusade Ministries of Madalitso Mbewe established the Calvary Family Church; both are today well-known Pentecostal churches in Malawi.

9   This also includes the establishment of a plethora of related organizations – e.g. 'crusade ministries', Bible schools, religious publication houses, music-studios producing songs, cassettes and the like which all contribute to the overall entrepreneurial style of this form of Christianity.

10 See Richards 1935; Marwick 1950; Willis 1968; Ranger 1972; van Dijk 1994a. See also Probst (1999) on the re-currence of *mchape*-like cleansing rituals in modern Malawi.

11 Eni visited Malawi in 1992. For these dimensions of Pentecostalism, see van Dijk 1997, 1999a.

12 Some street-preachers, whilst clearly 'Pentecostal' in their messages and oratory practices, portrayed themselves as being well-respected members of one of the established churches. For example, Linley Mbeta remained a member of the CCAP throughout her leadership of the successful 'Redemption Voice Ministry' which operated so effectively against witchcraft.

13 'Fighting Islam' is a common hallmark of these crusades in the Zomba area, generally assumed to be an Islamic stronghold in Malawi.

14 One of the Pentecostal groups very active in this style of proselytization was, for instance, called the 'Aggressive Mission Training Corps'.

15 One kind of critique that has been voiced against this dominant view of modern witchcraft is that although it lives on *within* modernity, it is not necessarily *about* modernity. It can be about many other issues. Sanders (2000), for instance, shows in his study on Tanzania how people make clear-cut distinctions between what they consider 'modern' and 'traditional'. They link witchcraft eradication activities to this ideological rupture. Sanders shows that their witchcraft concerns relate directly to problems they perceive as belonging to clearly demarcated traditions (in this case rainmaking rituals). However, again, this interpretation treats witchcraft only as a source of anxiety and does not bring in the possibility that it can be made subject to scepticism including a kind of conviviality.

16 *Nkhoswe* is the Chewa title for the guardian of the matriclan to whom all young men are subservient (see Phiri 1983).

17 Mandala (1990) has analysed in great detail the ever-changing fortune of gerontocratic rule over the younger generation in Malawi, for instance, by pointing to periods in the nineteenth and twentieth centuries when initiation rituals either grew in importance or were on the verge of disappearing. One factor explaining the rise and fall of such forms of ritual control over the younger generation was, he claims, the fluctuating demand for labour power.

18 This was E. Bwanali – at the time of these events aged 19 – who would step in for Peter Mbepula as a leader of the Fellowship when the latter was absent from Mulunguzi.

19 Witchcraft accusations have always been subjected to serious 'testing', such as was the case under the practice of the *mwabvi* poison ordeal, outlawed under colonial rule, whereby both the accuser and the accused had to drink the poison cup. This 'testing' must not be confused with the kind of scepticism that negotiates the structures of legitimate authority as was implied here.

Bibliography

Auslander, M. (1993) '"Open the wombs": the symbolic politics of modern Ngoni witchfinding', in J. Comaroff and J. Comaroff (eds) *Modernity and its Malcontents: Ritual and Power in Postcolonial Africa*, Chicago: University of Chicago Press.

Bastian, M.L. (1993) '"Bloodhounds who have no friends": witchcraft and locality in the Nigerian popular press', in J. Comaroff and J. Comaroff (eds) *Modernity and its Malcontents: Ritual and Power in Postcolonial Africa*, Chicago: University of Chicago Press.

Ciekawy, D. (1998) 'Witchcraft in statecraft: five technologies of power in colonial and postcolonial coastal Kenya', *African Studies Review* 41, 3: 119–141.

Comaroff, J. and Comaroff, J.L. (eds) (1993) *Modernity and its Malcontents: Ritual and Power in Postcolonial Africa*, Chicago: University of Chicago Press.

—— (1999) 'Occult economies and the violence of abstraction: notes from the South African postcolony', *American Ethnologist* 26, 2: 279–303.

Englund, H. (1996a) 'Witchcraft, modernity and the person: the morality of accumulation in central Malawi', *Critique of Anthropology* 16, 3: 257–281.

—— (1996b) 'Between God and Kamuzu: the transition to multiparty politics in central Malawi', in R. Werbner and T. Ranger (eds) *Postcolonial Identities in Africa*, London: Zed Books.

Fields, K.E. (1985) *Revival and Rebellion in Colonial Central Africa*, Princeton: University Press.

Fisiy, C.F. and Geschiere, P. (1991) 'Sorcery, witchcraft and accumulation: regional variations in South and West Cameroon', *Critique of Anthropology* 11, 3: 251–279.

Forster, P.G. (1994) 'Culture, nationalism, and the invention of tradition in Malawi', *The Journal of Modern African Studies* 32, 3: 477–497.

Gable, E. (1995) 'The decolonization of consciousness: local skeptics and the "will to be modern" in a West African village', *American Ethnologist* 22, 2: 242–257.

Geschiere, P. (1997) *The Modernity of Witchcraft: Politics and the Occult in Postcolonial Africa*, Charlottesville: University Press of Virginia.

Geschiere, P. and Fisiy, C.F. (1994) 'Domesticating personal violence: witchcraft, courts and confessions in Cameroon', *Africa* 64, 3: 323–341.

Geschiere, P. and Nyamnjoh, F. (1998) 'Witchcraft as an issue in the "politics of belonging": democratization and urban migrants' involvement with the home village', *African Studies Review* 41, 3: 69–91.

Gifford, P. (1991) *The New Crusaders: Christianity and the New Right in Southern Africa*, London: Pluto Press.

—— (1993) 'Reinhard Bonnke's mission to Africa, and his 1991 Nairobi crusade', in P. Gifford (ed.) *New Dimensions in African Christianity*, Ibadan: (AACC) Sefer Books.

—— (1998) *African Christianity: Its Public Role*, London: Hurst.

Lewis, I.M. (1975) *Ecstatic Religion: An Anthropological Study of Spirit Possession and Shamanism*, London: Penguin Books.

Kaspin, D. (1993) 'Chewa visions and revisions of power: transformations of the Nyau dance in central Malawi', in J. Comaroff and J. Comaroff (eds) *Modernity and its Malcontents: Ritual and Power in Postcolonial Africa*, Chicago: University of Chicago Press.

Mandala, E.C. (1990) *Work and Control in a Peasant Economy: A History of the Lower Tchire Valley in Malawi, 1859–1960*, Madison: University of Wisconsin Press.

Marshall, R. (1993) '"Power in the name of Jesus": social transformation and Pentecostalism in western Nigeria revisited', in T. Ranger and O. Vaughan (eds) *Legitimacy and the State in Twentieth-Century Africa*, London: Macmillan.

Marwick, M.G. (1950) 'Another anti-witchcraft movement in East Central Africa', *Africa* xx: 100–112.

Maxwell, D. (1998) '"Delivered from the spirit of poverty?": Pentecostalism, prosperity and modernity in Zimbabwe,' *Journal of Religion in Africa* xxviii, 3: 350–373.

Mbembe, A. (1992) 'Provisional notes on the postcolony,' *Africa* 62, 1: 3–37.

Meyer, B. (1998) '"Make a complete break with the past": time and modernity in Ghanaian Pentecostalist discourse', in R.P. Werbner (ed.) *Memory and the Postcolony*, London: Zed Books.

—— (1999) 'Commodities and the power of prayer: Pentecostalist attitudes towards consumption in contemporary Ghana', in B. Meyer and P. Geschiere (eds) *Globalization and Identity: Dialectics of Flow and Closure*, Oxford: Blackwell.

Ncozana, S.S. (1985) 'Spirit possession and Tumbuka Christians, 1875–1950', unpublished Ph.D. thesis, University of Aberdeen.

Phiri, K.M. (1983) 'Some changes in the matrilineal family system among the Chewa of Malawi since the nineteenth century', *Journal of African History* 24: 257–274.

Probst, P. (1999) 'Mchape '95, or, the sudden fame of Billy Goodson Chisupe: healing, social memory and the enigma of the public sphere in post-Banda Malawi', *Africa* 69, 1: 108–138.

Ranger, T.O. (1972) 'Mchape and the study of witchcraft eradication', paper presented at the conference on the History of Central African Religious Systems, 31 August – 8 September, 1972, Lusaka, Zambia.

Richards, A.I. (1935) 'A modern movement of witchfinders', *Africa* viii, 4: 448–461.

Ross, A.C. (1969) 'The political role of the witchfinder in southern Malawi during the crisis of October 1964 to May 1965', in R.G. Willis (ed.) *Witchcraft and Healing*, Edinburgh: University of Edinburgh Press.

Sanders, T. (2000) 'Rain-witches and analytic (un)certainties: reconsidering mystical malevolence in postcolonial Africa', paper presented at the 16th Satterthwaite Colloquium on African Religion and Ritual, Ulverston, 16–19 April, 2000.

Sansom, B. (1972) 'When witches are not named', in M. Gluckman (ed.) *The Allocation of Responsibility*, Manchester: University Press.

Schoffeleers, J.M. (1985) *Pentecostalism and Neo-Traditionalism: The Religious Polarization of a Rural District in Southern Malawi*, Amsterdam: Free University Press.

Shaw, R. (1997) 'The production of witchcraft/witchcraft as production: memory, modernity and the slave trade in Sierra Leone', *American Ethnologist*, 24, 4: 856–876.

Taussig, M.T. (1980) *The Devil and Commodity Fetishism in South America*, Chapel Hill, NC: University of North Carolina Press.

—— (1987) *Shamanism, Colonialism and the Wild Man: A Study in Terror and Healing*, Chicago: University of Chicago Press.

Tengatenga, J. (1996) 'Young people: participation or alienation?', in K.R. Ross (ed.) *God, People and Power in Malawi: Democratization in Theological Perspective*, Blantyre: CLAIM Press.

Vail, L. and White, L. (1989) 'Tribalism in the political history of Malawi', in L. Vail (ed.) *The Creation of Tribalism in Southern Africa*, London: James Currey.

van Dijk, R.A. (1992a) 'Young Malawian Puritans: Young Puritan Preachers in a Present-

Day African Urban Environment', unpublished Ph.D. Dissertation, ISOR, Utrecht University.

—— (1992b) 'Young Puritan preachers in post-independence Malawi', *Africa* 62, 2: 159–181.

—— (1993) 'Young born-again preachers in Malawi: the significance of an extraneous identity', in P. Gifford (ed.) *New Dimensions in African Christianity*, Ibadan: (AACC) Sefer Books.

—— (1994a) 'Foucault and the anti-witchcraft movement: review article', *Critique of Anthropology* 14, 4: 429–435.

—— (1994b) 'La guérisseuse du docteur Banda au Malawi', *Politique Africaine* 52: 145–150.

—— (1995) 'Fundamentalism and its moral geography in Malawi: the representation of the diasporic and the diabolical', *Critique of Anthropology* 15, 2: 171–191

—— (1997) 'From camp to encompassment: discourses of transsubjectivity in the Ghanaian Pentecostal diaspora', *Journal of Religion in Africa* xxvii, 2: 135–169.

—— (1998) 'Pentecostalism, cultural memory and the state: contested representations of time in postcolonial Malawi', in R.P. Werbner (ed.) *Memory and the Postcolony*, London: Zed Books.

—— (1999a) 'The Pentecostal gift: Ghanaian charismatic churches and the moral innocence of the global economy', in R. Fardon, W. van Binsbergen and R. van Dijk (eds) *Modernity on a Shoestring*, London: School of Oriental and African Studies.

—— (1999b) 'Pentecostalism, gerontocratic rule and democratization in Malawi: the changing position of the young in political culture', in J. Haynes (ed.) *Religion, Globalization and Political Culture in the Third World*, London: Macmillan.

Von Doepp, P. (1998) 'The kingdom beyond Zasintha: churches and political life in Malawi's post-authoritarian era', in K.M. Phiri and K.R. Ross (eds) *Democratization in Malawi: A Stocktaking*, Blantyre: CLAIM Press.

Willis, R.G. (1968) 'Kamchape: an anti-sorcery movement in south-west Tanzania', *Africa* xxxviii: 1–15.

Wyllie, R.W. (1973) 'Introspective witchcraft among the Effutu of southern Ghana', *Man* 8, 1: 74–79.

Chapter 6

Black market, free market

Anti-witchcraft shrines and fetishes among the Akan[1]

Jane Parish

Among the Akan of Ghana, anti-witchcraft shrines have always represented a means by which ambitious entrepreneurs may take advantage of innovative business opportunities offered by new types of commodities. It was against a background of moral anxieties generated by the presence in the local economy of different types of accumulation that anti-witchcraft shrines flourished in colonial Asante (McCaskie 1981; McLeod 1965, 1975).

Shrines were especially popular among those individuals seeking to take advantage of new business opportunities. Indeed, the 1930s and 1940s saw an increase in the number of shrines as witchcraft accusations escalated (Field 1937; Fortes 1948; Goody 1957, 1975; Ward 1956). The pursuit of wealth through the purchasing of fetish from anti-witchcraft shrines was seen as simultaneously dangerous and alluring and, indeed, witchcraft discourses were an implicit critical comment on industrial accumulation as young men were seen as pursuing individual enrichment at all costs (McLeod 1975).

The accumulation of wealth in postcolonial African states continues to be a complex relation embodied in discourses about materialism and witchcraft. Many scholars have described how a dynamic relationship is formed between witchcraft and the idiom of the market, with the expansion of an occult economy alongside the global and cultural forces of modernity (Auslander 1993; Comaroff and Comaroff 1999; Geschiere 1997; Parish 2000; Rowlands and Warnier 1988; Sanders, Chapter 8; Shaw 1997). Yet, it should not be presumed that the forces of modernity are everywhere the same and something which all local economies experience as either threat or enchantment (Englund and Leach 2000). Indeed, this dichotomy may often obscure the kaleidoscopic nature of what it means to be 'up-to-date' as when businessmen engage with sorcery and 'traditional' witches infiltrate money markets (Englund and Leach 2000: 228). Or as Comaroff and Comaroff have shown, 'looked at up close, then, modernity itself all too rapidly melts into air' (1993: xii).

What it means to be modern in postcolonial Africa, as in the pursuit of money and material desires, is an imaginative, provocative and highly specific journey which may often turn-on-its-head the expansive and taken-for-granted forces of capitalism (see Meyer 1998). This is illustrated when we look at the symbolic meanings attached to wealth and, by implication, poverty, in present-day Ghana. Power and influence are often looked upon with a particular mixture of admiration and suspicion, as Lentz found in her study of different groups of 'big' men in Northern Ghana (1998: 51). Meyer, too, illustrates how one man's opportunity may easily become his downfall, as in a popular Ghanaian story told in Accra of a businessman who sought the help of a fetish priest when his business began to decline. His wealth was regarded by his relatives as 'evil' because it was earned in league with the devil. The contradictory perception of the family as a source of need during times of poverty and insecurity, and a drain on the wealth of prosperous relatives, is well recognized as a source of tension and money may be seen as both a blessing and a curse. Meyer analyses how Pentecostal Christians in Accra dream of 'big' money from a safe distance through fantasies about satanic riches and witchcraft. In retribution, popular narratives tell of satanic bank notes put into the pockets of their intended victims to spirit their wealth away (Meyer 1995).

The presence of 'good' and 'evil' wealth highlights the tense relationship between economic aspirations and the legitimation of such wealth, even after death, as in Gilbert's analysis of the meanings attached to the burial of a Ghanaian millionaire (Gilbert 1988; Parish 1999). Amongst the Akan, this ambiguous message about materialism is echoed by clients who visit anti-witchcraft shrines. On the one hand, anti-witchcraft shrines are perceived by many as a means by which enterprising individuals may, through 'traditional' magical powers, overthrow the fetters of existing social and moral relations to accumulate and consume commodities in new ways. On the other hand, shrines may be described by their critics, such as urbanites who live in large cosmopolitan cities, as part of rural African superstition, representative of a heathen past from which they try to distance themselves.

In my own fieldwork in the Dormaa-Ahenkro district, Brong-Ahafo Region, shrines are visited by young clients who make witchcraft accusations which are quite often at odds with one another and reflect, among other things, contradictory opinions about economic accumulation and the consumption of global commodities (Parish 1999, 2000). In many instances, the shrine itself comes to represent several different cultural transformations all at once. This complex engagement of African spirits with aspects of capitalist development is most explicit in the contrasting hopes for the future of two loose circles of young men with mutual friends in the Dormaa district. Both groups see the prosperous routes offered them by commercial capitalism as blocked in different ways and their varied responses to these predicaments can be seen in their engagement with anti-witchcraft shrines in the district. While one group sees the anti-witchcraft shrine as helping them to overcome impoverishment and achieve financial success, the other sees the shrine as promoting the worst excesses of capitalist development and greed, and of corrupting their spiritual heritage. They seek to resurrect at the shrine traditional African values of goodness and respect which, they hope, will promote greater social wealth for all (Geschiere 1997).

Anti-witchcraft shrines in the Dormaa district

The town, Dormaa Ahenkro, is the capital of the district and a major cross-roads for the movement of people both between the villages of the district and between Dormaa Ahenkro and the large cities of Kumase, the capital of the Asante Region, Sunyani, the regional capital of the Brong Ahafo Region and Accra, the capital city of Ghana. There is also a bus which travels twice a week between Dormaa Ahenkro and Abidjan in the Cote D'Ivoire.

In Akan religion, at the top of the hierarchy is the creator God, *Onyame*, followed by the earth goddess, *Asasa Yaa*, and the ancestral spirits, *nsamanfo*. Access to *Onyame* is through the deities (*abosom*). There are currently twenty-three practising anti-witchcraft shrines or *abosom-brafo* (*abosom*, pl., deity *abrafo*, pl., executioner, judge) which, as Goody (1957) records, often spring up and then disappear, only to reappear in another Region. A shrine is made up of a small alter constructed from several copper pots and pans and made into a structure several feet high. Perched in one pan is the god (*abosom*) hidden amongst twigs and dirt. All living creatures are believed to possess a spirit (*sunsum*, sing.; *asunsum*, pl.). Non-human *sunsum* is called *sasa*. *Abosom* are believed to be pure *sunsum*. Hidden inside trees, they attract the attention of the person they are to possess by calling him or her into the bush. Subordinate to the gods are a lesser group of spirits or talisman (*suman*, sing.; *asuman*, pl.). A potential shrine-priest (*okomfo*) will vanish into the bush for several years and be taught how to communicate with the god before bringing the god to a village where a shrine is built (see Fink 1990; Parish 1999; Rattray 1927).

The most important function at the *abosom-brafo* shrines is possession when the god reveals, through the mouthpiece of the shrine-priest, remedies to the varying misfortunes of shrine-clients. If a witch (*obayifo*) is present during possession, the god will listen to her confess to her crimes and will symbolically remove her witchcraft (*obayi*) which appears as a snake from the vagina (Parish 1999). During possession the priest appears to be in a trance-like state, wearing a grass skirt with many charms to it. Outside of possession, shrines are open to anyone who seeks the help of a god. In the majority of cases, clients visit a shrine to purchase protective talismans (*asuman*) which not only bring financial success but also protect their owners from witchcraft and from evil magic and medicine (*aduto*).

Greed and wealth

The most popular of the practising shrines are the *abosom-brafo-mmoatia* belonging to the forest-dwelling dwarfs. It is at these shrines that perceptions of both cultural continuity and change is expressed most explicitly. This is especially the case at the shrines of the younger shrine-priests. Their shrines are stressed by them as being the most modern because their gods are able to traverse the globe and to be able to offer advice and talismans to deal with complex financial and marketing opportunities in the global economy. One young, male priest summed up the 'new' wisdom of his god in the following way:

> He reads many newspapers . . . international newspapers . . . which explain where to invest and attractive products to make a man wealthy . . . our talismans keep many secret ingredients which this god has hidden . . . buy this and be rich . . . other gods read the gossip and about football . . . At this shrine . . . we have international opportunities . . . we understand market wars!

The definitive feature of the modern vision of some of these gods is the knowledge they possess of all things economic, both locally and globally, and, subsequently, the protection and talismans they offer shrine-clients wanting to make money. As the above shrine-priest summed up, 'not all the gods understand how to find money'. For the anti-witchcraft shrine is a potential means of securing riches for those who, otherwise, are unable to capitalize on the economic possibilities offered by the market economy. However, for many young Christians attending orthodox churches in the Region, the shrine acts as a reminder of the worst social excesses of western capitalism and they are seen to encourage greed and individual accumulation at the expense of the good fortune of wider kin and those who work hard and who do not purchase talismans to achieve quick economic gratification. Thus a most unlikely bedfellow to join in the condemnation of 'rural' anti-witchcraft shrines is Sankofa, or Afrikania, a religious movement founded in Ghana 1982 by a former Catholic priest, Kwabena Damuah, which seeks to spread the word of African traditional religion. The legacy of colonialism, it is forcefully suggested, has devalued the traditional role of the shrine as a place to communicate with God and, instead, their main function has become selling dubious medicines and talismans to clients who use the *abosom* as a means to achieve great riches. Sankofa reprimands those 'quacks' who fetishize their shrines gods in the pursuit of greed and who tarnish the 'good' name of the shrine. This, Sankofa argues, is not the way to achieve political and economic progress. Rather, in a 'modern' Africa, shrine-priests will preach that their gods are angels of God and obey His laws. It is the views of wealth and greed, expressed by two different groups of young men, which are discussed next.

The young men described in this chapter are ones I met through Joe, the nephew of a prominent chief. Sitting in the shade in the hot afternoons, in a town in the district, Joe met with his friends, among whom were several related to local chiefs and others who were university educated. To this end, I shall refer to this loose circle of people as the young aristocracy. The sons and relatives of the 'old' political elite, they have got stuck in a town which they had hoped to leave for well-paid jobs in the city. Instead, as they see it, they are forced to look for interim work that does not match their educational qualifications or social aspirations. Often connected to one of the many stools in the district, their social status confers a certain respect but not financial reward. They feel that the postcolonial state has let them down, economically, and that their often low-paid bureaucratic work prevents them from fulfilling their real potential (see Ferguson 1999). At the same time, some also have wealthy kin who are able to finance their further studies, particularly in law, and they hope to travel abroad, although as yet they have failed to prove themselves at 'home'. Their sponsors are unwilling to bankroll studentships or careers until convinced of their loyalty, integrity and commitment to political office, and until these young men show signs of independent initiative and participate more fully in community affairs. The young aristocracy in the district are openly contemptuous of many of the witchcraft shrines of the *abosom-brafo*, which they accuse of robbing clients of money and giving the 'true' traditional shrine a bad name. Those who attend regularly an orthodox Christian church are adamant that they would never visit a shrine because the shrine encourages people to use evil medicines against one another. There are also some young aristocrats, such as Roy, who secretly believe that people of bad character are able to outwit them, financially, with the help of fetishes they have purchased, although they have no evidence of this:

> Many thieves and criminals possess *asuman* which cover up their sins and allow them to hide their illegal money from their relatives. They become very rich and then use . . . their bad medicines to take the prosperity . . . of good people . . . I am poor because they use secret medicines to harm me . . . I am sure of it . . . they try to make me fail.

As Joe once remarked, 'the shrines bring misfortune on us all . . . they allow bad men to succeed, not me'. Some members of the young aristocracy resent the sporadic financial success of their less educated peers and blame the shrines for giving 'greedy' men and women unfair market advantage. In other words, in the eyes of some aristocrats, the financial possibilities opened to various shrine-clients curtails the opportunities left to those 'good' men who do not purchase 'evil' talismans. The wealth of some and the poverty of others is connected.

Many young aristocrats believe that witchcraft is rife in rural areas such as Dormaa, and that witchcraft accusations inevitably result when people are greedy, or do not help less well-off kin when they have the money to do so. Others tell how the spread of colonialism was accompanied by vices such as deviousness and envy and that a witch is a woman who embodies these characteristics. Many Africans, however, in their view, fell into the clutches of Satan and turned their back on their own heritage at the expense of pursuing individual accumulation. Greed, they believe, is the white man's curse. It is precisely this type of immorality, they argue, which inhibits the spread of 'traditional' African values and leaves Ghana in a perilous socio-economic state. Kwesi, whose uncle is a local sub-chief, told how this type of behaviour characterised western countries: 'Western people are not always good. There are many murders . . . people turn away from God . . . They think only of much money. There were once many laws in Ghana . . . now there is not so much listening to the ancestors . . . we forget their words.'

George, Kwesi's nephew, agreed that greed is a characteristic today of those who seek to buy talismans at a 'rural' shrine. He thought that the role of the 'rural' shrine has changed. Whereas once it played an important function in community affairs such as helping sick people and promoting honesty and humility, today there are shrine-priests and shrine-clients who are blinded by their own thirst for money. He believed that if the shrine returned to its original function, to serve *Onyame* and practise kindness and humility, then many Christians would see that the shrine offers another way of praying, albeit an African way.

Joe had dropped out of school and had promised to return at a later date to take his A-levels. Over the years, as his friends and brothers returned to finish their studying in Accra and Kumase, Joe mingled with unemployed youths who enjoyed no formal education, nor shared his aristocratic background. Often Joe would sneak off to buy cigarettes from these youths, among them the street-sellers, aware that his mother, a prominent royal in the district, strongly disapproved of this behaviour. It was through one such cigarette seller that I met Kofi, an ice seller, in a town just outside Sunyani, the Regional capital. He lived with his grandmother and mother in an overcrowded compound where he shared a room with five siblings. He introduced me to other lowly paid youths who were equally dependent on relatives and who eked out a living selling among other things, iced water, or manning kiosks with their friends. Others travelled, selling western commodities which they had acquired on the black market. Black market commodities carry a certain glamorous chic for these young men, combining the danger of illegal smuggling with the image of luxury commodities which others, without an avenue to the black market, cannot afford, nor even locate. They pride themselves on being adventurers in search of big earnings and of being able to buy any commodity at a cheap price to resell at a profit.

These young men spoke about witchcraft in relation to their boasts about their sexual conquests. In most cases, I found, the unemployed youth interviewed believe that witches are ex-lovers whom, they complain, were never satisfied with their sexual performance, or ex-wives and relatives unhappy with the expensive luxury gifts they have bestowed on them (Parish 1999). They buy talismans to protect themselves from witches and from the 'bad' thoughts and actions of their enemies. Talismans may also be bought by them to overcome economic obstacles put in their way by corrupt businessmen who try to 'eliminate' potential market competition. For all objects infused with spiritual powers, will, believe many clients, strengthen their economic prowess in the face of tough economic competition in the market economy. For the purposes of this chapter, I shall call this loose group of young men, black marketeers.

It is not unusual to find gangs of such young marketeers regularly visiting the shrines in the villages, staying for three or four days at a time before returning to the Region's large towns and cities. Sometimes, one of them has a relative living in the locality whom they seek out. The slow pace of life in the village and particularly at the shrine makes it a comfortable place for youths who gather and pass the day sleeping on benches reserved for shrine-clients. They will banter with one another, smoking and drinking beer all day long, stopping only to pay the children a few coins to fetch them fu-fu or rice from one of the sellers cooking at the edge of the road. Now and then these youths move off, usually to a bar, returning the next day in search of other young men with whom to socialise.

Often, if the shrine-priest has no other business to conduct, each young man will be allowed to consult with the god for a minimum fee, or sometimes for free. They buy talismans to cover a variety of ventures: from the prediction of lottery numbers, to protecting get-rich-quick schemes, or to protect their intermittent wealth from jealous lovers and rival market competitors. For example, John, aged 23, had been caught smuggling foodstuffs in the boot of his car between different regions in Ghana by internal border patrols. He was convinced that his car was possessed by an evil spirit conjured by his ex-wife. He had visited many shrines in the Brong-Ahafo and Asante Region but felt that the car had taken on a life of its own, particularly after a near fatal accident involving a tractor. He bought a powerful talisman and hung it over the windscreen. David, aged 30, believed that people did not buy cigarettes from him because his ex-girlfriend, whom he alleged to be a witch, had cursed his business. He wanted to buy a talisman that would not only ward off any evil spirits set in motion by his enemies, but also bring him prosperity and great riches. One young street-seller, Ken, whom I met through Joe at a shrine in the Dormaa district, was from the large market town of Techiman in the Brong-Ahafo Region. He worried that the reason many of his schemes had been scuppered by the police was because a witch, a spiteful female aunt, was sapping his energy. He frequently felt tired and lacked the will-power to put his best ideas into practice. The witch was making him impotent and this he took as a sign of his decreasing influence in all areas of his life. He had bought a fetish, a secret mixture of herbs locked in a small bracelet which he had also convinced many members of his family to purchase and was convinced of its ability to turn his life around. In the next section, I look at how many of the young marketeers seeking help from the shrines in the Dormaa district perceive themselves as the representatives of a capitalist culture marked out by the interface between Africa and Euro-America.

Tradition and capital

In the eyes of the young marketeers seeking help from anti-witchcraft shrines, the distinguishing feature of western economies is the opportunity for a lot of people to make a lot of money. As one unemployed youth said to me, 'In England everybody is rich' (cf. Sanders 1999). They see themselves as possessing the ability to spot gaps in the market which their business acumen will fill and which will allow them to make vast amounts of money very quickly, the biggest scheme always being just around the next corner. The most ingenious of these money-making-schemes among some young marketeers involved an attempt to sell 'fetish' to Europeans and rich Africans and Americans in West Africa so that they may sample a bit of 'African traditional religion' and protect their wealth from 'their own evil spirits', said one marketeer, William. William, aged 20, like many of his contemporaries, often boasted about the money he had earned by selling 'ancient' African talisman to wealthy Europeans, and of the contacts he had in Abidjan and other African cities. He knew, he said, how and where to cross the border to the Cote D'Ivoire quite easily and undetected. To this end, it was decided to combine a smuggling trip with the selling of talismans to tourists in the Cote D'Ivoire. Thus, William, together with three of his friends, set about buying talismans from a particular shrine at a price agreed with the *okomfo* which, incidentally, involved cutting him in on a share of the anticipated future profit.

William, together with Joseph, Bulie and Kofi, set off early one morning for the border where three friends were waiting with a car to take them to their compound in Abidjan. Resting after their journey, they spent the evening drinking at home before retiring to their quarters. The next day, they wandered aimlessly around the city. In the busiest sectors they stopped and watched other young men mingling among the few Europeans and Americans already on the tourist trail. Selling a variety of commodities from lighters and biros, cassettes of African music, they set up stall. The next day, William and Kofi marked out their pitch to hassle the few tourists around into buying an 'authentic African fetish'. Their plastic shopping bags were stuffed to the brim with bits of herb, cattle tail onto which they had stuck beads and cloth in order 'to make it look like African spirits', and stickers bearing slogans such as 'I am Afraid Of My Friends, Even You' and 'No Condition Is Permanent'. They came to sell not only 'traditional fetish', but also wooden airplanes painted with the Ghana airline logo. Many foreign visitors seemed somewhat wary of the youth and had obviously been warned to be careful of thieves and beggars, which these young men gave the impression of being. Gordon, from Ohio, was approached by Kofi outside a bar. He had flown to west Africa on business and had seen it all before:

> Give them an inch . . . well, they are trying to make a living. Its par for the course. In Dakar, believe me, its worse . . . much worse . . . the bullshit . . . (laughter). I suppose there are mouths to be fed . . . these lucky charms . . . is that the word? Kind of like voodoo, New Orleans stuff . . . gifts for the kids . . . cheap, badly made . . . better to go to the official market . . . artisan stuff looks better value for money . . . I'll pass . . . my kids could have made it!

However, some African-American tourists were more readily seduced by the opportunity to buy a little bit of African tradition and felt reassured by the fact that, in their eyes, most Africans had left such superstitions behind and that they were being sold souvenirs or relics of this past. Eventually, at the end of three days, William had sold at a profit all of the talismans he had bought at the shrine, although later he played down his earnings when paying the shrine-priest his share. William also managed to purchase cheap alcohol to smuggle past state border patrols, to sell to his customers in remote Ghanaian towns and villages and give the priests at traditional shrines the cheap liquor used to pour libation to the ancestors. Trips back to Abidjan became a regular journey for these young men as they divided smuggling runs and the selling of talismans. Increasingly, however, they were inclined to combine fetish with more established 'tourist' objects, such as cloth, pots and Asante gold figurines which the foreign visitor recognized as 'African'. Their customers were simply not convinced that the shrine fetish was authentically traditional, nor, in their eyes, did it look convincingly spiritual!

Money and magic

These young marketeers reinvent and support the *abosom-brafo* shrine as a means of grasping financial success through magical means. They enjoy little 'official' support for their plans to flood a potentially lucrative tourist market with shrine 'merchandise', nor do they seek it. Those of their relatives who had heard of their exploits thought that they were tempting misfortune by dabbling with spirits and that their ancestral spirits would be angered by this. Others, with whom they spoke, simply dismissed their plans as another failed venture which would bring in no money. Some of their friends thought that there was money to be made in the future, but that there were not enough tourists presently visiting Ghana and those, for example, in the capital, Accra, called in at the official Arts Centres where Kente cloth and Asante gold figures could be purchased. This, however, in no way deters the young marketeers. Indeed, they prefer it this way because they are left to their own devices and they meet with little interference. The priest at the particular shrine where they traded simply desired to make money to support himself and his family and certainly did not want to have to share any profits with rival anti-witchcraft shrines.

Although there is a Dormaa Fetish Priest Association, none of the young marketeers saw this as an effective organization to involve in their schemes. Indeed, the association is relatively inactive even though many of the fetish priests in the district belong to this association and see it as a way of safeguarding their collective interests. Six priests arranged a meeting of the association several months into my fieldwork so that I might buy drinks for the gods of the district! Priests try to represent themselves as a lobbying group, for example, against government attempts to tax their earnings. However, with little money in their coffers, it proves difficult to arrange meetings, particularly as many priests are illiterate, elderly men who are a law unto themselves and their gods, and who suddenly disappear for several weeks without warning. Many also work at shrines found in isolated villages making communication with them time-consuming and expensive. Shrine-priests openly compete with one another and are very suspicious of one another, especially as the popularity of a shrine at any one time is fairly fragile.

Presently, shrines also have very little political support from chiefs who, as committed Christians, are keen to distance themselves from the more controversial aspects of 'traditional' religion, those they associate with witchcraft accusations and the buying of talismans to protect them from evil. In reality, chiefs tread a precarious path as they seek to accommodate all types of religious worship while upsetting no one and hoping that no controversy will arise which would involve them taking sides. They are willing to tolerate the presence of the shrines as long as their profile is kept low. Others simply dismiss the activities of these shrines as the last vestiges of superstition and believe that if people want to waste their money at such places, then so be it; they do no harm and do not wish to stop them, unless a crime is being committed.

Contesting tradition

Unlike their elders, many of the young aristocracy abhor how shrines undermine 'the goodness in us all'. The *abosom-brafo* dwell too much on *obayi* (witchcraft), suggested the son of one prominent chief in the district. The 'young aristocracy' decry the local *abosom-brafo* shrines, despite their evident vitality and sporadic commercial success, for casting shame upon their true African heritage 'by encouraging the worshipping of stones, rocks and other fetishes'. The shrines, in Joe's view, perpetuate European myths about African evil such as witchcraft and fetish. Ben, the nephew of a royal stool-holder, described these shrines as encouraging beliefs about witchcraft which have no place in twentieth-century Ghana. The priests at some shrines, they say, should play down references to witchcraft. In particular, references to fetish is frowned upon, for it is felt that this type of discourse has connotations with backward ideas prevalent in Dormaa district, with which the young aristocracy do not wish to be associated.

We may say that the continued existence and vitality of the anti-witchcraft shrine highlights the predicament in which the young aristocracy are caught. Their rejection of the 'local' shrine has much in common with the rejection of the past by the global prosperity gospels of charismatic Pentecostalism (Hackett 1998; Marshall-Fratani 1998). Yet, in opposition to the global condemnation of Africanisation by charismatic Pentecostalism, the young aristocrats are keen to stress that some African shrines are simply a natural predecessor to the Christian church. Local shrines should thus be encouraged to emphasize the presence of 'goodness' in the world and the word of God. Just as Christians in America pray, explained one young son of a prominent Queenmother, so the African uses the shrine as an African communication with God. Hence the aristocrats invent their own recent model of an authentic African traditional shrine, itself a hybrid model which is held up as representing a true African past. What counts at this 'model' shrine is the antiquity of the shrine and their own associations with a glorified past. The contemporary vitality of the shrine is perceived to be embodied in traditional objects such as royal stools, linguists' staffs and cloth, and a 'continually reconstructed history' (see Gilbert 1997). These objects embody the past metonymically, but also metaphorically, by connecting it physically to the present and by representing royalty and distinction.

It is this imagery, believed Ben, that should be stressed to foreign visitors who should not be allowed to roam around with pimps and criminals who draw attention to the worst characteristics of the wrong type of shrine and its associated forms of African worship. The *abosom-brafo* shrines of the district, along with their shrine-priests, are perceived by the young aristocracy as engaging in immoral behaviour which is a barrier to the rejuvenating of a culture under threat from immoral influences such as alcohol, crime and drugs. For, as noted by Gilbert among the Akuapim, Christianity has often led to a disdain of things traditional as backward (Gilbert 1997). Indeed, the authority of the old elite is under question by the next rulers of Akuapim. 'They do not want to go back to being "fetish" priests sitting on stones; they want to be like their former [colonial] rulers' (Gilbert 1997: 527). In the Dormaa district, the young aristocracy, unlike the old elite, denounce many of the shrines as fulfilling 'the white man's worst prejudices about witchcraft'. Kwame thought that white people who came to Ghana were keen to stereotype African religion as the worshipping of Satan, 'You see Satan all ways . . . it's all witchcraft you say'. He declared that shrines are located in rundown compounds which do not do justice to the great African gods: 'Religion began here in Africa . . . not with the white man.' Shrine-priests, he claimed, need to be updated about current religious practice, 'not the greedy witch . . . look at the good'. The need is for shrines to represent the 'right kind' of African tradition which in Kwame's eyes is about 'ancestors and their great acts'.

It is often in Accra and Kumase that, as students, young aristocrats first developed an interest in African 'traditional' religion, trampled underfoot, as they see it, by first European missionaries and now by the charismatic Pentecostal movement (see Marshall-Fratani 1998: 285). In Amasu, a town in the Dormaa district, the movement known as African Traditional Religion or Sankofa has a local branch which seeks to counter popular stereotypes about 'traditional' worship.

While not wanting to be seen as supporters of Sankofa for fear of upsetting the delicate balance between 'traditional' and Christian worship, some young aristocrats see its symbolism as a way in which local shrines can be repackaged. Thus the branch's compound is adorned with a large yellow cardboard bird which can be seen for miles. This is the Sankofa bird, the traditional emblem of African Religion. A common figure in Akan art, the Sankofa bird is depicted with an egg on its back, its head turned to gaze toward it. The significance of this in African Traditional Religion is that the bird is turning to look at the rebirth, reactivation and reorganization of traditional religion.

In reiterating the 'communal' aspects of religious practice, the symbolism Sankofa has developed relies upon powerful images of an African cultural heritage and reasserts a cultural independence that rejects the colonial prejudice which is said to have destroyed indigenous culture. 'Culture', it is assumed implicitly, is threatened by time. Upon visiting Africa in 1980, the Pope gave the message: 'Preserve your culture. Do not let it die. Keep it alive.' Converts to Sankofa frequently quote this exhortation as evidence that traditional culture is endangered by modern times. Mr Aboah, a policeman who could often be found at the compound, told me how it was necessary 'to think good and be honest in your thoughts . . . as the ancestors taught us . . . this will take us forward'. The Sankofa bird gazes wistfully at a cultural heritage of art, music and festivals celebrating past national triumphs and memories. Inattention to custom leads, according to one prominent local Sankofa follower, 'to laziness and carelessness among the young'. This has led to a desire to collect 'Culture', to preserve and display it.

'Culture' is especially represented at the shrine that followers of Sankofa have built in Amasu, a town in the Dormaa district. Resembling a Christian altar, to the left of a small bowl is the Afrikania flag. To the right is the Ghanaian national flag. The shrine constitutes a symbolic place which is both Ghanaian and African, a space of nationalism and virtue.

Visitors to Amasu are encouraged by young aristocrats to visit the head-quarters of Sankofa in order to see for themselves how the shrine can play a vital role in the creation of a better African future, a future that enables African Religion to compete on equal footing with the world religions represented throughout Ghana. Upon arriving at the compound, visitors are given small glasses filled with gin in order to pour libation to the ancestors of the district. Here Ben told me:

> We should be proud of ourselves . . . the shrines allow us to retrieve the past . . . not use *asuman* . . . harm each other . . . God created the shrines to help us make schools and teach us better ways to use our resources. The spirits at the shrines are God's messengers and he wants us to prosper and be thoughtful.

The old ways must be incorporated into the future. However, the active *abosom-brafo* shrines of the district, those visited to ward off evil and witchcraft, do not symbolize the past in a way that such a project can usefully engage with. They are simply not the 'right type' of pre-modern religious phenomena.

A sense of tradition can evolve out of a cosmopolitan knowledge that embraces an orientation towards the future but that nevertheless goes along with a concern for building respect for the past and past generations. A further twist in this contested terrain concerns the fact that in spite of the views of the old and new elite, the young *abosom-brafo* priests at the shrines popular with the marketeers actually see their shrines as representing the most contemporary powers of their gods as opposed to the demonized ways of the past. In the next section, I illustrate how their particular perception of the past has made some young shrine-priests prepared to join forces with the young marketeers as opposed to the young aristocracy.

Evil and misfortune

Two of the youngest, and in one instance, most recently appointed shrine-priests believe that their gods have a new potency. This is a power which derives from the powerful spirit of those gods who have with them a knowledge that travels frontiers, a knowledge that can be achieved by travelling outside of Ghana, so that the far can come to be viewed from nearby, apart from national politics. As one priest pointed out:

> The god who possesses me knows all about life today. He has travelled to London and Frankfurt . . . he can decide the cocoa price if he wishes . . . he is not like the other gods whose spirit has been attacked by witches and the officials who work for the government . . . at this shrine we can make powerful talismans and make them lose money.

The young priests tell how there are people who will lie and bribe. These people, they suggest, have forgotten how the local gods fought for them and their ancestors. They have neglected the shrines and the gods at these shrines, bar their own, are weak. To be free of such people it is necessary to watch them from afar, like those gods, whose knowledge has grown. Their knowledge is up to the minute and now stretches beyond Ghana's borders. Misfortune is everywhere, described one shrine-priest, because people wish ill on their rivals:

> There are too many bad thoughts . . . people no longer come to the shrines and they kill one another . . . there is too much witchcraft . . . and the gods at the other shrines cannot fight it . . . the spirits are angry and they bring misfortune . . . the spirits cause much trouble because people do not respect their wishes. We try to fight this because we understand how misfortune is working . . . We understand economic and political ideals . . . the talismans will guide you in this . . . the World Bank asks for our help.

Likewise, several young marketeers draw analogies between these newer gods and the Silver Surfer, a figure from an American comic book. This comic was discarded, only to be found by a marketeer, Rob, who kept it and told one particular shrine-priest about this character. The Silver Surfer, Norrin Radd, I later read, surrendered his freedom to become herald to the world-devouring Galactus in order to save his home planet, Zenn-La. The Surfer freely travels the vast universe. Possessed with cosmic power, he has the ability to channel energy through his body and release it at will and watches the earth from space. Kofi told me that the god at one particular shrine he visits soon realized that, like the Silver Surfer, his motives would never be comprehended by his enemies:

At this shrine the god knows about very new things which happen only today in Africa. He will make you a talisman so that you invest your money wisely . . . he knows about . . . currencies and . . . invests money . . . he knows about very fine opportunities . . . my uncle he says . . . no . . . he just take your money . . . my uncle . . . no way . . . he understands how to make his women love him like mine do . . . he is stuck . . . the Silver Surfer he is powerful . . . so is this god . . . the old people they do not understand that they are trying to help us and make us strong so that our spirit can overcome misfortune and all the problems in the world.

The Silver Surfer, therefore, like the god, has an overview of events, but he remains misunderstood by the nations of the earth who believe that he still works for Galactus; also, like the shrine-gods, he seeks to conceal his own corruption.

Talismans and the free market

Interestingly, the talismans bought by the marketeers to protect themselves from witchcraft and to make themselves rich differ from the talismans sold to tourists. In the eyes of one marketeer, Michael, the latter fetish bore little resemblance to the type of *suman* he used to protect his wealth from witches, although he found it difficult to pinpoint why:

No, No, No . . . it does not work . . . not like mine. The American buys it to move closer to God . . . It is not the real *sunsum*. Why? . . . the ingredients are mixed in a difficult way . . . the abosom would not listen to . . . be pleased with . . . (laughter) . . . maybe special mixture has been left out. . . maybe this does not matter because the American has not the same worries as me . . . It is not essential to them . . . They do not believe in the witchcraft . . . means nothing to them . . . they do not fear it. I treat it with respect . . . it worries me.

In seeking a remedy to the evil and misfortune that shrine-clients hope to overcome, some shrine-priests fashion powerful talismans which combine a mixture of natural 'bush' matter with bits of western commodities. Continuity with the past comes from the notion that powerful talismans are associated with spiritual sources found in the bush such as plants and bits of animal horn which the god instructs the shrine-priest to collect.

These natural ingredients are often fastened to 'foreign' objects, such as ballpoint pens, and made sacred by the priest who injects them with 'special ingredients' only known about by the shrine god. These talismans are worn about the body in order to bring the wearer good fortune and protect him or her from evil magic and medicine used by one's enemies. Talismans fuse the power of the local and the global in a deliberate mixture of material categories. The local assumption is that all natural matter is animated. This means that even the most exotic objects can be appropriated and made effectively local by refashioning and attributing 'local' *asunsum* to them.

Thus, of particular interest to the young marketeers are those objects obtained from rich businessmen and foreign tourists, their credit cards, American Express, for example. The *asuman* (talismans) fastened by young marketeers to American Express plastic gives the purchaser, it is believed, the power to overcome local enemies. It places the wearer in an international market place. It gives him the power to operate successfully against hidden market mechanisms. The credit card, the epitome of the modern global economy, will, for example, be plastered with herbs bought from a shrine-priest who has collected these from the bush in the district, traditionally the dwelling place of the most African of mythical creatures, the *sasa-bonsam*, a monstrous shaped monkey. The power of the local moral economy is injected into the global commodity. This can then be worn about the person to protect against attack by witches who are thought to be confused by the invisible workings of the card. It also guarantees protection against corrupt state officials and businessmen who seek to manipulate the 'local' market for their own interests and try to prevent others from earning a successful living.

To the young aristocrats, these 'hybridized European' charms do not carry the same power as 'authentic local' ones. The global commodity in some way undermines, in their view, the power of the 'local'. Anthony, aged 30, put this succinctly:

> The white man takes it all . . . their commodities have their place . . . not in African religion. This is a worshipping that has a long history. Do not ruin it and try to replace it with Christian ways of life. These credit cards carry no power at all. There is no god in them. The god has gone, and left us . . . anyhow . . . you confuse me . . . no *suman* should be sold . . . they are selfish people who buy these like the Europeans. Do not try to copy them.

For the tourist, on the other hand, the 'local' fetish sold to them by marketeers has no value either spiritually or in the global marketplace. It is merely a cheap memento. It is not easily recognizable and does not have the same international value as African masks, wooden animals and Kente cloth. Likewise, global products dressed up as 'authentic fetish' also have no appeal. They are not 'local' enough and as one tourist summed it up: 'It has no roots!' In thinking about talismans, their symbolic complexity has much to do with how competing values and sources of power come to be represented and confined in objects which bear, for some, highly charged connotations and associations. Talismans are pieces cut out of, or extracted from, larger worlds of meaning and action. Their transformative power derives both from their association with these different worlds and, sometimes, from forced conjuncture. The young marketeers or the aristocracy who speculate about these conjunctures are in different ways both cosmopolitan. They reach out imaginatively to other places and times in contrasting attempts to represent their past and command their present and their futures.

Conclusion

Contradictory social opinions expressed by marketeers and young aristocrats about the distinct role of anti-witchcraft shrines may be taken as illustrative of schisms in the way development and the market place itself is interpreted. The continual vitality of anti-witchcraft shrines illustrates, above all, the simultaneous existence of both cultural change and resistance. Young marketeers fashion talismans sold at shrines to resell to tourists in search of an authentic Africa. More importantly, they also purchase spiritual protection for themselves in the hope that this power may protect them from witchcraft and help them to secure untold riches in the market economy. In appearance, the talismans most spiritually valued by the marketeer would not appeal to the tourist because these fetishes are made up either of herbs and plants which the Euro-American does not value, or of global brands which the Euro-American consumer does not associate with an African sacredness, or both. However, for the young marketeer, the talisman he carries, attached to credit cards, the epitome of an international 'virtual' currency, enables the wearer to overcome obstacles which are placed in his way by an assortment of ex-lovers, corrupt businessmen and politicians at home who abuse their privileged position. It also enables its wearer to circumvent evil and, using the power of the anti-witchcraft shrine, exploit the free market for his own ends.

The young aristocrat wants to preserve an 'African' way of life at the shrine, free from the influence of both traditional African evils such as witchcraft and of western lifestyles which have no place in the African shrine of today. Ironically, this is also the kind of shrine which would appeal to the Euro-American tourist in search of African art purchases, though the aristocrat would never entertain such an idea. For he wants to keep at bay the corrupting economic and moral influence of capitalism, a corruption epitomized by the greed of the 'racketeer' who, as the aristocrats see it, uses the shrine for his own selfish ends. Development, in his eyes, demands that the 'traditional' values most associated with the shrine such as respect and sharing are inscribed in the heart of the nation and that western immoral attitudes are kept at arms length if the community at large is to enjoy prosperity. This project involves restoring the shrine to its former glory, dissociating it from African diabolicalization and making shrines a place where worshippers can communicate with *Onyame*, learn how to be good to their neighbours, and enact the religious and cultural traditions of a golden past.

Note

1 This paper is based on fieldwork carried out between 1990 and 1991 in Dormaa-Ahenkro district. All personal names have been changed at the request of the people cited. This is because of the illegal activities of the black marketeers and the desire of young aristocrats to preserve anonymity in order to avoid political dispute and possible social affront.

Bibliography

Auslander, M. (1993) '"Open the wombs!": the symbolic politics of modern Ngoni witchfinding', in J. Comaroff and J.L. Comaroff (eds) *Modernity and its Malcontents: Ritual and Power in Postcolonial Africa*, Chicago: University of Chicago Press.

Comaroff, J. and Comaroff, J.L. (eds) (1993) *Modernity and its Malcontents: Ritual and Power in Postcolonial Africa*, Chicago: University of Chicago Press.

—— (1999) 'Occult economies and the violence of abstraction: notes from the South African postcolony', *American Ethnologist* 26: 279–303.

Englund, H. and Leach, J. (2000) 'Ethnography and the meta-narratives of modernity', *Current Anthropology* 41, 2: 225–239.

Ferguson, J. (1999) *Expectations of Modernity: Myths and Meanings of Urban Life on the Zambian Copperbelt*, Berkeley: University of California Press.

Field, M. (1937) *Search for Security*, London: Faber and Faber.

Fink, H.G. (1990) *Religion, Disease and Healing in Ghana: A Case Study of Traditional Dormaa Medicine*, Munich: Trickster Wissenschaft.

Fortes, M. (1948) 'The Ashanti social survey: a preliminary report', *Rhodes-Livingstone Journal* 6: 1–36.

Geschiere, P. (1997) *The Modernity of Witchcraft: Politics and the Occult in Postcolonial Africa*, Charlottesville: University Press of Virginia.

Gilbert, M. (1988) 'The sudden death of a millionaire: consensus and conversion in a Ghanaian kingdom', *Africa* 58: 291–313.

—— (1997) 'No condition is permanent: ethnic construction and the use of history in Akuapim', *Africa* 67, 4: 501–534.

Goody, J. (1957) 'Anomie in Asante', *Africa* xxvii: 356–363

—— (ed.) (1975) *Changing Social Structure in Ghana: Essays in the Comparative Sociology of a New State and an Old Tradition*, London: International African Institute.

Hackett, R.I.J. (1998) 'Charismatic/Pentecostal appropriation of media technologies in Nigeria and Ghana', *Journal of Religion in Africa* xxvii, 3: 258–279.

Lentz, C. (1998) 'The chief, the mine captain and the politician: legitimating power in northern Ghana', *Africa* 68: 46–67.

McCaskie, T.C. (1981) 'Anti-witchcraft cults in Asante: an essay in the social history of an African people', *History in Africa* 8: 125–154.

McLeod, M. (1965) 'Survey of the literature on witchcraft in Ghana', unpublished BLitt thesis, Oxford University.

—— (1975) 'On the spread of anti-witchcraft cults in modern Asante', in J. Goody (ed.) *Changing Social Structure in Ghana: Essays in the Comparative Sociology of a New State and an Old Tradition*, London: International African Institute.

Marshall-Fratani, R. (1998) 'Mediating the global and the local in Nigerian Pentecostalism', *Journal of Religion in Africa* xxvii, 3: 278–316.

Meyer, B. (1995) 'Delivered from the powers of darkness: confessions of satanic riches in Christian Ghana', *Africa* 65: 236–255.

—— (1998) 'The power of money: politics, occult forces and Pentecostalism in Ghana', *African Studies Review* 41: 15–37.

Parish, J. (1999) 'The dynamics of witchcraft and indigenous shrines amongst the Akan', *Africa* 69: 426–448.

—— (2000) 'From the body to the wallet: conceptualising Akan witchcraft at home and abroad', *Journal of the Royal Anthropological Institute* 6: 487–500.

Rattray, R.S. (1927) *Religion and Art in Ashanti*, London: Oxford University Press.

Rowlands, M. and Warnier, J.P. (1988) 'Sorcery, power and the modern state in Cameroon', *Man* 23: 118–132.

Sanders, T. (1999) 'Modernity, wealth and witchcraft in Tanzania', *Research in Economic Anthropology* 20: 117–131.

Shaw, R. (1997) 'Production of witchcraft/witchcraft as production: memory, modernity and the slave trade in Sierra Leone', *American Ethnologist* 24: 856–876.

Ward, B.E. (1956) 'Some observations on religious cults in Asante', *Africa* 26: 47–61.

Chapter 7

Betrayal or affirmation?

Transformations in witchcraft technologies of power, danger and agency among the Tuareg of Niger[1]

Susan Rasmussen

Anthropology, witchcraft, and political economy

In the anthropology of religion, it is now recognized that so-called 'mystic' or ritual powers require careful deconstruction and recasting (Beidelman 1971, 1993; Crick 1976; Parkin 1985, 1991; Geschiere 1997; Pels 1998).[1] Studies of 'witchcraft', in particular, must be sensitive to problems of translation and also grounded in history and political economy. Among the Tuareg people of the Niger Republic – a traditionally stratified, semi-nomadic, Muslim people, who speak a Berber language – Tamajaq, so-called 'witchcraft' poses special problems for analysis and interpretation. Four types of power are often invoked to explain human social destiny: *togerchet*; *tezma*; *ark echaghel*; and *al baraka*. These powers often overlap, they are disputed in everyday practice, and have been trans-formed by recent socioeconomic and political turmoil.[2] The Tamajaq terms have only approximate translations in English. *Togerchet* denotes approximately 'evil mouth' or 'evil eye' (Nicolaisen 1961; Rasmussen 2001; Casajus 2000). *Tezma* most closely approaches classical anthropological definitions of 'witchcraft' (Douglas 1966, 1992), referring to a force unintentionally activated when a request for a gift, compensation, or pay is rejected; this usually involves conflict between a smith/artisan and a noble. Occasionally, however, nobles may activate this power. (*Ark*) *echaghel*, literally 'bad work', is often translated by local speakers into French as *la sorcellerie*, sorcery in English. Finally, *al baraka*, the power most widely described in the ethnographic literature of North Africa (Westermarck 1926; Gellner 1969; Norris 1990), refers to Islamic blessing or benediction, possessed primarily by Islamic scholars popularly called marabouts and by some respected elders, herbalists, and chiefs. It is particularly powerful in those maraboutique clans called *icherifan*, who claim descent from the Prophet and are credited with healing powers. Yet sometimes, local residents insist, *al baraka* can be misused and become corrupted, used to destroy, even kill. These negative transformations of *al baraka* have received less attention.

These forces are complex and defy conventional binaries and glosses. Like the more familiar English concepts of 'jinxed' situations or objects, or persons called 'Svengali-like', 'losers', or 'accident-prone', the Tuareg forces should not be overly-mystified or exoticized. They include very human, social, as well as spiritual agencies, and they straddle both sacred and secular domains (these latter not neatly separated). These four powers involve diverse agents, victims, and beneficiaries. Two of them – *togerchet* and (*ark*) *echaghel* – are generalized, and may apply (in agent and victim) to anyone. The other two – *tezma* and *al baraka* – tend to be more class-specific. Three powers are believed to cause primarily misfortune and ill luck; whereas the fourth, *al baraka*, similar though not identical to the Polynesian *mana*, usually brings good fortune through association with a benevolent leader. Yet *al baraka* can be misused and in fact, sometimes becomes converted into (*ark*) *echaghel*. Finally, while these forces are frequently invoked, local cultural concepts of personal destiny are not strictly 'fatalistic'. Many situations are attributed to the vagaries of nature or individual human frailties (Nicolaisen 1961; Rasmussen 1989, 1992, 1998, 2001; Spittler 1993).

Still, these 'mystic' powers are important. A comparative analysis of them sheds light upon anthropological studies of witchcraft and, more broadly, theories of causation and destiny in 'other modernities' (Geschiere 1997; Ciekawy and Geschiere 1998; Douglas 1966, 1992; Comaroff and Comaroff 1999). In my view, many recent studies, while correct in emphasizing wider political economy and historic factors, still need to account for witchcraft as a moral, philosophical force. Tuareg idioms of 'witchcraft' reveal how, among Tuareg as among many other Africans, the 'traditional' and the 'modern' are not so neatly opposed, and do not replace each other (Martin and O'Meara 1995; Hutchinson 1996; Comaroff and Comaroff 1993, 1999); rather, they coexist and continually inform each other. So-called 'modernity' is a very slippery, relative term, often distinct from Euro-American concepts of power, statehood, and 'development' in its cross-cultural formulations.

In many parts of Africa, witchcraft is explicitly linked to home and family (Ciekawy and Geschiere 1998: 4). Witchcraft has been described as the 'dark side of kinship . . . inherent in the kinship order but is at same time a betrayal of its boundaries' (Ciekawy and Geschiere 1998: 5). Among the Tuareg, it is often linked to threatening outsiders. In the Air Mountains of northern Niger, 'witchcraft' is the inversion of the stratified social order. It addresses the betrayal of socioeconomic boundaries and local trust in the traditional keepers and guardians of these boundaries, mediators and buffers who normally protect. For example, smith/artisans and nobles are ideally mutually supportive and symbiotic in their traditionally fictive kin-based, balanced and reciprocal client–patron relations; Islamic scholars (called *ineslemen* or marabouts) are ideally benevolent toward their trusting believer/followers; youths should obey or at least respect elder leadership; and husbands and wives are supposed to love and support each other. The invoking of mystic powers expresses concern with the undermining of traditional safeguards in social relationships, the selectivity and limitations of economic opportunities, and the differential enjoyment of benefits (Taussig 1980; Rowlands and Warnier 1988; Geschiere 1997; Englund 1996; Masquelier 1999).

Understanding witchcraft in relation to political economy still requires grappling with the problem of translation (Middleton 1960; Crick 1976; Beidelman 1993; Rasmussen 1992, 1998; Englund 1996; Bongmba 1998: 167). Use of both indigenous terms and non-indigenous terms, while never an exact translation, will facilitate understanding the phenomenon and situate it more within Tuareg, than Euro-American experiences of modernity (Englund and Leach 2000; Ferguson 1999). In this chapter, I show how Tuareg patterns of accusation of ritual powers and attributions of agency reflect social and economic turmoil: the breakdown of the pre-colonial stratified hierarchical system of nobles, tributaries, smith/artisans, and former slaves, the questioning of important cultural values in conduct between youths and elders and men and women. Many Air Tuareg are pressured to sedentarize by ecological disasters: irregular rains, diminishing pastures – and by colonial and postcolonial state policies. They also face political tensions and intermittent armed conflict with the central government.[3] There are disruptions in property balance, and material and spiritual resources. 'Witchcraft' accusations reflect enduring but contested cultural values: namely, respect, reserve, sharing and giving, obedience, restraint in eating, verbal reticence, and caution in praise. Thus in analysing these ritual powers of *togerchet*, *tezma*, *echaghel*, and *al baraka*, one must look to pressures in the contemporary socioeconomic system where wealth and descent no longer coincide exactly, and where the bases of prestige and status – for nobles, smiths, former tributary and servile men and women, marabouts, and elders and youths – are increasingly fluid, and these traditionally-distinct powers, particularly *al baraka* and *tezma*, are not stable or diametrically opposed in every context, but acquire new meanings and uses.

Socioeconomic turmoil, powers, and dangers among the Tuareg

In Niger as across the African continent, there has been a growing exposure to free market economics, privatization, and creation of small and medium-scale enterprises, all in the name of 'development' and 're-structuring' (Ndegwa and Stryker 1995; Geschiere 1997; Sanders, Chapter 8). 'Witchcraft' powers illustrate local perceptions of these processes and ways of coping with them, thereby revealing local idioms of so-called 'development', and how such idioms shape people's lived-in worlds in specific locales, but also how people actively respond to them. Interpersonal tensions are rooted in changing economic, political, and social conditions. Many rural Tuareg remain semi-nomadic, and continue to practise oasis gardening, herding, artisan work, and trading of salt, dates, and millet on caravans to Nigeria. Traditionally, occupations corresponded to inherited social status (of noble, tributary, smith/artisan, and former slave). Noble descent groups or clans wielded military domination over their client and formerly-servile populations.[4] The more nomadic pastoralist nobles collected tribute from the subjugated oasis populations, peoples of various degrees of servitude performed domestic, herding, and caravan labour for noble owners, tributaries raided and traded for nobles, and smith/artisans provided nobles with goods and services, with specific client–patron rights and obligations.

It is now difficult to live on nomadic stockbreeding alone, in the face of recurrent droughts and increasing monetarization. Nowadays, persons of diverse social origins practise occupations formerly associated with one or another social stratum, as well as new occupations of tourism, men's migrant labour, and itinerant trade of artisan products. In some Tuareg groups, despite official social stratum endogamy, there has been long-standing intermarriage between nobles and former slaves (Rodd 1926; Bernus 1981). Smiths remain the most endogamous. Although they ideally share a joking relationship with smiths as fictive cousins, most nobles still abhor marrying smiths because of lingering pollution beliefs. Many individuals still appeal to noble origins to justify certain conduct, chiefly noble and maraboutique clans attempt to arrange endogamous, politically-advantageous marriages between close cousins, and appeal to Islam in attempts to preserve traditional social prestige in the face of impoverishment from drought and danger from armed conflict.[5] There is sometimes, moreover, competition among marabout/Islamic scholars for influence within the community, and conflict between traditional and emergent leaders and elders and youths.[6] There are now upheavals in patterns of production, wealth, and consumption. Song verses, for example, lament that former slaves 'come and do what they want', warn against jealousy, gossip over success, and theft of property. Women criticize men for returning from migrant labour without money or presents for their families (Rasmussen 1995).

In the Air countryside, smiths continue to manufacture silver jewellery and leather, wooden, and stone tools for their patron nobles, assist in arranging nobles' marriages, act as 'ambassadors' for chiefs, and serve food and sing praise-songs at their nobles' rites of passage.[7] The traditionally symbiotic relations between nobles and smiths are now becoming more asymmetric, however. Rural nobles still depend upon smiths as a group for many goods and services; whereas smiths have alternate sources of patronage and income in the tourist trade. Many rural smiths today also practise oasis gardening, herding, and tailoring, as well as their traditional work of forge and rites of passage services. Until recently, many nobles were more reluctant to take up gardening and tailoring because of the traditional stigma of manual labour associated with them. In client–patron relationships in the countryside, smiths' work for nobles is remunerated in some combination of money, food, and tea. But nobles are now having more difficulty supporting smiths. Some nobles resent some smiths' economic success.

Islamic scholars act as scribes, healers, and legal adjudicators. Nobles require the blessing of marabouts' amulets and Qur'anic formulae before any dangerous undertaking (formerly raids, today caravanning, well-digging for oasis gardening, migrant labour, and most recently, the 1990–1995 Tuareg nationalist/separatist rebellion). Marabouts' amulets also protect against theft and *togerchet* powers of evil eye and evil mouth. Marabouts nowadays acquire animals through religious alms donations, in hospitality arrangements, and by ritual treatments requiring animal sacrifice. One source of marabouts' income is a religious tax, called *zakat*, paid for by all who worship at the local mosque (Keenan 1977: 166; Spittler 1993). Marabouts ideally act as 'men of peace' and, like smith/artisans, should act as mediators and refrain from fighting. Recently, however, there are hints of greater political activity among marabouts in two arenas: during the 1990–1995 Tuareg Rebellion, when their amulets against bullets were in great demand by rebel fighters, and recently during greater assertion, in the towns of Niger, by Islamic reform movements.

Cultural values of nobles emphasize dignity, reserve, respect/shame, and restraint from too-open or loquacious speech. Deeds are closely connected to words. The spoken word is a topic of great concern. *Tangalt*, which denotes 'shadowy' or indirect speech by allusion, metaphor, or symbol, is emphasized by nobles, both for politeness and for protection from vulnerability to misfortune (Casajus 2000: 32). In local attitudes toward destiny and causation, God or Allah is eternal, all-powerful, and good, but also punishes and condemns. Some inexplicable conditions, such as blindness without any discernible illness cause, are explained as the result of past sins. Other types of personal destiny are explained as caused by the actions of spirits, Qur'anic and non-Qur'anic, who often attack persons who become vulnerable during isolation in remote places (also metaphorically, in psycho-social loneliness and nostalgia) or during transitions (Nicolaisen 1961; Casajus 1987; Rasmussen 1995, 1997).

The contexts of these 'witch'-like powers are therefore complex. There are economic and ecological upheavals, as well as changing ideas about reproduction and production that place stress upon new wealth flows and forms of redistribution, yet there are some efforts to retain the older bases of power. New notions and practices of modernity and power affect Tuareg of different social origins in contrasting ways. In Niger until recently, the northern regions were not integrated into wider political or economic infrastructures, and Tuareg tended to be underrepresented in decision-making and benefits. Many Tuareg initially resisted colonial and postcolonial secular schools, regarding them as strategies to force them to sedentarize, and abandon local language and culture. French colonial policies tended to favour the interests of the southern regions and the farming peoples (Fugelstad 1983; Decalo 1996). There have been efforts to correct these regional disparities. Following the Tuareg nationalist/separatist rebellion, the terms of the 1995 Peace Pact have brought more aid organizations into northern regions and efforts to repatriate Tuareg, for example, integrate them into the army and government. Yet there remain problems throughout Niger: of privatization, unemployment, social 'banditry', and sporadic armed conflict between militia and former rebels. In the following sections, I argue that, while it is true that global forces trespass on local worlds, these local worlds also actively resist, re-fashion, and re-interpret global intrusions. The challenge for anthropologists now is to convey these processes in their full complexity. This task requires ethnographic portrayals that retain the depth and intimacy of small-scale community studies, but also address wider forces intruding into the local terrain.

Four ritual powers among the Tuareg

'Evil eye/mouth' (Togerchet)

Togerchet conveys the idea that back-biting gossip, as well as praises from envy or complacency, can wound people and animals. I was often struck by its effect upon ethnographic field research. While I, as anthropologist, continually sought clarification and precision in verbal descriptions, local cultural values often emphasized verbal restraint and caution due to fear of *togerchet*, which appears to outsiders as evasion or vagueness. For example, one is cautious about praises addressed to others' families or animals. Once, when I returned from the home of a sick baby I had treated with an anti-dehydration remedy for diarrhoea, I announced to my field hostess with satisfaction, that the baby was now better. She cautioned me that it is safe to say 'This baby is beautiful', but not 'This baby is healthy', when a baby is cured of an illness, because the latter stimulates *togerchet* and may cause the baby to relapse and die. Friends constantly warned me against revealing my true desires, preferences, and goals. For example, a field assistant explained to me, after we had eaten several dates, that, 'if someone with *togerchet* sees how many date pits you leave and gossips about how much you eat, this gives you a toothache'. Key themes here are envy, desire, proliferation of words, news, and opinions, flaunting of belongings, open eating, and tensions between sharing and hoarding. *Togerchet* has to do with perceived greed and hoarding, not sharing belongings, especially food.

One should be very little inclined to speak about what one does oneself. A hunter who prepares to leave on the hunt does not tell anyone, for if others see him leave and speak to him about it, the success of his hunt will be compromised (Nicolaisen 1961: 134). Once during a visit, conversation turned to my own work in anthropology and ethnography. Suddenly, a friend who had accompanied me stood up, and rather abruptly announced our departure. En route home, he expressed worry that I had begun 'to reveal the secrets of my life' to the woman we had visited. In another incident, while I was photographing a spirit possession ritual, my camera shutter stuck suddenly. I attributed this to the wind and sand, ubiquitous in the Sahara, but several women friends insisted that this was caused by the *togerchet* (or more generally, *awal*, denoting speech in general) emanating from negative gossip by several persons present at the ritual. Although I had requested and received permission to take these photographs, there were some persons there who perhaps coveted this new item of technology, then still considered a luxury, rarer than audio-recorders in the region. Some camera cases, moreover, resembled gun-holsters. They evoked unpleasant memories of attacks when Air villages were caught in the middle of battles between militia, separatist rebels, and 'bandits'.

These incidents and commentaries suggest the importance of verbal restraint: as with men's veiling of the face, nobles, especially, must follow the shadowy detours of indirect speech by allusion, especially in praise. In order to avoid being responsible for misfortunes, when one states an opinion, it is better to cry

'Bismillah', in the name of God or *'Taborak Allah'*, 'May God be blessed', thereby transferring toward the Creator the praise imprudently made to the human being.

Often at stake in *togerchet* warnings are wider concerns with property and success. One smith/artisan man, whom I will call Mounkaila, was born to the west of Agadez in a small nomadic camp, where he began the work of the forge for nobles at an early age. Later on he attended school in Agadez. He was bright and talented, and assisted a French ethnographer in the Agadez region, collaborating on a book. He also continued to manufacture beautiful Tuareg silver jewellery, and went to France to participate in artisan fairs. He was awarded a prize for a necklace he had made. His jewellery became popular with both Tuareg and Europeans, and he established a store in Niamey, the capital city. He also acted as a liaison in arranging for a fashion show to come to Agadez. This was highly publicized in newspapers, where models were photographed wearing ostrich feather costumes for a French fashion magazine. In July 1999, Mounkaila and a business partner came to the United States, visiting New York, Washington, Philadelphia, Atlanta, and Houston, where they stayed in my home as guests. During their visit, they sold their jewellery and their wives' leatherwork at Houston international fairs, import shops, and museums.

When Mounkaila's business partner returned to Houston in April 2000, however, he brought disturbing news. Mounkaila now suffered from a kind of 'mental block', which prevented him from creating jewellery. He also felt depressed, and his work declined. A marabout indicated that Mounkaila was suffering from *togerchet*, activated by the jealousy of some other smiths over his extraordinary success. The marabout made amulets for him from Qur'anic verses, and as of this writing, Mounkaila was feeling better and at work again.

Not solely smiths, but also nobles, may experience *togerchet*, but several highly successful smiths have suffered from particularly acute cases of this recently. *Togerchet* in these contexts appears to be emerging as a counterbalance to smiths' traditional power of *tezma*. In the past, smiths were the ones who were, reputedly at least, poor. As a smith man explained to me in the 1970s, 'I make jewellery for my noble women, but I do not wear it myself; I disdain jewellery. I do not imitate nobles, but (instead) I hover near them, buzzing around like a fly; I am a kind of nobles' journalist.' By contrast, in 1998 a smith employed by a noble to manufacture a wooden well pulley wore an elegant silver-cased amulet around his neck, which the noble pointed out to me disapprovingly. There are hints here that smiths, in order to comment critically upon and mediate between noble social groups, cannot become too much like nobles. But nowadays, increasingly, smiths themselves accumulate property they were once believed to covet from nobles.

Indeed, everyone is vulnerable to *togerchet* under certain circumstances: during transitions, for example, rites of passage, special precautions should be taken. At the name-day held for a third child by a noble man's second wife, a marabout wrote verses from the Qu'ran on a tablet, and the baby's father washed it off for the mother to drink to protect against *togerchet* from anyone there who might be jealous or resentful of the child and/or the mother. It was widely known that this man's first wife had been unhappy over his contracting of the second, polygynous marriage.[8] Significantly, songs at name-days and weddings, settings of joyful praises and admiration, often contain verses repelling *togerchet*. Good fortune and praise are desired, yet dangerous.

Yet there is often no single diagnosis of misfortune. Disagreements reveal considerable overlap between *togerchet* and other forces, for example, (*ark*) *echaghel* or 'bad work' ('sorcery'). One woman of noble origins, married to a retired school supervisor, suddenly fell ill with aches in her ribs and a fever and vomiting. A clinic doctor diagnosed her with high blood pressure and heart problems, and instructed her to get a series of shots. This woman took me aside and in hushed tones complained about additional problems: the *togerchet* gossip of some of her neighbours in the village, in a different descent group (*tawsit*), with whom her own had fought several years earlier. They hinted that her visits to the distant clinic included trysts with a lover. Later, this woman was accused by her husband of an extramarital affair with a smith/artisan man attached to noble families of the old rival *tawsit*. Smith/artisan men are in principle forbidden as husbands or lovers, and permitted only to be friends and confidants of noble women.

Here, the force of *togerchet* targets the breaking of social stratum sexual taboos: illicit sexual relations between noble and smith, in an extramarital liaison. Thus *togerchet* remains, as traditionally, active in cases of greed and ostentatiousness: in the acquisition of too much food, too much wealth, too many wives on the part of men, or too many (or inappropriate) lovers. But in this adultery case, there were new considerations: physical sexual taboos are traditionally intended to channel property in appropriate directions, and to convert reproductive energy into productive property relations. These paths became diverted and reproduction was endangered by becoming detached from productive wealth.

The connections between reproduction, wealth, and changing powers in modernity are also shown in the interplay of *togerchet* with other forces, for example, *echaghel* or sorcery. For example, one couple's marriage was threatened by a pact with the spirits promising wealth. One year, the husband, Ibrahim (pseudonym), obtained a magic for becoming rich. In exchange, he had to slaughter a rooster each Friday, because the magic was a spirit bull that nourished itself with its blood. If he did not do this, he would lose each child his wife, Fatimata (pseudonym), gave birth to. Ibrahim at first followed these instructions, but he eventually neglected to slaughter the rooster, and each time Fatimata gave birth to a child, as predicted, the child died. She sought a marabout's protection against her husband's magic, and the marabout killed this bull with sorcery (*echaghel*). Ibrahim then lost his magic, and Fatimata went crazy. Later he became polygynous. One herbalist Fatimata consulted diagnosed her as suffering from Kel Essuf spirits, *togerchet*, and *tuksi*, a generic category of 'hot' illness in the local counteractive medical system.[9] Fatimata's son-in-law sacrificed an animal in the hope of curing her, and Fatimata also underwent the possession ritual called *tende n goumaten*, whose possessing spirits are believed to be inherited matrilineally, transmitted through the mother's milk.[10] Many local men explained this family's misfortunes differently: they indicated that 'some women in that family have difficulty marrying because they cause men's herds to die'.

These disputes over power, causation, and agency address changing connections between wealth and reproduction. Husbands and wives are caught in conflicts over ambiguous property ownership in recent sedentarization and men's migrant labour. Over approximately the past seventy years, drought, colonial French and postcolonial Niger government policies, and aid 'development' programmes have pressured many Air Tuareg to settle down, and practise oasis gardening more intensively. Many men have been constructing adobe mud houses, which they own, next-door to their wives' tents, and try to bring wives to reside near husbands' kin while husbands are absent on long-term new travel. (Whereas in the past, many men felt wives were better off near their own kin while men went on the traditional caravan trade 5–6 months a year.) Many men have also constructed adobe houses. In more sedentarized communities, many men at first reside in their wife's nuptial tent near her parents, according to traditional custom, but later attempt to bring wives with them, preferably far from wives' parents' compound. Although Tuareg women retain the tent, and the right to eject the husband upon divorce, with these houses, men no longer fear being homeless.

There are additional marriage-related tensions. Polygyny, while still not prevalent among most Tuareg men, is becoming more common in semi-sedentarized communities among some chiefs, marabouts, prosperous gardeners, and merchants. Motives include men's seeking of new, wider political and economic alliances and different homes in their diverse places of work, and sometimes, also, younger wives to bear more children to assist with gardening tasks (Rasmussen 1997). Most gardens are owned by men; whereas women and men both traditionally own livestock animals. Many women now feel greater pressure to bear more children men insist they need in greater numbers, to assist with oasis gardening. Whereas by contrast, in the old, more pastoral nomadic economy, births were spaced: it was shameful to have another child when the youngest child was under 3 years old. Now, many women fear their husband will become polygynous unless they fulfil these increased demands of fertility. Female herbalists believe many fertility problems and birth defects are caused by a mother's anger while pregnant (*tourgoum*). Other women believe that Kel Essuf spirits may prevent children or cause their deaths. By contrast, in many male marabouts' viewpoint, 'only God does these things', or as some men say, 'Some women themselves (in matrilineal transmission), pass down certain misfortunes'. Thus more children now signify greater wealth, whereas in the past, more livestock herds – including some herds passed matrilineally through women – provided greater wealth and security for women. These forms of women's wealth, called *akhu huderan* ('living milk' property), in effect become symbolically inverted, and converted by some men in their comments regarding 'dangerous' women, into 'misfortunes for men'. Moreover, many postcolonial state legal arrangements now tend to position women as wards of men. For example, postal addresses in Niger refer to women as 'Madame + name of husband', school and clinic records refer to women with the surnames of their father, and houses are registered in the names of husbands.[11]

Ibrahim's new source of wealth, won and then lost, brings to light additional connections between witchcraft accusations, wealth, and sharing. Ibrahim, Fatimata's husband, was supposed to give offerings to his tutelary spirit, but he reneged on this obligation. Spirit pacts should be used to benefit others, not solely to enrich the individual. *Togerchet* is associated with pollution in food, sex, and medicine that threatens bodily and social boundaries, but these are not static or fixed. Moreover, *togerchet* and the more smith-specific power of *tezma* were traditionally somewhat complementary to each other, counterbalancing and reinforcing ideally reciprocal social relations between nobles and smiths. Now *togerchet* power increasingly expresses the newly problematic boundaries – of gender and social stratum and newly emergent class relations within and beyond the household – in the changing moral and social system: namely, boundaries between technologies of good and evil (e.g. cameras can resemble guns); between persons (nobles and smiths, husbands and wives, and members of different descent groups), as well as between substances (spirit pacts and Qur'anic verses may be either protective, or become poisons or burdens).

Smiths' mystic powers (tezma)

Tezma attacks a region of the stomach through the orifices, and is manifested by a swelling of the stomach, often fatal among children and animals. While evil mouth or eye comes from conscious envy or desire, the force of *tezma* comes from a smith, allegedly unconsciously, in automatic punishment if one does not give one's surplus or justly compensate for services rendered. Nonetheless, smiths are blamed (Nicolaisen 1961: 136). In the countryside, smiths may still ask for or merely see something they wish for, even outside ritual and technical work situations, and nobles should give to smiths. Violence against smiths is traditionally rare because they are a protected people, nobles' fictive cousins, against whom it is not appropriate to express anger without denigrating oneself (Rasmussen 1992). Recently, however, there are signs of increasing social tensions between some nobles and smiths. While some nobles and smiths are becoming business partners, many are rivals in an economic system where rewards are scarce, and some nobles view smiths' work for tourists as a distraction from their traditional duties toward nobles (Rasmussen 1998). Accusations of sexual transgressions and pollution appear as a kind of metonymy for other concerns. As shown in the case of alleged adultery between the noble woman and the smith man, alleged sexual offences figure in many of these tensions. In another incident, a smith man was accused of starting a ring of prostitution, and of engaging a young noble women in this for his own profit, in one rural community. Local residents reported that such organized prostitution had never existed in the countryside before, only in the towns. Outraged, they flogged him, and ejected him from the community.

Thus there is a changing political economy of wealth and of perceptions of value. Some smiths are apparently sexually successful (or feared to become so) with the wives and daughters of their traditional noble patrons, now that the former have greater access to wealth by selling jewellery to tourists and are no longer so dependent upon noble patronage. But how do smiths themselves view this *tezma* power and its extensions into current conflicts? Two elderly smiths I questioned explained, 'there is a verse of the Qur'an that cures illness caused by *tezma*, which marabouts can read'. Many also indicated that, related to belief in *tezma* is smiths' lack of reserve; the reason for this is 'so that they may accept compensation (remuneration) from nobles for their work, and therefore smiths and nobles must be kept separate. Smiths need this protection, in order to practise their work and receive compensation.' *Tezma*, in other words, comes from smiths' ideal lack of reserve in feeling free to ask nobles for goods, and from nobles' ideal reserve and hesitation to ask for something because of values emphasizing dignity and indirect speech as crucial to noble identity; it in effect validates client–patron roles and relationships. But these values are now more difficult for both parties to maintain, when many nobles find themselves in need, and many smiths are finding a new economic niche. Indeed, on rare occasions, nobles allegedly activate *tezma*, and this is believed stronger than that of smiths. According to two elderly smith men, however, 'With some people, [smiths'] *tezma* is so strong a belief, that if a smith comes even for a short time, if he leaves (without doing anything), they are going to say that he did *tezma*'.

One smith woman apparently experienced this 'self-fulfilling prophecy' when she was accused of *tezma* by one of her noble patron woman's daughters, who fell ill after the smith woman had asked for and been refused sugar at this household. The smith woman cried and vehemently denied this, but her client–patron relationship with this family was broken. The breakdown was somewhat disadvantageous for this smith woman, for several reasons. Most smith women have fewer alternative sources of income or customers than smith men in the new tourist trade, where there is greater demand for men's silver and gold jewellery than women's leatherwork. Although this woman was a popular praise-singer, an important role in the countryside, she was somewhat more impoverished than some other smiths. Furthermore, rather than marrying a close cousin according to the usual smith custom, this woman had married a former slave man. Although the couple were now divorced, marriage to a former slave is less stigmatized than in the past, and divorce does not bring any stigma to women, this smith woman had also broken a sexual taboo: she had two illegitimate children, disapproved of in Tuareg society despite tolerance of some pre-marital affairs. Thus this woman's alleged *tezma* seems to have been reinforced by her more general marginality in the community at a time of heightened tensions, when some search for scapegoats.

Figure 7.1 Herbal medicine woman divining to diagnose *tezma*-induced illness. (Photo by S. Rasmussen.)

I was frequently warned about smiths' alleged *tezma*, and advised to comply with their requests. On one occasion, my hosts surmised that I caught *tezma* from a smith man who was reputed to have particularly strong powers, in a puzzlingly violent but brief cold and fever I had suffered while I was staying in his village (see Figure 7.1). I had experienced an intense night sweat and smelled an odd odour, but these had vanished suddenly overnight. My hosts explained that, because I gave him food belatedly after he came by, the *tezma* had suddenly left me. Another friend believed this *tezma* was cast upon me by another, elderly smith man who had requested eye ointment from me, but whom I had to refuse reluctantly because I had left the remedy behind, in a distant village. Expatriates are replacing nobles in some contexts, in local client–patron relationships (Rasmussen 1998). Indeed, some Tuareg artisans in Niamey, the capital city, are now working for French entrepreneurs in artisan workshops. Relevant here are wider policies of the World Bank and the International Monetary Fund in Africa, which have imposed austerity measures and pressured the Niger economy toward privatization. While ostensibly 'cost-cutting', these measures have actually created unemployment, delay of salaries, devaluation of local currency (the West African CFA) by 50 per cent, and caused shortages of medicines (Rasmussen 2001). These conditions, as well as the intermittent violence of armed conflicts in the northern region, have forced men into more distant and prolonged migrant labour than previous travel (caravans, raids) required. Formerly, members of the social strata and the different age groups were seen as bound to each other by mutual rights and obligations, and, ideally, could rely on each others' protective, rather than destructive powers. Disputed interpretations and changing outcomes of *tezma* accusations reflect upheavals in these relationships.

'Bad work' or 'sorcery' (ark echaghel)

Ark echaghel, or what some ethnographers call 'black magic' (Nicolaisen 1961: 137), is considered a terrible force, sufficient to kill even from a distance. Some outsiders are believed to have this malevolent power, for example, some families of Tubu origins, called Ikarkawen, former slaves of the Kel Geres con-federation of Tuareg, are believed to cause and cure this. *Echaghel* is thus attributed to persons slightly more distant than the perpetrators of *togerchet* or *tezma*. *Echaghel* activation, however, requires the services of an expert, who knows the principal ingredients and methods of administration. The base ingredients are either fed to the intended victim, or thrown on the ground where he/she will tread. *Al baraka* can also come hand-in-hand with *echaghel*, and their boundaries – as friend and foe of the afflicted person – are by no means clearly demarcated. Thus social ties may be either affirmed or betrayed by this same power.

One smith/artisan man, whom I'll call Tafa, had been married for several years to a close cousin who resided in a neighbouring village where the couple resided uxorilocally. Tafa had been ill for three years with a stomach ache (one symptom of either *togerchet, tezma,* or sorcery – depending upon the context and diagnosis), body aches, 'craziness' apparently resembling our own notion of 'panic attacks', and also alleged spirit problems 'of the head'. Various diagnos-ticians disagreed, however, on the relative severity and primacy of these afflictions as causes of his malaise. Tafa initially saw marabouts, who diagnosed through Qur'anic divination a case of possessing spirits, but did not cure him. Tafa next saw a famous elderly female herbalist. She thought his mind was 'touched'. Also, she diagnosed him as having a 'hot' (inflammatory) illness called *tuksi*. This, she said, came about when he ingested too much marabout vegetal ink medicine, but she conceded that he also had spirits called *eljenan*. Tafa's most prominent symptom was fear. The herbalist said this meant he was also the victim of sorcery: she diagnosed this when she touched his head, which had become diminished. This also caused him to be restless. The herbalist commented that 'It is necessary to do marabout medicine in stages, gradually, not too fast; and also, one needs to trust a single marabout in this'. Tafa finally saw a male non-Qur'anic diviner called a *boka*. Tafa credited both the *boka* and the herbalist with having cured him, but the diviner insisted that he had chased his spirits away. The diviner divined with cowry shells, and said that a black spirit had struck Tafa on his way walking home, causing his feet to become heavy and making him collapse to his knees. In order to reinforce the cure for this, people must neither greet nor ask about the patient for fourteen days of the cure, from fear of *togerchet*.

Several months prior to his symptoms, Tafa had unwittingly accepted stolen goods from thieves from Mount Bagzan, and sold them in his store in his natal village. He had experienced some trouble with the police afterward. But the *boka* reassured him that all this was not his fault. He stated: 'Spirits can attack at random, like a thief; they can ask something of someone and kill him. You did not do anything bad to bring on your illness, you merely encountered a spirit at random, like a thief. For example, if goats go into the wild, the jackal can catch any goat by chance.' After fourteen days of treatment with the *boka*'s tree medicines, Tafa felt better, but still rested at the home of a male cousin and avoided his store which, since his illness, had been closed. Tafa had begun studying maraboutage, but did not yet practise it, although he had ambitions in this specialty and wrote verses at home. He and his wife had not yet become independent or moved away from this uxorilocal residence.[12] Tafa's economic situation was thus rather precarious. Professional rivalry over Qur'anic study may also enter into this case. There were hints that Tafa had overextended himself in Qur'anic studies and perhaps, attempted to claim too much competence for someone at his level of study. One prominent marabout in the region indicated to me that 'a truly great marabout should not seek glory; he is ideally a magnet for, or reflection of God'. There is often competition among holy men for followings (Gellner 1969), and concentrations of *al baraka* may be thereby converted into accusations of sorcery.

In this case, therefore, the sources of illness and cure and their boundaries are in dispute. There are hints that Qur'anic medicine can itself become poison or illness, if improperly used. Perhaps there was rivalry over the practice of maraboutism involving Tafa, or perhaps his potential for developing *al baraka* became polluted by his great ambition or his contact (however inadvertent) with the thieves, causing him much psycho-social stress. In the currently uncertain politics of the semi-autonomous northern region and more general unemployment and breakdown of security throughout Niger, some former fighters in the Tuareg Rebellion and other disaffected youths have turned to 'social banditry'. As with the boundaries of social agents, the boundaries of ritual powers and their agents are not clear-cut (Rasmussen 2001).

Highlighted in the foregoing material are connections between sorcery and Islamic scholars/marabouts. For sorcery to have a truly successful, fatal effect, the help of a marabout is imperative (Nicolaisen 1961: 137). Also required is the use of written, not solely oral words, in the form of curses drawn from verses of the Qur'an, or formulas of incantation drawn from Arabic manuals on magic. Thus *al baraka* is not always rigidly opposed to *echaghel*, and the targets, agents, and interpretations of these powers are being re-formulated in current political and economic upheavals. A marabout can practise sorcery either in order to avenge himself against someone, or upon demand from a third party. One friend in Agadez related to me an incident involving a noble man who was a renowned dancer in a cultural exchange troupe due to go to France for a performance. But this man loved the same woman a marabout loved. The marabout became jealous of him, so he activated a form of *echaghel* that caused his teeth to sink into his leg and wound it, and thus he was debilitated and could not go to perform with the dance troupe in France. Marabouts, ideally benevolent, nonetheless occupy a curious position among the Tuareg. Since medieval Tuareg nobles initially resisted Islam and valued valour in war, some compromise was necessary in the social system: the only sacerdotal class was confronted by moral dilemmas, and had to provide standards to transform a warlike society (Norris 1975: 20–21). Today in Air, marabouts are generally honoured for their wisdom and their *al baraka*, but also feared for their capability of using their knowledge in sorcery, or in other unexpected ways. Hence the ambiguity and indeterminacy of marabouts' *al baraka* power.

Marabouts' Islamic blessing or benediction (al baraka)

That life force, blessing, and benediction called *al baraka*, believed to be concentrated in prominent marabouts and chiefs, is therefore complex. Norris (1990: 167) defines *(al)baraka* as 'a divine blessing or grace bestowed upon Sufis in holy places, in their communal meals, in prayer from a specific and revered Shaykh, and also from the discarded *khirqa* (ritual Sufi) mantle'. The *icherifan* nobles who claim descent from the Prophet seek to establish a rapport with the force of *al baraka* and the chief of the clan also has this. Traditionally, there exists a connection between the responsibility of chiefs concerning the fertility of the country and their relation to *al baraka*. This applies particularly to the Sultan of Air, the Amenokal in Agadez who, it is said, keeps bones of his ancestors as amulets. Everything that is living, that grows, that is good, contains some *al baraka* (Nicolaisen 1961; Rasmussen 1991).

Even prestigious marabouts and *icherifan* who possess *al baraka*, are still supposed to be obedient and modest, as servants of those they heal. Marabouts manufacture many amulets to protect against thieves: for example, one was on the wall of an adobe house in the compound of my host family. It came from Nigeria, and was believed to cause a thief to lose his way. All these amulets are made from forms of Qur'anic divination, done only for people the marabout knows well, kin or like kin (see Figures 7.2 and 7.3). One marabout asked me if I wasn't afraid of local malevolent powers, and offered to make amulets for me. Ideally, therefore, 'good' marabouts make use of their *al baraka* as guardians of the local, 'home' cultural terrain. At night, marabouts' tombs with *al baraka* are believed to become dangerous with evil spirits and attack passers-by without protective metal, e.g. swords. Perhaps this belief is intended to discourage certain forms of anti-social behaviour, for example, the breaking of sexual taboos (couples may fear having trysts there), or perhaps, it may discourage outsiders from wandering about the local terrain. But now this terrain is disputed and often invaded. For example, one local chief and marabout forbade the cutting down of trees in a forest on Mount Bagzan, intending to benefit the local populations ultimately in preventing erosion, but some local herders resented this restriction, identifying it with a government agency called *Eaux et Forets* (Waters and Forests).

Figure 7.2 A marabout man working with verses which he will insert into an amulet. (Photo by S. Rasmussen.)

As guardians of sacred places in times of economic and ecological crisis, some marabouts take a stand against what they view as dubious benefits of central state edicts, international aid programmes, and tourism agencies intruding into Air. Following Niger's independence, during difficult years of drought, some marabouts' powers to bring rain were marshalled, but also threatened. When an aid agency installed rain gauges one rainy season on the plateau summit of Mount Bagzan, the rains did not fall as expected. Local marabouts insisted that it was these rain gauges that were causing the drought, by preventing the rain from falling. This veiled their fear of some political competition of outside influences from these postcolonial central state authorities, in the form of technical aid. There was a conflict of modernities here: in effect, the marabouts sensed the competition for technological control, and possibly also for political power from the aid agency, despite the general welcoming of some of its benefits.

Perhaps in response to such fears, some marabouts are rumoured to bury 'bad' sorcery amulets underground along some routes, to deter outsiders from entering the area. This was vividly shown during a dispute over when to begin to celebrate Biannu, a celebration of renewal for the coming year. Its date of onset is calculated by the lunar calendar, as are other Islamic holidays. One begins to celebrate it upon confirmation, by marabouts, on their sighting of the moon. During the regime of Seyni Kountche (1974–1987), the then-president of Niger declared that it was time to celebrate the holiday, that the moon had come. The leader of the Air marabouts, however, disagreed, and refused to follow the central

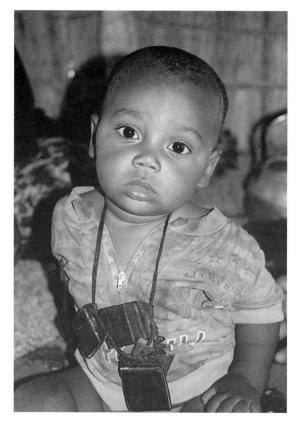

Figure 7.3 A child wearing special amulets which protect it against malevolent forces. (Photo by S. Rasmussen.)

government's declaration. Kountche sent several functionaries as representatives into the region to initiate the celebration, but each time a car set out, there was an accident and fatalities. Local residents insisted that this calamity was caused by the prominent marabout's *al baraka* against Kountche. Subsequently, the marabout declared the sighting of the moon, thereby overriding, allegedly at least, the late president's declaration of when to start Biannu celebrations.

These beliefs and incidents illustrate the transformations, but also continuities, in marabouts' *al baraka* powers during tensions between the northern Air region and Niamey, the capital, the seat of central state and international aid agency hegemonies. Marabouts, despite their traditional pacific roles, cannot avoid becoming involved in political debates over the effects of aid policies. Inter-mittently, their *al baraka* is drawn outward, and channelled into more contentious, outside upheavals, if not in 'fact', at least in *ex post facto* interpretations.

Some marabouts are rumoured to manufacture amulets protecting against bullets in the intermittent armed conflicts between some Tuareg separatists and government militia. During the rebellion, militia arrested some marabouts they suspected of sympathizing with and 'stirring up' rebels. One marabout, highly esteemed for his amulets believed to protect rebels from militia bullets, had two sons who nonetheless obtained guns from a rebel front, and at first they resisted the efforts after the Peace Pact to disarm. But many people believe that the (now former) rebel leaders, especially Rhissa Boula, have powerful maraboutique protection against bullets. Following the Peace Pact, interestingly, the government appointed Rhissa Boula, formerly a rebel leader, as a minister. To some extent, this appointment was one measure fulfilling the terms of the Peace Pact: to integrate more Tuareg (heretofore minorities underrepresented in the national infrastructure) into the militia and government and university. On another more unspoken, yet equally powerful, level, however, this leader's alleged protection by the *al baraka*-saturated amulets of prominent Air marabouts was also, surely, taken very seriously. Marabouts now publicly bless the political rallies of the Amana party, popular in the northern town of Agadez.

Some marabouts are drawn into religious sectarian conflicts. Izala, an Islamic puritanical-reformist sect, has gained some ground in Niger. There have been several shootings in Agadez between marabouts recently. In August 1995, a marabout in Agadez was killed in an armed robbery. Prior to this, there were only rarely attacks on marabouts, ideally men of peace who, like smith/artisans, traditionally must not be the victims of aggression. Thus marabouts play roles in new forms of political economy, based upon longstanding and transformed ideas about power and social relations.

Conclusions: the interplay of ritual powers and social agency

Beliefs about alleged mystical powers reveal alternately competing, aligned, opposed, complementary, and overlapping social agents in different contexts. Even before recent upheavals and turmoil, the holders of ritual powers have often inverted the popular images of their powers (Rasmussen 1989, 1992). In some contexts, marabouts' powers are transformed into sorcery, particularly in political resistance to outside intruders viewed as infidels. Smiths' powers, despite their alleged danger, can also sometimes confer protection from spirits, for example, converting natural into cultural substances such as metals. Marabouts' power, traditionally that of figurehead who pronounces the will of official authority, addresses wider political concerns of the breakdown of authority. Smiths also still have access to indirect power, through their control of unofficial negotiations surrounding marriage and their roles as political go-betweens and, increasingly today, also access to material wealth, whereas many nobles are becoming marginalized in the economic infrastructure. Yet the relationship between danger and opportunity is ambiguous. *Tezma* now has the added dimension of sexual pollution, and sometimes reverts back against the accused smith perpetrator, rather than acting to his/her advantage as purely an economic levelling device, as in the past. Smith/artisans are becoming more victims of this themselves; rather than a source of control over nobles, it appears to be converting into a source of danger for smiths (in more violent retaliation). Furthermore, as shown, some highly successful smiths are frequently afflicted with *togerchet*, suggesting their loss of status as a traditionally protected people. *Al baraka* is becoming more politicized in nation-state level violence, and also converted more easily into *ark echaghel* to protect local cultural autonomy interests. Yet the interpretation of *al baraka* appears to remain largely in marabouts' control; even cases of its conversion into alleged *ark echaghel* are not always viewed as anti-social, provided they are perceived as benefiting the community as a whole. On the other hand, when *echaghel* (or even *al baraka*) is associated with selfish, individual gain, as in corruption of a spirit pact or contamination by theft, it is believed to have dire consequences – in effect, 'blocking' fertility of women, decimating livestock, and ruining business.

More broadly, the four types of ritual powers among the Tuareg offer insights into processes of resistance and accommodation to historically momentous trends in institution building. The Tuareg data suggest ways of investing more complex meanings to cultural forms assumed to be generated by responses to capitalism (Taussig 1980; Willis 1981). Here, cultural forms arise from class positions in an institutional order that is changing, but not in neatly predictable or unilinear fashion. Clifford and Marcus (1986: 178) correctly observe that there has been some anthropological bias toward emphasizing 'pre-capitalist' dimensions of lives of ethnographic subjects. On the other hand, in my view there is also an equally problematic modernist bias in assuming that trans-nationalism and capitalism take the same form everywhere. Local cultural beliefs and political economy continually inform each other, and small-scale community studies add richness and depth to multi-sited ethnographies. Local narratives of ritual power, agency, and causation show local residents' creativity in the face of global changes. Yet local residents, in invoking these powers, are not acting solely in response to modernist schemes. The effects of these changes are very uneven, and bring to light inconsistencies of 'modernist' schemes. From this perspective, 'global culture' is a misnomer; there are only 'global cultures', in the plural.

Notes

1   This article is based on research between 1974 and 1998 among the Tuareg in the Republic of Niger, West Africa on spirit possession, ageing and the life course, herbal and diviner healing specialists, and comparison of rural and urban smith/artisans, supported by Fulbright Hays; the Wenner-Gren Foundation for Anthropological Research; the Social Science Research Council; National Geographic; Indiana University Grant-in-Aid; and University of Houston Limited Grant-in-Aid.

2   From the early 1980s, the World Bank and International Monetary Fund policies of 'restructuring' have been applied to many African countries, including Niger. These involve enforcing western-based concepts of free market conditions and loan repayment, including for example, privatization, 'democratization' and curtailing of

previous, more socialistic policies of some African governments of central planning and subsidies (see Sanders, Chapter 8). In Niger and elsewhere, many health-care benefits have been cut, there is widespread unemployment, and the poor have suffered most from these measures (Ndegwa and Stryker 1995). Additionally, Niger has been hard-hit by droughts (in 1969–1973, 1984, and 2000), and regional and 'ethnic' conflicts.

3 From 1990 to 1995, some Tuareg groups in the northern regions of Niger and Mali were embroiled in a nationalist/separatist armed conflict against the central governments of these countries. In April 1995, a Peace Pact was signed in Ouagadougou, Burkina Faso, but there have been numerous factions and sporadic military confrontations in some regions. Some former fighters have been integrated into the national infrastructure, for example, the army, but others have turned to 'banditry' from the combined effects of political turmoil and economic structural adjustments in Niger. Until recently, there were significant discrepancies in colonial and postcolonial 'development' policies in different regions of these countries, and while these often translated into 'ethnic' conflicts, in my view they are largely regionally based. From French colonial to recent times, diverse populations in the northern regions have lacked access to health care, education, and jobs. On the other hand, some Tuareg in the south of Niger have become more integrated into local Hausa and Zarma-Songhay societies; and not all Tuareg, even in the north, supported the rebellion. See Bourgeot 1994, Charlick 1991, Claudot-Hawad 1993, and Rasmussen 2001.

4 In pre-colonial Tuareg social organization, more nomadic nobles controlled the caravan trade and owned most weapons and large livestock. They had rights to tribute from servile groups in oases, as well as to domestic, herding, and gardening labour of newly-acquired slaves (*iklan*). Despite official social stratum endogamy, in some Tuareg groups nobles and former slaves have long intermarried. Some vestiges of traditional practices persisted even into the early 1980s, well after French manumission of slaves in the early twentieth century and official abolition of slavery at Niger's independence in 1960. By the mid-1990s, however, most of these privileges had completely broken down. More nomadic nobles (*imajeghen*) and more sedentarized oasis populations descending from servile and client groups (*ighawalen*) now trade, rather than practise traditional tribute (*tiwse*). Many leaders of the five-year rebellion and current cultural revitalization discourage emphasis upon traditional social origins, and encourage unity of all Tuareg, based upon common Tamajaq language (see Keenan 1977; Bernus 1981; Claudot-Hawad 1993; Nicolaisen and Nicolaisen 1997; Rasmussen 2001).

5 Tuareg vary in devotion to Islam. In some groups, particularly around Mount Bagzan in the Air, there are numerous clans of influential and respected Islamic scholars (*ineslemen*), and the more revered *icherifan*, who claim descent from the Prophet and are believed to have special blessing and healing powers (Norris 1975, 1990). In Niamey and the large towns, secular courts predominate, and in the countryside local councils of marabouts and elders adjudicate disputes according to Qur'anic law (*Sharia*), and local cultural interpretation, and recently, also, former rebel/peacekeeping forces participate in this. Currently in Niger there is some resurgence of Muslim puritanical/reform movements such as the Izala sect, from Nigeria and Sudan. This sect is particularly prominent in the towns and among the Hausa, although official Sharia law has not been declared nationally in Niger as of this writing. It is difficult to predict future Islamic reform influence in Niger (see Gregoire 1993).

6 In the pre-colonial political system, chiefs from noble descent groups elected an *amenukal* or sultan of their regional confederation. At the local level, councils of elders, chiefs, and marabouts adjudicated disputes. Beginning early in the twentieth

century under French colonialism, nomadic camps' political organization became more sedentarized and village-based. Some more paramount chiefs' powers were strengthened, reinforced by coercive force from the central government. Other chiefs' powers were curtailed, in allegiance to central state laws (Claudot-Hawad 1993). Traditionally, chiefs ruled by respect, not coercion, and have also depended upon belief in their *al baraka* power to rule. Recently, however, this power has been eroded for some, but also, as shown, reinforced for others. During the Tuareg rebellion, some traditional chiefs were killed and some elders were disobeyed, or at least their authority and decisions were questioned by many youths. Some fighters and 'bandits' in the turmoil in the north reportedly defied older leaders' attempts to enforce traditional warrior codes of dignified and honourable conduct: for example, important taboos against raping women and against harming those who do not resist raids. In the past, many Agadez festivals on holy days and national holidays took place in the Sultans' Palace courtyard, a place believed saturated with his *al baraka*. But since these conflicts, many festivals have shifted to the *Maison des Jeunes* (Youth House). Thus *al baraka*'s protection of self and others in some contexts remains effective, but in others, is breaking down.

7 Each noble family in the countryside still officially inherits a family of smith/artisans (*inaden*) as attached clients, and continues to rely upon them in rituals, hair-styling, and manufacture of jewellery and tools, and to some extent still, in marriage negotiations. Nobles traditionally owe their inherited smiths special meat parts of the slaughtered animal (*izouza*) at rites of passage; a portion of caravan trade millet; and sugar, tea, millet, and cash during smiths' praise-singing. Nowadays, there is greater flexibility in these arrangements: each individual noble can choose a personal smith on the basis of rapport or work preference for tools and jewellery. In the town of Agadez, these relationships have broken down further, where many smiths have inherited patron families still in rural areas, for whom some Agadez smiths now rarely work. Many Tuareg of diverse social origins hint of misuse of powers by both smiths and marabouts. Some local residents say cryptically that 'smiths give injections to women'. But many Tuareg agree that ideally, 'If a person is honest, he/she does not fight with a smith, because a noble does not fight with someone beneath them'. Traditionally, nobles regard smiths are 'next to slaves' or similar to slaves. Smiths themselves emphasize their difference from slaves. According to one elderly smith leader in a rural village, 'smiths are more important than slaves; slaves were bought; a slave cannot, in tradition, inherit a smith'. But following the manumission of slaves in Air oases, a few former slaves did, in fact, inherit smith client families. Smith status is therefore complex. They are also compared to women, who traditionally, among Tuareg, enjoy high status and prestige and economic independence, and to cousins; the latter share a joking relationship. Smiths are also identified with spirits: specifically, fire *djinn*, who work on tiny forges underground and play tricks on travellers (Nicolaisen 1961; Nicolaisen and Nicolaisen 1997; Saenz 1991; Rasmussen 1992, 1998).

8 While women sometimes divorce men who become polygynous, some couples remain together for their children's sake. Many more prosperous and prominent men (chiefs and Islamic scholars) in more sedentarized communities are acquiring second, and even third, wives (up to four are permitted by Islam). Many ethnographers agree that in general, Tuareg women have enjoyed traditionally high prestige and independent socioeconomic status. Women build and own the tent, are not secluded, may request divorce, and are not compelled to wear a veil. Rather, it is Tuareg men who wear a face-veil, a sign of modesty, reserve, and respect. Most Air Tuareg today practise bilateral descent, inheritance, and succession. There are vestiges of ancient matrilineal institutions, such as those forms of property called *akhu huderan* or 'living milk' property (herds, date palms) that can be transmitted only to sisters, daughters, or

nieces, sometimes referred to in English as 'endowments' (Worley 1991). Many Tuareg trace their early descent to a female founding ancestress, although in some groups, notably those with many influential clans of Islamic scholar/marabouts, men tend to highlight male and marabout founders. There have also been many recent upheavals in which women's rights are disputed. See Rasmussen 1995, 1997, 1998; Claudot-Hawad 1993; and Nicolaisen and Nicolaisen 1997.

9 This *tuksi*, 'hot' category of illnesses, opposed to the generic category of 'cold' illnesses (*tesmut*), is part of the more general counteractive local disease classification and healing system, which is similar to Moorish and Latin American systems. 'Hot' illnesses tend to refer to stomach and liver-related ailments, usually caused by exposure to 'hot' foods and other hot things like the sun and heated sand, and can also refer to anger and other imbalances from sources ranging from psycho-social to dietary, and thus includes many non-organic, as well as organic, illnesses. Its opposite, *tesmut*, refers to afflictions caused by cold, but this is likewise, extended metaphorically to include a whole range of problems, for example, many STDs and urinary tract infections. Ideally, women are 'cool' and men 'hot' (Figueredo, personal communication, Aix-en-Provence, France 2000; Rasmussen 2001; cf. Sanders 2000).

10 See Rasmussen 1995 on Tuareg spirit possession rituals, in which women predominantly, though not exclusively, participate in trance possession. Matrilineal imagery is apparent here and pervasive throughout many Tuareg healing rites (possession and herbalism, in particular). There is reference, for example, to the *akhu huderan* living milk property inheritance (n. 8).

11 The state has been frequently deleterious for nomadic women as households are forced to settle. See, for example, O'Kelly and Carney 1986 and Oxby 1977.

12 Usually, newly-married couples spend the first two or three years in uxorilocal post-marital residence, until the groom has completed bridewealth payments and work for his parents-in-law, in particular, until he has 'pleased' his mother-in-law and she permits the couple to decide where to live and her daughter detaches her own animals from her mother's herds. Many men attempt to bring wives to reside nearer their own relatives and/or place of work, which is sometimes a source of marital conflict (Claudot-Hawad 1993; Rasmussen 1997).

Bibliography

Beidelman, T.O. (1971) 'Nuer priests and prophets: charisma, authority, and power among the Nuer', in T.O. Beidelman (ed.) *The Translation of Cultures: Essays to E.E. Evans-Pritchard*, London: Tavistock.

—— (1993) *Moral Imagination in Kaguru Modes of Thought*, Washington DC: Smithsonian Institution Press.

Bernus, E. (1981) *Les Touaregs Nigeriens: Unite Culturelle et Diversite Regionale d'un Peuple Pasteur*, Paris: Office de la Recherche scientifique et technique d'outre-mer.

Bongmba, E. (1998) 'Toward a hermeneutic of Wimbum Tfu', *African Studies Review* 41, 3: 165–193.

Bourgeot, A. (1994) 'Revoltes et rebellions en pays touareg', *Afrique Contemporaine* 70: 3–19.

Casajus, D. (1987) *La Tente dans l'Essuf*, Cambridge: University Press.

—— (2000) *Gens de Parole: Langage, Poesie et Politique en Pays Touareg*, Paris: Editions la decouverte textes a l'appui/anthropologie.

Charlick, R. (1991) *Niger: Personal Rule and Survival in the Sahel*, Boulder: Westview Press.

Ciekawy, D. and Geschiere, P. (1998) 'Containing witchcraft: conflicting scenarios in postcolonial Africa', *African Studies Review* 41, 3: 1–15.

Claudot-Hawad, H. (1993) *Touareg: Portrait en Fragments*, Aix-en-Provence: Edisud.

Clifford, J. and Marcus, G.E. (1986) *Writing Culture: The Poetics and Politics of Ethnography*, Berkeley: University of California Press.

Comaroff, J. and Comaroff, J.L. (eds) (1993) *Modernity and its Malcontents: Ritual and Power in Postcolonial Africa*, Chicago: University of Chicago Press.

—— (1999) 'Occult economies and the violence of abstraction: notes from the South African postcolony', *American Ethnologist* 26, 2: 279–303.

Crick, M. (1976) 'Recasting witchcraft', in M. Crick (ed.) *Explorations in Language and Meaning*, New York: John Wiley and Sons.

Decalo, S. (1996) *Historical Dictionary of Niger*, Lanham, MD: The Scarecrow Press.

Douglas, M. (1966) *Purity and Danger*, London: Routledge and Kegan Paul.

—— (1992) *Risk and Culture*, London: Routledge.

Englund, H. (1996) 'Witchcraft, modernity and the person: the morality of accumulation in Central Malawi', *Critique of Anthropology* 16, 3: 257–279.

Englund, H. and Leach, J. (2000) 'Ethnography and the meta-narratives of modernity', *Current Anthropology* 41, 2: 225–239.

Ferguson, J. (1999) *Expectations of Modernity: Myths and Meanings of Urban Life on the Zambian Copperbelt*, Berkeley: University of California Press.

Fugelstad, F. (1983) *A History of Niger 1850–1960*, Cambridge: University Press.

Gellner, E. (1969) *Saints of the Atlas*, London: Weidenfeld and Nicholson.

Geschiere, P. (1997) *The Modernity of Witchcraft: Politics and the Occult in Postcolonial Africa*, Charlottesville: University Press of Virginia.

Gregoire, E. (1993) 'Islam and the identity of merchants in Maradi (Niger)', in L. Brenner (ed.) *Muslim Identity and Social Change in Sub-Saharan Africa*, Bloomington: Indiana University Press.

Hutchinson, S.E. (1996) *Nuer Dilemmas: Coping with Money, War, and the State*, Berkeley: University of California Press.

Keenan, J. (1977) *Tuareg: People of Ahaggar*, London: Allen Lane.

Martin, P. and O'Meara, P. (eds) (1995) *Africa* (3rd edn), Bloomington: Indiana University Press.

Masquelier, A. (1999) 'Money and serpents, their remedy is killing: the pathology of consumption in southern Niger', *Research in Economic Anthropology* 20, 97–115.

Middleton, J. (1960) *Lugbara Religion*, London: Oxford University Press.

Ndegwa, S. and Stryker, R. (1995) 'The African development crisis', in P. Martin and P. O'Meara (eds) *Africa* (3rd edn), Bloomington: Indiana University Press.

Nicolaisen, J. (1961) 'Essai sur la religion et la magie touaregues', *Folk* 3, 113–162.

Nicolaisen, J. and Nicolaisen, I. (1997) *The Pastoral Tuareg*, vols 1 and 2, London: Thames and Hudson, Rhodes International Science and Art Publishers.

Norris, H.T. (1975) *The Tuareg: Their Islamic Legacy and its Diffusion in the Sahel*, London: Fryson.

—— (1990) *Sufi Mystics of the Niger Desert*, Oxford: Clarendon Press.

O'Kelly, C. and Carney, L.S. (1986) *Women and Men in Society: Cross-Cultural Perspectives on Gender Stratification*, Belmont, CA: Wadsworth Publishing Company.

Oxby, C. (1977) 'Sexual division and slavery in a Tuareg community', unpublished PhD thesis, University of London.

Parkin, D. (ed.) (1985) *The Anthropology of Evil*, Oxford: Blackwell.

—— (1991) *Sacred Void: Spatial Images of Work and Ritual among the Giriama of Kenya*, Cambridge: University Press.

Pels, P. (1998) 'The magic of Africa: reflections on a western commonplace', *African Studies Review* 41, 3: 193–209.

Rasmussen, S. (1989) 'Accounting for belief: causation, evil, and misfortune in Tuareg systems of thought', *Journal of the Royal Anthropological Institute* 24: 124–44.

—— (1992) 'Ritual specialists, ambiguity, and power in Tuareg society', *Journal of the Royal Anthropological Institute* 27: 125–28.

—— (1995) *Spirit Possession and Personhood among the Kel Ewey Tuareg*, Cambridge: University Press.

—— (1997) *The Poetics and Politics of Tuareg Aging: Life Course and Personal Destiny in Niger*, DeKalb: University of Northern Illinois Press.

—— (1998) 'Ritual powers and social tensions as moral discourse among the Tuareg', *American Anthropologist* 100, 2: 458–468.

—— (2001) *Healing in Community: Medicine, Contested Terrains, and Cultural Encounters among the Tuareg*, Westport: Greenwood (Bergin and Garvey).

Rodd, F.R. (1926) *People of the Veil*, London: Macmillan.

Rowlands, M. and Warnier, J-P (1988) 'Sorcery, power and the modern state in Cameroon', *Man* 23: 118–132.

Saenz, C. (1991) 'They have eaten our grandfathers! The special status of Saharan smiths', unpublished PhD dissertation, Columbia University.

Sanders, T. (2000) 'Rains gone bad, women gone mad: rethinking gender rituals of rebellion and patriarchy', *Journal of the Royal Anthropological Institute* 6: 469–486.

Spittler, G. (1993) *Les Touaregues Face aux Secheresses et aux Famines*, Paris: Khartala.

Taussig, M. (1980) *The Devil and Commodity Fetishism in South America*, Chapel Hill, NC: University of North Carolina Press.

Westermarck, E. (1926) *Ritual and Belief in Morocco*, vols I-II, London: Macmillan.

Willis, P. (1981) *Learning to Labor: How Working Class Kids Get Working Class Jobs*, New York: Columbia University Press.

Worley, B. (1991) 'Women's war drum, women's wealth', unpublished PhD dissertation, Columbia University.

Chapter 8

Save our skins

Structural adjustment, morality and the occult in Tanzania

Todd Sanders

In the spring of 1999, in the southern reaches of Tanzania, police arrested two people for the murder of an 11-year-old schoolboy. Under ordinary circumstances such murders, though rare, would scarcely attract national – let alone international – attention. But these were no ordinary circumstances. For the boy's body was found skinned; the alleged murderers were attempting to sell the skin to a Malawian man. Within weeks, also in Mbeya Region, a second skin-less body was reportedly discovered. And in June, so said local papers, a third. By mid-July a total of six youths had purportedly been killed and skinned, 'the skins . . . allegedly offered for sale in Malawi, Zambia and the Democratic Republic of Congo for use in witchcraft activities', reported the London-based broadsheet, *The Guardian*.[1] For many Tanzanians, the rationale for such witchcraft killings was all too obvious: private economic and political gain. As one paper put it, 'The human skins and other body parts, including vaginas and penises, are said to be in demand by sorcerers who use them to make powerful concoctions, which are potent enough to make the rich richer, and the mighty mightier'.[2]

Alarmist and patently moralizing reports filled Tanzanian and regional newspapers, radio and television programmes, all recently liberalized under International Monetary Fund pressures for structural adjustment. 'Over the past three months', one among countless news stories reiterated in September 1999,

> the obnoxious trade in human skin has taken root in Mbeya region. Criminals are said to skin their victims after killing them and sell them to Zambia. It is said that an un-bruised human skin would fetch up to 5,000 US dollars in Zambia where it is used in witchcraft . . . [A] joint operation [with Zambian and Malawian police] included an elaborate plan to hunt down the criminals of this inhuman trade.[3]

Several months later, another report lamented that: 'Human beings were butchered by their assailants who later skinned their corpses to sell the "commodity" in Malawi and Zambia for 5,000 US dollars. Suspects who have been arrested say markets for un-bruised human skin can be found as far as the Democratic Republic of Congo, South Africa and Cameroon.'[4]

Sadly, such happenings may be more than illusory, as the front page photographs of at least one skinned victim grossly attested (cf. Scheper-Hughes 2000). Yet what is particularly striking is how these few incidents in Southern Tanzania – inhumane, inexcusable, deplorable, without a doubt – rocked the nation and fired the popular imagi-nation; how they captured and crystallized, if for a moment, a nationwide sentiment that said somehow, something, somewhere, had gone intolerably wrong.

When I visited Tanzania in the summer of 1999, urban and rural rumours had it that ruthless human skin traders were now searching out their victims not only in relatively remote villages, but also in the cities of Morogoro, Arusha and Dar es Salaam.[5] It was here, after all, in large urban sprawls, that people could be disappeared most easily, their skins sold for exorbitant prices, with little risk of detection. And even though, as far as I am aware, no skin-less victims have ever materialized in any Tanzanian city, rumours that they *had* ran rampant all the same.

Rumours about trafficking in human bodies and body parts for occult purposes are not unique to Tanzania, and are today recounted widely across Africa (Bastian 1999; Colson 2000: 340; Comaroff and Comaroff 1999; Harnischfeger 1997; Mabiriizi 1986; Scheper-Hughes 1996, 2000; White 1997). Nor is it obvious that such notions – which are not new – will fade into oblivion anytime soon. If anything, witchcraft and other 'occult economies' (Comaroff and Comaroff 1999) in their various guises and disguises appear to be rising, rather than declining, across the continent and beyond.[6]

This raises myriad questions, all of them pressing. Why here? Why now? For even though recent events are not without precedent (e.g. Jones 1951), the nagging question remains: Why, at this particular historical moment, have rumours about the occult-related transnational trafficking in human skins so captivated many Tanzanians? And many others across the continent? More fundamentally, perhaps, how can such beliefs survive, indeed, thrive in our global and globalizing world? At a time when the World Bank and the International Monetary Fund (IMF) structural adjustment policies insist on efficiency, transparent fiscal policies and good governance the world over, when expansive, liberalized media and markets span the globe, should not witchcraft and other occult beliefs simply wither away?

Of no less importance, should we in the west – morally, *can* we – divert our ever-limited attention and resources from the things that *really* matter, from the harsh realities of political economies that govern, often with painful clarity, many Africans' life-worlds? After all, the World Bank tells us, Sub-Saharan Africa is in 'crisis' (World Bank 1981, 1989). Among Africa's oft-cited troubles are 'high rates of population growth, low levels of investment and saving . . . inefficient resource use, weak institutional capacity and human resources, and a general decline in income and living standards' (World Bank 1989: 17). By focusing on recent rumours of occult trading are we not overlooking those things that matter most? This chapter suggests quite the opposite.

As we shall see, these two sets of concerns – human skin trading and occult forces, on the one hand, and the (de)pressing materialities of people's daily lives, on the other – are inexorably linked. Following recent poststructuralist concerns to deconstruct the development enterprise (Escobar 1991, 1995; Ferguson 1994), this chapter argues that the recent rise of occult idioms and practices in Tanzania is directly related to the way structural adjustment has been presented and implemented.

Over the past decade Tanzania has been thoroughly 'adjusted' by the IMF and World Bank: markets and media liberalized, government bureaucracies rationalized. These institutions have continually presented structural adjustment and the changes it has unleashed as a technical matter of means-ends calculation and 'efficiency', motored, in some matter-of-fact manner, by value-free economic theories. Such views render structural adjustment and social change, at least for its advocates, unproblematic, natural and amoral.[7]

Ordinary Tanzanians, however, reject such claims, insisting that recent changes raise a host of moral and moralizing questions that demand attention: at whose expense do market reforms come? Who wins? Who loses? Is this desirable? Is it acceptable? And it is here, in light of these and related questions, that popular ruminations over occult dealings raise pointed and morally-probing questions about the limitations and liberations of 'the market', the circulation of commodities across international borders, and the implications and desirability of such things both for individuals and for society as a whole. In this sense, 'the occult' – by which I mean unseen powers, positive or negative – provides a compelling local lexicon for re-moralizing sterile World Bank/IMF stories about structural adjustment and social change (Ferguson 1995).[8]

But 'the occult' is not just a way to contemplate the moralities and immoralities of a changing world. It also has very real material consequences in and on that world. For many Tanzanians, successfully managing occult forces has long been a logical prerequisite for gaining and maintaining status and wealth. For as long as there have been powerful and powerless, rich and poor people, there has been a ready-made market for occult powers. But today, with structural adjustment's relentless imposition of 'the free market', the possibilities for marketing the occult appear virtually limitless. Diviners now sell occult 'medicines' across the nation at large, 'liberalized' markets; African witches allegedly cross ethnic divides to exchange know-how and 'medicines' at conferences in Europe. Thanks to 'the free market' the occult itself has in recent years been commodified in ways previously neither possible nor imaginable.

Baldly stated, then, this chapter argues that structural adjustment has provided necessary and sufficient conditions for the rapid proliferation of occult discourses and practices in Tanzania. To make this point I use ethnographic material from the Ihanzu, those Tanzanians I know best.

The Ihanzu provide a particularly telling case since, for them, using human skin, genitalia or other human body parts to occult ends has no local resonance. No Ihanzu I know ever suggested that local occult users, of whom there are reputedly many, engage in such practices. And yet because the Ihanzu, like many Tanzanians, were patently gripped by the stories of trafficking in human skins for occult purposes, we must ask *why* they find such trafficking meaningful when the exact symbolic and practical linkages between human skins, occult forces and wealth creation remain elusive. The answer, as we shall see, lies in much broader understandings of occult forces, morality, the market and commodification. But first, before providing any specifics, we must consider two general, competing visions of the recent structural adjustment-induced changes in Tanzania.

Millennial moments in the Tanzanian postcolony: official and unofficial stories

In recent years Tanzania has undergone profound political, economic and social changes, driven by an array of internal and external forces (see Tripp 1997). Principle among the external forces have been the IMF and the World Bank, together with their policies of structural adjustment.

When Tanzania (then Tanganyika) gained independence from Britain in 1961, the nascent nation's first president, Julius Nyerere, forged and followed a unique path of 'non-Marxist socialism' (Tripp 1997: 62) known as *ujamaa*.[9] The nation's guiding *ujamaa* principles were explicitly formulated in the now-famous Arusha Declaration. Though fundamentally African in its philosophical outlook (Ferguson 1995: 134; Pratt 1976: 7; Stoger-Eising 2000), in practice *ujamaa* followed a Sino-Soviet model of state centralization, whereby administrative powers were highly concentrated in the central government and delegated to local level authorities in diminishing amounts. The Tanzanian state nationalized major commercial, financial and manufacturing industries; imposed severe import restrictions on foreign goods and currencies; and emphasized production within the nation, for the nation.

By the mid-1980s, for several reasons, *ujamaa* was on its last leg.[10] It was in 1986, under the Republic's second president, Ali Hassan Mwinyi, that Tanzania became fully committed to an IMF-led structural adjustment programme; a programme that would forever change the face of the nation.

So what is structural adjustment? Simply stated, structural adjustment is about market reform, and 'getting the price right'. It operates on the principle that less government intervention in the economy is better; that economies will work best, and most efficiently, if propelled by market forces rather than bureaucrats. Structural adjustment, then, is a move 'away from more autonomous, nationalistic, inward-oriented, import-substitution, state interventionist, and socialist models towards *laissez-faire* capitalism' (Sparr 1994: 2).

While at least initially structural adjustment was seen as being mainly about macroeconomic policies (e.g. World Bank 1981), the IMF, World Bank and others soon came to believe that 'good governance' and a politically 'enabling environment' were logical prerequisites for economic growth (World Bank

1989, 1994).[11] Thus, when structural adjustment policies failed to improve African economies, the IMF and other international agencies blamed inept African bureaucracies, assuming that '[t]he public sector lies at the core of the stagnation and decline in growth in Africa' (World Bank 1994: 99). Practically, this meant African countries would have to undergo fundamental political reforms before they would receive further foreign aid.

In Tanzania, beginning in the early 1990s under President Mwinyi, this dual insistence on economic and political restructuring ushered in an entirely new order (or perhaps more accurately, *dis*-order) commonly recalled as a *ruksa* or 'free-for-all'.[12] Emblematic of this (dis)order is the Zanzibar Declaration of 1991, as it later came to be known, which boldly challenged the 1967 Arusha Declaration and led to a number of consequential 'amendments' to it; amendments that, in reality, radically undermined rather than updated the Arusha Delcaration's original vision. The Zanzibar Declaration allows party leaders and civil servants to own shares in companies, rent property and to engage in business for private gain – all (legal) impossibilities under the Arusha Declaration. 'The symbolic importance of these changes', notes Tripp, 'cannot be emphasized strongly enough, for the Arusha Declaration was the central document in establishing the egalitarian, self-reliant, and socialist orientation that Tanzania adopted' (1997: 171). Other liberalizations followed suit: privatizing many parastatals; abolishing foreign exchange restrictions; legalizing private commerce and trade; allowing local and foreign newspapers and magazines, radio and television broadcasts to circulate freely.

Equally decisive in shaping the newly 'adjusted' nation was the Tanzanian National Assembly's passage of the 8th Constitutional Amendment Act in May 1992. This paved the way for Tanzania's first multiparty elections, held in 1995, when Benjamin Mkapa became the Republic's third president. In October 2000, Mkapa was re-elected for a second and final five-year term.

From the outset President Mkapa and his administration have enthusiastically supported structural adjustment measures. Much more so, in fact, than did Mwinyi. At home and abroad, with irrepressible determination, Mkapa has continually draw attention to the merits of 'good governance' and 'liberalization' as well as to the evils of 'corruption'. What is more, his proclamations have been matched every step of the way by further policy reforms.

Consequently, when Anupam Basu, the Deputy Director for Africa Department in the IMF, visited Dar es Salaam in December 2000 – his first visit to Tanzania since the 1980s – he found a radically changed world. The tangible signs of 'adjustment' were everywhere. The few government-owned newspapers, *Daily News*, *Uhuru* and *Mzalendo*, had been eclipsed by more than twenty-five local and international newspapers, magazines and tabloids, in both English and Swahili, available on many news-stands; the single state radio station had been joined by manifold others from near and afar; urban and some rural Tanzanians could watch the private television network ITV which broadcasts local and foreign serials and newscasts, as well as many American sitcoms, soaps and action movies. No fewer than thirteen political parties had registered; and two multiparty presidential elections had already taken place. Shops in Dar es Salaam, Arusha and across the country were bursting with foreign and domestic consumer goods; the informal economy was bustling.

From an official viewpoint, these have been unquestionably positive developments. In the Deputy Director's own words: 'I always urge with my colleagues that you cannot judge a country whether it has improved or not if you have not visited the country for ten or twenty years since your last visit. From what I have witnessed in your country I can confess that Tanzania has very much developed and changed.'[13] By all 'objective' indicators, too, according to official reckoning, Tanzania is today well-adjusted – or at least adjusting well. An IMF press release from April 2000 accurately captures the moment:

> Tanzania has made substantial progress in implementing economic reforms. During the past 4 years, inflation decreased to less than 7%, after many years of rates exceeding 20%, and the government has been repaying domestic debt, after many years of borrowing in excess of 3% of GDP annually. Tanzania has also made a strong structural adjustment effort in recent years, including far-reaching reforms in the external, financial, and public sectors.[14]

Due to Tanzania's 'good' fiscal and political behaviour all round, the IMF and World Bank in 2001 agreed to write off about one-half of Tanzania's debt-service obligations to the year 2003, and about one-third thereafter.

In official eyes, thanks largely to structural adjustment, Tanzania is rapidly becoming a success story. And I emphasize here a *story*, for the story of structural adjustment, as told in myriad IMF and World Bank publications, tells in so many ways of the triumph of the Market over the Command Economy; of capitalism's success and socialism's failure; of the righteousness of the west and the wrongheadedness the rest. It subscribes unabashedly to modernity's guiding masternarratives, the European Enlightenment-inspired notions of unilinear progress and development (Ferguson 1999; Englund and Leach 2000). This is a teleological tale, above all, of the triumph of neoliberal ideologies and policies in our contemporary world.

But it is not told that way, not officially anyway. Although in many places, especially in post-socialist places like Tanzania, capitalism and the market are presented 'as a gospel of salvation' (Comaroff and Comaroff 2000: 292; forthcoming) – displaying what billionaire philanthropist George Soros (1998) has dubbed 'market fundamentalism' – this has not been the story of structural adjustment. Rather, as Ferguson (1995) has incisively argued, structural adjustment's story is routinely told in cold, technocratic tones, where GDP, inflation figures and other macro-economic indicators reign supreme. Here, the confident rhetoric of social change is one of scientific objectivity, where 'facts' and 'findings' are endlessly (re)presented as authoritative, logical and rationally derived (Apthorpe 1986; Bernstein 1990; Brydon 1999: 382). Official analyses are allegedly driven by considerations of 'efficiency', 'pragmatism', 'hardheaded analysis' and the like (e.g. World Bank 1989: 162, 189; 1994: 204). The IMF and World Bank have remained dogmatically committed to the idea that they have no dogma.

Telling stories in this way does several things. For one, it suggest there is a scientific, no-nonsense bottom-line, discernible through the careful application of macro- and microeconomic theories (Heilbroner 1973; Mehmet 1999). Moreover, it naturalizes 'structural adjustment' and 'the market', making them appear inevitable and beyond reproach (Pottier 1999: 98; Williams 1999). Finally, and not inconsequentially, telling stories this way allows 'structural adjustment', 'the market' and 'social change' to present themselves as amoral – as neither good nor bad, but simply the natural, unavoidable course of events. It would be just as foolish, so the reasoning goes, to lament the sun's rising in the east as it would the advent of the free market. Both just happen. 'The morality of the market', notes Ferguson, 'denies its own status as a morality, presenting itself as mere technique' (1995: 139). And so it goes with structural adjustment.

Alternative visions of the moment

While structural adjustment presents itself as scientific, natural and therefore morally unproblematic, the radical changes it has wrought as so obviously positive as to merit no serious discussion, ordinary Tanzanians tell a different tale. Underpinning it are some different facts and figures about the effects of structural adjustment policies, which:

> frequently compound many of the hardships, resulting in inflation induced by devaluation and massive layoffs due to closures of uncompetitive industries. The inability of the state, generally the major source of employment, to provide adequate incomes and employment prompted individuals, groups, and mutual-aid organizations to seek alternative solutions to their worsening economic situations. The decline in real wages, coupled with rising rates of unemployment, led many urban dwellers to seek informal sources of income to supplement their wages or to leave their jobs altogether and go into private business or farming.
>
> (Tripp 1997: 22)

Indeed, not a few scholars of Tanzania have argued that structural adjustment has 'forced a majority of people [in Dar es Salaam] to use the informal sector as a survival strategy' (Lugalla 1997: 440; also Lugalla 1995; Mbilinyi 1990); and occasioned a nationwide increase in religious and ethnic tensions (Kaiser 1996). Equally, in rural areas, 'in "liberalized" Tanzania, farmers are growing more crops, risking more in marketing them, spending more in cultivating them, and earning less from their sale' (Ponte 1998: 339).

Lest we forget, Tanzania remains one of the poorest countries in the world today. Per capita income is estimated at $120 annually, with nearly 40 per cent of Tanzanians living on less than $0.65 per day[15] – which explains why so many Tanzanians today spend such exorbitant amounts of time and energy 'getting by' (Tripp 1997). Small wonder, really, that former President Mwinyi's *ruksa* or 'free-for-all' has now given way to the era of *ukapa* (after President Mkapa): a term coined and used in popular parlance which roughly translates as 'lots of goods, no money to buy them' (cf. Brydon 1999: 378–379). For many, it appears that this has been the austere outcome of Tanzania's being 'adjusted' by the IMF, other international agencies and the government itself for more than a decade. As one Tanzanian recently lamented: 'Deep down . . . everybody is groaning at the economic hardship.'[16]

On the other hand some Tanzanians *have* benefited – some astonishingly so – from this recently arrived and liberalized world of goods. New Pajeros, Land Cruisers and Range Rovers travel the roads like never before; businessmen and others are sometimes seen in smart Armani and Hugo Boss suits. Problem is, for the vast majority, participating in such a world is a veritable impossibly – which only heightens, with tedious regularity, the *relative* poverty those denied access to this new world routinely experience under structural adjustment's reign.[17]

Unlike the IMF's confident metanarrative, then, the popular tale many Tanzanians tell about the current moment is one of queries, not convictions; of grave uncertainties about the nation's present and future trajectory; of ever-increasing structural adjustment-induced hardships and poverty (Campbell and Stein 1992). This tale speaks to the capriciousness of the market, the erratic rise and demise of individual fortunes, the promises and the perils of the newly adjusted nation. Moreover, as we shall see, this tale is told in an entirely different tenor, concerned as it is with the moralities and immoralities of recent changes. It suggests that 'debates about market regulation and liberalization are not simply about the mechanics of economic transactions . . . but are embedded deeply in normative discourse about social relations and political values' (Gould and von Oppen 1994: 4; also Appadurai 1986; Gudeman 1986; Parry and Bloch 1989). This is not just a story of woes, but of both hope and despair, of prosperity and austerity, one that seriously reflects on both the virtues and vices of the country's rapidly-shifting economic, political and moral terrain. Rather than speak in generalities about such things, I focus here on the Ihanzu, implying throughout that their experiences with recent changes resonate with those of many other Tanzanians.

The Ihanzu and market (im)moralities

The Ihanzu number around 30,000. Most lead an agricultural life in Singida Region, north-central Tanzania, the place they have called 'home' for over a century. This rural homeland area is far from Tanzania's major urban centres. It is a nearly two-day drive from Dar es Salaam; and a long day's drive from Arusha.

The Ihanzu are inveterate travellers. This has been true since at least colonial times when, beginning in the 1910s, many were forced to trek vast distances to carry out migrant labour (Adam 1963), a trend that continues today. In the 1930s Lutheran missionaries entered the area and they, too, cleared pathways that a number of Ihanzu converts have since travelled: relocating to other rural areas to spread The Word, or to Tanzanian cities for higher education, employment and sometimes permanent settlement. In Dar es Salaam, Arusha and Singida, one can today find second- and even third-generation Ihanzu (many of them Christians), who, though born and raised in the cities, consider themselves 'Ihanzu'. Such urbanites frequently maintain links with their 'home' villages, where some occasionally visit kin, attend funerals and are buried.

Whether urban or rural, Ihanzu experiences with recent macro-level changes in the political-economy have been remarkably similar: nearly all feel that, of late, life has grown increasingly intolerable. In the words of one young Ihanzu Dar es Salaam-based businesswoman who I interviewed in late 1999: 'Under [President] Mwinyi some things worked. But today, with [President] Mkapa, it has become impossible to do business: taxes are collected by force, and we can't afford to pay them. If you follow the law, you can't succeed in business today.' And from another interview that year, in the words of an Ibaga-village guesthouse owner (who only began doing business in Ihanzu in 1991, after being made redundant from his Dar es Salaam job as a medical statistician):

> In 1991 business was *very* good; . . . By 1995 things began to decline. 1996 wasn't so good; and 1998 was just mediocre, but better than today. . . . Today, business is extremely bad for everyone . . . because we're all locked together by one thing, a thing called 'money'. And the circulation of money – even at the national level – the nation itself is sticking (*kwama*) and is bemoaning (*lalimika*) the fact that there's no money. . . . I'm a businessman. But here in Ibaga, there's no money and no business. You'll find another with a shop, also moaning 'there's no money'. . . . We're all ruled by the circulation of money.

Such have been the deleterious effects of IMF-led restructuring on most, perhaps all, Ihanzu – and on many other Tanzanians. Based on my own experiences in Tanzania through the 1990s, I believe my informants when they tell me such things, when they say that life has grown increasingly difficult all round. But my aim is not to 'prove' this. I offer no hard economic data from 'before' and 'after' to argue that the Ihanzu, or any others, have been hard done by structural adjustment. My first concern, instead, is with what the Ihanzu *say* about the nation's rapidly-shifting economic and political terrain, and with how they say it. And this means discussing 'the occult'. My second concern is with how, in the era of structural adjustment, 'the occult' has itself been commodified and thus vastly expanded, both in the popular imagination and in its practical reach.

Markets, moralities and occult forces

The Ihanzu, like many peoples across Africa, divide their world into two distinct realms (Nyamnjoh, Chapter 2). The first is the manifest world, the world that is visible, plain and 'obvious' to all. Herein lies the stuff of people's everyday existence: farming, herding, fetching water and firewood; political happenings and economic transactions. The second world runs parallel to the first and is unseen. This is the realm of witchcraft (ũlogi), ancestral spirits (alũngũ) and god (itunda). This occult (ushirikina or mazingara) realm is very much a part of the Ihanzu's everyday lives – albeit an invisible part – which they understand as pedestrian and commonplace (cf. Ashforth 1996).

These visible and invisible realms are thought to be causally linked in that the former is animated by unseen forces from the latter. Invisible forces determine visible outcomes. Thus, as with the logical of conspiracy theories, the Ihanzu maintain that most or all everyday activities are guided and shaped in fundamental ways by unseen forces. Our everyday world is simply a façade that masks a deeper, more 'real reality,' one that lies beyond our immediate comprehension, one that harbours the engine of all this-worldly events (Ashforth 1996: 1220; Douglas 1970: xvi).

Because occult forces shape the Ihanzu's daily lives, control over these forces is crucial. There are many ways to tap into, harness and manage hidden forces of the universe. One popular way is by using 'medicine'. Medicine (ikota, or dawa in Swahili) is a broad term. It can refer to the concoctions of diviners, rainmakers or witches as well as to western medicines – including illegal drugs – and dehydrated and compressed foods eaten by soldiers and astronauts. As already noted, the notion of using human skins or body parts for occult medicine is foreign to the Ihanzu. Even Ihanzu witches, people say, have no knowledge of such things. However, few would deny that others across the country, region and the continent routinely use human skins and body parts to generate illicit wealth through occult means.

For the Ihanzu, it is common knowledge that people use certain 'medicine' to amass wealth and to gain political position, as well as to protect such things once acquired. As one Christian Ihanzu man named Marko, a long-time resident of Dar es Salaam who holds a Master's degree from a prominent UK university and is today director of a large Tanzanian parastatal, told me: 'Whenever a government position becomes vacant, you will notice lots of people going to [diviners in] Bagamoyo for medicine. The government knows about this but remains silent.'

There is nothing inherently problematic about employing occult forces in this way. In both urban and rural settings, for instance, it is commonly assumed that people use medicine called kĩsumba to attract such things as material wealth, customers, lovers, rain, fish or, as Marko mentioned, even a better job. This might be seen as 'good luck medicine', or a 'medicine of attraction'. Since kĩsumba is said to harm no one, it can theoretically be used without fear of social reprisal. Another medicine, called *kinga*, is similarly considered morally tenable. *Kinga*, people say, functions solely to protect its user against more malevolent occult forces. It is common, many mention, for shopkeepers, businesspersons, politicians, farmers, herders and myriad others to fortify their persons and property medicinally in this way.

But medicine can also be put to more nefarious ends, as when witches use it to destroy the wealthy and politically powerful and to amass illicitly wealth and power for themselves. For example, Ihanzu witches purportedly use medicine to kill people so that they can transform them into zombies (*atumbũka*) who then toil at night on the witch's plot. By killing and creating a nocturnal zombie labour force, witches misanthropically reroute others' reproductive powers to their own illicit ends. Needless to say, such exploitation of occult forces is morally objectionable all round.

Another apparent witch favourite, equally devastating in its effects, is ndagũ. Those who use *ndagũ* (a sort of 'medicinal pact with a diviner') reputedly benefit, but only at the immediate expense of others. Thus, an *ndagũ* user might gain political prominence, or become extremely wealthy in cattle, crops or shops, but only by first sacrificing one or several close kin. In Marko's words: 'In Dar es Salaam, there are people with, say, four children. They are told to choose the one they love most and kill him or her to get [for example] a job! This really happens, to get a good opportunity or to become rich.' From other Ihanzu I have heard many such stories, often told in moralizing tones: a young man from Dodoma who allegedly sacrificed his brother for wealth; a Regional Trade Officer who gave up his child for the same. In this zero-sum universe, the witch's gain is the moral man's bane (Sanders 1999).

The Ihanzu Christian minority, who make up around 20 per cent of the total Ihanzu population, has a slightly different take on these matters. No Ihanzu Christian doubts the efficacy of 'medicine' or that people regularly use it. Neither, as Marko makes clear, would any deny the veracity of witchcraft – many indefatigably noting that 'witchcraft is in the Bible'. Yet their religion teaches them, as did early missionaries, that 'traditional medicine' and witchcraft are this-worldly manifestations of the devil which must therefore be steadfastly avoided. To steer occult forces, then, Christians must instead pray to Jesus or directly to God – the most potent and benevolent of all unseen powers. The Christian god thus overpowers rather than replaces other occult forces like witchcraft (van Dijk, Chapter 5; Meyer 1992; Wild 1998). For Christians, then, drawing on any occult forces, their own god(s) notwithstanding, is seen as evil and immoral. In any case, Ihanzu Christians share with the non-Christian majority the notion that occult forces must be managed; they differ only over how best to do this, and in their moral evaluations of the different methods.

There is a rather obvious difficulty here – and this is the point. Since no ordinary Ihanzu has direct access to the hidden realm of powers, the ultimate causes of this-worldly events can only be inferred, never once-and-for-all known. The operation of power between invisible and visible worlds thus remains profoundly ambivalent (Arens and Karp 1989; Geschiere 1997). And this ambivalence, in turn, makes it is impossible to know whether or not any particular this-worldly event is the result of moral or immoral conduct (cf. Middleton 1960). Is a man rich because he prays to Jesus, because he uses a (for non-Christians) morally tenable medicine like *kĩsumba*, or because he uses *ndagũ*, which all agree demands a human sacrifice and is thus irredeemably immoral? Is a politician powerful because he uses socially-sanctioned *kinga* to protect himself, or because, through some dubious medicinal doings, he kills off his adversaries? Does he feed people or feed *on* people?

The manifest signs provide clues, but no definitive answers. Which is why the occult, in Ihanzu and across Africa, provides a compelling local vocabulary for deliberating over issues of entitlement and morality. By definition occult idioms raise the issues: Who gets what and why? At whose expense? And, How desirable is this? (Auslander 1993; Bastian 1993; Comaroff and Comaroff 1993; Rasmussen 1998). Let me provide an example of how the Ihanzu discuss 'the market' and the rise and demise of individual fortunes in terms of occult forces; and how this is, simultaneously, a discussion about morality.

Bonifasi and his wife Maria, both of Chagga ethnic origin and devout Roman Catholics, first came to Ihanzu to do business in the 1960s. They opened a small shop in the western village of Chem Chem and, some years later, moved to Ibaga village. Their business grew slowly at first, and boomed in the late 1980s and early 1990s with the demise of *ujamaa*. They soon opened a shop in Dar es Salaam, and began to amass a considerable fortune by selling Ihanzu-bought maize and beans for a healthy profit in Dar, while acquiring modern consumer goods in Dar and selling them in Ihanzu. Over the past five years, however, coinciding with recent shifts in the political-economy, their businesses in both locations have faltered. They recently sold their shop in Dar es Salaam. These developments have not gone unnoticed by Ihanzu villagers, and have occasioned much discussion and speculation.

Bonifasi and Maria, for their part, publicly attribute their personal fortunes and misfortunes to God alone. Bonifasi insisted to me, as he has to others, that we can only pray to the all-knowing God for success and protection against others' ill-doings. He claims never to have used non-Christian occult forces of any type to gain or maintain his wealth and to have no knowledge of such things. Others beg to differ. This is how Hamisi, a 64-year-old farmer and former Ibaga village businessman, explained Bonfasi's recent misfortunes to me:

> Bonifasi was the wealthiest in the village, but he was bewitched! His children became drunks and wasted their father's money. His wife now has a strange illness that causes her to be epileptic. She has withered a lot, and their wealth is beginning to end. They had cars, but now they are all ruined. He used to live in Dar [es Salaam] but has now failed. He's returned [to Ibaga] now to run the business himself, but it's ruined. It's not like in the past. And these things surprise us. We see that this man was intelligent.

Why has this happened to him? We know this is because of witchcraft of locals who see modernity [and destroy it].

When I asked Hamisi about how Bonifasi had become rich in the first place, he did not hesitate: 'He used *kĩsumba* of course; and he used *kinga*, too, to protect himself, his family and his riches.'

Halima, a middle-aged woman from a nearby village, offered a somewhat different perspective:

> Bonifasi has something witch-like about him (*mazingara yake*). *Lots* of people say this. His witchcraft is that he doesn't want others to get anything, that he [wants to] get everything for himself. . . . After trying [with witchcraft] to ruin a particular [business?] person, he saw the effects of [counter-] witchcraft on his wife. She has become crippled, epileptic. She's still alive all right, like an ordinary human being, but her mind has been ruined by witchcraft!

Other villagers told me that Bonifasi had made an *ndagũ* pact at his wife's expense (or at the expense of other unspecified villagers), causing her to become half mad and epileptic for the sake of material riches – a pact that had apparently gone terribly wrong, since even the riches had now vanished.

The point worth stressing is that such witchcraft rumours speak directly to issues of morality, and more specifically, to the morality of the market. They pose difficult questions about who gets what, how they get it, and at whose expense. Hamisi's explanation highlights the fact that accumulation is not immoral *per se*, but fraught with difficulties. He claims Bonifasi used medicines to acquire and protect his wealth and sees no moral dilemma with this. Bonifasi, after all, was only attracting business, and riches, and protecting himself against other evil-doers. The difficulty, however, arises when envious others turn their witchcraft against him, which occasioned the loss of Bonfasi's wealth and his wife's health. Hamisi's is a commentary on the perils of prosperity, the inherent dangers of doing business in an intensely competitive economic climate. And he should know: Hamisi blames his own failed business ventures on fellow villagers' witchcraft, which he says made his children ill and caused two owls to dance on his doorstep – a definitive warning, in his mind, of worse things to come, which eventually did.

Halima's explanation and ones similar to it are more ominous. And more damning. They suggest that Bonfasi's economic rise and demise resulted from his own gluttonous desires, expressed at the immediate expense of others. He was either done in by his competitors' superior witchcraft or for having agreed to an *ndagũ* that went horribly wrong. His actions are deeply disapproved of, and said to be wholly evil (*mbĩ tai*).

Note that from all viewpoints 'the market' and people's engagements with it come only at a price: the lives and livelihoods of fellow businesspeople; of innocent villagers; or even of themselves. No one gets something for nothing. Seen in this light, there is nothing at all 'free' about the so-called *free* market (*soko huria*). By its very 'nature' the market extracts a heavy toll in human lives. Far from being 'natural', 'obvious' and 'amoral', as modernity's mouthpieces insist it is, the market is laden with ambiguities, uncertainties and profound moral dilemmas. One's involvement in it, these days unavoidable, is as dangerous as it is potentially rewarding.

With the recent wave of liberalizations that has washed over Tanzania the possibilities for personal enrichment through the Market have increased manifold. This has also meant increased competition and conflict over scarce resources (cf. Kaiser 1996) as well as greater economic differentiation. Consequently, the occult has featured even more prominently. Niko, a middle-aged Christian man from Kirumi village, explained it like this:

> I've been to Arusha and Shinyanga and all over the place and, from what I've heard, it's true: everyone uses medicines to attract business! Also it doesn't matter whether they are Ihanzu, Sukuma, Chagga or whatever. They *all* use medicine. There's no other way in this difficult economy. Everyone is selling but very few are buying. There's little money to go around. No one has money. But everyone is trying to sell things to make a living. It is much worse in the cities than here [in the villages]. This is because there are too many people selling things, and there are never enough customers. They have to be resourceful, they have to use medicine to attract customers. . . . Don't think it's ok. It's not. It's *very* bad. But what can they do?

> [Witchcraft] is much worse today than ever before. . . . In the past people wanted only a few things. . . . Today there are too many things that people want. . . . cars, bicycles, radios, nice houses, etc. . . . Everyone wants to develop (*kuendelea*). But think about it. . . . How is this possible? People become jealous of what others around them have. Maybe that one has a radio and that one doesn't, but he wants one. . . . He might be so angry that he bewitches the neighbour and his stupid radio. He might try to knock him down, to cause him to go backwards (*kurudi nyuma*) so that he will not develop. This is why today witchcraft is much worse. It is development itself that brings witchcraft. More development means more witchcraft.

Such comments speak volumes about ordinary Tanzanians' yearnings for a meaningful modernity (in this case, an *equitable* distribution of wealth) and, conversely, of their lack of interest in numerically-impressive but socially vacuous statistics on GDP and inflation. Such remarks also speak to the logical inconsistencies in structural adjustment dogma, namely, the notion of infinite wants in a universe of finite possibilities.

If the advent of the free market in Tanzania has increased speculation about 'the occult' – about how best to connect means and ends, actions and outcomes, and to evaluate the morality and immorality of these nebulous processes – it has also provided the very mechanism by which such ideas and practices are spread. After all, the 'free' market is a place where, for a price, anything and everything can be had, occult medicines and powers included.

Commodifying the occult

I have spoken to many Ihanzu diviners (*aganga*), acknowledged experts in 'medicine' for sale, who claim that their business has, in recent years, skyrocketed. All claim they deal in 'good' occult medicines rather than 'bad' witchcraft-related ones, even if they also regularly imply an intimate knowledge of both.

Tanzanians today travel great distances to buy 'medicines' from diviners in faraway villages. I have met clients of one well-known Ihanzu diviner who came from as far away as Dar es Salaam, Arusha and Tanga, many well-educated and economically and politically well-to-do. Some suggested that, by visiting diviners far from home, it was easier to remain discrete – always an issue when positive occult forces can all too easily be mistaken for negative ones.

Many diviners at the turn of the millennium do reasonable business not only at home in the villages but across the country. Saidi, a well-known Ihanzu diviner, today spends much of his time travelling around the country overtly and covertly practising his trade. Since the early 1990s, he claims, he has been secretly summoned on several occasions by district-level government officials in Kiomboi, who paid him for medicinally protecting them against witchcraft. He also says he was paid for medicinally fortifying butcher shops, small hotels, bars and scores of everyday businesses en route. The fact that his humble home is packed full of blankets, radios, chairs and other such modern wares suggests there is more to his stories than mere entertainment value. Other diviners I know are similarly well-off, and tell similar tales.

These days, too, many diviners openly traffic their goods across the country at large, travelling markets (*minada*; sing., *mnada*), markets that owe their very existence to the recent wave of liberalizations. Such markets, which are now numerous, are made up of small convoys of large lorries that follow regular circuits around each district. On the same date each month, at regular locations along their route, they set up market. Literally thousands attend these markets. For some, it is simply to look and to visit with friends and relatives. For others, notably those in remote areas, it is because these markets are the only place to buy things for miles. To the furthest, most remote corners of the country *minada* bring a host of consumer goods and goodies: pots, pans and plastic wares, dried fish, fresh meat, second-hand clothes. And occult 'medicine'.

Since the mid-1990s one such market has made a monthly visit to Ihanzu and set up just outside Ibaga village. Figure 8.1 shows a diviner at the Ibaga market, a man from Tabora (western Tanzania), consulting with an Ihanzu client. Before them lie his medicines: various bits of root, bark and bottled-substances. Figure 8.2 shows a large, cloth banner standing beside him which reads: 'Senior Traditional Diviner, Elder Kipara, S.L.P. Igunga [village] Tabora'. Then follows a

Figure 8.1 A diviner from Tabora District, western Tanzania, practising his trade at a travelling martket (*mnada*) in Ihanzu, June 1994. (Photo by T. Sanders.)

list of illnesses and symptoms he claims to treat, and some of the medicines on offer. To take just a few: (1) epilepsy; (3) shooting pains; (11) swollen feet; (19) love medicine; (29) bloody nose; (30) fertility medicine; (33) skin disease; and (34) dizziness. Also on offer are: (20) medicine to protect individuals against witchcraft; (21) business medicine; (47) medicine to protect a home against witchcraft; (55) removal (lit. 'shaving') of witchcraft; and (58) medicine to raise the dead. Clearly, with the 'free' market, marketing the occult has become big business.

This is one reason, as countless Ihanzu have told me, the occult is not what it used to be. 'Witchcraft has gone mad (*ovio*) these days', noted one elderly Ihanzu villager. 'It used to follow [within] the clan, but today you can buy it from anyone, anywhere, anytime.' Another from Matongo village remarked similarly: 'In the past, only a few elderly women understood such things; today anyone can buy medicine.'

Such comments conjure the distinction Evans-Pritchard (1937) long ago made, based on his time among the Azande, between 'witchcraft' and 'sorcery'. Witchcraft, Azande believed, formed part of a witch's innermost make-up and was transmitted genetically. Sorcery, on the other hand, was a technique that could be acquired and used by anyone. Though the Ihanzu, like many Africans, do not distinguish linguistically between 'witchcraft' and 'sorcery' – they call both *ũlogi* (Swahili, *uchawi*) – it is clear that they *do* today draw this distinction conceptually. And what their comments clearly say is this: 'witchcraft' is declining, but 'sorcery' is increasing dramatically. With the democratization of

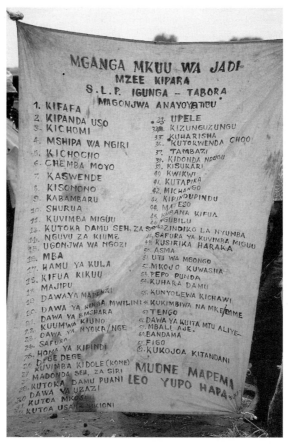

Figure 8.2 The Tabora diviner's make-shift, cloth banner which lists some of the symptoms
he treats and the medicines available for sale, including medicine to get rich
in business, to protect one's self and home against witchcraft and to raise the
dead (*dawa ya kuita mfu alive*). (Photo by T. Sanders.)

the nation has come the democratization of the occult. Through the all-
pervasive 'free' market, anyone who can afford it now has instant access to
occult forces. Note, the logic here goes beyond just 'new market access', to
explore the depths of the market's apparent operation.

Across Africa, the occult has always been about controlling the powers of
production, reproduction and growth. This is as true for 'positive' and theoretically unproblematic occult forces as it is for 'negative' ones, like witchcraft,
where such control nearly always implies direct predation on others. Through
occult means, wealth and power can be produced, replicated and reproduced.
Negative replication routinely requires illicitly rerouting one person's reproductive powers and life-substances to the benefit of another. The difference now,
it appears, is that occult powers of replication have themselves become, like the

'free' market, self-replicating. In ways previously unimaginable the occult now appears to expand, and reproduce itself, quite of its own volition.

Interestingly, since the market is now more vocally translocal and 'freer' than ever before, so, too, are the possibilities for this expansion and the exchange of occult powers. Newspaper and popular stories abound about occult practitioners moving and trading on a truly global scale (cf. Parish 2000). One Ihanzu man, born and raised in Dar es Salaam, told me about a troublesome Tanzanian who allegedly bought 'medicine' from a Ghanaian witch at a World Health Organization conference in Switzerland. The moral of these stories? 'The market', and its promises and perils, have now expanded to global proportions. No longer is the market – or the occult – subject to limitations.

Conclusion: structural adjustment, the occult and trafficking in human skins

I have argued that structural adjustment and the changes it has unleashed are themselves responsible for the recent rise of occult idioms and practices across Tanzania. There are two principle reasons for this. First, the fact that structural adjustment presents itself and the changes it has wrought as categorically amoral, even though they are not, has compelled people to turn to alternative, more familiar registers – like the occult – to raise and debate the (im)moralities of recent changes. Second, the fact that structural adjustment has, by using foreign aid carrots and sticks, indefatigably forced the 'free' market on Tanzanians and led inescapably to the commodification of the occult itself.

In making this argument my aim has been to unsettle one of modernity's comfortable masternarratives, to show how and why – pace any number of social theorists – 'modernizing' forces in one particular time and place have generated the very 'enchantments' they should in theory eliminate. In this context, it is perhaps worth considering what or who, exactly, has been enchanted. For it appears that structural adjustment itself possesses untold powers of self-mystification which bespeak modernity's many enchantments. Neither is it obvious that 'the occult' is some pre-logical, 'traditional', unchanging relic from the past that, against all odds, lives on in the present. On the contrary, recent developments in Tanzania and elsewhere suggest that witchcraft and other occult forces and discourses are profoundly malleable, dynamic and modern, indicative of a deeply engaged collective imagination about the world and people's place in it. Wherever it is found, the occult frequently provides a moralizing discourse of the moment.

But how, to return to our initial questions, is trafficking in human skin implicated in the magical generation of wealth?' Why, just now, has human skin trading to occult ends so captured the Tanzanian popular imagination? And what meaning could such things possibly have for the Ihanzu and others like them, who have a symbolically and practically impoverished understanding of the precise mechanisms at work?

The answer is surprisingly straightforward. 'Why not?', lamented one elderly Ihanzu woman. 'There are no limits to what people will do these days for money'. No limits indeed – which brings us to the crux of the matter. Tanzanians' frenzied musings over the marketing of human skins for wealth production are, I submit, musings over the (il)logical conclusion of unbridled liberalization – a world where *everything* is commodified through and through, a world where society, culture, history and humanity itself have fallen victim to the caprices of The Market. At issue here is 'a fear of the creeping commodification of life itself. . . . of a relentless process that erodes the inalienable humanity of persons and renders them susceptible as never before to the long reach of the market' (Comaroff and Comaroff 1999: 291), indicative of 'just how vulnerable people feel in a system which they see as draining them of their resources to the benefit of remote others' (Colson 2000: 341). These skins, corporeal tropes of sorts, are being traded to far-off, transnational places to the benefit of a few, at the expense of many. If Mauss was correct in suggesting a relationship between individual and social bodies, then we might say that Tanzania is losing her social skin: it is being systematically traded away, obliterated in the name of prosperity, much as the skins of the unfortunate victims of the human skin trade. Structural adjustment insists on free trade across Tanzania's borders to enrich the nation; ruthless occult traders reputedly remove and sell human skins for personal gain. The magic of removing boundaries to generate wealth apparently works on many levels. Human skins, in this sense, are plainly 'good to think with'.

Yet for many, these are stories less about skins than stories told with and through skins (cf. White 1997). At least for the Ihanzu, and presumably for others, there is no 'deep' cultural logic to be uncovered about skins and magical wealth production. In fact, it is precisely because such notions lack specific cultural moorings that they can become meaningful across such a vast region. Ihanzu collective groanings about an occult-related trafficking in human skins are ruminations over the perverse extremes to which some Tanzanians are apparently prepared to go to get rich – or just to get by – in the new millennium's deeply unsettling economic climate. The language itself is telling. 'Obnoxious', 'inhuman', 'grotesque', 'evil', these terms recur in newspapers, on radio and television, and in the stories people tell around town, in the cities and in the villages about the human skin trade. These caustic commentaries point to the potentially disastrous consequences of liberalization run amuck, to a particular postcolonial (dis)order gone catastrophically wrong. They insist on interrogating the logic and limitations of liberalization, how trade is conducted and, most of all, the parameters and desirability of vastly expanded social, political and economic horizons. These are all deeply moral issues about social change that sterile development donor discourses studiously avoid.

This does not mean that, through such occult ruminations, Tanzanians are necessarily 'resisting' things modern. Across Tanzania and across Africa people are simultaneously taunted and tantalized by 'modernity'. Its promises of prosperity for all are too good to be ignored and, as many discover, too good to be true.

Instead, what Tanzanians and many others are after is an 'indigenization of modernity, their own cultural space in the global scheme of things' (Sahlins 1999: 410; Piot 1999). This is a meaningful modernity, a modernity that makes sense, a modernity on their own terms. And there is no other way to get it than by raising and debating the morally troublesome questions that 'modernity' and 'development' inevitably pose.

In probing such questions, occult idioms provide few definitive answers. The answers to questions of who wins and who loses, of who is deprived and who is depraved, of what is acceptable and what is not, are rarely straightforward. As we saw with Bonifasi and Maria, even the same this-worldly events may be interpreted differently by different actors, suggesting that the (im)moralities of social changes are at the very least murky. Even so, while 'the occult' may not answer such complex questions, it nevertheless provides a persuasive idiom – one among several (e.g. Campbell and Stein 1992) – in which to raise, discuss and debate them.

Official stories of structural adjustment tell of a better life for all Tanzanians found in The Free Market, and in a world of expanded and expanding horizons and opportunities that accompany it. This 'opening up' is natural, rational and so obviously amoral and desirable that it scarcely merits attention, let alone discussion. From the sidelines, ordinary Tanzanians tell a decidedly different story of the present through and with human skins and the occult. This is a present of ever-increasing uncertainty, where hard questions must be asked, and tough choices must be made. The fact that Tanzanians voice such concerns, albeit in different registers, makes one thing clear: we would do well to scrutinize 'structural adjustment', its decidedly cultural claims and its not always congenial consequences, rather than denying that such things matter.

Notes

1 As reported on BBC World News, Africa: 'Tanzania's deadly skin trade', Monday 21 June 1999; see also BBC World News, Africa: 'New arrests in witchdoctor skin murders', 16 July 1999; 'Operation to rout out human skin business successful', *Panafrican News Agency*, 21 July 2000.

2 'Dismembered head linked to witchcraft killings', *Panafrican News Agency*, 8 August 2000.

3 'Police hunt human skin traders', *Panafrican News Agency*, 24 September 1999.

4 'African human skulls retrieved from Tanzanian rain maker', *Panafrican News Agency*, 8 February 2000. See 'Minister acknowledges trafficking in human organs', *Panafrican News Agency*, 15 December 2000, for a view from Mozambique; and 'Human skins a hit. . .', *Times of Zambia* (Lusaka) 26 June 1999, from Zambia.

5 This chapter is based on fieldwork in Ihanzu between 1993 and 1995, and especially that between July and September 1999 in Dar es Salaam, Singida and Ihanzu. The 70 tape-recorded interviews I conducted that summer on modernity/development (*maendeleo*), political economy, social change and witchcraft are to be archived with the ESRC, to whom I am grateful for financial support. I thank Henrietta Moore, Albert Schrauwers and Katherine Snyder for their helpful comments on a preliminary draft of this chapter.

6 On Africa, see, e.g., Ashforth 1996; 1998; Auslander 1993; Bastian 1993; Colson 2000; Comaroff and Comaroff 1999; 2000; forthcoming; Geschiere 1997; Rowlands and Warnier 1988.

7 I am not arguing that capitalist ideologies cannot speak in moralizing voices. Clearly they can, and do (Comaroff and Comaroff 2000). Rather the point is that 'structural adjustment' presents itself as being principally about science and objectivity, and thus being amoral.

8 Of late, Foucauldian-inspired approaches to 'development' (e.g. Escobar 1991; 1995; Ferguson 1994; Sachs 1992) have been criticized for presenting development discourses as unduly monolithic and unchanging (Gardner and Lewis 2000: 19; Leach and Fairhead 2000; Moore 1999: 656). I am not arguing that structural adjustment has remained unchanged. My point is that while policy contents may have changed, the rhetorical stance – the pretensions to scientific objectivity and hence amorality – has remained constant.

9 On Nyerere's political thought and how it translated into policy, see Pratt 1976: 63ff. For more general perspectives on *ujamaa* see Hyden 1980 and Shivji 1995.

10 For more detailed accounts of this transition period and beyond, see Campbell and Stein 1992 and Tripp 1997: ch. 4.

11 See Schatz 1996 who argues that 'good governance' and good economic performance need not go hand-in-hand; and Boafo-Arthur 1999 who, using Ghana as an example, explores the contradictions between imposing economic restructuring while insisting on democracy.

12 For more details on these reforms see Kiondo 1992; Stein 1992; and Ndulu and Mwega 1994.

13 Quoted in 'Tanzania's foreign exchange reserve increases three times – IMF', TOMRIC Agency, 18 December 2000.

14 Press Release No. 00/26, 'IMF and IDA support debt relief for Tanzania', International Monetary Fund, 5 April 2000.

15 John A. Corrie, Co-president of ACP/EU Joint Assembly, 'Focus on the plight of the poor, EU tells Tanzania', The East African (Nairobi), 4 January 2001.

16 Michael Okema, 'Happiness in a time of monetary austerity', The East African (Nairobi), 18 November 1998.

17 The question of whether structural adjustment has on balance made Tanzanians worse off, in some *absolute* sense, must remain for another time. For varied views on this issue, see Booth 1994; Campbell and Stein 1992; Lugalla 1995, 1997; Mbilinyi 1990; Ponte 1998; Tripp 1997.

Bibliography

Adam, V. (1963) 'Migrant labour from Ihanzu', Conference Proceedings from the East African Institute of Social Research, Makerere College.

Appadurai, A. (ed.) (1986) *The Social Life of Things: Commodities in Cultural Perspective*, Cambridge: University Press.

Apthorpe, R. (1986) 'Development policy discourse', *Public Administration and Development* 6, 4: 377–389.

Arens, W. and Karp, I. (eds) (1989) *Creativity of Power: Cosmology and Action in African Societies*, Washington DC: Smithsonian Institution Press.

Ashforth, A. (1996) 'Of secrecy and the commonplace: witchcraft and power in Soweto', *Social Research* 63, 4: 1183–1234.

—— (1998) 'Reflections on spiritual insecurity in a modern African city (Soweto)', *African Studies Review* 41, 3: 39–67.

Auslander, M. (1993) '"Open the wombs!": the symbolic politics of modern Ngoni witchfinding', in J. Comaroff and J.L. Comaroff (eds) *Modernity and its Malcontents: Ritual and Power in Postcolonial Africa*, Chicago: University of Chicago Press.

Bastian, M.L. (1993) '"Bloodhounds who have no friends": witchcraft and locality in the Nigerian popular press', in J. Comaroff and J.L. Comaroff (eds) *Modernity and its Malcontents: Ritual and Power in Postcolonial Africa*, Chicago: University of Chicago Press.

—— (1999) ' "Diabolic realities": narratives of conspiracy, transparency and "ritual murder" in the Nigerian popular print and electronic media', paper presented at the workshop Transparency and Conspiracy: Power Revealed and Concealed in (the) Global Village(s), London School of Economics, 28–29 May.

Bernstein, H. (1990) 'Agricultural "modernisation" and the era of structural adjustment: observations on Sub-Saharan Africa', *Journal of Peasant Studies* 18, 1: 3–35.

Boafo-Arthur, K. (1999) 'Ghana: structural adjustment, democratization, and the politics of continuity', *African Studies Review* 42, 2: 41–72.

Booth, D. (1994) 'Economic liberalization, real markets and the (un)reality of structural adjustment in rural Tanzania', *Sociologia Ruralis* xxxiv, 1: 45–62.

Brydon, L. (1999) ' "With a little bit of luck . . .": coping with adjustment in urban Ghana, 1975–90', *Africa* 69, 3: 366–385.

Campbell, H. and Stein, H. (eds) (1992) *Tanzania and the IMF: The Dynamics of Liberalization*, Boulder: Westview Press.

Colson, E. (2000) 'The father as witch', *Africa* 70, 3: 333–358.

Comaroff, J. and Comaroff, J.L. (1993) 'Introduction', in J. Comaroff and J.L. Comaroff (eds) *Modernity and its Malcontents: Ritual and Power in Postcolonial Africa*, Chicago: University of Chicago Press.

—— (1999) 'Occult economies and the violence of abstraction: notes from the South African postcolony', *American Ethnologist* 26, 2: 279–303.

—— (2000) 'Millennial capitalism: first thoughts on a second coming', *Public Culture* (special issue: *Millennial capitalism and the culture of neoliberalism*) 12, 2: 291–343.

—— (forthcoming) 'Alien-nation: zombies, immigrants, and millennial capitalism', in G. Schwab (ed.) *Forces of Globalization*, New York: Columbia University Press.

Douglas, M. (1970) 'Thirty years after *Witchcraft, Oracles and Magic*', in M. Douglas (ed.) *Witchcraft Confessions and Accusations*, London: Tavistock.

Englund, H. and Leach, J. (2000) 'Ethnography and the meta-narratives of modernity', *Current Anthropology* 41, 2: 225–239.

Escobar, A. (1991) 'Anthropology and the development encounter: the making and marketing of development anthropology', *American Ethnologist* 18, 4: 658–682.

—— (1995) *Encountering Development: The Making and Unmaking of the Third World*, Princeton: University Press.

Evans-Pritchard, E.E. (1937) *Witchcraft, Oracles and Magic among the Azande*, Oxford: Clarendon Press.

Ferguson, J. (1994) *The Anti-Politics Machine: 'Development', Depoliticization, and Bureaucratic Power in Lesotho*, Minneapolis: University of Minnesota Press.

—— (1995) 'From African socialism to scientific capitalism: reflections on the legitimation crisis in IMF-ruled Africa', in D.B. Moore and G.J. Schmitz (eds) *Debating Development Discourse: Institutional and Popular Perspectives*, New York: St Martin's Press.

—— (1999) *Expectations of Modernity: Myths and Meanings of Urban Life on the Zambian Copperbelt*, Berkeley: University of California Press.

Gardner, K. and Lewis, D. (2000) 'Dominant paradigms overturned or "business as usual"? Development discourse and the White Paper on International Development', *Critique of Anthropology* 20, 1: 15–29.

Geschiere, P. (1997) *The Modernity of Witchcraft: Politics and the Occult in Postcolonial Africa*, Charlottesville: University Press of Virginia.

Gould, J. and von Oppen, A. (1994) 'Of rhetoric and market: the "liberalization" of food trade in East Africa. Introduction: Representing "the Market"', *Sociologia Ruralis* xxxiv, 1: 3–12.

Gudeman, S. (1986) *Economics as Culture: Models and Metaphors of Livelihood*, London: Routledge.

Harnischfeger, J. (1997) 'Unverdienter Reichtum: Über Hexerei und Ritualmorde in Nigeria', *Sociologus* 47, 2: 129–159.

Heilbroner, R.R. (1973) 'Economics as a "value-free" science', *Social Research* 40, 1: 129–143.

Hyden, G. (1980) *Beyond Ujamaa in Tanzania: Underdevelopment and an Uncaptured Peasantry*, London: Heinemann.

Jones, G.I. (1951) *'Diretlo' Murders in Basutoland (Presented by the Secretary of State for Commonwealth Relations to Parliament by Command of His Majesty)*, London: H.M. Stationery Office.

Kaiser, P.J. (1996) 'Structural adjustment and the fragile nation: the demise of social unity in Tanzania', *The Journal of Modern African Studies* 34, 2: 227–237.

Kiondo, A. (1992) 'The nature of economic reforms in Tanzania', in H. Campbell and H. Stein (eds) *Tanzania and the IMF: The Dynamics of Liberalization*, Boulder: Westview Press.

Leach, M. and Fairhead, J. (2000) 'Fashioned forest pasts, occluded histories? International environmental analysis in west African locales', *Development and Change* 31: 35–59.

Lugalla, J.L.P. (1995) 'The impact of structural adjustment policies on women's and children's health in Tanzania', *Review of African Political Economy* 63: 43–53.

—— (1997) 'Development, change, and poverty in the informal sector during the era of structural adjustment in Tanzania', *Canadian Journal of African Studies* 31, 3: 424–451.

Mabiriizi, D. (1986) 'Reflections on the socio-economic content of medicine murder in Lesotho', *Zimbabwe Law Review* 4, 1/2: 43–59.

Mbilinyi, M. (1990) '"Structural adjustment", agribusiness and rural women in Tanzania', in H. Bernstein *et al.* (eds) *The Food Question: Profits Versus People?*, London: Earthscan.

Mehmet, O. (1999) *Westernizing the Third World: The Eurocentricity of Economic Development Theories*, London: Routledge.

Meyer, B. (1992) '"If you are a devil, you are a witch and, if you are a witch, you are a devil": the integration of "pagan" ideas into the conceptual universe of the Ewe Christians in Southeastern Ghana', *Journal of Religion in Africa* xxii, 2: 98–132.

Middleton, J. (1960) *Lugbara Religion: Ritual and Authority among an East African People*, London: Oxford University Press.

Moore, D.S. (1999) 'The crucible of cultural politics: reworking "development" in Zimbabwe's eastern highlands', *American Ethnologist* 26, 3: 654–689.

Ndulu, B.J. and Mwega, F.W. (1994) 'Economic adjustment policies', in J.D. Barkan (ed.) *Beyond Capitalism Vs. Socialism in Kenya and Tanzania*, Boulder: Lynne Rienner Publishers.

Parish, J. (2000) 'From the body to the wallet: conceptualizing Akan witchcraft at home and abroad', *Journal of the Royal Anthropological Institute* 6, 3: 487–500.

Parry, J. and Bloch, M. (eds) (1989) *Money and the Morality of Exchange*, Cambridge: University Press.

Piot, C. (1999) *Remotely Global: Village Modernity in West Africa*, Chicago: University of Chicago Press.

Ponte, S. (1998) 'Fast crops, fast cash: market liberalization and rural livelihoods in Songea and Morogoro Districts, Tanzania', *Canadian Journal of African Studies* 32, 2: 316–348.

Pottier, J. (1999) *Anthropology of Food: The Social Dynamics of Food Security*, Cambridge: Polity.

Pratt, C. (1976) *The Critical Phase in Tanzania, 1945–1968: Nyerere and the Emergence of a Socialist Strategy*, Cambridge: University Press.

Rasmussen, S. (1998) 'Ritual powers and social tensions as moral discourse among the Taureg', *American Anthropologist* 100, 2: 458–468.

Rowlands, M. and Warnier, J.-P. (1988) 'Sorcery, power and the modern State in Cameroon', *Man* 23: 118–132.

Sachs, W. (ed.) (1992) *The Development Dictionary: A Guide to Knowledge as Power*, London: Zed Books.

Sahlins, M. (1999) 'Two or three things that I know about culture', *Journal of the Royal Anthropological Institute* 5: 399–421.

Sanders, T. (1999) 'Modernity, wealth and witchcraft in Tanzania', *Research in Economic Anthropology* 20: 117–131.

Schatz, S.P. (1996) 'The World Bank's fundamental misconception in Africa', *The Journal of Modern African Studies* 34, 2: 239–247.

Scheper-Hughes, N. (1996) 'Theft of life: organ stealing rumours', *Anthropology Today* 12, 3: 3–10.

—— (2000) 'The global traffic in human organs', *Current Anthropology* 41, 2: 191–224.

Shivji, I.G. (1995) 'The rule of law and *ujamaa* in the ideological formation of Tanzania', *Social and Legal Studies* 4, 2: 147–174.

Soros, G. (1998) *The Crisis of Global Capitalism: Open Society Endangered*, New York: Public Affairs.

Sparr, P. (1994) 'What is structural adjustment?', in P. Sparr (ed.) *Mortgaging Women's Lives: Feminist Critiques of Structural Adjustment*, London: Zed Books.

Stein, H. (1992) 'Economic policy and the IMF in Tanzania: conditionality, conflict, and convergence', in H. Campbell and H. Stein (eds) *Tanzania and the IMF: The Dynamics of Liberalization*, Boulder: Westview Press.

Stoger-Eising, V. (2000) '*Ujamaa* revisited: indigenous and European influences in Nyerere's social and political thought', *Africa* 70, 1: 118–143.

Tripp, A.M. (1997) *Changing the Rules: The Politics of Liberalization and the Urban Informal Economy in Tanzania*, Berkeley: University of California Press.

White, L. (1997) 'The traffic in heads: bodies, borders and the articulation of regional histories', *Journal of Southern African Studies* 23, 2: 325–338.

Wild, E. (1998) '"Is it witchcraft? Is it Satan? It is a miracle": Mai-Mai soldiers and the Christian concepts of evil in north-east Congo', *Journal of Religion in Africa* xxviii, 4: 450–467.

Williams, D. (1999) 'Constructing the economic space: the World Bank and the making of *Homo Oeconomicus*', *Millennium* 28, 1: 79–99.

World Bank (1981) *Accelerated Development in Sub-Saharan Africa: An Agenda for Action*, Washington DC: World Bank.

—— (1989) *Sub-Saharan Africa: From Crisis to Sustainable Growth*, Washington DC: World Bank.

—— (1994) *Adjustment in Africa: Reforms, Results, and the Road Ahead*, New York: Oxford University Press (for the World Bank).

Chapter 9

Witchcraft in the new South Africa

From colonial superstition to postcolonial reality?[1]

Isak Niehaus

> No person with a background in Western science can admit the reality of witchcraft or the 'breath of men' as defined by the Nyakyusa. . .The only solution is to kill the belief in witchcraft. As we have shown, it is somewhat weakened by elementary education and Christian teaching; and we believe that its disappearance turns on increased technical control, particularly in the field of disease, on scientific education, and on the development of interpersonal relations.
>
> (Wilson 1967 [1951]: 135)

> I do not believe in it [witchcraft] myself, but I do not have disdain for the people who believe in it like most of our society seems to have. I understand it from the cultural roots. . . . We [the black consciousness movement] do not reject it. We regard it as part of the mystery of our cultural heritage. . . . Whites are not superstitious; whites do not have witches and witch doctors. We are the people who have this.
>
> (Biko cited in Woods 1978: 166–167)

> Belief in witchcraft and related practices form part of a basic cultural, traditional and customary principle of Africans in South Africa, and Africa as a whole.
>
> (Ralushai *et al.* 1996: 45)

In the Northern Province of South Africa the execution of suspected witches has reached alarming proportions. According to an informed estimate more than 389 witchcraft-related killings occurred between 1985 and 1995.[2] In one gruelling episode during April 1986, members of the Sekhukhuneland Youth Organisation 'necklaced' 43 alleged witches. Police uncovered their corpses in pits and in bushes. A man told reporters that he had seen his wife burnt to death while her assailants sang 'freedom songs'.[3]

Such episodes raise the crucial questions: 'What is to be done about witchcraft in the new South Africa?', and, 'What legislative changes can be implemented to end violence against alleged witches?' As anthropologists we might imagine that we are legislators, and formulate proposals we believe present satisfactory solutions, but we seldom have real power to enforce our prescriptions. In any case, I believe that there is no generally acceptable solution to this particular set of problems. Any action against witchcraft beliefs, witchcraft accusations, and the killing of witches is based on prior assumptions about the meaning and morality of these phenomena. It is unlikely that a consensus would emerge between those who perceive witchcraft as a real danger, those who regard witchcraft as superstition, and others for whom witchcraft beliefs, but not witch-killings, have positive value. In a fundamental sense, witchcraft involves political contestation. Under these circumstances the anthropologist might well make a more appropriate intervention by elucidating cultural meanings and politics that are encoded in actions on witchcraft and by assessing their likely consequences.[4]

Against the backdrop of these assumptions this chapter provides a critical overview of the Ralushai Commission of inquiry into witchcraft.[5] The Commission was appointed in March 1995 by the Executive Council of the Northern Province to investigate the causes of witchcraft-related violence; to review criminal cases pertaining to witchcraft over the previous ten years; and to recommend measures to be undertaken by government to combat such violence. I shall comment on the report in the light of novel ways of dealing with witchcraft that have emerged elsewhere in postcolonial Africa, and with reference to my own ethnographic fieldwork conducted in the Bushbuckridge area of the Northern Province for intermittent periods from 1990 until the present.[6]

Dederen (1996) criticizes the Ralushai report for failing to meet the requirements of rigorous academic research and writing. He describes the report as based on dubious fieldwork; as poorly edited and structured; flawed by the inclusion of unsourced facts from the literature; as containing rare attempts at the critical analysis of data, and as including many unresolved contradictions. The report, he asserts, 'fails to probe beyond the veil of mystery created by accounts of witches, witch-familiars, and zombies' (Dederen 1996: 3).

While I share Dederen's reservations about the scholarly merits of the report, I do not believe that we can underestimate its political significance. I endeavour to show that the Ralushai report presents an important shift in official discourses about witchcraft. I argue that during the eras of segregation and apartheid – from about 1900 to 1994 – the civilizing mission of colonialism that demanded the eradication of witchcraft informed the state's position on witchcraft. By contrast, the ideas expressed in the Ralushai report signal the advent of counter-colonial discourses in the post-apartheid era – since 1994. The new discourses 'subvert the self-confident rationality of imperial science' (Ranger 1996: 271), accept witchcraft as real, and appropriate it as a marker of African identity. Yet I suggest that the official recognition of witchcraft is by no means unambiguous: new lines of contestation are likely to emerge as witchcraft becomes embroiled in politics of African nationalism.

Colonialism, apartheid, and witchcraft

During the eras of segregation and apartheid the civilizing mission of colonialism demanded no compromise with any belief or practice pertaining to witchcraft. These were perceived as repugnant, baseless, and even as diabolic pagan superstitions, which are deeply ingrained in the lives of 'primitive people', and will only disappear with the spread of western civilization, education, and Christianity.[7] Colonial states also saw the prosecution of witches as a challenge to their authority.

In the early colonial period, colonial regimes made a concerted effort to end the trials of witches. The German administration of Tanganyika (now Tanzania) hanged several diviners for naming a person as a witch, who was later killed, and also condemned the killers to death (Mesaki 1994: 50). British administrations outlawed well-known methods of determining witches' guilt such as the poison ordeal.[8] In pre-colonial Africa, witchcraft was a crime. For colonial rulers, it was a superstition, and the African judges and executioners of witches became murderers (Fields 1982: 572).

Since about 1900, British colonial administrations systematized the legal control of witchcraft throughout Africa. They enacted a series of laws that prohibited witchcraft accusation and attempts to practise witchcraft. These laws were, however, implemented with different degrees of severity. In Northern Rhodesia (now Zambia) people pretending to be witches, witch-finders, and even those who commented that illness was caused by 'non-natural' means could be fined £50 and/or be imprisoned for three years. In terms of the 1922 Witchcraft Ordinance of Tanganyika, the High Court could impose fines of up to £200 and/or prison sentences of up to five years. Ugandans could even be punished for wearing charms.[9]

In South Africa, the Suppression of Witchcraft Act No. 3 of 1957, as amended in 1970, consolidated earlier colonial laws into unified legislation for the whole country.[10] In terms of the Act, anyone who indicates another person as being a witch, or attempts to practise witchcraft, can be fined up to R2,000, imprisoned for up to ten years, and/or whipped up to ten strokes. If a person accused of witchcraft was killed, the perpetrator could be jailed for up to twenty years. A second category of offenders are persons who approach 'witch-doctors' to 'smell out' others as witches; advise others how to bewitch, supply them with the 'pretended means of witchcraft', or attempt to put into operation processes calculated to injure other people or things. These offenders can be sentenced to a fine not exceeding R500 and/or imprisoned for a period not exceeding five years. Even those who claim to possess the powers of divination can be fined R200 or imprisoned for two years.

In practice, however, the manner in which colonial states dealt with witchcraft often contradicted the ideals of the civilizing mission. Fields (1982) suggests that colonial regimes could not afford large-scale policing to rule solely by force. Nor was there sufficient commonality between the rulers and the ruled that would have enabled the exercise of legitimate authority. In this context, she argues, order could only be sustained by not upsetting routine ways of thinking and behaving. Hence the maintenance of African authorities, redeployment of African institutions, and preservation of indigenous culture, thus became paradoxical conditions for achieving the civilizing mission (Fields 1982: 569).[11]

In South Africa such ambiguities were pronounced. Whilst the National Party government certainly possessed the coercive capacities to enforce adherence to the Suppression of Witchcraft Act, the segregationist policy of apartheid ostensibly ensured African self-government. As in the case of British indirect administration, the South African state reserved land for exclusive African occupation, and allowed chiefs to enforce 'Native law and custom' on a daily basis. In Parliament, speakers of the United Party opposition pointed out that by 'reverting to the tribal system' government impeded that progress towards civilization that would lead to the demise of witchcraft.[12]

In Bushbuckridge, Northern Sotho and Tsonga-speakers were guaranteed rights of residence beneath the Moholoholo mountains by the 1913 Land Act, and by the proclamation of Native Reserves and Bantustans. In such areas Act 38 of 1927 entrenched the authority of chiefs over their subjects. Such juridical autonomy enabled chiefs to accede to the demand by villagers for the control of witches. Out of sight and earshot of the Native Commissioners, chiefs tried cases that touched on witchcraft, and mediated in witchcraft accusations among commoners. Chiefs authorized witch-diviners to determine the guilt of the accused, condoned the ritual humiliation of those identified as witches, and ensured that the bewitched were compensated in cattle for the crimes committed against them. Chiefs and their councillors also sought out and punished witches who stopped rain. By managing misfortune in this way and by protecting their subjects from harm, chiefs tapped a potent source of political legitimacy.

The Native Commissioners seemed to have ignored these infringements, perhaps because they involved minimal violence. Only with the establishment of Bantu Authorities in 1958 did chiefs become more directly accountable to Bantu Affairs Commissioners. This, and also the unfortunate killing of a man who had allegedly bewitched chief Seganyane II in 1959, placed chiefs under greater pressure to comply with the stipulations of the Suppression of Witchcraft Act. But chiefs and headmen still occasionally intervened in cases of suspected witchcraft, in defiance of the Commissioners.

The position of the colonial state was, moreover, not without ambiguity. Mesaki (1994: 50) comments that colonial laws did allow the accusers formally to bring charges of witchcraft before magistrates and the courts. The British Witchcraft Ordinances of 1928 and 1958 empowered District Officers to deport alleged witches to specific localities. Moreover, line officers of the colonial administrations often revised formulations of the witchcraft laws when implementing them.[13] Fields (1982: 85) notes that the *bamcapi* witch-cleansing movement, which swept large parts of central Africa in the 1930s, led to manifold violations of the witchcraft laws, colonial administrators maintaining a policy of 'watchful tolerance' and allowing chiefs to have their localities cleansed. Occasionally, the officers themselves utilized 'traditional expertise' to deal with witchcraft. In the 1940s, increased witchcraft accusations prompted the District Commissioner of Ulanga, Tanganyika, to send *mganga* to conduct mass shavings. (These were thought to suppress the powers of witches and to protect people against bewitchment.) Within village communities a perception even arose that colonial governments had appointed anti-witchcraft specialists for purposes of development (Green 1994: 29).

Officers of the South African government, too, could not consistently ignore witchcraft beliefs. In the 1950s, a prominent chief of the Eastern Cape complained to the Chief Native Commissioner that a man had been seen riding around his kraal at midnight, mounted on a baboon. The Commissioner saved the alleged witch from serious injury by having him removed to another district.[14] Since the early 1990s the South African Police Service have regularly intervened in accusations of witchcraft in Bushbuckridge and have protected the accused from harm by confining them to a locality behind the Acornhoek police station (Niehaus 1998). The Ralushai Commission of inquiry documents cases elsewhere in which police officers have actually investigated allegations of witchcraft. For example, in 1994 police took statements after a 5-year-old boy had disappeared from his home in the Tafelkop area of Lebowa. The boy returned to his parents with a cut on his foot. Inside the wound was a small stone, a piece of wood and herbal substances. The boy's nails and hair had been cut, and he claimed that a man had pushed a piece of wire into his penis. On 27 January 1995 teachers in Lebowa complained to the police that a soot-like substance was sprinkled into a schoolgirl's food. The police sent the food to the Forensic Chemistry Laboratories in Johannesburg for analysis, but no toxic substances could be detected. Neither case resulted in an arrest (Ralushai *et al.* 1996: 99, 188–190).

During the apartheid era the Suppression of Witchcraft Act was implemented very inconsistently in areas currently comprising the Northern Province. The Ralushai Commission compiled 211 cases relating to witchcraft that appeared in police dockets or that were brought before the courts between 1985 and 1995. Very few of these cases resulted in prosecutions in terms of the Act, and the sentences that were imposed on those who were tried and convicted were very uneven. Only 47 (25 per cent) of the 190 persons accused of having named others as witches, and of having threatened them with violence, were found guilty.[15] Suspended sentences were given to 9; 1 was sentenced to receive strokes with a light cane, 5 were sentenced to imprisonment (for periods varying from three to ten months); and 32 to an option of a fine or imprisonment (ranging from R60 or two months, to R1,000 or twelve months). Of the 230 persons accused of having perpetrated violence against alleged witches 71 (31 per cent) were prosecuted for contravening the Act, or for common assault, attempted murder, malicious damage to property, or arson.[16] Suspended sentences were given to 21; 8, strokes with a light cane; 4 were ordered to pay R175 in damages; 5 sentenced to imprisonment (for periods of between three months and two years); and 33 given the option of a fine or imprisonment (ranging from R30 or ten days, to R1,000 or eight months.)

Between 1985 and 1995 the courts prosecuted 109 (52 per cent) of the 209 persons accused of participating in witch-killings.[17] Suspended sentences were given to 12; 4, strokes with a light cane; and 84 were imprisoned (for periods varying from 18 months to life). Judges often treated the belief in witchcraft as an extenuating circumstance. In the case of *State* v. *Mathabi*, Justice van der Walt considered sentencing to death four accused who had pleaded guilty to murder but he accepted their claim that they had thought the deceased was a witch and reduced the penalty to five years' imprisonment, of which two years were suspended.[18]

Witchcraft beliefs were also treated as a suitable ground for appeal, and at times their recognition contributed to the passage of very light sentences. In 1985 Neledzani Netshiavha was woken by a scratching sound on his door. He picked up an axe, walked outside, and chopped down an animal hanging on the rafters of his roof. After it fell to the ground, Neledzani chopped it a second and a third time. Villagers, who came to see the 'animal', described it as a donkey or a large bat, but it later assumed the shape of an elderly man who was a reputed witch. Neledzani had killed this man. A judge of the Venda Supreme Court sentenced him to ten years' imprisonment for culpable homicide. The Bloemfontein Appeal Court, however, reduced his sentence to four years.[19] In 1991, six men who had stoned and burnt to death four alleged witches, were convicted of the murder, but sentenced to only five years' imprisonment, wholly suspended on condition that they underwent 100 hours' community service.[20]

Hence the tensions between the civilizing mission of colonialism and systems of indirect rule such as apartheid were profound. Such tensions gave rise to various contradictions and ambiguities that undermined the efforts of the South African State to act decisively against witchcraft beliefs. In certain respects legislation such as the Suppression of Witchcraft Act No. 3 of 1957, was more important as a symbolic statement of the state's ideological commitment to modernization, than as a legislative attempt to eradicate witchcraft accusations. Postcolonial critics of the civilizing mission seldom give sufficient weight to these contradictions.

Regulating witchcraft in post-apartheid South Africa

Independence saw increased agitation in many parts of Africa that the state should no longer remain indifferent to witchcraft. Some African intellectuals, who perceive witchcraft as real, have even reproached the courts for refusing to sentence witches. However, postcolonial governments have not responded in a uniform manner. While governments, such as those of Tanzania, retained the colonial outlook and legislation (Abrahams 1994), state courts in Cameroon have freely convicted witches (Fisiy and Geschiere 1990), and in Malawi a system of 'traditional' courts have dealt with witchcraft (Motshekga 1984: 12–13). Independence thus inaugurated new lines of contestation.

The report of the Ralushai Commission, which is likely to be a centrepiece in official debates about witchcraft in the new South Africa, presents a decisive break from the civilizing mission of colonialism. It is informed by the works of John Mbiti, a theologian; Gordon Chavunduka, former Principal of the University of Zimbabwe, and President of the Zimbabwe National Traditional Healers' Association (ZINATHA); and Mathole Motshekga, a legal scholar. These influences are apparent in lengthy citations and in some passages that follow the sources very closely.

Mbiti (1970: 9–10) castigates the colonial assumption that witchcraft is a myth which only exists in the mind of the ignorant, and appropriates it as a marker of African identity. He asserts that witchcraft is a traditional religious concept that continues to dominate the background of African people.

Chavunduka (1982: 4) finds the definition of witchcraft, by Rhodesian law, as 'the throwing of bones, use of charms and other devices' to be misplaced. The Ndebele and Shona terms *umthakati* and *muroyi* rather denote troublemakers, poisoners, and those who eat corpses, dance naked and cause misfortune. Chavunduka concedes that some claims – such as the one that witches can fly – are purely mythical, but he insists that other activities could be factual (Scheper-Hughes 2000). Poisoning has been verified by the examination of substances. Confessions about witchcraft, with a striking degree of corroboration between witnesses, are also commonplace.[21] For example, three women separately stated in court that they killed the husband of one woman by feeding him roots, snake skin, and powder from a lion's heart, in his sleep (Chavunduka 1982: 13). Since the witnesses were not forced to confess, nor were they insane, and could not possibly have dreamt the same dream, Chavunduka concludes that such statements could be valid. Verbal threats and the placing of objects in footpaths can also have deadly consequences. The belief that one had been bewitched might induce prolonged tension, shock, a fall in blood pressure, and food refusal – leading to death.[22] While Chavunduka acknowledges that the laws prevent innocent people from being accused, he asserts that they do not solve the problem of witchcraft. 'It is as if one were to tell a physician engaged in public health work that he could eradicate malaria by merely denying its existence' (Chavunduka 1982: 19).

Motshekga (1984) claims that in assessing blame for criminal cases involving witchcraft, colonial courts model their judgements on European standards of 'reasonableness'. He cites the example of a Kenyan court that, in 1922, sentenced 70 men to death for killing an old woman whom they believed to have been a witch. Likewise, a South African court convicted a male youth of culpable homicide. He had lived in a community haunted by the *tikoloshe*, entered a hut, and dealt several blows to the supposed *tikoloshe* with a hatchet. When he dragged it out he discovered that he had killed a small child, his nephew.[23] In both cases judges rejected claims by the defence that the accused had acted in 'imaginary self-defence', and argued that witchcraft cannot be recognized by English or Roman Dutch law.[24] Motshekga notes that the judgements did not express a humanitarian concern for the reformation of criminals, but a utilitarian objective of effecting social change through exemplary deterrence. He contends, however, that existing laws have hitherto proven ineffective in eradicating the blight of witchcraft (Motshekga 1984: 11).

These scholars advocate a new legal approach, in which Africans are judged by African norms, and witchcraft comes under the purview of the law. Chavunduka and Motshekga envisage an important role for 'traditional courts'. Chavunduka (1982: 17) proposes that traditional courts should deal with the social aspects of witchcraft accusations, reconcile the disputing parties, and encourage deviants to conform; while formal courts should focus on the legal aspects of such cases.[25] Motshekga (1984) commends the Malawian system of traditional courts. He cites the example of a man who, in 1974, threatened to send a swarm of bees to the hostel where a schoolgirl lived, and to bury 'medicines' at the entrance to cause all the schoolgirls to run amok. After an outbreak of mass hysteria at the hostel, a Malawian traditional court found him guilty of imitating witchcraft. Motshekga (1984: 13) regards this judgement as 'exemplary', but regrets that the Malawian courts admit only to the 'pretence' of witchcraft.

The membership of the Ralushai Commission ensured a wide representation of African voices, previously unheard in the formulation of witchcraft laws. The commissioners, who were headed by Prof. Ralushai (a social anthropologist and retired deputy principal of the University of Venda) also included Prof. van Heerden (a professor of law), Pastor Masingi (a former magistrate), Mr Ndou (an attorney), Mr Mphaphuli (a chief), Mr Mathiba (President of a South African Council of Traditional Healers), Ms Madiba (a theologian), Brig. Mokwena (of the South African Police), and Mr Matabane (a former ANC representative in Washington).

Their lengthy report (288 pages) consists of data generated from fieldwork, some recommendations, and 150 pages of court material, pictures, and maps. The commissioners undertook what Dederen (1996: 1) calls a 'magical mystery tour' to interview representatives of 173 communities (including Acornhoek) and 43 different organizations. The latter were associations for *dingaka* (diviner/herbalists), churches, health workers, policemen, civic organizations, chiefs, students, and political parties. They also attended eight peace rallies, and three rallies of chiefs. These investigations enabled the authors to claim that the belief in witches is virtually omnipresent among Africans. Educated people reportedly cited Shakespeare to justify their beliefs. Zionist church members quoted Exodus 22, Deuteronomy 18, and Acts 8. Only the leaders of European-controlled churches 'condemned witchcraft beliefs in the language of the missionaries', and spokespersons for a few isolated communities doubted the existence of zombies (p. 18).

In presenting this data the commissioners dissolve the spectrum of opinion into impersonal phrases, such as 'it is believed' (Dederen 1996: 1). This mode of presentation supports the report's contention that witchcraft is an expression of a uniform and unique African culture. Though Indians marginally participate in these practices – for example by selling *dihlare* (herbal potions) to Africans – whites are neither perceived to be the perpetrators or victims of witchcraft (p. 25). By consistently using atemporal concepts, such as 'traditional', the authors also represent witchcraft as primordial, and obscure changes in belief. The report states that: 'our forefathers regarded witchcraft as an integral part of our lives'; 'traditionally' mainly women were accused; 'traditional healers' sniffed out witches; and 'traditional courts' punished witches by shaving their heads, imposing fines, drowning them, or by roasting them in fires (pp. 13, 21, 28). The authors claim that traditional beliefs moulded Christianity rather than *vice versa*. Religious teaching reportedly had little impact, and church people 'still adhere to traditional beliefs relating to witchcraft and the ancestors' (p. 50). In short the authors invoke the past to explain the present.

The report only contains a short description of contemporary witchcraft beliefs. Witches inherit a craving for evil-doing from the maternal side, or buy poisons from 'traditional healers' (p. 23). The deeds ascribed to them include the uttering of life-threatening curses; the causing of misfortune, illness, abortions, and death; and the sending of lightning to destroy people's property. Numerous familiars and items of witchcraft are listed, but their symbolic meanings are left unexplored (p. 22).[26] There is also hardly any mention of wealth, reproduction, and fertility.

The authors insinuate that these beliefs are factual with reference to two perplexing accounts of zombies.[27] In one account four naked women called a man from his sleep, and took him to a tree where they forced him to drink 'medicine' that tasted like oil. At a house he was shown people who had died long ago. Villagers later found the man in a kraal (p. 18). Another account concerns Jack Mafikeng, an alleged zombie, who returned to his family 25 years after he was buried (p. 19). The authors contemplate no alternative explanations for these events.

The report none the less condemns the recent witch-hunts and killings as 'senseless', 'brutal', 'uncivilized' and 'barbaric' (Ralushai *et al.* 1996: 62, 121, 270). It is estimated that at least 389 alleged witches were killed between 1985 and 1995. This figure is acknowledged to be a vast underestimate, as many respondents were reluctant to give information about the killings in fear of victimization. The authors also condemn the destruction of the homes of alleged witches, their banishment, and the refusal to allow their children to attend school.

The report does not offer a clear explanation for the violence, but lays blame at the door of the entire community. Male youths, known as Comrades, are recognized to have been at the forefront of the violence, and it is acknowledged that political motives were sometimes involved. The execution of witches was apparently informed by the killing of 'political undesirables' in the urban areas, and aimed to discredit Bantustan governments and chiefs who had become upholders of apartheid (Ralushai *et al.* 1996: 32). However, the authors argue that adults manipulated the youth. Adults reportedly delegated responsibility for punishing witches to the youth because the courts treat juvenile offenders more leniently (Ralushai *et al.* 1996: 32). In fact, the authors suggest that local communities saw the youth as 'heroes and protectors'.

'Traditional healers', who sniff out witches on the receipt of money, are identified as key actors in the commission of these crimes (Ralushai *et al.* 1996: 29). The authors none the less empathize with the healers, and explain how youths forced many healers to point out witches. Despite the missionaries' condemnation of traditional healing, they observe that there are about 10,000 healers in Johannesburg whom 85 per cent of black households occasionally consult (Ralushai *et al.* 1996: 47). Most inherit their skills from their ancestors, are clean and well-educated. Current disarray in the practice is seen to result from improper control by rival associations of healers, with conflicting rules of conduct. The associations do not always ensure that their members are well qualified, and clients who are exploited cannot lodge complaints to the associations.

The authors criticize law enforcement agencies as ineffective. Due to the concentration of police stations in white residential areas during the apartheid years, African rural areas are deprived of effective policing. The arrests of witch-killers has also been impeded by the fact that existing police stations are manned by the members of local communities, who are reluctant to investigate cases which involve their relatives. Many police believe in witchcraft and feel that witches impose an unnecessary burden on them. Moreover, the courts have not been able to build strong cases because witnesses are reluctant to testify. Consequently, serious offenders are easily released.

For the authors the Suppression of Witchcraft Act is an unacceptable solution to the problems of witchcraft and witch-killings. Respondents perceived the Act as unjust because it does not aim to punish witches, but those who name others as witches. Some condoned the killings. Others felt that witches should be kept in special places, perhaps with the wild animals in the Kruger National Park (Ralushai *et al.* 1996: 17). 'Traditionalists' believed the 'old order' should be restored, and that chiefs and diviners should be empowered to deal with witchcraft. 'Modernists' felt witch-killings should be ended by means of education, the church, and the mass media (Ralushai *et al.* 1996: 15).

The Commission makes the following recommendations:

1 *Education*   It urges government to embark upon a programme of education that would 'liberate people mentally', so that they would refrain from perpetrating violence against witches. Workshops, rallies, music competitions, and media programmes should be organized to show the futility of witch purges; and 'experts on African customs' should design courses in

school syllabi (Ralushai *et al.* 1996: 60). The report emphasizes that churches can play a valuable role, and commends the Zion Christian Church who formed their own commission of inquiry into witchcraft. The Zion Christian Church assured the Member of the Executive Council for Safety and Security of their co-operation in the fight against witchcraft-related violence, stated that they disapproved of consultations with *dingaka*, and condemned the use of violence for political purposes (Ralushai *et al.* 1996: 50).

2 *Research*   According to the Commission, the development of sound policies on witch-killings requires more accurate information. Legal experts and eminent scholars – such as Gordon Chavunduka and Jean La Fontaine – should be invited to participate in educational programmes. The police should regularly submit more reliable statistics to the Member of the Executive Council (MEC) for Safety and Security, and witchcraft should be researched on a more regular basis. 'Our universities, specifically the historic-ally black universities, should embark upon an intensive research program dealing with witchcraft and ritual killings as most students in these univers-ities come from communities in which these practices are still prevalent' (p. 62).

3 *Legislative Changes*   The report proposes that the Suppression of Witchcraft Act be repealed and replaced by a Witchcraft Control Act. In terms of the new Act, those who practise witchcraft would receive the harshest punish-ments. Any person who creates 'reasonable suspicion' that he/she practises witchcraft; puts into operation any process, which is calculated to damage another person or thing, professes knowledge of witchcraft, advises another person how to bewitch, or supplies him/her with the 'means of witchcraft' would be liable to imprisonment for up to four years and/or a fine of up to R4,000. Persons who 'without any reasonable or justifiable cause' name, or employ 'witch-doctors' to indicate another person as a witch, would be liable upon conviction to a fine not exceeding R3,000 and/or a prison sentence not exceeding three years. People who collect money to employ 'witch-doctors' to indicate others as witches, or force 'witch-doctors' to indicate other persons as witches, would be liable to a fine of up to R2,000 and/or imprisoned for up to two years.

4 *The Control of Traditional Medical Practitioners*   The Commission proposes that, as in Zimbabwe (Chavunduka 1986), a Traditional Medical Practi-tioners' Council be established to regulate the practice of 'traditional healers' in the Northern Province. The council is to be a corporate body comprising twelve members – a chairman, vice chairman, five members elected by trad-itional healers, and five members appointed by the Minister.[28] The Minister shall also appoint a registrar to serve as secretary of the council, with the right to dismiss councillors who fail to comply with their duties. The proposed council is to maintain a register of traditional healers and to hold inquiries for purposes of the Act (Ralushai *et al.* 1996: 66). Only registered healers would be allowed to practise for gain and to use the title 'Traditional

Medical Practitioner' or 'Spirit Medium'. If found guilty of improper conduct the healer could be ordered to pay a fine, suspended, or expelled. Unregistered healers who practise for gain, falsify certificates, or use unauthorised titles could be fined up to R2,000 and/or be imprisoned for two years.

The Commission also proposes that a National Traditional Healers' Association, headed by an executive of 25 members, be established to unite all 'traditional healers', 'spirit mediums' and 'faith healers' into one body. Its aims would be to prevent quackery, promote traditional medicine and the beneficial aspects of African culture, and to co-operate with ministries and other organizations involved in the field of health.

Dederen (1996: 6) describes these proposals as too vague and general to qualify as meaningful solutions. He laments the lack of specific information about the educational programmes and questions whether the condemnation of witchcraft-related violence by churches would have much of an effect, particularly in the light of the earlier assertion that religious teachings have had little influence on witchcraft beliefs. Dederen states that it remains an unresolved riddle how the Witchcraft Control Act would counter witchcraft-related violence while nurturing the very ideologies in which they are rooted.

To these criticisms one can add that the proposals make no reference to the status of the courts of chiefs. Neither do they address the question of evidence. How would 'reasonable suspicion' of practising witchcraft, or 'justifiable cause' for naming another person as a witch, be determined? For example, could a similar solution be adopted as the one in the East Province of Cameroon where diviners are allowed to act as key witnesses in state courts (Fisiy 1990; Fisiy and Geschiere 1990, 1996)? The proposals about traditional healers do not specifically refer to the pointing out of witches. The inclusion of the distinctively Zimbabwean category 'spirit medium', and the lack of any distinction between diviners and witch-diviners, raises further concern. So does the neglect of witchcraft attributions by Christian prophets, and the assumption that Christian healers would sedately accept membership of a national body for 'traditional medical practitioners'.

Witchcraft as postcolonial dilemma

Though not a blueprint for action, the Ralushai report none the less indicates a general direction in the formulation of policy that might guard against the worst pitfalls that have arisen from modernization strategies embarked upon elsewhere in Africa, such as in Tanzania. After independence, the Tanzanian government vigorously implemented *ujamaa* villagization schemes and replaced chiefs with appointed officials. They retained the British witchcraft laws to demonstrate their opposition to the whole complex of beliefs and practices, and made hardly any official provision for witchcraft accusations. This strategy has had disastrous effects, and has led to fierce contestation between village communities and the state. In the absence of any institutional support, Tanzanian villagers have resorted to self-help to eradicate witchcraft. In Sukumaland 3,072 witch-killings occurred between 1970 and 1988. Yet state courts have only prosecuted seven people for these killings (Mesaki 1994: 52). In the 1970s, 12 people died when the security personnel of Sukumaland rounded up 897 suspected witches and criminals. In response the Tanzanian government imprisoned four police officers, forced two Regional Commissioners and two Ministers to resign, and threatened to take severe actions against the diviners who continued to identify witches (Mesaki 1994: 57). Yet these repressive actions did not have the desired outcome. In the 1980s the killings resumed, as Sungusungu vigilante groups arrogated the authority for administering justice (Bukurura 1994).

Evidence from Bushbuckridge, South Africa, shows a correlation between the non-recognition of witchcraft by political authorities and the advent of witch-killings. Hardly any killings occurred before the 1960s, when nearly all chiefs actively mediated in witchcraft accusations between commoners. Chiefs encouraged household heads to report suspected witches to their courts. When hearing a witchcraft case, the chiefs required both the accuser and the accused to deposit a stake of five cattle for safekeeping at the royal kraal. The chief and each party then elected representatives to accompany the accused to a witch-diviner in Phundu Malia, near Venda. (They walked the entire distance, 200 kilometres, each way.) If the witch-diviner pronounced the accused to be a witch, he would cut holes into his or her clothes and would shave his or her hair in a rough manner. The accuser would then collect the cattle from the royal kraal. If the accused was found not guilty, he or she blew a goat's horn upon entering the village, and would be awarded cattle in compensation for being wrongfully accused.[29] This measure dissipated the accusers desire for vengeance, and gave those accused of witchcraft a chance to prove their innocence.

In the 1960s growing dependence on migrant labour, villagization, and the emergence of new forms of inequality heightened suspicions of witchcraft. The implementation of Bantu Authorities exacerbated these problems. When chiefs were prohibited from intervening in witchcraft, a perception arose that chiefs sided with witches. This, paradoxically, brought about greater violence as villagers took justice into their own hands and took revenge against those whom they suspected of witchcraft. The prosecution of witch-killers only enhanced conflict between villagers and government. In 1986, political activists, known as Comrades, exploited popular discontent, and killed more than 36 suspected witches in an attempt to eliminate evil, and so to attain legitimacy as a political movement. Indeed, these attacks became linked to a broader challenge to the state's control of local government, the courts, and schools (see Delius 1996; Niehaus 1993; Ritchken 1995; Van Kessel 1993).

The unbanning of the ANC in 1990 did not bring an end to witchcraft accusations or to witch killings.[30] Yet it is significant that no loss of life occurred in the public witch-hunts that took place during the period of my fieldwork. In these dramas alternative forms of punishment came into play. For example, in

December 1990, after several mysterious deaths occurred in the village of Green Valley, Comrades took about 100 suspects to a witch-diviner in Mbuzini, near Swaziland. Thirty-five elders were identified as witches and were ritually punished – they were beaten behind the neck with a switch, were commanded to undress, painted with black oil, and their hair was shaven in a rough manner.[31] At home ANC leaders ensured that no further harm was done to the alleged witches, but forced them to burn their herbs.[32] Six years later Patrick Mnisi, a resident of Rooiboklaagte who worked as a malaria control officer at the Department of Health, started a truck to collect the other workers from work. Only 100 metres from his home two armed men stopped the truck, shot Patrick dead, and fled into a nearby forest. After Patrick's death rumours circulated that he had been a notorious witch and that the kin of his victims had hired the assailants. In contrast to the Green Valley witch-hunt in this case, the accusers' desire for vengeance found expression in homicide.

While the institutional provision for witchcraft accusations may well suppress witch-killings in the short term, experiences in the East Province of Cameroon show that state intervention too can have dire consequences. Here individuals who protest their innocence have been imprisoned for periods of ten years on the basis of testimony provided by certified diviners (*nkong*). Diviners have also searched the homes of suspects for evidence and dragged them before the courts. Fisiy and Geschiere (1990) see this practice as indicative of deepening economic inequalities and of a novel alliance between state elites and the diviners. Since independence, elites have relied on the occult powers (*djambe*) of diviners to strengthen their positions, outwit their rivals, and to mediate between them and judges. In the eyes of the elite, witchcraft presents an anti-modern barrier to progress. Those convicted of witchcraft have invariably been the less fortunate who supposedly attack successful persons out of envy.[33] Ordinary villagers, who are alienated from the process of accusation, continue to fear witchcraft. They view the diviners as ambivalent figures, who can only help against witchcraft because they too are representatives of *djambe*. By recognizing diviners the government has thus strengthened the very forces it tries to combat (Fisiy and Geschiere 1990: 153). Villagers fear that the destructive tendencies of the diviners may get the upper hand. They also perceive imprisonment as an ineffective sanction because witches can learn new forms of witchcraft in jail. This diverges from their expectation that the *nkong* should render the powers of witches harmless.

As in Cameroon, witchcraft accusations in the Bushbuckridge area of South Africa are intimately related to deepening economic inequalities. Since the 1960s these accusations increased dramatically, partly due to the implementation of villagization schemes that made people completely dependent upon migrant labour. The greater inequities of a migrant labour economy were fertile breeding grounds for feelings of envy and resentment, and for suspicions of witchcraft. Residents of Bushbuckridge conceive of witchcraft as the destructive power of the subordinate. According to villagers, witches were deprived, marginal, and poorer persons, who were so envious and resentful that they attacked more fortunate kin and neighbours. My analysis of 291 witchcraft accusations in the village of Green Valley in Bushbuckridge shows that 18 (6 per cent) occurred between cognates, 120 (42 per cent) between relatives by marriage, and 153 (53 per cent) between non-kin. Those accused have primarily been neglected parents, siblings who have been deprived of their inheritance, wives who suffer excessive domination, affines with no rights to the children of their daughters, jilted lovers, and unsuccessful neighbours who fail to make ends meet. Villagers believed that any sign of success could motivate attacks from envious neighbours. For example, when Florence Nokeri took her ill child to a diviner, she was told that a noise at her home attracted the attention of her neighbours. Florence asked the diviner whether it could be the music system that her husband had recently purchased. The diviner replied, 'Yes. This can make such a sound. Be careful! Your neighbours are on your heels!'

Witchcraft accusations have reinforced rather than challenged social privilege. Persons of relatively greater status and influence could manipulate this cultural fantasy to their own advantage. By accusing poorer neighbours of witchcraft, educated young men who held well-paid jobs defended social inequality. They legitimated their own success and defined their neighbours' desires for a better life as illegitimate and evil. After he had obtained a BA degree from the University of the North, Ruben Malatsi held an ostentatious graduation party, but did not invite Ena Sekgobela his next-door neighbour who was much poorer than himself. When Ena asked whether she could see Rubin's cake, his sister believed that Ena wanted to poison the cake and chased her away. In this manner witchcraft accusations excused uncharitable behaviour.

Stadler (1994) and Comaroff and Comaroff (1999) correctly highlight the generational dimensions of witchcraft in South Africa. The supposed victims of witchcraft have often been youngsters, and the most notable perpetrators of violence against witches – the Comrades – are predominantly initiated but unmarried men. In contrast, those whom they have accused of witchcraft have predominantly been middle-aged and elderly persons. This pattern of accusations does not diverge from the above-mentioned inequalities. Whilst the Comrades, themselves, might well be poor and unemployed, the local character of the struggle was such as to give them considerable political power. Elders have become politically subordinate. Their power of adulthood slips away into infertility and infirmity, and their status rests purely on their control of esoteric knowledge (cf. Heald 1986). The association of elders with witchcraft reflects perceptions of increasing political marginalization.

Hence, as in the case of Cameroon, it is likely that in the condoning of witchcraft accusations the South African state would entrench social inequality. Moreover, in the South African lowveld the regulation from above of diviners – who have until now derived their powers from ancestors and alien spirits rather than from political authorities – could fundamentally alter their basis of legimacy.[34] It could also accord the Minister, who would effectively become the chief of all diviners, new powers in the realm of the occult.

Conclusions

The control of witchcraft by postcolonial states may well be as ambiguous and impractical as the suppression of witchcraft was in colonial times. Postcolonial discourses have, in important ways, failed to transcend the central assumptions of the colonial civilizing mission, which is that witchcraft is a residual survival of a preliterate African culture. In the postcolonial vision of the Ralushai Commission, beliefs in witchcraft are no longer stigmatized, but are still a marker of a unique and primordial African identity.[35] This claim is not only inaccurate, but it is as improper as the argument that racism is an expression of Afrikaner culture.

Witchcraft beliefs are not unique to Africans. They are also encountered in pre-revolutionary Russia (Worobec 1995), in India (Bailey 1997), France (Favret-Saada 1980), and in tales of satanic child abuse in the United States and in England (Comaroff 1994, 1997; La Fontaine 1998). In South Africa the *tokkelosie* has on occasions been described as Afrikaner folklore (Coetzee 1938: 59), while fears of satanism and consultations of 'witch-doctors' are common present-day concerns among whites (Chidester 1992: 60–66; MacCullum 1993). Indeed, after I participated in a discussion about witchcraft on the television programme *Two Ways* I received several telephone calls from distressed white residents of Johannesburg's affluent suburbs who earnestly believed that they had been the victims of witchcraft. As evidence the callers referred to consistent illness and misfortune, herbal substances they uncovered in their sitting rooms, and inexplicable cracks in their swimming pools. In December 1999, Laviena Human, an Afrikaner woman from Louis Trichardt in the Northern Province, pleaded guilty in court to attempted murder after she paid a fellow African employee R7,000 to get a concoction from a herbalist to kill her husband. Her husband, Jasper Human, became violently ill after she sprinkled the smelly mixture in his food, but he survived.[36]

Neither is the belief in witchcraft primordial. In the lowveld, these beliefs have been marked by radical changes through time. During the earlier period of subsistence agriculture witchcraft accusations were inhibited by the vital import-ance of solidarity between the members of *metse* (extended households) and their neighbours. By attributing misfortune to ancestral displeasure or states of pollution, people shifted the burden of blame onto forces that were less disruptive of interpersonal relations. With villagization, the fragmentation of *metse* into smaller households, and increased labour migration, these inhibitions disappeared. Conflict between kin and neighbours and new forms of inequality favoured more personalized theories of misfortune causation. At the same time the emergence of a this-worldly and dualistic Christian worldview led to the formulation of witchcraft as the most concrete manifestation of evil (Niehaus 1997).

While witchcraft may not be a discourse about modernity *per se* (Englund 1996), it can none the less only be understood within the frame of contemporary social and political concerns. As I have argued elsewhere, the symbolic meanings of witch-familiars, such as the ape-like *tokolotši* and the snake-like *mamlambo* are intimately related to a people's participation in the modern capitalist economy as migrant labourers (Niehaus 1995). Fears of the *tokolotši* – which is used by single adults to rape those whom they desire sexually – arose in the context of an economic system which obliges wage-earning men to live apart from their spouses for the greatest part of their working lives. The belief in the *mamlambo* – which brings wealth, but demands human sacrifices in return – reflects upon the deprivations and the all-consuming desire for money which are keynotes of the monetary economy. Stories of the occult also refer to witches who keep white persons as familiars, and use dangerous technologies described as *sekgowa* ('ways of the whites'). These include chemical poisons, trains, automobiles, and even remote-controlled devices. This symbolic association between witches and whites contains important elements of a critique of white domination (Niehaus 1997: 123–159). Witchcraft accusations arise from contemporary predicaments in South Africa's rural areas such as the frailty of marriage; tensions about the diffusion of migrant wages; conflict over inheritance; competition for residential stands; rivalries among businessmen and church leaders; and enmities between richer and poorer neighbours. Witch-hunting occurred alongside other campaigns of the Comrades in their struggles for national liberation.

Finally, colonial and postcolonial representations alike construct witchcraft as a bounded total system, torn loose from any social context.[37] This vision does not capture the fluid manner in which villagers situationally invoke witchcraft beliefs as they encounter perplexing events – such as the appearance of snakes in their homes – experience prolonged conflict in marriage, or suffer unspeakable misfortune – such as the untimely deaths of close kin. For villagers witchcraft has less to do with civilization and African identity than with their experiences of misery, abjection, illness, poverty, and insecurity in South Africa's over-crowded former Bantustan areas (Ashforth, Chapter 10). Similarly, as Ashforth (1996, 1998, 2000) shows, the resurgence of witchcraft in the black urban area of Soweto indicates increased inequality and the frustrations of 'revolutionary expectations' in the post-apartheid era, rather than retribalization.

In these contexts, the law may well be more of an irrelevance than a decisive influence. It is unlikely that either the existing Suppression of Witchcraft Act or the proposed Witchcraft Control Act would stem witchcraft accusations. The best option for the state may well be a minimalist one: to allow local level processes that limit violence against witches to proceed, to repeal all legislation related to witchcraft, and to charge those who perpetrate violence against witches under existing laws which deal with assault and murder. There can be no lasting solution to witchcraft-related violence if the predicaments, fears, and anxieties of the believers are not addressed.

Notes

1 An earlier version of this paper was published in *African Legal Studies* (2), 2001. I
   thank John Hund for permission to republish the paper. I also wish to thank Dianne
   Ciekawy, Gotfried Dederen, Peter Geschiere, Adam Kuper, Eliazaar Mohlala,
   Henrietta Moore, Joanne Pannell, Todd Sanders, Owen Sichone, Hal Scheffler, John
   Sharp, Kally Shokane, Andrew Spiegel and Jonathan Stadler for their assistance and
   helpful suggestions. All local concepts and expressions in this chapter are in Northern
   Sotho and I use pseudonymns to disguise the identity of local persons.
2 Ralushai *et al.* (1996: 191–239) note that 312 witchcraft-related killings were
   reported to the former Lebowa police, that respondents in Gazankulu recounted 57
   killings, and that court records from Venda reveal 20 killings. These are obviously
   vast underestimates. According to police sources more than 73 people were killed as
   witches in Lebowa alone in 1993 (*New York Times*, 18 September 1994).
3 *Sunday Times*, 20 April 1986.
4 I have tried to emulate Ferguson (1990) who, in his study of development initiatives
   in Lesotho, focuses on discourses, their politics, and their real intended and unin-
   tended social effects.
5 The Ralushai Commission was also required to investigate ritual murders. Yet the
   entire report refers to only eight criminal cases pertaining to ritual murders (pp.
   257–267), and makes no recommendations about this phenomenon. This is because
   the Commission chose to emphasize witchcraft. In the Northern Province ritual
   murder is a topic of considerable importance.
6 My research was conducted primarily in Green Valley, a village in the Setlhare
   chiefdom of Bushbuckridge with an estimated population of about twenty thousand
   Northern Sotho and Tsonga-speaking residents.
7 For the parliamentary discussions of on the Suppression of Witchcraft Act see
   Debates of the House of Assembly (Hansard), 18 January to 22 June, 1957, pp.
   243–268, 328–330.
8 In the ordeal, chiefs administered poison to alleged witches. Those who died were
   allegedly guilty, while the survivors were absolved of blame. See Evans-Pritchard
   1937, Douglas 1963, and Mombeshora 1994.
9 See Ode Brown 1935, Malinowski 1961: 94–99, Fields 1982: 577, and Mombeshora
   1994: 75 for more extensive overviews of British colonial witchcraft laws.
10 The earliest witchcraft laws in South Africa were: Act 24 of 1886 and Act 2 of 1895
   (Cape of Good Hope); Law 19 (Natal); Proclamation 11 of 1887 (Zululand); and
   Ordinance 26 of 1904 (Transvaal). No witchcraft laws existed in the Orange Free
   State. The Suppression of Witchcraft Act retained the essential clauses of the earlier
   laws, but provided for the imposition of harsher penalties (previously penalties
   ranged from £2 or fourteen days' to £10 or three months' imprisonment).
11 Fields (1982: 574) argues that missions could not provide the solution required by
   African strategists. Missions produced African advocates for the empire, but also an
   acculturated elite who opposed colonialism. Moreover, converts were set aside from
   the moral community of the masses.
12 See the speeches in parliament by Dr D.L. Smit, Mr Stanford, Mr Mitchell, Mr
   Sutter, and Mr Hughes. *Debates of the House of Assembly (Hansard)*, 18 January to 22
   June, 1957, pp. 246–266.
13 Frank Melland, a District Officer in Northern Rhodesia, adopted a sensitive stance
   towards witchcraft beliefs and produced an amateur ethnographer's treatise, arguing
   for the coherence of witch beliefs, nearly fifteen years prior to Evans-Pritchard's
   (1937) *Witchcraft, Oracles and Magic among the Azande*. Melland (1923, 1935)
   criticized the colonial witchcraft laws as 'politically foolish' and pointed to flaws such
   as the lumping together of 'witches' and 'witch-doctors'.

14 This case was brought to the attention of parliament by Dr D.L Smit, speaker of the United Party. See *Debates of the House of Assembly (Hansard)*, 18 January to 22 June, 1957, pp. 246–247.

15 The charges against 65 persons were withdrawn, 13 of the accused could not be traced, and 59 were found not guilty. Two cases were transferred to chiefs, and four cases were still under investigation.

16 In many cases there was insufficient evidence as the assaults were usually perpetrated late at night by groups of men. Consequently the charges against 29 persons were withdrawn, 119 of the accused were found not guilty, and police failed to trace 11 of the accused.

17 No penalties were imposed against 94 persons. Charges against 13 persons were withdrawn, 65 were found not guilty, 1 was referred to the supreme court, 14 received postponed sentences, and the results of 16 cases were still outstanding.

18 See *State* v. *Mathabi* and six others, Venda Supreme Court, 19–20 February 1991, sitting at Thohoyandou before Justice Van der Walt (cited in Ralushai *et al.* 1996: 237–239).

19 See *State* v. *Netshiavha*, Venda Supreme Court, Case No. A20/1987; and *Netshiavha* v. *State* 1990 (3), SACR. 331 (AD) (cited in Ralushai *et al.* 1996).

20 *State* v. *Hlanganani* and others Cr No. 96/12/91, Supreme Court Case No. CC253/93, sitting at Tzaneen before Justice Botha (cited in Ralushai *et al.* 1996: 240).

21 See Crawford 1967 for a discussion of confessions about witchcraft in the state courts of Rhodesia (now Zimbabwe).

22 Here Chavunduka (1982) draws on Cannon's (1942) study of 'voodoo death'.

23 The case of *R* v. *Mbombela*, 1933 (cited in Motshekga 1984: 10).

24 In the light of the earlier discussion we can only conclude that Motshekga's (1984) critique is somewhat misplaced. The cases he cites may be representative of the legislative ideals, but not of actual legal practice.

25 Chavunduka (1982: 18) claims that divination, the boiling water test, and the poison ordeal are unsatisfactory methods for detecting witches that could lead to the punishment of innocent individuals.

26 Familiars listed by the report are the owl, bat, muswoo, cat, hyena, crocodile, snake, goat, jackal, duiker, donkey, tortoise, scorpion, pig, dog, leopard, tokoloti, monkey, and baboon. Articles used in witchcraft are purported to be razor blades, mirrors, sticks, brushes, pot lids, plates, horns, ball pens, gramophone records, books, mirrors, loaves of bread, and spoons (Ralushai *et al* 1996: 22). A curious omission is the *mamlambo*.

27 See Comaroff and Comaroff (forthcoming) for a discussion and analysis of the beliefs in zombies in South Africa.

28 In terms of the proposed legislation 'Minister' means the Minister of Health or such other Minister to whom the Provincial Premier may from time to time assign the administration of the Act (Ralushai *et al.* 1996: 66).

29 Cattle were widely recognized as a form of compensation for the loss of human life. This was apparent in the case of bride wealth – where cattle were exchanged for wives – and also in homicide – where murderers compensated the families of their victims with ten head of cattle. The resolution of blood feuds amongst the Nuer followed a similar logic.

30 Comaroff and Comaroff (1999) argue precisely the opposite. They suggest that 'appeals to enchantment' have intensified in the South African 'postcolony'. The roots to such appeals can be found in a mixture of hope and hopelessness, and of promise and its perversions. In the postcolonial situation glimpses of vast wealth are accompanied by a chilling desperation of being left out of the promise of prosperity. Comaroff and Comaroff see moral panics as symptoms of an occult economy – the

deployment of magical means for material ends. This view has considerable merit, despite the overt economism of their claims.

31 These actions can be interpreted as symbolic killing. Lowvelders consider the back of the neck as the body's most vulnerable part. This is where oxen are stabbed when slaughtered. The haircut is an essential part of funeral rites. Relatives of the deceased shave the corpse's hair and place it in the coffin. Moreover, corpses are buried naked and are wrapped only in white linen. By painting the witches in black oil, the witch-diviner tainted them with the colour of death and decay.

32 See Niehaus 1993 for a more extensive discussion of the Green Valley witch-hunt.

33 Fisiy and Geschiere (1990: 149) contend that, despite the totalitarian pretensions of Cameroon's Ahidjo regime, there was no concerted effort by government against witchcraft. This practice was triggered by accusations from within villages, and courts intervened at the request of local elites and the *nkong*.

34 See Lan (1987: 207–222) for a brief, but informative discussion of the effects of the bureaucratization of spirit-mediums in postcolonial Zimbabwe.

35 This contrasts with the manner in which witchcraft beliefs are appropriated elsewhere. The witch-museum of Salem, Massachusetts, stands as a symbol of intolerance, which reminds us, by virtue of its contrasts, of American democratic ideals.

36 *Sunday Times*, 12 December 1999.

37 See Thornton 1988 and Amselle 1998 for critiques of the bounded view of culture.

Bibliography

Abrahams, R. (1994) 'Introduction', in R. Abrahams (ed.) *Witchcraft in Contemporary Tanzania*, Cambridge: African Studies Centre.

Amselle, J.-L. (1998) *Mestizo Logics: Anthropology of Identity in Africa and Elsewhere*, Stanford: University Press.

Ashforth, A. (1996) 'Of secrecy and the commonplace: witchcraft and power in Soweto', *Social Research* 63, 4: 1183–1214.

—— (1998) 'Reflections on spiritual insecurity in a modern African city (Soweto)', *African Studies Review* 41, 3: 39–68.

—— (2000) *Madumo: A Man Bewitched*, Chicago: University of Chicago Press.

Bailey, F.G. (1997) *Witch-hunt in an Indian Village or the Triumph of Morality*, New Delhi: Oxford University Press.

Bukurura, S. (1994) 'Sungusungu and the banishment of suspected witches in Kahama', in R. Abrahams (ed.) *Witchcraft in Contemporary Tanzania*, Cambridge: African Studies Centre.

Cannon, W.G. (1942) 'Voodoo death', *American Anthropologist* 44, 2: 169–181.

Chavunduka, G. (1982) 'Witches, witchcraft and the law in Zimbabwe', Occasional Papers 1, Harare: ZINATHA.

—— (1986) 'The organisation of traditional medicine in Zimbabwe', in M. Last and G.L. Chavunduka (eds) *The Professionalisation of African Medicine*, Manchester: University Press.

Chidester, D. (1992) *Shots in the Streets: Violence and Religion in South Africa*, Cape Town: Oxford University Press.

Coetzee, A.J. (1938) *Die Afrikaanse Volksgeloof*, Amsterdam: N.V. Swets and Zeitlinger.

Comaroff, J. (1994) 'Contentious subjects: moral being in the modern world', *Suomen Antropologi* 19, 2: 2–17.

—— (1997) 'Consuming passions: child abuse, fetishism, and the "New World Order"', *Culture* 17, 1–2: 7–19.

Comaroff, J. and J.L. Comaroff (1999) 'Occult economies and the violence of abstraction: notes from the South African postcolony', *American Ethnologist* 26, 4: 279–303.

—— (forthcoming) 'Alien-nation: zombies, immigrants, and millennial capitalism', in G. Schwab (ed.) *Forces of Globalization*, New York: Columbia University Press.

Crawford, J.R. (1967) *Witchcraft and Sorcery in Rhodesia*, London: Oxford University Press.

Debates of the House of Assembly (1957) *Hansard*, Pretoria: Government Printers.

Dederen J.M. (1996) 'Killing is easier than paperwork . . . A critique of the Report of the Commission of Inquiry into witchcraft violence and ritual murders in the Northern Province of the Republic of South Africa', paper presented at the PAA/AASA Conference, Pretoria: University of South Africa.

Delius, P. (1996) *A Lion Amongst the Cattle: Reconstruction and Resistance in the Northern Transvaal*, Johannesburg: Ravan Press.

Douglas, M. (1963) 'Techniques of sorcery control in central Africa', in J. Middleton and E.H. Winter (eds) *Witchcraft and Sorcery in East Africa*, London: Routledge and Kegan Paul.

Englund, H. (1996) 'Witchcraft, modernity and the person: the morality of accumulation in central Malawi', *Critique of Anthropology* 16, 3: 257–279.

Evans-Pritchard, E.E. (1937) *Witchcraft, Oracles and Magic among the Azande*, Oxford: Claredon Press.

Favret-Saada, J. (1980) *Deadly Words: Witchcraft in Brocage*, Cambridge: University Press.

Ferguson, J. (1990) *The Anti-Politics Machine: 'Development', Depoliticization and Bureaucratic State Power in Lesotho*, Cape Town: David Philip.

Fields, K.E. (1982) 'Political contingencies of witchcraft in colonial central Africa: culture and State in Marxist theory', *Canadian Journal of African Studies* 16, 3: 567–593.

Fisiy, C.F. (1990) 'Le monopole juridictionnel de l'État et le reglement des affaires de sorcellerie au Cameroon', *Politique africaine* 40, 1: 60–72.

Fisiy, C.F. and Geschiere, P. (1990) 'Judges and witches, or How is the State to deal with witchcraft', *Cahiers d'Études africaines* 118, xxx: 135–156.

—— (1996) 'Witchcraft, violence and identity: different trajectories in postcolonial Cameroon', in R. Werbner and T. Ranger (eds) *Postcolonial Identities in Africa*, London: Zed Books.

Green, M. (1994) 'Shaving witchcraft in Ulanga: *kunyolewa* and the Catholic church', in R. Abrahams (ed.) *Witchcraft in Contemporary Tanzania*, Cambridge: African Studies Centre.

Heald, S. (1986) 'Witches and thieves: deviant motivations in Gisu society', *Man* 21, 1: 65–78.

La Fontaine, J.S. (1998) *Speak of the Devil: Tales of Satanic Abuse in Contemporary England*, Cambridge: University Press.

Lan, D. (1987 [1985]) *Guns and Rain: Guerrillas and Spirit Mediums in Zimbabwe*, London: James Currey.

MacCullum, T.G. (1993) *White Woman Witchdoctor: Tales from the African Life of Rae Graham*, Johannesburg: Struik.

Malinowski, B. (1961) *The Dynamics of Culture Change: An Inquiry into Race Relations in Africa*, New Haven: Yale University Press.

Mbiti, J.S. (1970) *African Religions and Philosophy*, New York: Doubleday.

Melland, F. (1923) *In Witchbound Africa*, London: Secley, Service and Co.

—— (1935) 'Ethical and political aspects of African witchcraft', *Africa* viii, 4: 495–503.

Mesaki, S. (1994) 'Witch-killing in Sukumaland', in R. Abrahams (ed.) *Witchcraft in Contemporary Tanzania*, Cambridge: African Studies Centre.

Mombeshora, S. (1994) 'Witches, witchcraft and the question of order: a view from a Bena village in the southern highlands', in R. Abrahams (ed.) *Witchcraft in Contemporary Tanzania*, Cambridge: African Studies Centre.

Motshekga, M.S. (1984)'The ideology behind witchcraft and the principle of fault in criminal law', *Codicillvs* xxxv, 2: 4–14.

Niehaus, I. (1993) 'Witch-hunting and political legitimacy: continuity and change in Green Valley, Lebowa, 1930–93', *Africa* 53, 4: 138–160.

—— (1995) 'Witches of the Transvaal Lowveld and their familiars: conceptions of duality, power and desire', *Cahiers d'Études africaines* 138–139, xxxv, 2–3: 513–540.

—— (1997) 'Witchcraft, power and politics: an ethnographic study of the South African Lowveld', unpublished PhD thesis, University of the Witwatersrand.

—— (1998) 'The ANC's dilemma: the symbolic politics of three witch-hunts in the South African Lowveld, 1990–1995', *African Studies Review* 41, 3: 93–118.

Ode Brown, G. (1935) 'Witchcraft and British colonial law', *Africa* viii, 4: 481–487.

Ralushai, N.V, Masingi, M.G, Madiba, D.M.M. *et al.* (1996) *Report of the Commission of Inquiry into Witchcraft Violence and Ritual Murders in the Northern Province of South Africa* (To: His Excellency the Honourable Member of the Executive Council for Safety and Security, Northern Province). No publisher given.

Ranger, T. (1996) 'Postscript: colonial and postcolonial identities', in R. Werbner and T. Ranger (eds) *Postcolonial Identities in Africa*, London: Zed Books.

Ritchken, E. (1995) 'Leadership and conflict in Bushbuckridge: struggles to define moral economies within the context of rapidly transforming political economies', unpublished PhD thesis, University of the Witwatersrand.

Scheper-Hughes, N. (2000) 'The global traffic in human organs', *Current Anthropology* 41, 2: 191–224.

Stadler, J. (1994) 'Witches and witch-hunters: witchcraft, generational relations and the life-cycle in a Lowveld village', *African Studies* 55, 1: 87–100.

Thornton, R. (1988) 'Culture: a contemporary definition', in E. Boonzaier and J. Sharp (eds) *South African Keywords*, Cape Town: David Philip.

Van Kessel, I. (1993) '"From confusion to Lusaka": the youth revolt in Sekhukhuneland', *Journal of Southern African Studies* 19, 4: 593–614.

Wilson, M. (1967 [1951]) *Good Company: A Study of Nyakyusa Age-Villages*, Boston: Beacon.

Woods, D. (1978) *Biko*, Harmondsworth: Penguin.

Worobec, C.D. (1995) 'Witchcraft beliefs and practices in pre-revolutionary Russian and Ukranian villages', *The Russian Review* 54: 165–187.

Chapter 10

On living in a world with witches

Everyday epistemology and spiritual insecurity in a modern African city (Soweto)

Adam Ashforth

The quintessential predicament of living in a world with witches was once summarized for me in a conversation with the woman I long ago came to know as 'mother' in Soweto, MaMfete:

> You know, Adam, this thing [witchcraft] comes from a bitterness in somebody's heart, like a poison, causing jealousy and hatred. And you can never know what's inside someone's heart. You can think you know somebody, but you don't. And people who have this spirit of hatred, this bitterness, they can do anything.
>
> (Ashforth 2000: 74)[1]

The presumption that the people amongst whom one lives have capacities for extraordinary action in the form of witchcraft creates an epistemological double bind. On the one hand, one can never really know who has the motive for malicious action. The 'bitterness' in the heart, to adopt MaMfete's terms, is secret. On the other hand, one can never really know what they are capable of, nor can one know how they achieve their evil ends for their methods and means are secret. All one can be sure of is that if people have the motive, they can and will act.

Amidst the poverty, violence, and general hardship of life in Soweto, there is no shortage of plausible evidence that evil powers are at work. And despite the fact that the secrecy of witchcraft precludes certainty, when witches are experienced as posing a real and present danger their potential for causing harm makes discovering what they are up to imperative. In this chapter I intend to tease out some of the implications of this double bind through a rudimentary sociology of knowledge focusing on problems of spiritual insecurity in Soweto.

'Witchcraft', as most people with whom I have discussed the matter in Soweto seem to understand it, is a term loosely applied to the field of illegitimate action engaging capacities of human persons to cause harm or accumulate wealth and power by mysterious means. In common Sowetan usage, the term – whether expressed in English, or its Sotho (*boloi*) or Zulu (*ubuthakathi*) equivalents –

refers to practices wherein human action directed towards evil ends engages with invisible forces that are variously conceived of as either physical, human, or extra-human (spiritual) in nature.[2] Amongst other things, 'witchcraft' can refer to the malicious manipulation of the powers of herbs and other substances generally referred to as *muthi* (the same word as used for healing medicines), to pacts with devils and demons, to innate supernatural powers, or to collective action by persons engaging all of these forces. When people speak of witches at work, they typically say people are 'using *muthi*' although they may have radically different understandings of the active power of *muthi* as anchored in either chemistry, magic, or demonic powers.[3]

Many uses of occult power and interactions with invisible forces or entities are considered legitimate in Soweto, most notably in prayer, divination, and healing. Sometimes, too, suffering can be inflicted upon people by invisible powers as a form of legitimate punishment. Ancestors, for example, are thought to impose hardships on the living to remind them to pay respect to the dead (Kiernan 1982). Spirits can take possession of a person as a way of calling them to become healers (Campbell 1998).[4] When something is described as witchcraft, however, the import of the statement is that a human interaction with unseen forces has taken place which is unambiguously evil and directed towards causing serious harm to others.

The misfortunes that witches can cause are unbounded: illness, death, unemployment, car accidents, divorce, family discord are all within their capacities. Ultimately, witches aim at death and destruction, and it is this that distinguishes their action from the salutary punishments of tutelary powers and renders witchcraft essentially illegitimate (cf. Berglund 1976: 269). The distinguishing feature of 'witchcraft' as a means of accumulating wealth or power (as distinct from commonplace and legitimate occult procedures geared towards the same end) is the killing of others.[5] Knowing when to ascribe an unfortunate event to witchcraft, however, is no easy task. Typically, the action of a witch is surmised in retrospect after the onset of illness or affliction and confirmed by the diagnosis of a diviner. Even in the absence of marked misfortune, however, everyday life is lived with a lively sense of the potential of others to cause harm through witchcraft and a general awareness that this must be guarded against, both by being careful not to stimulate the motive of 'jealousy' and by securing supernatural protection from healers.

Sowetans generally are aware that there were, and perhaps still are, a great many 'traditions', in what they refer to as 'culture', about the powers and dangers of witches and other matters of life and death, particularly concerning relations with ancestors, dangers of spiritual pollution, and customary prohibitions. Most of the particularities of these traditions, however, have been long neglected.[6] The majority of the population (84.1 per cent) are under 40 (Morris 1999: 2.2) and few have grown up in families where the traditions of the ancestors were well known and rigidly adhered to. In any event, tradition is not something undisputed. A great variety of Christians – European and African, Catholic and

Protestant, Black, White, and Brazilian – have for more than a century been preaching such a variety of theological responses to indigenous cosmologies and religious practices that no-one can say, without fear of contradiction, what is, or once was, authentically 'African' (see Niehaus, Chapter 9). Furthermore, almost everyone in Soweto has some formal schooling, with at least an introduction to elementary science. Everyone lives amidst the technologies of the modern world. Consequently, the variety of opinions about witchcraft is every bit as diverse as the variety of religious beliefs about a personal god that responds to human prayer. And while most people do not have access to sophisticated and fully elaborated cosmologies which they could present to inquisitive outsiders fully formed, they are generally mindful of the fact that they live in the world with witches. Sometimes they discover that this fact needs to be taken very seriously. If all this were not enough to complicate the enterprise of interpreting relations within these domains of power and their attendant feelings of insecurity, speculation about the powers of invisible forces in post-apartheid Soweto also takes place within a context marked by a stark socio-economic differentiation between 'Blacks' and 'Whites' that makes difficult the articulation of cultural differences without presuming, or confirming, historically iniquitous presumptions of African inferiority.

My concern in this chapter is to examine, through reflection on fieldwork conducted during the 1990s in Soweto, problems of spiritual insecurity, that sense of danger, doubt, and fear arising from troubled efforts to manage relations with invisible forces deemed responsible for misfortune. I will suggest that the epistemological dimensions of the problem of spiritual insecurity complicate life and heighten the sense of vulnerability and exposure to unmanageable powers. Before attempting this, however, I will sketch a few broad historical and sociological features of life in Soweto, focusing particularly upon those aspects of life that might be thought conducive to a general sense of insecurity.

Soweto

Soweto is a conglomeration of dormitory townships to the southwest of Johannesburg (Pirie 1984b). Home to above a million people, Soweto covers an area of about 30 square miles. In apartheid South Africa, Soweto was the biggest, most ethnically and socio-economically diverse and the most politically significant of the black townships. As Walter Sisulu, veteran leader of the African National Congress and lifetime Sowetan, says (with characteristic Sowetan exaggeration): 'the history of Soweto is the history of South Africa' (Sisulu 1998: 7). Though created by government officials responding, in a thoroughly modern style, to the imperatives of African urbanization by building racially segregated public housing for poorly paid black workers, Soweto came over the years to resemble something living in shape and character and, despite its inauspicious beginnings, Soweto became a place of homes.

At the dawn of the twenty-first century, most Sowetans are either at school or are unemployed. Almost everyone between the ages of 7 and 20, about a quarter of the total population, is at school (Morris 1999: 2.2), and many of the younger children are in pre-schools and crèches. About two-thirds of the adult population have spent ten years or more in school, although fewer than half of those who sat for their final matriculation examinations during the 1990s passed (South Africa Ministry of Education 1999). Although older women are likely to have had less schooling than men, by the 1990s girls were attending school in equal numbers to boys and were more likely to sit for their matriculation examinations (although less likely to pass). The quality of Soweto's schools is generally poor.

Most Sowetans are poor. About 60 per cent of households surveyed in 1997 had incomes less than R1,500 ($300) per month (Morris 1999: 9), the average wage for an urban semi-skilled worker in formal employment. In 1997, the estimated subsistence level for a family of five was R1,293 ($465) (Morris 1999: 9): a loaf of bread cost about R2.50, a bottle of beer R3.5, a medium sized television R3,000, and a second-hand car R40–50,000. While many slept hungry, virtually no-one was starving, and virtually everyone had access to a television – either at home, in a friend's or neighbour's house, or in their local shebeen – that was constantly bombarding them with images reminding them that they were not prospering despite the election of a government promising 'A Better Life for All'.

In relation to the socio-economic profile of South Africa as a whole, Soweto is somewhere in the middle. There are many places where conditions are far worse. Black people in rural areas for example have much lower household incomes (less than R1,000 per year [Whiteford and Van Seventer 1999]) and far inferior access to services. Indeed, Soweto has a slightly higher socio-economic profile with a more substantial middle class than most other black townships (Morris 1999: 11). In comparison with the formerly segregated (and still mostly white) suburbs, however, conditions in Soweto – even in the relatively desirable parts – are inferior.

For the past decade the black middle classes have been fleeing Soweto for houses in the suburbs and new housing developments outside the townships. Over the same period, socio-economic inequalities among black South Africans have increased to match the aggregate income difference between black and white (Whiteford and Van Seventer 1999). Most families have at least some relatives who are prospering, but it would be very difficult to find a financially successful person in or from Soweto who has no relatives that are poor. The impact of this growing black income inequality has been felt in virtually every family. All of the families I have been close to over the past decade have been wracked in the last few years by conflicts over money and resentments about the redistribution of resources to less-well-off relatives.

Most 'breadwinners' in Sowetan households are male (67.4 per cent [Morris 1999]), and the ideology of family life is strongly patriarchal, with fathers claiming the right to govern women and children absolutely. In practice, however, mothers dominate family life. Given the scarcity of cash in this place and the absence of other resources upon which to found their manhood, such as land or cattle, it is extremely difficult for most males, especially young men, to live up to the predominating ideals of masculinity grounded upon the capacity to support and dominate women and children (Ashforth 1999). Older women, particularly, are inclined to view men in general as being 'useless'. I once asked the women in the house where I stay their opinion of the fathers in the 30 houses lining our street. Only three of the 30 families had fathers who were still in residence with their families and not adjudged 'useless'. Poverty is particularly hard on the status of fatherhood. When children sleep hungry, though their mother suffers with them, she is no less a mother for their pain. In fact, sharing the suffering of her family makes her more of a mother in the eyes of the community. A father whose family suffers, however, is by definition a failure. For it is a father's duty to provide. Not surprisingly, many men flee the constant reminders of their failings. Paternal flight also makes more difficult the responsibility of maintaining relations with the father's ancestors, who are the principle source of welfare for the family.

Most Sowetan breadwinners view themselves as 'urban' people (Morris 1999: 4.11). Because the years of 'high' apartheid, during the 1950s to the 1980s, were marked by ever-increasing efforts by the authorities to control the movement of people to towns, and the fact that public housing construction in Soweto essentially stopped after the late 1960s, most of the older sections of Soweto are populated by families whose youngest members are the descendants of several generations of urban dwellers. The children in the house where I stay, for example, are fourth generation Sowetans whose great grandparents came to Johannesburg in the 1930s and whose grandparents settled in the street when it was built in 1964. The history of a family's migration to the urban areas has enormous significance for the character of life within a household. More recent migrants are more likely to live in poorer neighbourhoods, with lower quality housing (Morris 1999: 9.10), and they are more likely also to have stronger knowledge of and attachments to rituals and traditions of rural life. Native-born Sowetans tend to view their country cousins with disdain, although they are mindful of the rural basis of what people refer to as 'culture' and the attendant reputation of distant parts for powerful witchcraft and healing.

In 1954, the national government decreed that henceforth all township housing should be segregated along ethnic lines (Pirie 1984a). About two-thirds of the townships of Greater Soweto are thus segregated, divided broadly into those dominated by Zulu- and Xhosa-speaking households, and those where Pedi, Sotho, and Tswana predominate. One township, Chiawelo, was set aside for Tsonga- and Venda-speaking families. The oldest townships, such as Orlando and Pimville, were not ethnically segregated and neither were the newer suburbs built since the 1970s. Broad linguistic divisions remain throughout Soweto. From childhood, however, most Sowetans learn at least some variety of both the main African language groups of the region (Sotho/Tswana and Nguni) as well as English. Most younger people, in their daily encounters, speak a distinct urban argot known as *iscamtho* which is all but incomprehensible to speakers of 'pure' versions of the regional languages (Ntshangase 1993). Just as their language borrows from diverse sources to create something new and constantly changing, so do the concepts expressed therein, including that of 'witchcraft'.

Virtually all Sowetans are at least nominally Christian. Like black South Africans more generally, approximately one-third of Sowetans affiliate themselves with particular 'Mainline' (European mission) congregations and another third with 'Independent' (or 'African Initiated') congregations (Froise 1996: 21).[7] The vast majority of regular churchgoers are women and girls. As well as being Christians, however, and in many instances despite the formal teachings of their church, most Sowetans also participate in at least some rituals associated with indigenous practices of ancestor reverence and most will also consult a 'traditional healer' when the need arises. The commonly cited figure for consultation with a traditional healer countrywide is 80 per cent of black South Africans (Select Committee on Social Services 1998). My experience in Soweto would confirm at least this rate. I would also estimate that the number of such healers in Soweto is approximately 10,000. In addition, a similar number of Independent church 'prophets' are probably active in healing work in Soweto.

There are two hospitals (one public and one private), 12 public clinics offering low-cost medical services, one private clinic, and about 30 or 40 private medical practices. Treatment at public clinics is much cheaper than treatment by 'traditional healers'. Healer-prophets of the African Initiated Churches tend not to charge as much as traditional healers, although participation in their churches can involve major investments of time and life-style change. In 1997, most people (76.7 per cent) reported themselves as in good health, although a significant proportion (13.4 per cent) said their health had been 'bad' in the past month (Morris 1999). Of women over the age of 50, 29.5 per cent reported their health as bad (compared with 20 per cent of men) and 14.4 per cent of older people suffered from hypertension (Morris 1999).

In 1998, 20 per cent of pregnant women attending ante-natal clinics tested positive for HIV-1. At the end of 2000 the seroprevalence rate for HIV amongst pregnant women countrywide was 24.5 per cent (Department of Health 2001). When I first began talking to people in Soweto about AIDS in the early 1990s, the disease was laughingly referred to as the 'American Invention to Discourage Sex' and the government's programme to dispense free condoms through clinics was seen as a ploy to keep the black birth-rate down in the interests of white supremacy. By the end of the 1990s, however, death from AIDS was beginning to become commonplace in Soweto although there was a strong stigma against acknowledging the disease as the cause of death. South Africa at the turn of the century is estimated to have the fastest growing rate of HIV infection and all indications are that the death rate from AIDS will increase dramatically in the next decade (Whiteside and Sunter 2000). Few people know their HIV status, and when symptoms of illnesses associated with AIDS begin, many people identify them as witchcraft-associated (Ashforth 2001).

Soweto is a dangerous place. Each year more than 1,000 people are murdered there, with another 15,000 attempted murders. Until 1994, political murders and repressive state violence were also a major concern.[8] Approximately 13,000 violent assaults, 2,500 or more rapes,[9] and more than 4,000 burglaries of residential properties are reported annually (South African Police Service 1998). Sowetans have always been worried about crime and have always taken precautions in everyday life to secure themselves against criminals. All houses have bars on their windows; most have at least barbed wire fences and locked gates. Approximately one in three households is affected by serious crime each year, and slightly more than one in ten is affected by violent crimes.[10] More than two-thirds of respondents surveyed in 1997 thought that crime had increased in the previous five years. And the crimes that most people were most worried about were rape (34.1 per cent of respondents placed it at the top of their list of worries) and murder (26.4 per cent) (Morris 1999: 7.2). There are 12 police stations in Soweto. The officers working in them are struggling against not only the legacy of their reputation as enforcers of apartheid, but the legacy of the generalized disregard for lawfulness that system instilled, not to mention the temptations of bribery and the deep-seated incompetence of a poorly managed and ill-prepared force. Victims of crime in Soweto rarely turn to the law enforcement system with any real expectation of receiving justice.

On top of all the dangers of crime, the streets of Soweto are part of a network of roads throughout South Africa that have one of the world's highest rates of death per vehicle mile travelled (Ministry of Transport 1997). Some 10,000 people die on South African roads annually, with between 35,000 and 40,000 suffering serious injuries. Approximately twice that number suffer minor injuries (Ministry of Transport 1997). I have no specific figures for Soweto, but have seen enough carnage on the roads there to suspect that the Sowetan rates of road death and injury are commensurate with those of the rest of the country.

Alcohol abuse contributes significantly to the mayhem on the roads, as it does to the general scourge of violence in homes and neighbourhoods (Parry and Bennetts 1999). Researchers report that South Africans are amongst the heaviest drinkers in the world and that some 30 per cent of urban Africans are at risk from alcohol abuse (Parry 1997). My experience in Sowetan shebeens – those unlicensed drinking houses, one of which can be found within about 100 yards of any given point in the township – certainly confirms this finding. Surveys of criminal suspects and crime victims show a strong correlation between alcohol consumption and violent crime, with one reporting more than 70 per cent of victims and suspects in assault cases under the influence of alcohol (Shaw and Gastrow 2001). Serious drug abuse most often takes the form of Mandrax (methalqualone, a.k.a 'quaaludes') tablets, a heavy tranquillizer which, when smoked with marijuana (a combination favoured by young men and boys in Soweto), produces hallucinations and is addictive.[11] To avoid unnecessary injury in Soweto, the first thing to do is to avoid places where young men are drinking.

Considerations of security intrude into virtually every aspect of ordinary life in Soweto although they are not reckoned in the same way by everyone (young women, for example, factor the possibility of rape into their every move; young men calculate the risks of assault). Woven into the fabric of social life, particularly through the responsibilities of kinship, is the fundamental requirement of mutual aid and protection. For young men, particularly, 'brotherhood' means a willingness to risk your own life for that of your friends. On the streets of Soweto, young men are rarely far from situations where that commitment might be tested. Few people feel secure walking the streets at night.

As well as living behind well-secured gates and doors, most Sowetans and their houses have, at some time or another, been protected against the threat of witchcraft through, amongst other things, the application of herbs to incisions in the skin at joints (an operation known in Zulu as *ukuqiniswa*), the protection of a house from assaults by witches and evil spirits by means of healers spreading herbal mixtures around the property, or the presentation by healer-prophets of the African Initiated Churches of coloured cords to wear around the waist and water that has been prayed over (cf. Ashforth 2000).

In sum, then, Soweto is a working-class city where life is tough but not impossible. Generally, people are poor but most live in a solid house and have access to drinkable water and electricity. Most households also have a phone, or a family member with a cell phone; all have access to public phones in the near vicinity. With some 60 per cent of households earning barely sufficient to meet subsistence, most people live a financially precarious existence often made worse by addiction to alcohol. Many Sowetans, however, are thriving. Those who are not financially strapped have relatives whom they are expected to assist financially, far too many such relatives to help them all. And every family is intimately acquainted with a victim of disease, assault, fatal violence, and road death. Of all the families I have known since 1990, I know not a single one that has survived the decade without someone in the not-too-extended family dying of a preventable illness, in a crime of violence, or on the roads. I know none who can unambiguously proclaim themselves to be well off and free from suffering.

Spiritual insecurity and the struggle for life

The existence of something we might call spiritual insecurity is not easy to demonstrate. When people build walls braided with razor-wire around their houses, as they do in Soweto, it is easy to conclude that they do so to enhance their feeling of security. When they attend a church or visit a traditional healer, can we conclude they suffer from spiritual insecurity? Obviously not. The variety of motives and meanings in religious and spiritual experience cannot be reduced to questions of 'security' without injustice to the richness and complexity of life. Yet, on those occasions when life is experienced as subject to malicious forces bent on causing harm and misfortune, forces to be dreaded and fought, then questions of security do come to the fore amongst other consolations of religious life.

However, the fact that the crowded field of healing in both the 'traditional' and 'prophetic' faith-healing domains encompasses activities directly related to providing security from forces deemed bent on causing harm indicates that the matter of spiritual insecurity in Soweto is not insignificant. Moreover, while individual healers vigorously assert the legitimacy and integrity of their healing practice, in the popular imagination a person who knows how to manipulate the powers of herbs and others substances to heal is also, potentially, one capable of using that knowledge to evil ends.[12]

Most of the time, however, questions of spiritual insecurity in Soweto are not predominant. Unless being interviewed for some research project or debating the plausibility of some story doing the rounds, people mostly talk about witch-craft for amusement and all the malicious pleasures of scurrilous gossip (van Dijk, Chapter 5; Ashforth 2000: ch. 11). On occasion, however, the laughter and philosophical speculation disappears and witchcraft, or some other matter involving the action of mysterious powers, becomes a matter of life and death. These moments may be rare, but for the social researcher they are extremely problematic, particularly in relation to the misfortunes suspected as deriving from 'witchcraft'. For the moments when witchcraft is most significant in people's lives is also the time when it is least discussed. Moments, such as the birth of a child, when families are most vulnerable to occult assault, are treated with great confidentiality. Indeed, to talk openly at such times is to court catastrophe. For if word gets out that you are vulnerable, your enemies will make their move. If a witch knows that you have been attacked, the witch can easily switch to a new strategy of attack. And if others know you are already vulnerable, they may add their own curses to your burden.

While living in Soweto I have witnessed many occasions when dread of unseen powers has come to dominate friends' lives, causing them to expend precious emotional energy and money combating evil powers. For example, Mama C once met an *inyanga* in her neighbour's kitchen. When her asthma worsened shortly thereafter she became convinced that she was bewitched. None of the healers we visited could alleviate her suffering or the stress created by her fear of the neighbour's sorcery, all of which contributed to her hyper-tension. Convinced that nobody comes out of a hospital alive, she resisted medical treatment until it was too late. She died of heart failure within the year. She was 56 years old. I have also witnessed occasions when friends have been wracked with anxiety and anger after being suspected or accused outright of practising witchcraft. After my friend M built her mother a house, some neighbours who still lived in shacks, seemingly beside themselves with envy, accused the mother of using witchcraft to cause the death of a local family who had died the year before in a car accident. M's mother, shunned by her old friends and fuming at the injustice of the accusations, began attending church regularly as a precaution. Experiences such as these convinced me of the importance of examining questions of witchcraft as insecurity. And because the management of dangers and dread named under the rubric 'witchcraft' requires the engagement of a host of other powers and forces, from the inherent properties of physical substances to the miraculous powers of Jesus and the Holy Spirit, I think it not improper to treat witchcraft as a phenomenon in the general domain of spiritual insecurity.

Witchcraft and motive: the presumption of malice

Kenneth Burke in his famous exposition of 'dramatism' identified five 'basic forms of thought . . . which are exemplified in the attribution of motive' (Burke 1969: xv). These he summarized as: Act, Scene, Agent, Agency, and Purpose. Burke spent an enormous amount of time demonstrating that statements about each of these were always invoked whenever 'we say what people are doing and why they are doing it' (Burke 1969: xv). I want to paraphrase Burke's question and ask: what is involved when Sowetans say people are doing witchcraft and why they are doing it? And I will pilfer his five key terms of 'dramatism' to use as a framework for identifying the key epistemological problems of everyday life in a world of witches.

When Sowetans talk about acts of witchcraft, the talk typically centres on events surrounding premature death or events that could potentially have led to death, such as serious illnesses, accidents, or brushes with violence. While there are many ways of dying, three predominate: illness, murder, and motor vehicle accidents. Any occurrence of such an event is an occasion for speculation about witchcraft. The character and intensity of such speculation will depend primarily upon the relation of the interlocutors to the victims; for strangers and distant acquaintances, the tone might be one of idle speculation; for close relatives and loved ones, the matter can be so serious it might not be spoken of at all. The key to construing a death or potential death as an act of witchcraft is the imputation of agency to a perpetrator motivated to harm the victim. This perpetrator is rarely an agent in the ordinary sense. Thus, a young man might be murdered by schoolmates for reasons of their own, and the incident might thus be treated – by the police, the media, and whatever 'public' might exist for the narrative – as yet another story of murder and senseless violence. The same event, however, especially if it follows on the heels of other familial tragedies, may spur private speculation about the agency of others orchestrating the events of which the immediate agents, the murderers, were mere unwitting puppets.

The scene, or background situation within which acts of witchcraft are almost always played out in Soweto, as elsewhere in South Africa, is the household. Indeed, witchcraft is more often than not conceived of as an assault upon a family. The other players in the drama are all situated within intimate networks of relatives, friends, neighbours, schoolmates, church congregants, workmates, and so on. Acts of witchcraft are not usually perpetrated by strangers. Essentially the limiting factor in determining who is potentially part of the scene, or agent in the drama, is the extent of face-to-face community bounded by possibilities of *personal* motives for malice. Impersonal agencies of misfortune, such as the Apartheid regime, were not generally thought to be responsible for witchcraft-related suffering, although the people commanding powerful agencies can be thought to bolster their strength through sorcery.[13]

In principle, anyone can be a witch. All that is required to be, or become, a witch is the desire to kill and the capacity or know-how to do so. The desire at the heart of otherwise ordinary human agents that transforms them into a witch, the 'bitterness in the heart', is the source of the jealousy and hatred that is their motive for acting. And this desire is hidden. Not only is it hidden by virtue of the fact that one can never truly penetrate the depths of another's being, but if the bitterness motivating the desire to perpetrate witchcraft is in fact present, the witch, in order to avoid counteraction or punishment of his or her evil deeds, will keep it secret. When people speak of witchcraft as inherited, as they sometimes do, the thing that is passed down through generations can be either this bitterness, or the secret knowledge of *muthi*, or both.

Given that the motive for witchcraft is secret, and considering that the perpetrators have a strong incentive to conceal their motives, one way to determine the identity of the agent behind a particular act of witchcraft is to assess the probability of particular persons possessing the motives of jealousy and hatred. There are two basic ways of doing this: first, to assess the distribution of jealousy across particular social roles and correlate it with access to other means of causing harm, most notably violence; and, second, to assess the possible motives of particular individuals by inference from their other words and deeds. Broadly speaking, capacities for witchcraft and capacities for violence are typically perceived to be inversely related. Young men, for example, who are the most violent category of individuals, are seldom thought responsible for perpetrating witchcraft. Older women, on the other hand, who have few direct physical outlets for their malicious desires, or for revenge, are prime suspects when it comes to the covert action that is witchcraft.

When asked, Sowetans speak of all social roles as if co-existing on a spectrum of possibilities between pure witchcraft and pure violence. A jealous husband, for example, is presumed more likely to beat his wife and fight her lovers with fists, knives, and guns rather than punish them with witchcraft; a wife, on the other hand, if spurned, will have fewer options for violent retaliation and is therefore presumed more likely to resort to 'using *muthi*', that is, witchcraft. While the propensity for jealousy and envy are generally presumed to be evenly distributed across populations, certain social roles are deemed more conducive to the emotion than others. For example, mothers are considered more likely to be jealous of the achievements of other people's children than fathers because success in motherhood is rated primarily in relation to their children, while fathers are expected to build their own status as individuals. No matter how the propensity for motives conducive to witchcraft is inferred, however, the secrecy of the act and the secrecy of the inner motive determine that there will always be doubt regarding a witch's identity. To penetrate this secrecy, divination is needed. To be sure about a diviner's knowledge, however, a confession is required. Given the essential secrecy with which the truth about 'bitterness' in the heart is masked, the only truly reliable way of obtaining knowledge about the potential for witchcraft of any particular individual is through their positive confession (see Bastian, Chapter 4). Denials must always be doubted, for what else would a true witch do but deny? Positive confessions, on the other hand, especially because they expose the person making the confession to potentially serious sanctions, are valuable – even if, in fact, they are false or preposterous.[14] Only a positive confession of the desire to do evil can suffice to pre-empt suspicions of that desire (see Berglund 1976).

The agency of witchcraft, is, of course, witchcraft. Again, the tautology is meaningful because the act is premised on secrecy. Nobody knows how witchcraft works, except the witch. Thus, if an event is deemed to result from witchcraft, the means of causing it can only be named and countermanded, never comprehended. In contemporary Soweto there are certain conventional techniques that are imagined to comprise the witch's craft. These include such procedures as blowing herbs in the wind, placing them in food or drink, laying them in the path of an intended victim, creating familiars such as the legendary *tikoloshe* with his enormous genitals, domesticating certain animals in the service of evil, transmitting medicines through the sex act, and so on. The conventional repertoire of imagined witchcraft procedures mimics to some extent the practices of traditional healing. However, the techniques of witchcraft are by no means considered as limited to tried and tested traditions. The presumption these days is that witches are constantly innovating their techniques, and that the 'African science' of witchcraft is every bit as up-to-date and potent as 'White science'.[15]

In the absence of confession, life in a world of witches must be lived on a presumption of malice and with constant vigilance. Underlying all narratives of witchcraft that I have encountered in Soweto is the presumption that everyone is jealous of everyone else, regardless of appearances. Thus it is wise to presume malice in community life, even despite appearances to the contrary. Indeed, this presumption of malice is wise *especially* despite appearances of comity, for witches will bewitch simply because they can. In the event of good fortune befalling your family, it is wise to avoid any appearance of pride such as might make neighbours feel their feelings of envy justified them taking occult action.

Insecurity and uncertainty

Clearly there are 'objective' aspects to danger and, thus, fear and insecurity. Similarly there are purely subjective fears that may never find an objective correlative and generalized anxieties that need no object to evoke paralysing fear. Although it is generally not helpful to insist upon separating objective from subjective perceptions of threat, it is clear that conscious endeavours towards seeking security are predicated upon interpretation of the nature of threats and risks. The distinctive features of spiritual security arise, it seems to me, from the character of the epistemological problems they generate. These consist of a pentad of uncertainties – ambiguity, indeterminacy, secrecy, privacy, and mystery – produced amidst a superabundance of interpretive authority.

For people who live in a world of witches, the fact that evil forces are not ordinarily visible in no way diminishes the possibility of accurately discerning their action in shaping the fortunes and misfortunes of life (Nyamnjoh, Chapter 2). Invisibility, however, does present definite problems of interpretation. Typically, revelation of the action of invisible forces involves the interpretation of visible, audible, or generally tangible and intelligible signs. But these signs are themselves inherently ambiguous, for the sign is not the power itself. The sign is always originated by something else, the hidden reality that lies 'behind' the appearance of its manifestation. An illness characterized by persistent symptoms of coughing, for example, might be the sign that ancestors are displeased. Or it might be a sign of witchcraft at work in the form of *isidliso* ('poisoning'). It might also be tuberculosis, which in turn might have been brought on by an unseen virus named HIV sent by a witch. On the other hand, it might just be the result of a nasty cold causing bronchitis for which nobody is responsible and which a visit to the doctor might relieve. So the work of interpreting signs is plagued by indeterminacy.

As no-one but the witch can know the precise means of their illicit craft, so those who would seek to counteract this evil work must gain knowledge from access to 'higher' powers, beings such as ancestors or the Holy Spirit who can penetrate the secrets of the witch's craft without compromising their own moral character (and who can communicate this knowledge to human specialists in turn without compromising them). But penetrating evil secrets is dangerous work, and not open to all. Emerging from the secrecy undergirding the perpetration of witchcraft is the problem of privacy in authorizing the procedures of divination so central to the struggle to contain evil. The knowledge required to counteract the witch's secret power or divine the intentions of ancestors or other beings transmitting information about the dangers lurking in unseen domains is necessarily private, deriving from particular communication with higher beings. Both traditional healers and prophets (I will refer to them both, here, as 'diviners') partake in aspects of this privacy by founding their authority and power upon particular and personal relations with spiritual beings. Their healing and restorative practices are not premised upon generalizable, or even generally verifiable, public principles or institutions. Rather, diviners work through private communications with personal empowering spirits: dialogues in which only they have access to the interlocutor. The 'truth' uncovered through these conversations is then opened to participation and corroboration in dialogue with the client. A communication from a diviner's spirits will be deemed true if it accords with a privately known fact of the supplicant's life to which the diviner had no previous access or if the divination reveals a future course of events which subsequently comes to pass. While a diviner might gain a reputation for great power and ability in such a manner, his or her authority in counteracting evil will always remain limited because of the personal and private nature of the essential authorizing relationships upon which that power is founded.[16]

Matters pertaining to questions of witchcraft also intrude upon considerations of what might be termed a theological problem of 'unknowing' in relation to unseen powers. I would argue that it is necessary to countenance something akin to the phenomenon known in religious experience as the Mystery in relation to these matters pertaining to unseen powers, that is an engagement with something transcendent beyond human apprehension. This domain of mystery ought not be confused with that which is merely secret or hidden from view, for the idea of mystery invokes a concept of the unknowable pertaining to those realms of being wherein lie the 'interior' domains of personhood variously known in the west as 'mind', 'spirit', 'soul', and what my friend Madumo describes as 'the whole set-up of unseen powers'. That is to say, the putative action of witchcraft, along with the very real fears relating to them, spring from, relate to, and are located in, realms of being which are both ineffable and open to transcendence – that are not subject to forms of knowledge adequately represented by clear and distinct ideas (Nyamnjoh, Chapter 2). 'Witchcraft', in its broadest sense, refers to ways of being that are meaningful in connection with an orientation of openness to relations with the ineffable – that unknowable and unrepresentable something that is both 'out there' (in the rivers, the mountains, the heavens, the cosmos. . .) and 'in here' (in the 'heart', the 'soul', the 'spirit'. . .) as well as, as some would have it, 'amongst us'. It is, in a word, a religious phenomenon. This sense of metaphysical openness can also coexist with a sense of vulnerability, such as is confirmed by the widespread presumptions about the powers of witches, that can result in intense anxiety relating to struggles to manage the action of invisible forces upon the course of life.

Epistemic anxiety and the struggle against belief

There is no such thing as a simple 'belief' in witchcraft in twenty-first century Soweto. With most people I know well, the recognition of the reality of witchcraft is coupled with a belief that, somehow or other, one ought not to believe in witches. For example, a neighbour says she 'partly' believes in witchcraft: 'Witchcraft. . . it partly exists. That's true. But me, I don't believe'. That is to say, she does believe, but would rather not. Yet she is alert to the dangers that can emanate from invisible domains. So when her house was hit by lightning, she was quick to seek protection from a local prophet. My neighbour's attitude to these matters is by no means unusual.

This second order 'belief' (if it can be called that) regarding the undesirability of believing in witches has a very complex structure, impinging upon people's attitudes to occult forces in a multitude of ways. In some instances, it takes the form of a secular modernist assertion of the primacy of science. A visit to the clinic that leads to a clear medical diagnosis coupled with swift and effective treatment, for example, can trump suspicions of witchcraft. Similarly, a faith in chemistry can help alleviate the anxiety that might otherwise follow recognition of signs of sorcery in action, such as the time when my friend MC, in the middle of a battle with an aunt for possession of the family home, found white powder sprinkled on the kitchen floor in a suspicious manner. Although recognizing that the situation was dangerous, he told himself that he was immune to such nonsense, and, after a few drinks to bolster his courage, impressed his friends by dancing over the powder.

Some resist the pull of witchcraft beliefs by embracing a 'mainline' Christian insistence on the power and love of Jesus, while nurturing their faith in the power of Jesus to triumph over the forces of evil such as might be evidenced in the form of witchcraft.[17] Evangelical and Pentecostalist congregations, along with the huge variety of African Initiated Christian churches, tend to engage with the struggle against Satan and witches more explicitly and, hence, their adherents seem to have less concern with denying the belief in witchcraft than with combating the dangers it presents (van Dijk, Chapter 5).

Sometimes, a deliberate reluctance to 'believe' in witches is seen as a practical way of avoiding the psychological snares that await anyone seeking signs of occult forces at work. When we once found a substance resembling mud smeared on the wall in front of the house in Soweto, everyone made a conscious decision to resist the temptation to think that it contained *muthi*, preferring to think of the act as vandalism rather than witchcraft. If, however, the discovery of the mud had been accompanied by some serious mishap in the house, it might not have been easy to discount the possibility of occult attack.

Another reason for resisting the pull of witchcraft explanations for misfortunes is the belief that witches themselves can use your own mind to act against you. A person who becomes obsessed with questions of witchcraft might be laying themselves open to attack by weakening their mental defences against occult action. Thus my friend Madumo was instructed that 'westernizing' his mind could help in reducing the actual power of real witches seeking to destroy him. Ignoring the witches in this view does not make them disappear into that realm of nothingness we call the 'imagination', as a good westerner might believe, but merely renders them less effective. Living in a world of witches in a place like Soweto at the turn of the century, then, almost always involves a struggle *against* believing in witches despite the plenitude of evidence of suffering. During ordinary times, when the forces of misfortune seem manageable, the '*akrasia*' (incontinence of the will) regarding beliefs about witches, the failure of the will to refuse belief, is of little import.[18] When calamity strikes, however, the struggle can become all-consuming.

When I have witnessed friends in Soweto faced with problems of spiritual insecurity, when they have battled with a pressing need to manage the forces considered responsible for their suffering or those shaping their destinies and fate in detrimental ways, the plethora of available interpretative schemes often resulted in heightened anxiety about the nature and character of those powers. Given the widespread extent and uneven distribution of material hardship and violence in Soweto, it is not difficult to understand how the effort to find meaning in misfortune and to make suffering bearable (Geertz 1973) might readily lead to suppositions about witchcraft, even amongst people who might be inclined to scepticism.

In the eyes of those predisposed to detect such signs, evidence of malicious powers at work is everywhere. Indeed, were one so inclined as to perpetrate witchcraft oneself, the probability of misfortune befalling the intended victims or their loved-ones within a few months is sufficiently high to lend credence to conjectures of supernatural causation, whatever the actual efficacy of one's witchly efforts. None of the families I was intimately connected with throughout the 1990s survived the decade without experiencing serious problems they could not help but associate with witchcraft. But were their worries about witchcraft merely a product of living in an insecure world?

I believe that if people in Soweto could live lives free of worries about money, illness, and early death they would be less concerned about other people being able to afflict them through witchcraft. Poverty and material insecurity make people feel more exposed to risks they are unable to manage, in ways that are not only conducive to fearful speculations about supernatural powers, but which also exact a more mundane toll of depression and hopelessness. I also suspect that if greater material security prevailed, the rituals, prayers, ceremonies, and healing procedures that in times of crisis can become life-and-death struggles against evil forces might perhaps serve more as markers of a renascent African identity or joyful celebrations of community. Were everyone healthy, safe from violence, and financially secure, concerns about witchcraft might even come to be subsumed under categories of individual 'psychological' disturbance.

Such days, however, are not on the horizon. In the meantime, in addition to worrying about the ordinary woes of a hard life, people in Soweto must also grapple with distinct problems of spiritual insecurity, particularly the fear that others – who, despite all appearances to the contrary – might be harbouring evil intentions. And the ways in which these problems of security are resolved, or not resolved, through a presumption of malice can have serious ramifications in the lives of individuals, families, and communities, and perhaps also in the democratic state itself.

Notes

1   My discussions with people in Soweto about these matters have continued since my first visit in 1990. During the early 1990s, I spent most of my time living in Soweto. Since 1994, I have visited for three months each year. For an account of my engagement with the place and a description of some of the people who have made it possible for me to live there, see Ashforth 2000. When I speak of 'friends' these are the people of whom I speak. When I speak of 'experience', this is where it happened.
2   Many Africans object to the terms 'witch', 'witchcraft', and 'witchdoctor', arguing

that they are derogatory and misleading. This is undoubtedly so, but the words are unavoidable. Not only are the English words common in African usage, but the indigenous terms such as the Zulu *ubuthakathi* have long been inflected with notions deriving from Europe as much as Africa. Nor is it possible to insist on definitional clarity and precision without obscuring the ways in which the words are actually used in everyday practice. I prefer to use the terms loosely, much as my friends in Soweto do, while teasing out from investigation of the context what they might mean.

3   The term 'sorcery' is unknown in everyday parlance in Soweto. It could, however, be substituted for 'witchcraft' in most of what follows, since there is no firm distinction in these parts, such as reported by Evans-Pritchard (1937: 21) in the 1930s Sudan between 'witchcraft' as an innate capacity and 'sorcery' as the skill of manipulating substances.

4   In a Christian context preoccupied by demons, spirit possession can be problematic and people undergoing the symptoms of such possession that would traditionally have been interpreted as a call to heal are often subject to exorcism. Oosthuizen (1992) reports that such exorcisms, often in the form of repeated baptisms, are commonplace in African Initiated Churches. See also Jonker 1992 for discussion of the demonizing of ancestral spirits in Zambia.

5   Killings related to these forms of 'witchcraft' are typically thought to take three forms: '*muthi*-murders' (also known as 'ritual killings') in which body parts are used in medicines (Commission of Inquiry into Witchcraft Violence and Ritual Murders 1996); zombie-making, in which a victim is reincarnated as a slave double (Comaroff and Comaroff 1999; Niehaus n.d.); and human sacrifices to mystical beasts such as the snake *maMlambo* who is said to require the flesh of a relative (preferably one's own child) in recompense for her grant of wealth and power (Wilson 1961). For accounts of *muthi*-murder in the 1980s and 1990s, see the Report of the Ralushai Commission on Witchcraft Violence (Commission of Inquiry into Witchcraft Violence and Ritual Murders 1996).

6   My point is not that there has been a 'loss' of culture. Rather, in the vibrant worlds of urban life, there is a superabundance of interpretative authorities seeking to give meaning to life (Mugo 1999).

7   For discussion of the Independent churches in Soweto, see West 1975. On the AIC movement more generally, see Sundkler 1960 and Oosthuizen 1992.

8   In the first four years of the 1990s there were some 6,361 deaths attributed to political violence in the region around Soweto (Bornman *et al.* 1998: 18).

9   The statistics on rape are notoriously unreliable. South Africa has the highest incidence of reported rape in the world (Human Rights Watch 2001). A survey of women in the south of Johannesburg, the region encompassing Soweto, found that 20 per cent of young women experienced sexual abuse by the age of 18 (Anderson *et al.* 2000).

10 I arrive at this estimate by dividing the number of crimes reported in 1997 by the SAPS for Soweto (24,464 violent crimes; 67,765 including crimes against residential property) (South African Police Service 1998) by the number of households (178,338 including in this number those with backyard structures) estimated by the Wits Survey (Morris 1999). These are rough approximations only and probably underestimate the incidence of sexual and domestic violence. The 'household' unit here contrived gives a rough approximation of the social universe most directly affected by crimes. When the Wits survey asked respondents to rank the 'problems' faced by their households, 27.7 per cent rated being a victim of crime as their biggest problem (University of the Witwatersrand Department of Sociology 1997: 6.2.4).

11 A survey of drug use amongst criminal offenders found that 56 per cent of young male offenders under the age of 20 were using this combination (Louw and Parry 1999).

12 For an example of these sensitivities, see the account of the healer Sarah Mashele's attitudes in Simon 1993. When arrests are made in connection with 'ritual murder' cases involving human body parts, the stories typically refer to the involvement of 'traditional healers'. For example, see the South African Press Association report 'Ritual Murder: Healers in Court' (SAPA 18 May 2001).

13 During apartheid, there was widespread suspicion that 'traditional authorities' were using 'muthi' to maintain themselves in power at the people's expense (Commission of Inquiry into Witchcraft Violence and Ritual Murders 1996). In the late 1990s, too, I heard many rumours that the leader of the Zion Christian Church, the biggest religious organization in the region, Bishop Lekganyane, maintained a storeroom of human body parts which he drew upon to secure the success of his church.

14 For an example of a self-proclaimed African witch's confession, see Bannerman-Richter 1984.

15 Perhaps the most powerful analogy lending plausibility to the witchcraft paradigm today is that of western science against which is posited the equal potency of 'African science' as practised by witches and healers. Living in a world where the miracles of remote control and mobile telephones are everyday realities and images of nuclear explosions or space travels commonplace, no-one doubts the power of science to effect action at a distance and transform the world and its inhabitants. Commodities embodying such science, however, just like the classes in Physical Science taught in schools, images of industrial and technological power, or the doctors staffing clinics and hospitals, have an irreducibly alien feel in this context. They are not indigenous, not African. They are 'things of Whites'. Even when the scientists or doctors are black and African, they are not practising *African* science. African science is another, secret, sphere of knowledge. While no-one will admit to having mastered African science, to doubt that it is every bit as powerful as 'White' science is tantamount to betraying a lack of faith in the African 'race'.

16 In historical times the king, whose ancestors ruled over the fortunes of the whole people, employed the services of diviners who, by virtue of their standing (sometimes hereditary) in relation to the king were viewed as possessing powers capable of preserving the fortunes of the whole nation and diminishing their enemies (Pettersson 1953). Such arrangements may persist in some of the rural polities, but people in urban areas, especially those long-settled in towns beyond the purview of chiefly rule, have no access to such spiritual power outside churches.

17 Christian evangelists have long wrangled with questions of how best to engage with beliefs and practices associated with witchcraft. For a good overview of their approaches in South Africa, see Hayes 1995.

18 The term comes from Aristotle's *Ethics* (Aristotle 1953: bk 7, ch. 1). See also Rorty 1983.

Bibliography

Anderson, N., Mhatre, S., Mqotsi, N., and Penderis, M. (2000) *Beyond Victims and Villains: Culture of Sexual Violence in South Johannesburg*, Johannesburg: CIETafrica.

Aristotle (1953) *The Ethics of Aristotle*, London: Penguin.

Ashforth, A. (1999) 'Weighing manhood in Soweto', *Codesria Bulletin* 3/4: 51–58.

—— (2000) *Madumo, A Man Bewitched*, Chicago: University of Chicago Press.

—— (2001) 'AIDS, witchcraft and the problem of public power in post-apartheid South Africa', School of Social Science Occasional Paper, Princeton, Institute for Advanced Study.

Bannerman-Richter, G. (1984) *Don't Cry! My Baby, Don't Cry! Autobiography of an African Witch*, Winona, MN: Apollo Books.

Berglund, A.-I. (1976) *Zulu Thought-Patterns and Symbolism*, Bloomington: Indiana University Press.

Bornman, E., Eeden, R., and Wentzel, M. (1998) *Violence in South Africa*, Pretoria: HSRC.

Burke, K. (1969) *A Grammar of Motives*, Berkeley: University of California Press.

Campbell, S.S. (1998) *Called to Heal: African Shamanic Healers*, Twin Lakes, WI: Lotus Press.

Comaroff, J. and Comaroff, J.L. (1999) 'Occult economies and the violence of abstraction: notes from the South African postcolony', *American Ethnologist* 26, 2: 279–303.

Commission of Inquiry into Witchcraft Violence and Ritual Murders (1996) *Report of the Commission of Inquiry into Witchcraft Violence and Ritual Murders in the Northern Province of the Republic of South Africa (Ralushai Commission)*, Ministry of Safety and Security, Northern Province, South Africa.

Department of Health, Directorate of Health Systems Research and Epidemiology (2001) *Summary Report: National HIV Sero- prevalence Survey of Women Attending Ante-Natal Clinics in South Africa*, Pretoria: Department of Health.

Emdon, E. (1993) 'Privatisation of state housing, with special focus on the greater Soweto area', *Urban Forum* 4, 2: 1–13.

Evans-Pritchard, E.E. (1937) *Witchcraft, Oracles and Magic among the Azande*, Oxford: Clarendon Press.

Froise, M. (1996) *South African Christian Handbook 1996–97*, Pretoria: World Mission Centre.

Geertz, C. (1973) 'Religion as a cultural system', in *The Interpretation of Culture*, New York: Basic Books.

Hayes, S. (1995) 'Christian responses to witchcraft and sorcery', *Missionalia: the Journal of the Southern African Missiological Society* 339–354.

Human Rights Watch (2001) *Scared at School: Sexual Violence Against Girls in South African Schools*, New York: Human Rights Watch.

Human Sciences Research Council (HSRC) (1999) 'Employment Forecasts till 2003' Media release 25 August 1999. <http://www.hsrc.ac.za/corporate/media/1999/aug 25_1.html> (accessed 5 July 2001).

Jonker, C. (1992) 'Sleeping with the Devil: Christian re-interpretation of spirit possession in Zambia', *Etnofoor* 5, 1–2: 213–233.

Kiernan, J. (1982) 'The "problem of evil" in the context of ancestral intervention in the affairs of the living in Africa', *Man* 17: 287–301.

Louw, A. and Parry, C.D.H. (1999) *The MRC/ISS 3–Metros Arrestee Study*, Tygerberg: Medical Research Council of South Africa.

Ministry of Transport (1997) *Second Draft White Paper on the Road Accident Fund*, Pretoria: Ministry of Transport.

Morris, A. (ed.) (1999) *Change and Continuity: A Survey of Soweto in the Late 1990s*, Johannesburg: Department of Sociology, University of the Witwatersrand.

Mugo, M.G. (1999) 'African culture in education for sustainable development', in M.W. Malegapuru (ed.) *African Renaissance: The New Struggle*, Cape Town: Mafube and Tafelberg.

Niehaus, I.A. (n.d.) 'Witches and zombies in the South African lowveld: symbolic discourse, accusation and subjectivity', unpublished manuscript.

Ntshangase, K.D.J. (1993) 'The social history of Iscamtho', unpublished MA dissertation, University of the Witwatersrand.

Oosthuizen, G.C. (1992) *The Healer-Prophet in Afro-Christian Churches*, Leiden: E.J. Brill.

Parry, C.D.H. (1997) *Alcohol Misuse and Public Health: A 10–point Action Plan*, Tygerberg: Medical Research Council.

Parry, C.D.H. and Bennetts, A.L. (1999) *Alcohol Policy and Public Health in South Africa*, Cape Town: Oxford University Press.

Pettersson, O. (1953) *Chiefs and Gods: Religious and Social Elements in the South Eastern Bantu Kingship*, Lund: CWK Gleerup.

Pirie, G.H. (1984a) 'Ethno-linguistic zoning in South African black townships', *Area* 16: 291–298.

—— (1984b) 'Letters, words, worlds: the naming of Soweto', *African Studies Journal* 43: 43–51.

Rorty, A. (1983) 'Akratic believers', *American Philosophical Quarterly* 20, 2: 175–183.

Select Committee on Social Services (1998) *Report of the Select Committee on Social Services on Traditional Healers, 4 August, 1998*, Cape Town, Parliament of the Republic of South Africa, No.144–1998.

Shaw, M. and Gastrow, P. (2001) 'Stealing the show? Crime and its impact in post-apartheid South Africa', *Daedalus* 130, 1: 235–258.

Simon, L. (1993) *Inyanga; Sarah Mashele's Story*, Johannesburg: Justified Press.

Sisulu, W. (1998) 'Foreword', in B. Philip and S. Lauren (eds) *Soweto: A History*, Cape Town: Maskew Miller Longman.

South Africa Ministry of Education (1999) *Status Report for the Minister of Education*, Pretoria: Ministry of Education.

South African Police Service 1998, *CIMC Quarterly Report 1/98*.

Sundkler, B.G.M. (1960) *Bantu Prophets in South Africa*, London: Oxford University Press.

University of the Witwatersrand Department of Sociology (1997) *Soweto in Transition Project (Preliminary Report)*, Johannesburg, Soweto in Transition Project.

West, M. (1975) *Bishops and Prophets in an African City: African Independent Churches in Soweto, Johannesburg*, Cape Town: David Philip.

Whiteford, A. and Van Seventer, D. (1999) *Winners and Losers: A Report on South Africa's Changing Income Distribution in the 1990s*, Pretoria: Wharton Econometric Forecasting Associates.

Whiteside, A. and Sunter, C. (2000) *AIDS: The Challenge for South Africa*, Tafelberg: Human and Rousseau.

Wilson, M. (1961) *Reaction to Conquest: Effects of Contact with Europeans on the Pondo of South Africa*, London: Oxford University Press.

Chapter 11

Witchcraft, development and paranoia in Cameroon

Interactions between popular, academic and state discourse

Cyprian F. Fisiy and Peter Geschiere

To both of us it was, somewhat surprisingly, 'development' that forced us to study 'witchcraft'.[1] In the early 1980s, when Cyprian Fisiy was just recruited as a researcher for the new Institute of Human Sciences in Yaoundé, this institute was officially charged by the Ministry of Internal Affairs with starting a large-scale research project on *Sorcellerie et Développement* (Witchcraft and Development). The main goal of the research programme was to gather empirical evidence on witchcraft phenomena and its impacts on development – more precisely, to come up with policy prescriptions on how best to fight such phenomena. At the outset, a critical assumption, based on anecdotal evidence, was that witchcraft was a major barrier to development in the country. For reasons that are quite interesting in themselves, as we shall see in the second half of this chapter, the project never really took off. Yet it triggered a long series of articles by Fisiy on 'witchcraft', especially on the judicial aspects of the government's efforts to deal with it.

For Geschiere, the confrontation came somewhat earlier, when he started anthropological fieldwork in the early 1970s in a set of neighbouring Maka villages in the East Province. The aim of his project was not to study 'witchcraft'. The focus was rather on changing relations between villagers and the state; and development projects, as possible bones of contention, were to provide concrete points of entry into understanding these relations. However, one of his more startling findings was that it was state officials who, when addressing development issues, constantly referred to witchcraft. Indeed, a recurring theme in their admonitions – harangues might be a better word – to villagers was that they should stop sabotaging the state's projects, or *le développement* in general, with their witchcraft. At least initially, villagers were somewhat reticent to discuss *djambe* (now generally translated as *sorcellerie*). But once they agreed to discuss this more hidden side of everyday relations, there seemed to be no end to the stories they told about the working of occult forces, notably in more 'modern' contexts (school, football, the rise of a new elite, etc.).

Our personal experiences, therefore, correspond to an initial suggestion by this volume's editors that 'development' might offer a more concrete starting point – than, for instance, the broad notion of 'modernity' – to explore the resilience of witchcraft representations in modern contexts. One could object that development has become as vague a notion as modernity (or witchcraft). However, this was different in the 1970s and early 1980s. In those days 'development' still provided a confident metanarrative, anchored firmly in powerful institutional settings (Ferguson 1999; Escobar 1995). In some sort of rebound with this firm notion of development, even witchcraft seemed, at the time, to acquire clearly outlined contours: it figured in this context as a threatening, levelling mechanism – a hidden, traditionalist refusal of everything development stood for. In conjunction with a dirigiste state agenda, development discourse was conceptualized as a linear process, the ultimate destination of which was the production of modernity, a modern state. Anything that stood in the way, witchcraft beliefs and practices included, was considered a legitimate target for state intervention.

Since the 1980s, matters have seemingly become more complicated. The perception of development as a destination which should be pursued collectively by the state as part of the common good has been muted. The pursuit of modernity has become a personal enterprise based on the accumulation of individual wealth. The old role-model of the *fonctionnaire* with his school certificates and his career in government service tends to be replaced by people's fascination with the *feymen* of Cameroon or the 419s of Nigeria – unscrupulous fixers who have become dazzlingly rich.[2] And these shadowy figures are often related to a very different aspect of 'witchcraft', to what could be called its 'accumulative' side.

This apparent shift in the way 'witchcraft' is linked to 'development' – from a supposedly levelling force in the 1960s and 1970s to more emphasis on its accumulative capacities in more recent times – is especially intriguing. Elsewhere (Fisiy and Geschiere 1991; Geschiere 1997) we tried to show that it is precisely this ambivalence of being a force for both levelling and accumulation of power and riches that explains why witchcraft remains such an omnipresent image in present-day Africa, despite all modern changes. Witchcraft is often associated with jealousy – that is, with hidden aggression by the weak against the rich and powerful. It is this levelling side that mostly comes to the fore in formal accusations when those in power accuse people in a weaker position of trying to bring them down. However, at a more hidden level, witchcraft is equally associated with those who are doing well. Rumours also link it to the rich and powerful who allegedly owe their success to the use of varied occult sources and forces. Even if this supposed link between accumulation and witchcraft is not often expressed in public accusations – how could the weak dare accuse those in power? – this association seems to be currently accepted as self-evident. It is this ambivalence of witchcraft, its Janus-faced character, in relation to the new inequalities that makes these beliefs so all-pervasive and resilient. It is also clear that the emphasis can shift from one side to the other – from people being more preoccupied with the levelling side of witchcraft to more gossip about its accumulative side and vice versa, depending on the context and time. To what extent did such a shift occur in the relationship between witchcraft and development, and what were its implications?

Both parts of this chapter are based on personal experiences: Geschiere's during the early stages of his fieldwork among the Maka and Fisiy's during the difficult start of the *Sorcellerie et Développement* project. Therefore, we propose to write them in the I-form: the 'I' in each part referring to the researcher concerned. 'We' refers to our joint interpretations.

Fieldwork among the Maka: witchcraft as popular reaction or officials' paranoia?

When I (Geschiere) began fieldwork among the Maka in East Cameroon in the 1970s, I was determined to follow more 'modern' currents in anthropology. For one thing, I wanted to move beyond the restrictive focus on 'the local' that had, to then, featured so integrally to the ethnographic enterprise. At the time, the notion of 'local level politics' (Swartz 1968) was quite fashionable: anthropologists should learn to study the politics in 'their' community not as local affairs, but rather as part of a broader political framework – most notably, that of the state. My aim was therefore to study how local relations of authority were affected by broader political changes, especially de-colonization and the formation of the postcolonial state. This also meant, so I thought, that only limited attention could be paid to the more 'traditional' aspects of village life. I was prepared to take kinship seriously, as an important framework for local structures, but I was less interested in topics like bridewealth, witchcraft and so on.

It soon turned out that, as far as bridewealth was concerned, there was little chance of my ignoring it. The people of the lineage that adopted me because I came to live in their part of the village – to them it was self-evident that this made me *mwane Andjag*, child of Andjag – simply insisted I attend all their bridewealth negotiations. The least I could do in return for their hospitality, after all, was to strengthen their numbers at such negotiations with my presence as a *tangue* (lit., a pink one). This meant my sitting for many long afternoons through rowdy confrontations between the bride's and groom's groups, drinking too much palm wine, and feeling rather uncertain about my role in all this tumult.

With witchcraft, things were somewhat different. At the time, no one spoke too much or too openly about *la sorcellerie*. The ideology of the one-party state – that certainly had some local resonance, albeit often at unexpected moments – emphasized that *la sorcellerie* was something backward that had to be overcome as quickly as possible.[3] One of the local village elites where I lived, a regional inspector for education who also held high positions in the Party and the municipality, had an admonishing notice above the entrance to his office: 'Be brief. We have to do in four decades what Europe did in four centuries.' Talking about witchcraft – certainly for an anthropologist – meant primitivizing Cameroon and denying it the progress it had made towards development. I thus found it all the more surprising that none other than the *sous-préfet* himself raised the issue on one of his visits to the village to inspect a development project.

The main reason I had settled in this particular village was precisely because of this development project. Just before my arrival in the East, the government had launched a new co-operative organization, ZAPI (*zone d'action prioritaire integrée*), with strong support of French development experts. ZAPI was strongly influenced by the ideology of *animation*, the French version of 'community development'. Its aim was to strengthen peasants' involvement in the development of cash-cropping (particularly cocoa and coffee). For this, the peasants had to be organized and encouraged to take responsibility for running their own co-operatives. Of course, this more democratic approach was difficult to reconcile with the highly authoritarian and bureaucratic approach of the one-party state, and, for this reason, the *sous-préfet* kept a keen eye on developments in the ZAPI area. The ZAPI people asked me to work in one of their new zones, so that I could write reports on issues of importance to their projects (e.g. access to land, relations between the villages, but especially issues of leadership). The *sous-préfet*, whose authorization I needed for all my activities, seemed to see me as a welcome informal source of information on what ZAPI was up to in this zone.

In the village where I settled, ZAPI wanted to establish a pilot project they hoped would demonstrate to locals the advantages of their approach. The village had asked for a new school building. ZAPI provided the necessary funds for building materials, and villagers themselves promised to do the necessary work. Not unexpectedly, this latter part proved to be the weakest link in the project. Every Thursday – then officially the day for communal work in the whole country – the village chief paraded up and down the village in search of labourers, but mostly in vain. Most people left early for their own plantations in order to avoid the *corvée* for the school building. Apparently, they were more interested in working for their own benefit than for the village school. It was in this stalemate that the *sous-préfet* intervened, clearly delighted to show that his authoritarian approach was the only effective one. Yet, his interpretation of the problem was somewhat unexpected. He made the village chief announce that the following Thursday he himself would survey the school works and that everybody had better be there. Indeed, that Thursday quite a crowd gathered – in those days, people's fear of the *gendarmes* still lent force to the words of a *sous-préfet*. The latter arrived as usual in a hurry and his speech was, again as usual, brief but effective: the government was following the school project with great impatience, the village people had to take it more seriously; otherwise he had to intervene.[4] Yet, towards the end of his speech, he was suddenly impassioned as he shouted at the crowd: 'I'll tell you one thing. You have to stop sabotaging everything the government is trying to do for you with your damned witchcraft! The persons who are behind all this may think they remain invisible. Well, I see them and I know how to get them.'[5]

To this official, *la sorcellerie* was apparently the main impediment to development. This preoccupation with *sorcellerie* as anti-development may have been general in Cameroon in those days, but the East Province of the country was always cited as the most blatant example of this. It was seen as one of the most backward parts precisely because it was supposed to be infested with witchcraft. A brief scene, quite comical but at the same time shocking, illustrates this point.

> In 1971, at the start of my fieldwork, Mr Ayissi-Mvodo, then Minister of Territorial Administration and often mentioned as a possible crown-prince to President Ahidjo, came to visit the East Province. The UNC, the one-party, had organized an impressive welcome at Abong-Mbang, the main town in Maka land. The school children stood ready in their uniforms waving small flags. Shops and offices had been closed and the *gendarmes* saw to it that everybody had joined the crowd to welcome the venerable guest. After making the people wait for two hours in the hot sun, the minister arrived. He mounted the platform decorated with palm branches. The national hymn was played (luckily from a tape, since the crowd did not join in – clearly this was not even expected of them in the strictly directed ceremony). Then the minister started his speech. The first phrase was a strong one: 'Before I came to the East I had the impression that the people here were only interested in *arki* (local liquor) and *sorcellerie*.' Clearly, the minister wanted to go on to say that this prejudice had now been dispelled. But, unfortunately, before doing so, he paused briefly. The applause master, interpreting this as a sign for him to become active, beckoned the crowd with furious gestures to applaud, which they did obediently. Whatever the minister's intentions, he had once again confirmed the usual stereotype about the East.

At the time, this association with *sorcellerie* had specific, political implications. The one-party ideology of the Ahidjo regime, simple but repeated *encore et toujours* at any official occasion, was based on a Manichaean opposition of two basic themes: 'unity' versus 'subversion', with 'vigilance' as the crucial link. The special circumstances of Cameroonian independence – marked by a tenacious guerrilla movement of the UPC-opposition (the first nationalist movement in the country) in the Centre and west of the country – made for a heavy emphasis on an omnipresent danger of hidden 'subversion' that, supposedly, threatened the admirable national ideal of 'unity' behind President Ahidjo. Indeed, under the strict police control that the regime imposed on the nation, a simple accusation of 'subversion' could be enough to occasion someone's disappearance – probably (but one was never sure) to Tcholliré, Ahidjo's feared concentration camp in the North. The official insistence on 'vigilance' as the main duty of all party members and, indeed, of all Cameroonian citizens further reinforced the idea that 'subversion' lurked everywhere. Moreover, the emphasis on the hidden character of 'subversion' made it easy to link to *sorcellerie*. Since the early 1970s, the Ahidjo regime had succeeded in suppressing nearly all forms of open resistance against the new state. Its 'hegemonic project' (Bayart 1979) assumed ever more totalitarian pretensions, aiming to control strictly all aspects of daily life. In this extremely centralized conception of a complete bureaucratic surveillance of society – a conception that had concrete effects, even if reality was often quite different – *la sorcellerie* remained an uncomfortable exception: apparently very real to the people, yet very hard to control because of its hidden and diffuse character.

Like the *sous-préfet* quoted above, Minister Ayissi-Mvodo was, therefore, evoking a heavily charged topic when he linked the East to *la sorcellerie*. Particular aspects of the societies of the area can help explain why officials made this link so easily. Maka society, like other forest societies, was up until the colonial conquest (1905–1910) extremely segmentary in nature. Small patrilineal segments formed autonomous villages under the leadership of elders. Common descent but even more marriage and affinity created links between the villages, but these could at any time be ruptured by feuds. There were no central positions of authority above the village level. Moreover, village life was (and is) characterized by strong levelling tendencies: the ever-present tendencies towards fission implied in the kinship organization, and the impact of jealousy and witchcraft.[6] This mixture of segmentary tendencies and powerful levelling forces made these societies very problematic for colonial attempts at 'pacification' (see Geschiere 1982; Wirz 1972). In postcolonial times, with the rise of an ideology of development and *animation*, the same traits led to a quite frantic search for 'responsible leaders'. Typically one of the first topics that ZAPI (the parastatal co-operative in Maka land, mentioned above) required me to research was *comment déceler de vrais leaders?* (how to detect true leaders?). To the ZAPI people, their more participatory approach to involve the peasants in projects to raise the productivity in the zone – in contrast to the high-handed bureaucratic approach of both the colonial and the postcolonial state – required first of all to find 'real leaders' who could speak on behalf of the peasants and ensure their commitment to ZAPI goals and projects. But the contradiction between a strongly egalitarian ideology at the village level[7] and the extremely authoritarian impositions by the (post) colonial state seemed to make the quest for such leaders illusory.

The Maka discourse on *djambe* (now generally translated as *sorcellerie*) reflects the segmentary and levelling implications of this loose, socio-political order. *Djambe* is a highly diffuse and open notion. Like *evu* (the parallel notion among the Beti, the Maka's western neighbours who now play a prominent role in the state under 'their' President Paul Biya), it encompasses myriad hidden forces. The *djambe* imaginary has a horrible, black core: the image of witches (*mindjindjamb*) leaving their bodies at night and flying off to meet their fellow witches. Each witch must take his or her turn in 'offering' a relative for a cannibalistic feast. The victim will then fall ill and die unless a traditional healer (*nganga*) removes the spell.[8] It is the betrayal of kinship, even more than the act of cannibalism, that is most shocking to the Maka. But such imaginings do not preclude that the *djambe* can also be brought under control, for instance by the good services of a *nganga*, who actually himself can only help since he has learnt to restrain his powerful *djambe* and use it for healing. Indeed, once the *djambe* is brought under control, it becomes a positive asset and can be used for all sorts of constructive purposes. For this reason, one can even use the term to mean a special kind of energy as, for instance, when someone compliments a host for preparing a nice reception by saying that his *djambe* allowed him to do it. Moreover, the Maka tend to believe that, potentially, virtually everyone has a *djambe* in his or her belly; but that only some endeavour to develop it to gain access to special kinds of powers. Because *djambe* is such a diffuse notion – because it covers such an array of aspects, both negative and positive – it is, in practice, decidedly a-moral. Again, this contrasts starkly with the more hierarchical societies of the west (Bamileke, Bamenda) where the witchcraft discourse is much more 'compartmentalized', and various institutional mechanisms serve to separate, at least conceptually, more destructive from more constructive expressions of the occult, even though in practice these are often more confused.[9]

For the Maka, *djambe* can therefore take many forms. But it is clear that one of its basic expressions is closely linked to jealousy. In this sense, *djambe* is a consequential levelling force. It must have been this strain of *djambe* discourse that figured in official discourses – of both state officials and developers – as a fundamentally anti-development force. For villagers, too, *djambe* had such implications. It was supposed to function as a weapon of the weak and the jealous against their more successful kin. Therefore, since development clearly brought new inequalities, *djambe* was, indeed, seen as an acute danger to those who tried to profit from the new opportunities.

My fieldwork provided many examples of this. A striking one was the *gbati*, a new form of witchcraft that had suddenly spread in the area, a few years before my arrival in 1971 (see Geschiere 1980). People were still searching frantically for ways to combat this new threat, that would have come from the Mvelle to the northwest of the Maka region. It was especially frightening since it was carried by young boys. Normally, elders were seen as the undisputed masters of the secret world of *djambe* but, with *gbati* the young were suddenly the masters of the old! I witnessed palavers that were strongly reminiscent of the Salem witchcraft trials in eighteenth-century New England, in which young girls played a central role. Similarly, in the *gbati* trials, young boys confessed to hideous crimes: some claimed to have eaten holes in the local village school teacher's heart; or to have buried bamboo splinters under the doors of their parents' houses to make them ill or even die; or to have stopped the Presbyterian pastor from preaching at the village chapel (van Dijk, Chapter 5). This formerly unknown evil was so new that established *nganga* were at an utter loss for how to combat it. My good friend Mendouga, a prominent *nganga* along the *piste*, lost her reputation because she was wholly incapable of dealing with this novel threat. In fact, during one of the *gbati* palavers she claimed to have been nearly overcome herself – she was only saved by her dog whose furious barking had warned her only just in time, or else she would have been *ligotée* (tied up) by these treacherous child-witches. But a new *nganga* emerged, Ayindale, from a neighbouring village, who knew how to deal with this threat: during a big palaver, he forced the boys to eat enormous quantities of very greasy food (lots of oil and meat) until they vomited. From their puke, he produced several pieces of cord with knots in them – each knot stood for one victim.[10] The story of *gbati* is a continuing one: *gbati* has evolved and it still crops up, now and then, in village rumours, though it has lost much of its frightening character; people have become accustomed to it. In the context of this chapter it is of special interest that this *gbati*, when it entered the region at the end of the 1960s, had such a strong anti-developmental stance. The *gbati* boys directed their anger against everything that stood for development in the village: the school, its teacher, the church, the village elite.

A similar example of witchcraft directed against development was a popular saying that several people, especially elderly ones, quoted to me in 1971 – though even then they insisted that it applied more to former days than to the present: 'No man who plants a cocoa tree will live to reap its fruits.' This is, indeed, a strong threat since normally a cocoa tree begins producing only four years after being planted. The implication was clear. Cocoa was the first successful cash-crop in the forest area (it spread rapidly especially since the late 1940s). Thus it symbolized the new riches of ambitious *planteurs*. However, my informants remembered that, in former times, people were afraid to follow the government's admonitions to join in the cocoa boom. Was it not dangerous to kindle the jealousy of poorer relatives? The admonition that '. . . you would not live to reap the fruits' was, at the time, a powerful caveat. Again, this provides a clear example of witchcraft as a barrier to development. However, in this case, the double meaning of witchcraft is quite apparent. My first reaction when I heard this particular popular wisdom was to point out that since the 1950s many villagers had planted cocoa trees, and with considerable success. Since the 1960s, each village in the region could boast of a new elite of *grands planteurs*, who were proud of their extensive cocoa plantations. At this, my informants normally replied that, indeed, people had understood that this witchcraft ban on cocoa was nonsense. However, on closer inspection, this common-sense explanation turned out to be far too simple. Striking was that, in one way or another, nearly all the *grands planteurs* were easily associated with witchcraft. Indeed, as one of my most valuable informants – a true 'peasant intellectual' – remarked: how could they be 'innocent' if they had dared to brave the threat of jealousy, that is witchcraft, of their poorer relatives by joining in the race for the new cocoa riches? They must have had some sort of occult protection. Such suggestions clearly indicate that witchcraft had not only levelling implications in relation to development.

Yet, in general, it is clear that to villagers as well *djambe* could have levelling effects. Less clear is whether they really saw *djambe* as a 'subversive' force directed against the state and its projects, or against *le développement* more broadly. On the contrary, ordinary villagers seemed rather taken aback by the *sous-préfet's* and other officials' accusations against them. Moreover, I never heard any rumours that villagers were actually using, or were trying to use, secret forces to undermine such ambitious projects (which is striking in itself, given the sheer number of constantly changing witchcraft rumours on every topic imaginable). Rather, occult assaults were supposedly directed against specific persons, mostly relatives – which, indeed, corresponds to the highly personalized nature of *djambe* discourse and the emphasis on the close links between *djambe* and kinship (*bjel*).[11] It seems, therefore, that the image of *la sorcellerie* as the supreme form of subversion was more the result of official paranoia than of anything else. The link officials made between 'witchcraft' and 'subversion' – supposedly directed against the state, the new national order and, therefore, development – clearly corresponded to the rigid one-party ideology, obsessed as it was with the need for constant vigilance against omnipresent but hidden subversion. For villagers, *djambe* was rather about hidden aggression against individuals and, more specifically, aggression from 'within the house'.

We will return in this chapter to the subsequent collapse of the development dream in the region with the crisis of 1987, and the implications for witchcraft discourses. As already noted, witchcraft then seemed to show another face in relation to development. But first we want to explore how the official vision of witchcraft as a barrier to development manifested itself in other fields.

The state against witchcraft: the search for rationality in the occult

Apart from occasional harangues, as illustrated above, by *préfets* and *sous-préfets* on the anti-developmental nature of witchcraft and the government's determination to fight these practices, there was little in the state's armoury to carry out such a fight. The basic strategy for dealing with the topic was to approach it as a matter of law and order, and to classify witchcraft as a crime against individual safety and group security. In fact, the attempt to incriminate such practices was captured in the loosely-worded Article 251 of the 1967 Penal Code as follows:

> Whoever commits any act of witchcraft, magic or divination liable to disturb public order or tranquillity, or to harm another person, property or substance, whether by taking a reward or otherwise, shall be punished with imprisonment for from two to ten years, and with a fine of five thousand to one hundred thousand francs.

Practical guidance given to magistrates on how to apply the law stressed that the incriminating facts should be those that are liable to disturb public order and tranquillity or to harm another person and/or his property. What the constitutive elements of the crime were, in terms of *actus reus* and *mens rea*, were never fully specified. It should therefore come as no surprise that this legal instrument for dealing with witchcraft proved to be a rather blunt and ineffectual tool for fighting anti-developmental tendencies. The ambivalence in the interpretation of this text was such that it could be used to persecute alleged witches but also those members of the community who devoted their time to fight witchcraft as 'witch-doctors', so long as their acts could be classified as falling within the realm of witchcraft, magic and divination.

The fundamental question is why the law insisted on incriminating an activity or belief which the law itself could not even define. To what extent did the practices enunciated in Article 251 disturb public order and tranquillity? I (Fisiy) would argue that the concept of public order and tranquillity is at the centre of this offence and that it has to be seen as an extension of state control over local communities. Any alternative source of power not mediated by state institutions was seen – especially by local level bureaucrats such as the *préfet* and *sous-préfet* – as undermining the core attribute of command and control. The elusive nature of the witchcraft enigma and the lack of materiality in its practices and manifestations rendered it even more ominous to the administration. It was perceived as a countervailing force that could not be handled in a command and control power context.

Almost twenty years after the enactment of the Penal Code, the limits of this instrument became obvious to the politico-administrative elite. Despite the law, stories of witchcraft accusations and counter-accusations provided the basic content of local tabloid newspapers. It had simply become a major societal virus with no cure. It is therefore not surprising that with the persistence of witchcraft discourse and praxis, the government commissioned the Institute of Human Studies (IHS) in 1985 to investigate to what extent witchcraft was a hindrance to development and what should be done about it. An interdisciplinary approach was adopted, bringing together social scientists, economists, philosophers, and lawyers to assess the impact of 'the belief in witchcraft' on development programmes.

Framing the issue this way, in terms of the 'belief' in witchcraft, was already a subtle departure from the initial question. First, the location of the study within the Anthropological Department (*Centre de Recherches en Anthropologie* – CREA of the IHS) was quite indicative of the field of study. Second, the predominance of philosophical research at this centre, headed by a philosopher, structured the manner in which the witchcraft problematic was presented. In fact, *a priori* assumptions led to the framing of witchcraft discourse and research proposal in terms of belief. Preliminary discussions among the philosophers on the team drifted towards more general notions of African belief systems and cosmology.

Rather than pose the witchcraft problematic in terms of cause and effect research questions, researchers instead sought to establish the causal link between the relative underdevelopment of certain regions of the country and the preponderance of witchcraft beliefs. The challenge was not how to establish this link, it was one of seeking solutions to sever this link. A more probing approach would have been to pose the initial question suggested by the Ministries of Territorial Administration and Social Affairs – to ask whether witchcraft was a barrier to development. However, my colleagues seemed to assume that this was, indeed, the case. Thus the main question for the team became rather how to help the government fight witchcraft since it was seen to be a self-evident roadblock to development. The search for effective instruments for dealing with witchcraft became the object of study. This entry point justified my own focus on how to establish proof in witchcraft cases.

Furthermore, anecdotal evidence suggested that educated elite from certain parts of the country, including the East Province (where Geschiere did his fieldwork and the examples above come from), were particularly prone to witchcraft attacks and were therefore reluctant to return to their home areas for fear of being 'eaten' by witches. In fact, there was a common saying in those parts of Cameroon that the tombstones in front of every beautiful modern house were the last abode of elites who ventured to build in their home areas, but who were immediately killed by their jealous kin. Getting elite sons of the land to invest in their home areas was seen as a major developmental challenge. This would account for the backwardness of especially the forest regions of the country. Moreover, this fear of the homeland would be a major factor contributing to the rural exodus.

This was the background to the aforementioned research programme. Initially, my colleagues were quite excited at being called upon to research and propose policy changes on how to deal with witchcraft. But their enthusiasm soon faded when we began to carry out our programme and numerous conflicting commitments emerged. In fact, during the few meetings on the topic, some colleagues expressed their reservations about whether they really wanted to be associated with the study. Some claimed that all those who studied witchcraft were either witches themselves or would be consumed by the phenomenon and would consequently die. For me, as the law expert on the team, it was much easier to approach the study from a technical platform that sought to establish proof in witchcraft cases. By avoiding broader epistemological questions, I could continue to examine court files, and talk to judges and expert witnesses.

Although the local papers were full of witchcraft accounts, most of these accounts reported incidents of mob justice, lynching, and/or trial by ordeal procedures implemented by traditional authorities. There was little systematic evidence that the courts had pursued a rigorous anti-witchcraft policy. On closer analysis of why the courts were not aggressive in their pursuit of witchcraft cases, it became evident that their main problem was how to establish proof beyond a reasonable doubt. The judges had to deal with the dead weight of binding precedent bequeathed by the colonial legal system. A comparative analysis of the colonial and the postcolonial legal systems highlighted some striking differences. The colonial courts invariably situated witchcraft accusation within a discourse of modernity. As Seidman (1965a: 1140) pointed out, for witchcraft accusations to stand in court, 'the threats must be physical not meta-physical. The threat must be such that a reasonable Englishman would recognize, not the sort which would seem frightening only to an African steeped in the culture of the bush.'[12]

The colonial assumption was that witchcraft beliefs were based on a 'pre-scientific' perception of events. If only the people were better informed about the laws of causation, they would give up such pre-scientific ideas and adopt rational behaviour. Consequently, the colonial strategy was to emphasize the importance of education, especially of women, who were seen as the primary educators at home, and as agents of change for future generations. A broader modernization programme – as part of the civilizing mission of the colonial powers – was supposed to bring about the eradication of witchcraft. Belief in the latter was attributed to the forces of darkness; hence the expectation that the introduction of electricity would bring an end to the entire witchcraft phenomenon. From the standpoint of the colonial courts, the belief in witchcraft was therefore a result of knowledge deficit. Broadening the knowledge base through education would be the answer. Seidman (1965b: 59) postulated that 'the Africans who now control their countries, educated as they are to the highest standards of European culture, will not accept a pre-scientific standard of knowledge and behaviour' (see Nyamnjoh, Chapter 2).

After independence the official perception of witchcraft began to change. It was no longer seen as just a form of pre-scientific knowledge that would disappear with modernization, but rather as active resistance against modern-ization and development. The new Penal Code of 1967 – and the way it was enacted – constituted a turning point. Under the colonial system, witches were systematically set free when charged with the practice of witchcraft because it was impossible to prove the crime in court; instead those who used traditional means of proof against alleged witches were sentenced for assault or related crimes. No wonder the local population saw the colonial legal system as an ally of the witch against the people. However, people expected this to change with independence and the Africanization of the state apparatus. And, indeed, after some initial hesitation, it became increasingly clear that under postcolonial rule the courts began to approach the same offence differently (see Niehaus, Chapter 9). It was notably the vision of witchcraft as an anti-developmental force that encouraged the forces of orders to try and act against it.

By framing the belief in witchcraft as a developmental challenge – and not as a modernization problem that would disappear with the acquisition of European culture – the administration and the judiciary crossed some critical thresholds: witchcraft ceased to be seen as only a threat that originates from 'the intimacy of the house' (Geschiere 1997: 46). It had now been transformed into a broader societal crime that the courts were mandated to punish. Thus, the predominant notion that witchcraft was based on some form of mystical cannibalism of kin, was expanded; witchcraft was now seen increasingly as a broader societal challenge whereby witches used their occult powers to thwart development projects. It was especially this broadening of the scope of witchcraft beyond kinship bonds to cover a much wider array of unexplainable happenings that tipped the scales in favour of using the law to protect development. However, by turning the judicial system into an instrument of a development agenda, the new nation-builders also undermined the basis of the law as a neutral arbiter in regulating societal interactions. Moreover, it is quite clear that, even though there was heavy pressure on the courts to intervene, any action against witches was complicated by considerable judicial problems – notably the question of how to establish proof in this shady domain. For this, clearly, a judge would have to go directly against colonial precedence.

I decided, therefore, to focus my research for the larger IHS programme mentioned above on *Sorcellerie et Développement* on a series of court cases in the Eastern Province that had attracted considerable nationwide attention. Around 1980, the Eastern Courts quite abruptly began to condemn 'witches' to quite drastic punishments: up to ten years in jail and substantial fines. In Cameroon, people generally saw this as a major breakthrough: finally the law showed itself ready to deal with this major threat. But the general sentiment was also that it was no wonder that these cases took place in the East – a place where, after all, everybody knew witchcraft was running wild. Eventually, I was able to gain access through personal contacts to a set of thirty files on recent witchcraft trials before the Court of Appeal of Bertoua (the capital of the East Province), including reports on earlier judgements by various *tribunaux de première instance* in the East.

Elsewhere we published a more extensive analysis of these files, focusing particularly on the crucial role of local 'witch-doctors' (*nganga*) as key witnesses for the prosecution in these cases (see Fisiy and Geschiere 1990; Fisiy 1990a, 1990b). For the present chapter, two aspects of these files are of particular interest. First is the emphasis both judges and state attorneys put on witchcraft as a major threat to development – completely in line with the examples above – in order to justify their drastic interventions against this hidden threat. Striking is, for instance, the almost passionate appeal of the state attorney before the Bertoua Court:

> We are all Africans. We should not pretend that witchcraft does not exist. It is very much alive here in the East Province. We cannot allow all these primitive villagers to threaten government agents who are transferred to work here in the East. It is witchcraft that is drawing back development in this province.
>
> (Fisiy 1990a)

A second relevant aspect of these files is the thorny issue, already referred to above, of how to establish proof. The courts' problem here is perhaps best summarized by the judge of the *tribunal de première instance* of Batouri (also in the East Province) in his summing up of the case against a woman who was involved in an extramarital affair with a policeman in 1984; she was accused of rendering him impotent – or, in any case, incapable of having sexual relations with any other woman except her. In the judgement, the Court of Appeal said, *per curiam*:

> Considering the fact that witchcraft cannot be established scientifically;
> Considering the fact that modern medicines was ineffective in this case;
> Holds that only the firm conviction of the judge can guide him during the submissions in court.

This is a classic example of how the courts try to reconcile different forms of knowledge. It acknowledges that witchcraft cannot be proved scientifically, but it also emphasizes that modern medicine was ineffective in order to justify its conclusions that the impotence must therefore have been caused by witchcraft. The court decided, indeed, that a genuine case had been established, and the accused was convicted and sentenced to eight years in prison. The final proof in this case, as in many others, rested on the nebulous concept of the judge's firm conviction (*l'intime conviction du juge*) (Fisiy 1990a).

The wide discretionary powers of the judge were based on a new form of missionary zeal to fight anti-developmental practices which rendered certain regions inhospitable to civil servants and resistant to the state's agenda. The court felt that by meting out such harsh punishment it would soften the grounds and make it much more conducive for foreigners to live in the locality. It should be borne in mind that this wave of witchcraft incriminations was targeted against supposedly anti-communitarian occult practices.

This case shows again how witchcraft was shifted from a domestic affair to an offence against public order and tranquillity. To justify this, the courts usually applied Article 251, cited above (p. 234), in conjunction with Article 228 that punishes 'dangerous activities'. But even a combined reading of both articles does not provide the courts with any clear guidance on what course of conduct to follow. Hence, the interpretation and incrimination of the offence of witchcraft under the law has remained essentially discretionary, dependent on the judge's whims and caprices. This might also explain the considerable regional variations in the judicial action against 'witches': quite common in the East since 1980, but until now much less so in other provinces.

All this raises the question of whether the law is, in fact, an appropriate instrument to regulate culturally-grounded beliefs like witchcraft that are considered anti-developmental. The judicial basis of such actions seems to be very shaky. In our earlier article (Fisiy and Geschiere 1990) we also pointed to more practical reasons for doubting the efficacy of the judicial action on this score. Towards the end of the 1980s, some of the 'witches' who had been convicted and jailed reached the end of their term and were released. However, this raised the colossal question of their re-integration into society. The normal way to deal with dangerous witches is to invoke a *nganga*'s assistance to neutralize witches' dangerous powers. The state's sanctions have proved much less effective. Sending people to jail does not neutralize their powers. On the contrary, people say that this is where one meets *really* cunning *marabouts* who teach unknown secrets. No wonder the return of convicted 'witches' has created enormous practical problems. There is, indeed, good reason to doubt the state's capacity to deal with witchcraft.

The collapse of development: a new face of witchcraft?

In the end, it may not have been witchcraft that brought down the dream of development in the area, but rather some dramatic changes in the broader economic and political environment. Especially after the onset of the crisis in June 1987, formally announced by President Biya on TV and radio, it became clear that development – in any case, the recipe tried out until then, roughly summarized as a combination of cash-cropping and jobs in public service – was rapidly collapsing.

The first signs were the increasing difficulties in the 1980s of ZAPI – the co-operative that had a monopoly to buy the main cash-crops, cocoa and coffee – to pay farmers. There were constant rumours about financial malversations. The withdrawal of the French *agents techniques* made it all the easier for those in power, from inside but especially from outside ZAPI, to 'borrow' from its funds and use them for other purposes. During the annual cocoa and coffee campaigns, ZAPI was regularly forced to pay farmers with certificates that were of highly questionable value. However, people managed to circumvent this by smuggling their harvests out of ZAPI zones – for instance, by bringing them across the river – to districts where private traders were still allowed. The real blow came in 1989 and subsequent years when world market prices for both cocoa and coffee collapsed. The national *caisse de stabilisation*, whose job it was to accumulate levies during years of high prices in order to compensate farmers in years when prices fell, proved to be empty. Again, it was quite clear that the funds accumulated during the preceding years had been used for other purposes. The consequences were dramatic. In some villages, bags of cocoa stood rotting by the roadside since no one came to buy them. In 1991, the people of 'my' village asked me desperately whether I might be able to organize some way for them to sell their cocoa and coffee since nobody seemed to want it anymore.

During the 1990s, this implosion of the cash-crop sector was complemented by the crisis of the state. Whatever structural adjustment may have done in Cameroon, it dramatically effected the position of civil servants. The shrinkage of the state apparatus led to dismissals and forced retirements on a large scale. Many civil servants had the shock of suddenly receiving, without warning, a 'zero pay-slip', meaning that their employment had come to an abrupt end. Especially at the beginning of the decade, salaries were not paid for months on end. But it was, above all, the dramatic decrease of the salaries that had a lasting effect. Due to several consecutive cuts, by 1993 salaries had been reduced by as much as 60 per cent. The subsequent devaluation of the FCFA (by more than

50 per cent) further reduced the real value of civil servants' income.[13] Even the *filles libres* of Yaounde started to complain that it was no longer any use to go out with a *fonctionnaire*.

All this meant that the notion of development has acquired an ironic – or rather a sarcastic – ring, even in Cameroon.[14] It is quite striking that in this context 'witchcraft' also became much more ambiguous in its daily implications. The rather simplistic, official version of witchcraft as a levelling force and as a barrier to development is no longer tenable. As already noted, the witchcraft discourse is much richer in its implications – or, to evoke a less positive image, it is like the many-headed Hydra snake of Greek mythology, producing a new head each time Heracles chopped one off. In a similar vein, witchcraft discourses are apparently capable of producing ever-new meanings: there are obvious levelling overtones, but they can easily acquire accumulative implications as well. Among the Maka, *djambe* – like *evu* among the Beti – is, for instance, seen as indispensable to any chief or leader. Under certain circumstances it encourages and protects the accumulation of wealth instead of undermining it. It seems that the development ideology of the 1960s and 1970s, with its Manichaean contrast between 'the modern' and 'the traditional' – combined with a one-party ideology with parallel accents – imposed a specific reading of witchcraft as basically anti-development and, therefore, anti-modern; but subsequent developments have tended to favour other interpretations.

Lately the rumours of *Radio Trottoir* dwell on different themes: secret ways to get rich; access to global, occult networks; the cunning of entrepreneurs – especially younger ones – who dare to go outside the established frameworks of the formal economy (Parish, Chapter 6). The increasing ambiguity is reflected in rumours about the 'new witchcraft of wealth', differently named in the different regions of the country – *ekong* in Douala, *nyongou* around Mt. Cameroon, *famla* or *kupe* in the West and North West, *kong* in the forests of Central and East Cameroon – but referring to a similar set of representations (Fisiy and Geschiere 1991). Ardener (1970) reports on the emergence of such notions on the slopes of Mt. Cameroon in the 1950s and de Rosny (1981) shows that in Douala, the *ekong* goes back as far as the eighteenth century. Yet, especially over the past few decades, these representations have become country-wide preoccupations. Moreover, people insist that these are new forms of witchcraft, as compared to 'normal' forms of the 'witchcraft of eating' where witches give their relatives to their fellow witches for nocturnal cannibalistic banquets. In contrast, *ekong*, *famla* and other variants are about a witchcraft of labour. This new type of witch reputedly turns victims into zombies that are forced to work on 'invisible plantations' on Mt. Kupe (in the South West, more than 100 kms to the north of Douala).[15] This, in effect, is the secret of their riches, for *ekong*, *famla* and the other novel forms of witchcraft are invariably associated with the *nouveaux riches*.

In such conceptions, the levelling version of witchcraft representations remain. They express people's shock about the supposedly illegitimate ways the new rich have attained such dazzling wealth. Ardener (1970) details how such representations can discourage people, at least for some time, to profit from new opportunities for enrichment. However, these rumours' message is clearly double. For the rumours also express people's fascination with secret get-rich methods. Leaflets on how to get rich, with Mt. Kupe's magic profile on the cover, sell very well indeed on the free markets (see Sanders, Chapter 8). In his seminal study of *L'Esprit d'Entreprise au Cameroun*, Warnier (1993) notes that nearly all successful representatives of the new Bamileke bourgeoisie from the western part of the country, who now supposedly control the national economy, are popularly associated with *famla* (the local variant of the new witchcraft of wealth). But he adds that such rumours do not seem to affect their prestige. *Famla* is increasingly seen as a current aspect of entrepreneurial success.

This fascination with the riches such occult forces can bring comes even stronger to the fore in popular rumours about the *feymen*, the young successful entrepreneurs (see p. 227), with their dandy-like behaviour and their amazing wealth that seems to come from nowhere. This whole notion is very new; it is a Pidgin term, stemming from *faire quelqu'un* in Cameroonian French, meaning 'to trick someone'. The term *feyman* only gained currency in the mid-1990s, but within only a few years the *feyman* has become a new role model, especially for the young.[16] In his challenging research proposal, Ndjio (2000) quotes a sketch from a popular Cameroon television programme, 'Just for Fun': an ageing *fille libre* decides to disclose to her children the identity of the various men who have engendered them. The eldest child is dismayed to hear his father is a *professeur*; the second is equally unhappy that his father turns out to be a journalist; the third nearly attacks his mother when he hears his father is a military man; but the youngest is overjoyed when he learns his father is a *feyman*.

An essential element in the many stories about *feymen* is the magical quality of their wealth and the global span of their operations. The archetype, Donatien Koagne, may now suffer in a prison in Yemen, but he is rumoured to have conned several heads of state in Africa and leading French politicians with his false money tricks. Actually he would have been immediately executed by the Yemenites, were it not for the heavy pressure by the French who, at all costs, want to lay their hands on his carnet that contains such vital secrets (cf. Malaquais 2001). In Cameroon, his reputation was solidly established through his magnanimous and well-published contributions for the preparation of the national football team for the World Cup in 1994. Other *feymen* also enhanced their prestige through their ostentatious *largesse* on occasions like the recent France–Africa summit in Yaounde or in support of the Biya regime at election time. No wonder the national leadership is prepared to accord all sorts of favours to the organizations in which *feymen* are supposed to participate – like SYNES-JAPCAM (*Syndicat des salles des exploitants des salles de jeux et d'amusement publics au Cameroun*) or ASSOJHAC (*Association des jeunes hommes d'affaires du Cameroun*).

The contours of this enigmatic group are still far from clear.[17] Yet it is clear that the magical qualities attributed to their enigmatic accumulation of wealth make the official version of 'witchcraft' of the 1970s as a levelling force severely outdated. Apparently, the forms of enrichment that have come with economic liberalization have given witchcraft discourses yet another new lease on life.

Is the link with development helpful to grasp witchcraft? Can it account for witchcraft's surprising resilience and polyphony in present-day Africa? The foregoing has shown that linking witchcraft to development highlights how directly these enigmatic and volatile discourses relate to mundane and practical problems. Especially in the 1960s and 1970s, at a time when 'development' seemed a self-evident notion, 'witchcraft' as its counterpoint seemed to be equally unequivocal a notion. The subsequent proliferation of witchcraft and its many ambiguities seems to reflect the disappearance of a confident metanarrative about development's trajectory. Of course, such growing uncertainty is not particular to Africa, and cannot easily be separated from a broader loss of faith in the possibilities of social engineering. Similar uncertainties seem to become a general phenomenon in our globalizing world with the defeat of the state – whether of the welfare or the authoritarian type – by the requirements of 'the market', leaving society at the mercy of an economy that seems increasingly unpredictable and out of control. No wonder that, at the beginning of the twenty-first century, magic seems to become a fixed corollary of modernity, not only in Africa, but also in the richer parts of the world.[18]

Notes

1 We fully realize that both terms raise serious terminological problems. We use 'development' not so much as an ideological term but rather to denote a set of institutions and practices that have become an integral part of everyday life in many parts of Africa (as Chauveau 1994 puts it: *le développement est un dispositif*; also Olivier de Sardan 1995). While we realize that 'witchcraft' (like *sorcellerie* and other Western terms) is an unfortunate translation of African notions that often have a broader and more ambivalent set of meanings and associations, we prefer to retain this term due to its popularity in many parts of Africa (see also Geschiere 2000).

2 We will return to these enigmatic figures, see p. 242 and n. 16.

3 In the 1970s it was still the UNC (*Union Nationale Camerounaise*) of Ahmadou Ahidjo, Cameroon's first President, that monopolized politics from the national top down to the local level. After 1984 it was succeeded by the RDPC (the *Rassemblement Démocratique du Peuple Camerounais* of Paul Biya, Cameroon's second President), that was equally centralistic and authoritarian. The latter party is still in power, despite the formal political liberalization since 1990. In retrospect, the heavy, not to say obsessive, one-party jargon of the 1970s and 1980s may seem to have been artificial and even clumsy (see also p. 230). Yet Mbembe (1992) convincingly showed how deeply it affected the relations between political elites and *les masses populaires*. Elsewhere (Geschiere 1997), I tried to show that it created a political atmosphere that was highly conducive to witchcraft rumours: it was often hard to distinguish stories about secret machinations within the one-party-top and political confrontations behind closed doors, from the popular rumours about nightly confrontations between the witches.

4 There was (and is) a striking difference between the dry and authoritarian tone of State officials and the long, dramatic shows of eloquence of local leaders in the village palavers (see Geschiere 1982).

5   This is a good example of the ambiguity of witchcraft discourse. The *sous-préfet's* remark that he could 'see' the witches was certainly interpreted by the villagers as an allusion that he, too, had acquired a 'second pair of eyes' – which in this part of Africa, as in many others, is seen as the first and indispensable phase in one's initiation into witchcraft. The Maka say that someone who sees witchcraft everywhere is like the owl: he is the first to leave for the witches' nightly meetings. In practice this means that it is very difficult to talk about witchcraft without being implicated in it oneself.

6   Cf. the contrast implied by Warnier, in his magnificent study on *L'Esprit d'entreprise au Cameroun* (1993), between the levelling impact of kinship in the Cameroonian forest societies and the *stratégies de désaccumulation*, permitted by the kinship norms among the Bamileke of West Cameroon (from whose ranks an enterprising economic bourgeoisie emerged since the end of the colonial period).

7   The emphasis here, of course, is on egalitarian *ideology*; in practice these societies were (and are) certainly not egalitarian; indeed, there are marked inequalities between elders and young men, and even more between men and women. However, there is a strong emphasis on the basic equality of adult men that time and again serves to bring down all-too-ambitious leaders (Geschiere 1982).

8   *Nganga* (singular and plural) can be both men and women.

9   See Geschiere 1997: 209–210, where I tried to show that the basic ambiguity of witchcraft discourse always turns such attempts at compartmentalization into a fairly precarious struggle. This ambiguity gives witchcraft discourse a subversive quality: its capacity to dilute and confuse each and every apparently clear-cut opposition makes it the despair of anyone who tries to control or at least to systematize it (including the academic observer). In view of some criticisms on my book on this point (e.g. Toulabor 2000), it might be worthwhile trying to clarify the point I am trying to make on these pages. It certainly seems that Maka or Beti discourse on 'witchcraft' (*djambe/evu*) is extremely fluid, covering an array of images, both extremely negative and rather positive ones; other societies seem to go to greater lengths to distinguish ('compartmentalize') more morally acceptable and less acceptable manifestations of occult forces. However, it seems that such distinctions are always under heavy pressure and subject to constant re-interpretations. I think it is important to emphasize this, since many anthropologists and social scientists tended (and tend) to take such normative oppositions as givens, rather than asking *how* such normative distinctions are maintained in practice in the slippery domain of the occult and *how* such distinctions are reproduced in the face of constant change. The ambiguity of witchcraft categories – their poly-interpretability that may be precisely the source of their remarkable power and resilience in the face of great changes – tends to undermine such distinctions and make them subject to constant struggles.

10 This cure highlights a recurrent element in the *gbati* stories: the *gbati* boys were obsessed by things they did not (yet) have access to. Young boys normally only get the leftovers of the adults' meals, hardly any meat or oil. A fixed element in the *gbati* imaginary is also that it can only stay with boys who are virgins. In the 1980s I recorded a case of a *gbaticien*, a bachelor in his fifties (indeed, quite old compared to the *gbaticiens* of the 1970s who were only teenagers) who claimed that his *gbati* allowed him to leave his body at night and sleep with any woman he wanted to; after he had had intercourse with her she would remain sterile for the rest of her life.

11 This is also one of the reasons why the characterization of *djambe* as a 'popular mode of political action' – the notion is Bayart's (1979) – is somewhat difficult to maintain (Geschiere 1988).

12 In practice, however, even the colonial authorities were often less unequivocal in their policies. For instance, there were also in those days protracted debates among

civil servants on the issue of whether a 'witch-doctor' who had acted against 'witches' really should be persecuted for manslaughter (see Fields 1982; Geschiere 1997).

13 Characteristically, the only salaries that remained stable or rose were those of the police and the army. See Margaret Niger-Thomas (2000) for an evocative image of what all this meant to people's daily life.

14 We should add that over the past few years there are some signs of economic recovery. Official figures indicate substantial economic growth (5 per cent), though this seems – even in the realm of formal figures – to be largely outdone by the continuing rise of poverty. For the forest part of the East, involvement of the local population in the rapidly expanding exploitation of tropical hardwood seems to offer a new promise for enrichment. However, compared to cash-cropping, this is a far more adventurous road. Even though the forest law (1994) recognizes the local communities as important stakeholders, it is not at all clear how, in practice, they will profit and, especially, how it can be guaranteed that the exploitation – either by logging companies or local communities – can be 'sustainable'. Until now, the wood economy rather seems to correspond to popular images of magic money-makers like the *feymen* (see p. 242 and n. 16): sudden windfalls for a few clever persons and hardly any benefits for most of the people.

15 A recurrent element is also that the zombies are 'sold' to other employers. Hence the serious implications of expressions like 'I'll sell you'. Such expressions highlight the link with the trauma of the former slave-trade (see de Rosny 1981; Shaw, Chapter 3).

16 Compare the rapid emergence of the similar notion of '419s' in Nigeria. 419 is the article in Nigerian law against various forms of fraud. Like *feymen*, 419s are supposed to specialize in abuse of confidence – in particular with computer tricks on a global scale: these are the Nigerian 'businessmen' who reputedly empty European and American bank accounts through electronic means (also Apter 1999).

17 But compare the very interesting research by Dominique Malaquais (2001) and Basile Ndjio (2000).

18 See Comaroff and Comaroff (2000) on 'occult economies'; Meyer and Pels (forthcoming) on 'magic and modernity'; Geschiere (forthcoming) on 'witch-doctors and spin-doctors'.

Bibliography

Apter, A. (1999) 'IBB = 419, Nigerian democracy and the politics of illusion', in J. Comaroff and J. Comaroff, *Civil Society and the Political Imagination in Africa*, Chicago: University of Chicago Press.

Ardener, E. (1970) 'Witchcraft, economics and the continuity of belief', in M. Douglas (ed.) *Witchcraft Confessions and Accusations*, London: Tavistock.

Bayart, J.-F. (1979) *L'Etat au Cameroun*, Paris: Fondation nationale des sciences politiques.

Chauveau, J.-P. (1994) 'Participation paysanne et populisme bureaucratique: Essai d'histoire et de sociologie de la culture du développement', in J.P. Jacob and P. Lavigne Delville (eds) *Les Associations Paysannes en Afrique: Organisation et Dynamiques*, Paris: Karthala.

Comaroff, J. and Comaroff, J.L. (2000) 'Millennial capitalism: first thoughts on a second coming', *Public Culture* (special issue: *Millennial Capitalism and the Culture of Neoliberalism*) 12, 2: 291–344.

Escobar, A. (1995) *Encountering Development: the Making and Unmaking of the Third World*, Princeton: University Press.

Ferguson, J. (1999) *Expectations of Modernity: Myths and Meanings of Urban Life on the Zambian Copperbelt*, Berkeley: University of California Press.

Fields, K. (1982) 'Political contingencies of witchcraft in colonial central Africa: culture and the State in Marxist theory', *Canadian Journal of African studies* 16, 3: 567–593.

Fisiy, C. (1990a) *Palm Tree Justice in the Bertoua Court of Appeal: The Witchcraft Cases*, Leiden: African Studies Centre.

—— (1990b) 'Le monopole juridictionnel de l'Etat et le règlement des affaires de sorcellerie au Cameroun', *Politique africaine* 40: 60–72.

Fisiy, C. and Geschiere, P. (1990) 'Judges and witches, or how is the State to deal with witchcraft? Examples from southeastern Cameroon', *Cahiers d'Études africaines* 118: 135–156.

—— (1991) 'Sorcery, witchcraft and accumulation: regional variations in south and west Cameroon, *Critique of Anthropology* 11, 3: 251–278.

Geschiere, P. (1980) 'Child witches against the authority of their elders', in R. Schefold *et al.* (eds) *Man, Meaning and History: Essays in Honour of H.G. Schulte Nordholt*, The Hague: Nijhoff.

—— (1982) *Village Communities and the State: Changing Relations in Maka Villages of Southeastern Cameroon*, London: Kegan Paul International.

—— (1988) 'Sorcery and the State: popular modes of political action among the Maka of southeast Cameroon', *Critique of Anthropology* 8, 1: 35–63.

—— (1997) *The Modernity of Witchcraft: Politics and the Occult in Postcolonial Africa*, Charlottesville: University Press of Virginia.

—— (2000) 'Sorcellerie et modernité: retour sur une étrange complicité,' *Politique africaine* (special issue, F. Bernault and J. Tonda (eds) *Pouvoirs sorcier*) 79: 17–33.

—— (forthcoming) 'On witch-doctors and spin-doctors: the role of "experts" in African and American politics', in B. Meyer and P. Pels (eds) *Magic and Modernity*, Stanford: University Press.

Malaquais, D. (2001) 'Arts de feyre au Cameroun', *Politique africaine* 82: 101–119.

Mbembe, A. (1992) 'Provisional notes on the postcolony', *Africa* 62, 1: 3–38.

Meyer, B. and Pels, P. (forthcoming) *Magic and Modernity*, Stanford: University Press.

Ndjio, B. (2000) 'Famla and Feymen', research proposal for WOTRO, Leiden University.

Niger-Thomas, M. (2000) 'Buying futures', unpublished PhD thesis, Leiden University.

Olivier de Sardan, J.-P. (1995) *Anthropologie et Développement: Essai en Socio-Anthropologie du Changement Social*, Paris: Karthala.

de Rosny, E. (1981) *Les yeux de ma chèvre: sur les pas des maîtres de la nuit en pays douala*, Paris: Plon.

Seidman, R.B. (1965a) '*Mens rea*' and the reasonable African: the pre-scientific world-view and mistake of fact', *International and Comparative Law Quarterly* 15, 1135–1164.

—— (1965b) 'Witch murder and *mens rea*: a problem of society under radical change', *Modern Law Review* 28, 46–61.

Swartz, M.J. (1968) 'Introduction', in M.J. Swartz (ed.) *Local-Level Politics*, Chicago: Aldine.

Toulabor, C. (2000) 'Sacrifices humains et politiques: quelques exemples contemporains en Afrique', in P. Konings, W. van Binsbergen and G. Hesseling (eds) *Trajectoires de liberation en Afrique contemporaine*, Paris: Karthala.

Warnier, J.-P. (1993) *L'Esprit d'entreprise au Cameroun*, Paris: Karthala.

Wirz, A. (1972) *Vom Sklavenhandel zum kolonialen Handel: Wirtschafsräume und Wirtschafsformen in Kamerun vor 1914*, Zürich: Atlantis.

Index